DATE DUE NOV 0 6

GAYLORD			PRINTED IN U.S.A.

Praise for *The Opt-Out Revolt*

"If you want to understand what the fuss about the 'new careers' is all about, you have to read this book. It pulls together all the relevant theory and research, plus lots of stories of real people, and paints a compelling picture of the new career landscape. This book will be an important part of my syllabus the next time I teach my seminar on careers."

—Douglas T. Hall, Morton H. and Charlotte Friedman Professor of Management, Boston University School of Management

"Compelling, comprehensive, and insightful, this book advances our understanding of changes affecting the career patterns of both women and men and offers a fountain of advancement advice. The authors offer insightful evidence of gender-specific approaches to careers based on the proposition that a career pattern is not a predetermined trajectory but a kaleidoscope, where a change in any one element—structure, the work itself, and the striving for challenge and family balance—immediately affects everything else. Enlivened by firsthand illustrative personal accounts, their well-sourced and empirically researched study sets their work at a cutting edge and is invaluable for anyone anxious to explore a successful career strategy."

—Dorothy Perrin Moore, PhD, Distinguished Professor of Entrepreneurship, The Citadel; author, *Careerpreneurs*

"In this valuable book, Mainiero and Sullivan weigh in on an important and timely issue. They offer fascinating and useful discussion of the implications of the three dimensions of careers for how women and men may have more rewarding careers and lives."

—Gary N. Powell, Professor of Management, University of Connecticut; coauthor, *Women and Men in Management*

The Opt-Out Revolt

THE
OPT-OUT
REVOLT

WHY PEOPLE ARE LEAVING
COMPANIES TO CREATE
KALEIDOSCOPE CAREERS

LISA A. MAINIERO & SHERRY E. SULLIVAN

WITHDRAWN
Jackson County Library
SURPLUS OR OBSOLETE

·D|B·

Davies-Black Publishing
Mountain View, California

JACKSON COUNTY LIBRARY SERVICES
MEDFORD OREGON 97501

Published by Davies-Black Publishing, a division of CPP, Inc., 1055 Joaquin Road, 2nd Floor, Mountain View, CA 94043; 800-624-1765.

Special discounts on bulk quantities of Davies-Black books are available to corporations, professional associations, and other organizations. For details, contact the Director of Marketing and Sales at Davies-Black Publishing; 650-691-9123; fax 650-623-9271.

Copyright © 2006 by Davies-Black Publishing, a division of CPP, Inc. All rights reserved. No part of this book may be reproduced, stored in a retrieval system, or transmitted in any form or by any means, electronic, mechanical, photocopying, recording, or otherwise, without written permission of the publisher, except in the case of brief quotations embodied in critical articles or reviews. Davies-Black and its colophon are registered trademarks of CPP, Inc.

Visit the Davies-Black Publishing web site at www.daviesblack.com.

10 09 08 07 06   10 9 8 7 6 5 4 3 2 1
Printed in the United States of America

Library of Congress Cataloging-in-Publication Data
Mainiero, Lisa A.
The opt-out revolt : why people are leaving companies to create kaleidoscope careers / Lisa A. Mainiero and Sherry E. Sullivan.—1st ed.
  p. cm.
Includes bibliographical references and index.
ISBN-13: 0-89106-186-1 (hardcover : alk. paper)
ISBN-10: 0-89106-186-X (hardcover : alk. paper)
1. Quality of work life—United States. 2. Work and family—United States. 3. Career changes—United States. 4. Self-actualization (Psychology) 5. Social change—United States. I. Sullivan, Sherry E. II. Title.
HD6957.U6M27 2006
306.3′6—dc22

                                                          2006014561

FIRST EDITION
First printing 2006

This book is dedicated to my two children, Michael-David and Mariana Mangini, who will no doubt have future Kaleidoscope Careers of their own, and to my husband, David Mangini, who is starting to realize a Kaleidoscope Career may be something to consider after all. I love all of you so much.

—LISA A. MAINIERO

This book is dedicated to John I. Sullivan. Thank you for the bedtime stories, throwing back each fish we caught, the tea parties in the playhouse, the snowball fights, the sled rides . . . and for just always being there. I love you, Dad.

—SHERRY E. SULLIVAN

Contents

Preface   xi
Acknowledgments   xvii
About the Authors   xxi

1 Why Work Doesn't Work Anymore   1
2 Why Women Walk Away   21
3 Off with the Male Straitjacket   67
4 Kaleidoscope Careers   105
5 The Quest for Authenticity   155
6 The Search for Balance   187
7 The Drive for Challenge   215
8 No More Business as Usual   241

Appendix A: Research Methods
              and Study Information   299
Appendix B: Statistical Support
              for the Research   307
Notes   313
References   343
Index   367

Preface

Media coverage on "the opt-out revolution," a term coined to describe the alarming talent drain of highly trained women who choose not to aspire to the executive suite, has been explosive and controversial. As researchers, we grew interested in this phenomenon when we realized there was more to the story than news reporters were suggesting. We began this book as a journey to discover why women were leaving the workforce in alarming numbers and what their new career patterns might be. Along the way, we discovered that men's careers were also undergoing change and that we needed to examine the patterns for both.

We completed five studies to identify underlying patterns in women's and men's careers that would help us understand the opt-out phenomenon. Looking at these patterns from a gender lens, at first we found a disturbing sexist trend. On the surface, it appeared that men were remaining in the workforce while women were quitting their jobs to take care of their families. But when we looked deeper, we found fascinating complexities in the careers and lives of women and men. We found that men valued balance in their lives but often were caught in a straitjacket imposed by society, which many are desperate to get out of. We found women who were caught in an equally difficult bind: facing discrimination in the workplace, with no options for advancement or flexibility in their jobs, they were deciding to leave their aspirations behind and focus on the relationships in their lives.

Does this mean women lack ambition? We think not. Instead, we conclude that the structure of society, and especially the structure of corporations, forces women and men to make impossible choices between work and family. Many women and some men, therefore, are rejecting standard corporate careers. A new career pattern—that of the Kaleidoscope Career—has taken hold. Women and men are defining careers that allow them to work outside corporate boundaries, using technology as their tool, in ways we have never seen before. They are using creative thinking to construct new career patterns rather than merely accepting what corporations offer. They are finding ways to meet their needs for money, security, family balance, and autonomy outside of corporate boundaries and, in so doing, are creating uniquely different career patterns than we have seen before.

In our opinion, the "revolution" the media speaks of is much more a "revolt" against the standards of corporations that demand too much time and too many hours from reasonably minded people. Something has to give. Because most organizations have not acted, individual workers have acted instead. Women and men are working within and outside corporate boundaries to better blend their own needs for authenticity, balance, and challenge. These men and women are making adjustments to their careers to find a regression line that balances work and family. They are developing new definitions of success.

In our development of the Kaleidoscope Career model, we are indebted to researchers in the areas of work and family, career stage development, and the role of gender in organizations who have contributed to the literature. We see our work as building on the foundation of research in psychology, sociology, organizational behavior, and human resources disciplines that began in the 1970s and continues today. We are especially indebted to the fellow members of the Academy of Management upon whose work our model is based. Our research triangulates aspects of gender, careers, and human resources strategy in a way that we hope readers will find helpful.

To those who have left corporations to forge a career outside company boundaries, the message is clear: you are not a failure. Rather, you are a courageous trailblazer in a new age of Kaleidoscope Careers. To those human resources managers and organizational leaders who don't know why they are seeing more and more talented women—and men—walk out the door, here is our explanation. And, more important, here are strategies and examples used successfully by companies to turn around this costly trend.

The Opt-Out Revolt addresses the current trends affecting women's *and* men's careers. The book presents the results of a groundbreaking study that deconstructs women's and men's career patterns. We highlight three key parameters—authenticity, balance, and challenge—that influence women's and men's work and family priorities and that suggest different career directions. We argue that organizations need to reconsider how to design work and create a culture that encourages loyalty, retains talent, and perhaps even increases profitability.

The book addresses the influence of gender on the roles taken by modern-day careerists. Chapter 1 sets the stage by describing how the career landscape has changed over time. Job security is a thing of the past. Workers must embrace new attitudes and behaviors. Baby boomers, especially those who entered the workforce under the old career model, may find these changes confusing—and they may be further confused by the younger generation of workers who seem to have a much different work ethic from their own. Many factors, including globalization, rapid technological advances, and increased competition, have forever changed the American workplace. But where does this leave the typical working man and woman?

Chapter 2 illustrates how many women have created nontraditional career and life patterns that have escaped corporate radar. Although in the past women were restricted to the traditional career paths generated by the manufacturing dictates of the twentieth century, many women have discovered that their needs do not mesh with the confines of corporate realities. Women have also discovered that the relational skills they excel at—but that are not always valued by corporate America—are better suited to a more flexible, interactive environment. Women emphasize flexibility, team management, knowledge growth, and participative leadership—all skills well suited to alternative career models, including success outside of corporate America.

Chapter 3 identifies how men's careers remain more linear than not, but often change as a result of changing circumstances, such as downsizing or parenting. Our research shows that men are bound by the same parameters as are women: they want balance i00n the0ir lives, as well as challenge, and hope to find meaning (authenticity) in their work. But the order in which men pursue these goals is different than that of women. This chapter examines how men think about their careers, their lives, and themselves. The voices of stay-at-home dads and corporate men, detailing their career decisions and the role of family, are prominent in this discussion.

Chapter 4 introduces the concept of Kaleidoscope Careers. Like a kaleidoscope that produces changing patterns when the tube is rotated and the glass chips fall into new arrangements, women shift the patterns of their careers, rotating the different aspects of their lives to rearrange their roles and relationships. Women's careers, like kaleidoscopes, are relational. Rather than separate the concept of "career" from "family," we integrate both into a meaningful model that resonates with modern-day women. Each action taken by a woman in her career has profound and lasting effects on those around her. Each career action, therefore, is evaluated in the light of the impact such decisions may have on her relationships. The model also applies to men, but in different ways. Women's and men's careers are not boundaryless, as the popular academic literature suggests, but operate inside three major parameters: the need for authenticity, balance, and challenge—the ABC model of new careers.

Chapters 5, 6, and 7 detail the parameters of the ABC Career Kaleidoscope model. The first parameter of the ABC model, authenticity, is discussed in chapter 5. Workers today are looking for more than advancement through the standard corporate career. Even those women and men who have achieved success by any measurable standard still find they are searching for ways to be fulfilled while being true to themselves. Sometimes this quest takes the form of spirituality and the search for greater truths. Other times this need is fulfilled by personal self-actualization. We found a consistent and growing need to be genuine in women, especially as they approached midlife and "mellowed." As one of our interviewees said: "I've done things everyone else's way, and now it is my turn to be me." Men mellowed, too, but moved toward a more integrated lifestyle, rather than away from it, at midlife.

Chapter 6 examines the issues and conflicts surrounding balance, the second parameter of the ABC model, otherwise known as the "modern holy grail" for women. Many women leave corporate boundaries behind because they are suffering the stress of working long days and traveling. They need flexibility to nurture and care for a family, but flexibility is counterindicated by the demands of corporate careers. Even those men who persist in coping with the inflexible boundaries of linear careers find they must identify strategies of balance, handling nail-biting stress concerning children and rectifying household disequilibrium. The trade-offs are immense in consequence: If I work, what will happen to my children? If I don't work, how will I feed, clothe, and shelter them? This chapter details the daily struggles faced by women and by men as they negotiate to balance work demands with nonwork needs.

Chapter 7 looks at challenge, an important motivator in the early career period and the third parameter of the ABC model. When all is said and done, workers want to learn, to grow, to find new experiences, gain new skills, and stretch capabilities. But the nature of the challenges faced by women and men changes as they move through the stages of the life cycle. Challenges are defined by workers' personal concepts of success. The career transitions women and men make over time reflect their personal needs as well as work-driven ambitions. This chapter illustrates how women and men make major shifts and transitions in their careers to pursue new challenges, either personal or professional.

Finally, Chapter 8 examines the corporate imperative. We look at what corporations should be doing to create a more flexible, kaleidoscopic workplace. Corporations need to reshape, rebuild, and redesign their cultures to emphasize flexibility and eliminate face time. Workers must be viewed as individuals—with a life outside the office. The fundamental ways of doing business that have been used for decades must be reexamined. And the methods that no longer work in the new business environment must be quickly discarded. This chapter profiles companies that have successfully offered alternative career paths for workers, and forward-thinking firms that address the issue of flexibility. We offer prescriptive ideas for human resources professionals and decision makers to arrest the outflow of talent as women and men decide to take their careers in their own hands.

The purpose of this book is to demystify the complexities of women's and men's modern-day careers. By reading and using the ideas presented here, the individual worker will

- Gain a greater understanding of why a career is no longer a "career" as traditionally defined

- Realize which factors are most salient in the career transitions individuals make

- Understand how authenticity, balance, and challenge can be achieved

Likewise, managers and human resources professionals will

- Discover the reasons for America's opt-out revolt

- Understand how women and men make career choices and the factors that influence these choices over the life cycle

- Learn strategies for stemming the drain of talented individuals by creating a corporate culture that encourages authenticity, balance, and challenge

The landscape of our workplace is rapidly changing, and individuals and organizations must adapt to these changes. The opt-out revolt has occurred among women and men because corporations have not kept pace with these employment trends. The Kaleidoscope Career model offers a fresh new approach to understanding these career transitions and changes. We hope you find this book useful as you negotiate your Kaleidoscope Career. Please visit our Web site at www.theoptoutrevolt.com to offer comments, share your career stories, and find additional resources and updates on our continuing research.

Acknowledgments

The research that underscores this book was five years in the making, and we have many people to thank for their time, patience, and responsiveness to us as we inquired incessantly about their careers. First, let us thank our colleagues. Many friends and colleagues helped shepherd this work along its way through conversations about the research and reviews of our work. The first-place award goes to Monica Forret, who tirelessly and without complaint ran numerous statistics for us, often in the wee hours of the morning, as we put together the information for this book. Monica's dedication to our research and her delightful commentary on our chapters make her a superb colleague and friend. We are also grateful to Gary N. Powell, a longtime friend, collaborator, and colleague to both of us. We acknowledge Gary's contribution as one of the forerunners to this work; his original coauthored article with Lisa on the river of time metaphor sparked an interest in exploring this area at a future point. Rosabeth Moss Kanter is a professional colleague, mentor, and friend who cheered us on when she read our original research and graciously accepted the task of reading chapters and offering commentary about our conclusions. We are very grateful to her for acknowledging our research efforts and were happily surprised when we discovered we were thinking along similar kaleidoscope lines. We also acknowledge Bob Ford's strong support of our research and his useful comments on earlier versions of the model. Bob pushed us to refine our original ideas so that others would understand how this theory of careers is differentiated from previous research. Many thanks to Dot Moore, who has been a longtime supporter of our work. Madeline Crocitto has been a tireless cheerleader for this effort and has offered many fascinating insights on the chapters she read for us.

It is important that we thank the people who directly contributed to the research in this book as well. We must begin by offering a huge thank-you to Hugh Davis, who was of major assistance in conducting the two surveys through Greenfield Online. Hugh has been a friend to Fairfield University since his undergraduate days, and he is a strong alumni supporter of the university and faculty research. We had the good fortune to work with Hugh on developing two of the surveys that went into this research, and we are grateful to the entire staff of Greenfield Online for their professionalism and dedication to our work. We also thank the women in our original Web site survey who took the time to respond to our inquiries about their careers and offered their career histories as a starting point for our research. Their career stories jump-started our thinking about the ABCs of kaleidoscope careers, and we are forever grateful for their insights and commentary. A group of dedicated MBA students deserve acknowledgment here as well. These students were participants in an online EMBA course for a seven-week period, and we had the most intimate and revealing discussions online concerning their careers, their families, and their hopes and ambitions for their futures. We would be remiss not to thank Katie Kovorovic, a longtime neighbor and family babysitter, who along the way grew up into a smart, intelligent young woman who aided the coding process of the qualitative data and offered her insights as well. We also thank former thesis student Janis Slavic, who became our colleague and friend, for her tireless assistance in ensuring the completeness of all our references and citations.

Many people participated in the interviews for this book, and we thank them all for their commentary and insights. We would especially like to thank Jim Silver, Ronnie DiNucci, Mim Schreck, Tucker O'Connell, Deborah Ann Backes, Dick Kleine, Julie Roberge, Maureen Smith, Kim Vasquez, Roslinda Dunlap, Ann Storm, Barbara Pasternack, Tina Heinzman, Madolyn Johnson, A. Thomas Kelly, Bruce Miller, Gary Vasquez, Karen Nordberg, Pat Gagione, Paul Robert, R. Keith Martin, Patti Hutton, Jerri Leinen, Heidi Hammel, Nancy Killie, Robin Ostrosky, and Terry Ali. We also thank all the interviewees who contributed quotations in the surveys, online discussions, and interviews who wished to remain anonymous. We are especially grateful for access to the Ridgefield Women's Network. We are grateful to Lisa Belkin and the Connecticut chapter of the Society for Human Resource Management (SHRM), whose networking meeting sparked ideas and provided many interview contacts for the research. We also thank our colleagues in the Academy of Management and the Southern Management Association who provided feedback and who helped spark new ideas throughout the course of our five-year project.

We are thankful for our many students, who continue to amaze us on a daily basis. Our Gen X and Gen Y students have taught us that new generations of workers are afoot who plan on doing things much differently than the generations that came before. We hope this book provides you with some guidance as you embark on your Kaleidoscope Careers.

We are grateful to the entire team at Davies-Black Publishing, who marshaled the resources to put this book into production. First, our utmost thanks to Connie Kallback, whom we met at an Academy of Management meeting. Connie, we discovered, liked the kaleidoscope metaphor even before we started talking about a book on Kaleidoscope Careers. We were so comfortable with her as a potential editor that we had many conversations with her about the project before we submitted our original proposal. She became a strong supporter of our ideas, an advocate for our vision for the book, and a professional par excellence. We wish to thank Jill Anderson-Wilson and Stacey Lynn, who shepherded the book through the production process. We also want to express our gratitude to Laura Simonds, with whom we initiated conversations about the marketing for the book even before it had gotten off the ground. Laura was patient with our questions and efforts, and responded to our inquiries quickly and professionally.

From Lisa: I thank my family for their patience during my sabbatical, in which I was largely chained to the computer writing the chapters that underscore this book. Special acknowledgment goes to my husband, David Mangini, who not only commented on the theory and reflected on the concepts about men in ways that provided great insight but also took on the task of completing the graphics and charts for the entire book. In addition, he provided a system, the likes of which we had never seen before, to track all the quotes that you see in this book. He is the best graduate student assistant, helper, supporter, confidant, and fellow researcher whose contribution to this effort has been largely unseen and, until now, unrecognized. Thank you, David. I also thank my children, Michael-David and Mariana, who had to wait for their lunches on Saturday mornings while their Mom was busy writing, and who were quite surprised to learn their mom was writing an *entire* book, from start to finish. When they saw the volume of pages coming off the printer, their estimation of their mother's capabilities went up several notches. Above all, I acknowledge and thank my co-author, Sherry E. Sullivan, for her support throughout the process of writing this book. Sherry did not even flinch when I told her I wanted to travel to Italy on sabbatical. Instead, she said, "Let's find a way to get this done before you go." Thanks, Sherry, for letting me relax in Tuscany in peace and quiet, untethered to the Internet. For that gift of time I will always be grateful.

From Sherry: I thank my loving parents, John and Eileen Sullivan, who made countless sacrifices so that I could pursue my dreams of studying careers. You are truly the best parents ever; I can never do or say enough to thank you for all you've done and taught me over the years. Thank you to my brother, Terry; his wife, Kathy; and their children, Colin and Erin; as well as to my sister, Cindy; her husband, George; and their boys, Ryan and Jack. Your active, loving families provided me with a lens through which to view work-family interactions and inspired me to examine how corporations can and should do better by their workers. My special thanks to each of you for your love and support. Much appreciation to the women of the Golden Girls' Farm, who have offered continuing encouragement, friendship, and help whenever asked. You are simply the best; thank you, S. Gayle Baugh, Madeline Crocitto, and Monica Forret. I also acknowledge my longtime coauthor, friend, and partner in crime, Howard S. Tu. Special appreciation to my friends Shawn Carraher, Suzanne de Janasz, Lisa Mainiero, Saroj Parasuraman, and John Wanous, who always inspire me to achieve my best by their own examples of excellence, perseverance, and kindness. Thank you, Arnon Riechers—you are the finest mentor, role model, and friend a PhD student ever had. And thanks to Devil Dog for enforcing regular breaks and bedtimes during the writing process, and for reveling in each day.

About the Authors

Lisa A. Mainiero earned her PhD in organizational behavior from Yale University. She is the author of *Office Romance* (Macmillan, 1989) and is a sought-after lecturer and consultant, with appearances on *Good Morning America,* the *Oprah Winfrey Show, Larry King Live,* and numerous other radio and television programs. She is a professor of management at the School of Business at Fairfield University in Fairfield, Connecticut. Mainiero has published articles on women in management, office politics, and career strategies for technical professionals in *Administrative Science Quarterly,* the *Academy of Management Review,* the *Academy of Management Executive, Organizational Dynamics,* the *Journal of Management, Personnel Journal,* and the *Training and Development Journal.* She served as the research translation editor for the *Academy of Management Executive* and was a member of its editorial board. She has served as division chair, preconference chair, and program chair of the Women in Management Division of the Academy of Management. She is the co-author (with Cheryl L. Tromley) of *Developing Managerial Skills: Exercises, Cases, and Readings in Organizational Behavior* (Prentice-Hall, 1989). She lives with her husband, son, and daughter in Ridgefield, Connecticut.

Sherry E. Sullivan earned her PhD from The Ohio State University. She is a tenured associate professor at Bowling Green State University and a director of the Small Business Institute. She also taught at Memphis State University. She has published articles in the *Journal of Management,* the *Journal of Applied Psychology,* the

Journal of Vocational Behavior, Group and Organization Management, and *Academy of Management Executive.* She was division chair, program chair, and newsletter editor for the Academy of Management's Career Division, served on the Gender and Diversity in Organizations (GDO) Board, twice served on the Board of Southern Management Association, served as the Southwest Academy track chair for Entrepreneurship/Small Business/Consulting, served as program and division chair of the International Division of the United States Association for Small Business and Entrepreneurship, and served as treasurer and Human Resource Management/Careers/Organizational Development track chair for Midwest Academy. She is a recipient of the Academy of Management's GDO Division Janet Chusmir Outstanding Service Award and a Fellow of Southern Management Association.

CHAPTER 1

WHY WORK DOESN'T WORK ANYMORE

Mim Schreck is a former fast-tracker. At midlife, she left her hard-earned dream position as an executive vice president at Nine West Group to enjoy life at home while pursuing her passions for golf, tennis, and charity work.

Tucker O'Connell is a free agent. He has moved through a collection of twelve distinct jobs—some investment related, others marketing and sales related, still others operations related—while rearing his family of five children. Recently he started his own entrepreneurial logistics and transport firm.

Jim Silver is a stay-at-home dad. A Harvard Law School graduate and former practicing litigator, he made the decision to leave his lucrative career when he and his wife, a doctor, decided they wanted a parent at home full-time to rear their three children.

Ronnie DiNucci is a "boomerang" (an employee who opts out of a corporate job and returns to the firm, often years later). She left a managerial job at IBM during the boom and bust years of the early 1990s. After working a series of smaller, less taxing jobs in the town where she reared three children with her husband, also a former

IBMer, Ronnie returned to IBM sixteen years later, taking a job in the same department but at a lower level.

Deborah Ann Backes is a "recycler" (someone who reexamines his or her career at midlife and changes occupations). After years invested in law school, both Deborah and her husband tired of the practice of law. They mutually agreed to leave their respective law practices to begin new careers as the owners of a chocolate-making business.

What do these people have in common? They found work, defined in terms of the linear, "up is the only way" career model, to be limiting. Rather than follow the corporate career model, they decided to pursue alternative options to find more fulfilling jobs that better fit their lives, their families, and their interests.

An exodus of amazing proportions is quietly overtaking corporate America. Tired of the inflexibility of standard work hours and the lack of concern for work-family balance, employees are leaving corporate positions in favor of more flexible work options. Employees today are defining success on their own terms—and opting out of the 7 a.m. to 9 p.m. rat race. Instead of living to work, people are now working to live. A successful career is no longer viewed as working for a single firm forever. Rather than define their lives and self-worth in terms of a preordained, often constraining, career track, workers are creating their own patchworks of job experiences to suit their lives.

Workers today are rejecting the standard corporate contract in droves. Stories of women exiting high-level posts pervade the media. The Bureau of Labor Statistics reported that although the number of employed mothers with children increased from 47 percent to 73 percent from 1975 to 2000, their participation rate decreased slightly to 71 percent in 2004.[1] There are slightly more two-parent families in which only the husband is employed in 2004 than in 2000.[2] Despite the increasing number of women earning advanced degrees, surprisingly, still more men (89 percent) than women (76 percent) with college degrees are employed.[3] However, of those women who are in the labor force, the number of self-employed women increased from 27 percent in 1976 to 38 percent in 2004. Over the last thirty-five years, the number of women working part-time (fewer than 35 hours per week) has remained fairly constant while the number of men working part-time slightly increased, as has the number of stay-at-home dads.[4] More people than ever are working from home. Approximately 8.6 million workers are independent contractors, consultants, or free-lancers—and it's by choice: an overwhelming 83 percent of them prefer freelance work.

But why? Is it all about family and work life balance? We think not. The answer behind the opt-out revolt lies in more complex issues and trends resulting from a paradigm shift in how careers are developed, created, and shaped—by both women and men—that will be a defining force in the future of work.

We have written this book because a seismic shift is taking place in the world of work, a shift that others have only begun to notice. The book presents the results of a groundbreaking five-year study that examines women's and men's career patterns. Our research shows that the interplay of work and family, and work and self, are inexorably intertwined. Separating out career decisions from other life decisions is a relic, an artifact of twentieth-century old-line manufacturing thinking.

The media has focused only on the issue of work-family conflict by showcasing a number of high-profile women who left corporations to spend time with family, calling this a new workplace revolution. But there is much more to the story. The issue affects men as well as women. We argue that it is more of a "revolt" than a revolution that is going on. It is true that people, especially women, are protesting against work environments that don't permit them to have a balanced life. People are also revolting against organizations that don't permit them to be true to themselves or don't provide challenging work. Not only issues of work-family balance have ignited this change; a complex interplay among issues of authenticity, balance, and challenge is causing a workplace revolt of mass proportions. *The Opt-Out Revolt* points out the need for a new business model that allows workers the flexibility to work at home and provides off-ramps and on-ramps to attract and retain talent in the years to come. It also calls for a deeper examination and reformulation of the basic fabric of corporate culture so that individuals are provided work that is not only challenging but personally meaningful. Work, as defined by the parameters from the twentieth-century manufacturing model, no longer works for everyone.

CAREER PATHS, PAST AND PRESENT

Dick Kleine spent thirty-eight years working for the Midwest manufacturing company John Deere, and he rose to the position of general manager of one of the company's prominent divisions. His career describes a solid, upwardly mobile track through a series of assignments in industrial engineering. As early as high school, Dick decided to develop his skills so one day he could manage a factory. He attended Saint Louis University and majored in industrial engineering, believing an engineering degree would provide the best route for entry into management:

> *Setting a career vision early on is what helped me achieve my goals. I knew that I wanted to be an engineer since I felt that would be the best route to management of a factory; I didn't want to end up sitting at a drawing board. I knew I had the potential for management and could handle the responsibilities. Setting a career vision is powerful. Everything you do, consciously and unconsciously, contributes to accomplishing that vision.*

After graduating from college, Dick completed a three-year ROTC commitment to the U.S. Air Force and in 1960 went to work in the industrial engineering department of John Deere. During his early years with the company, he was promoted every two to three years. He held various engineering and management positions at six different Deere locations, assuming more management responsibility with each promotion. He described what motivated his climb up the corporate ladder:

> *What drove me is the challenge of the next position. I needed maybe the satisfaction of accomplishment; the money side never entered my mind. I figured I would be paid according to my next position and the company would be fair about that,*

and they were. I had enough self-confidence to always think I could handle the next position. I knew I could make a difference in the organization.

Dick's wife, Mary Lou, supported his career vision and ascent. About work-family balance, he said:

Things were a lot different back then. We didn't see the career conflicts that people see today. My wife has a college education and taught school for a year. But she stayed at home and was very supportive of my career; she was there for me. I worked my twelve-hour days and half days on Saturday, but I always attended my son's basketball games, and other events. I didn't work the whole day Saturday, and I didn't work Sunday. I'm not sure why all these people today work all day Saturday and Sunday. Maybe it's the computer—they never get any relief—or maybe they are not well organized. I tend to think it is the latter.

When the firm's business cycle slowed, so did the rate of Dick's promotions. Despite alternative job opportunities, Dick remained committed to Deere and was eventually named general manager (GM) of the Hay and Forage division in 1983; he became the GM of the larger Harvesting, Seeding, and Cylinder division in 1987, and, finally, vice president of quality for the corporation. He described his thirty-eight years with the company.

When your progression slows, it's your own fault. It's not the company's responsibility. There are not many cases when really outstanding performers aren't recognized through upward movement. Other people in the organization recognize this too, that the best performers get promoted. Organizations rarely make mistakes—they rarely overlook the right people and rarely promote the wrong person. If the company does make a rare mistake, everyone in the company knows it. I stayed with Deere for thirty-eight years. People say if you work for John Deere you have "green blood." A lot of employees' children end up working for Deere. My son worked for the company for fourteen years; he now owns five John Deere dealerships. If people don't stay with a company, that company is doing something wrong.

Soon after his retirement from John Deere, Dick was invited to serve on a number of nonprofit boards. He readily volunteers his time and has assumed the leadership of several groups or projects, including an expansion project at his church and establishment of an executive leadership institute to develop future leaders in the city where he lives. He described his retirement.

When it comes time to retire, nobody does that rocking chair bit. But most people are poorly prepared for retirement. I sure wasn't going to do nothing. . . . I had a relatively simple vision of my career when I was in high school—I wanted to manage. During my thirty-eight years at John Deere, my vision was to be continually challenged as I took on more management responsibility. Now, my career vision in retirement is to utilize my talents to help others. I want to continue to be challenged, but I also want to give back. I find satisfaction in giving back. A person needs to be challenged and be satisfied in his work. I have to be personally satisfied that I'm being a productive member of society even in retirement. There are so many things I want to accomplish for others.

Contrast Dick's traditional career pattern with that of Julie Roberge. Julie graduated from college with an MBA and promptly went to work in the field of human resources. She landed an assignment at Saab-Scania of America, where she started in the personnel function and later became the company's manager of human resources. Julie explained: "At Saab, I started in an entry-level assistant type of job, and over the almost ten years I was there, I worked my way up to being second in command of the department." At the time, she had no immediate plans to leave the company. "I liked what I was doing, but unfortunately, they [were] acquired by another firm and relocated their headquarters to Atlanta."

As part of the human resources function, Julie had the job of outplacing the workers at her division and then paying herself a severance package. When she closed the doors at Saab-Scania, she decided to do something different. She took a job assignment with a private school in Connecticut as director of human resources. This job offered a real challenge—the opportunity to create a human resources department from the ground up, and to professionalize human resources in an educational institution.

> *My husband and I were not interested in relocating, since our first child was coming in October and we wanted to stay around family. So I lined up my next job, which involved centralizing and developing the human resource function at a private school. It was a wonderful move up in the field, and a chance to really develop as a manager. Looking back, I definitely did not anticipate the degree of challenge I was in for. To say there was resistance is an understatement.*

As part of her effort to push the envelope at her new job, Julie was instrumental in establishing an on-campus child care center. Her daughter attended the center, allowing Julie to bring her daughter with her to work. "That turned out to be one of my most important career achievements. . . . Not only did it make lots of faculty happy but I was able to bring my daughter to school with me, know she was right next door, and have some input into how the center was managed." But while the work was steady, she and her husband had just the one child and longed for another. "I asked myself, is this the right place for me now?" said Julie. "The hours got longer, the work less rewarding, and the politics fierce, so I decided to resign." She quit her job to reduce stress, and her son arrived almost two years later.

But she did not return to work right away. While her son was young, she freelanced with a human resources consulting firm for four years, and took the real estate license exam. "But it is difficult to work from home when you have a baby, at least it was for me. Home chores and the baby distract you from working. I wound up working at night, after everyone else had hit the sack. I didn't get enough sleep, or make enough money." After many trials and tribulations with freelance work, Julie took a full-time entry-level position with another independent preparatory school, at a salary far lower than what she previously had earned in her years as director of human resources. Asked why she took a pay cut, she replied simply,

> *I wanted a job where I could make a valuable contribution, but with less stress than in human resource management. I wanted to come into the office and leave behind the work at the end of the day. My family needed medical insurance, and my husband required it due to his health situation. My primary focus has always been on my family, and these hours were perfect so I could drive [the kids] to school and get home at a reasonable hour.*

Julie and Dick represent very different career patterns. Dick's career was based on postwar values. Shaped by the manufacturing age and feeling fortunate to have solid career prospects, Dick relished the opportunity to work for the same firm, year in and year out, for many years. Julie's career, in contrast, is based on the values and ideologies of the new millennium. For her, caught in a decision between career and family, family won out over pay and long hours.

In the twenty-first century, individual employees are no longer bound to the idea of a career with one firm, and are motivated more by self-fulfillment and balancing their work with their family lives than by the emphasis on stability and security of the past.[5] They define success not only in terms of high salary and status but also in terms of respect, recognition, and self-satisfaction. Employees want to learn, grow, and develop in their jobs—asking the question, "If I take this job, what will I learn from it?" They regularly reexamine how work fits into the overall gestalt of their lives.

THE DEATH OF THE LINEAR CAREER

In the manufacturing days of the twentieth century, the gold standard of career models was the linear career such as that followed by Dick Kleine at John Deere. But nowadays, workers like Julie Roberge are developing what researchers call a "boundaryless career." The term "boundaryless career" describes a collection of related skill-building work experiences, knowledge, and perceptions that are marketed and shaped into an integrated, meaningful career path.[6] Employees who pursue boundaryless careers are concerned with developing portable skills, knowledge, and abilities across multiple firms. They want personal identification with meaningful work.

Researchers Mike Arthur and Denise Rousseau used the metaphor of the boundaryless career to recognize the increasing permeability and blurring of career boundaries. Boundaryless employees do not identify with the corporation for which they work. Instead, they take jobs that emphasize on-the-job action learning, the development and enrichment of their network of contacts, and the ability to learn from peers. Often they stay in the jobs for only a short time. Boundaryless employees may reject career opportunities within a corporation for personal reasons and may prefer to take individual responsibility for their own career management. They may work as innovators, moonlighters, knowledge-based professionals, originators of services, troubleshooters, entrepreneurs, contract workers, or in a multitude of other roles.

Today's employees are developing boundaryless careers outside the confines of traditional corporate structures as never before. As the economy evolved from supporting large, hierarchical firms to leaner, more flexible firms, organizations downsized many employees who had relied on the firms' implied promise of long-term job security. Continuous learning and growth replaced job security as the goal of many employees. Reporting relationships and rules within firms also changed. Physical movement between organizational levels and job functions became more common. Employees were as likely to move sideways or downward or realign themselves for a new job function as they were to move up.[7] Some employees broadened their networks, seeking validation through professional associations rather than from their employers. As job security decreased, individuals became less loyal to their firms (and more cynical about the possibilities for career advancement). The number of strictly brick-and-mortar organizations has decreased as virtual organizations enabled by technology have arrived on the corporate scene. Workers now move more freely not only between firms but between industries, occupations, and even countries.

In the new millennium, the boundaries between work life and private life have become increasingly blurred. Employees are declining promotions to spend more time with friends and family. Others are leaving corporate America and starting small businesses to gain control of their schedules and thereby better balance work and caring for children or elderly relatives. To try to capture the increasingly fluid nature of careers, scholar Tim Hall introduced the metaphor of the protean career.[8] Based on Proteus, the mythological Greek god who could alter his form at will, Hall's concept suggests that individuals can shape their careers into many different forms in response to changing environmental and personal circumstances. Protean careerists are able to repackage and market their skills, moving from firm to firm or project to project and gaining increased independence from employers. Because these protean careerists are more likely to change jobs, organizations, or even occupations more frequently than traditional linear careerists, they must adopt a new mind-set. Instead of passively relying on employers for training and learning opportunities, protean careerists take control of their own career development to ensure continued employability.

Newer models of careers are moving away from traditional inside-the-box, linear thinking to a more complex set of dimensions that allow for change, permeability, and multiplicity across the lives of individuals. These new approaches offer a greater understanding of women's careers, as the careers of women typically don't follow a traditional, linear pattern. Rather, women have forged boundaryless and protean careers ahead of their time, following their own paths, outside of the confines of a corporation.

MEN, WOMEN, AND CAREERS

Although attempts have been made to apply the linear, upward-driven male career models of the twentieth century to women, the general consensus has been that women's lives do not fit within a linear set of guidelines.[9] The fact that career theorists have been unable to profile women as neatly as they have men should come as no surprise. There is no overarching pattern to women's careers as a group. Instead, women's careers are marked by shifts, changes, transitions, compromises, and sharp bifurcations much too complex to fit into any existing career model.

Men's careers used to be more predictable, with most men, like Dick Kleine, following the traditional, linear career path. The careers of men are currently undergoing great shifts and upheavals. It is no longer possible to count on working for the same firm for a given length of time. Men find they are uprooted more often than expected and must face career changes, and life changes as well. These career changes can be devastating to the male ego and psyche, prompting reorientation about the meaning of "career." A trend is also emerging of the stay-at-home dad, who stays home full-time to watch the kids, and also the work-at-home dad, who can get the children off the bus, while the wife has a high-flying corporate career.[10] Although changes in information technology have allowed for a more flexible work-at-home career for many men, such arrangements often truncate their opportunities for promotion.

As we explored the issues, we discovered that although many static models of career development exist, most ignore gender as a defining feature of the life pattern. Although it may not be politically correct to admit it, women and men do respond to societal influences associated with their roles. Although a woman can easily bring home the bacon and fry it up in the frying pan, when it comes to household chores and child rearing, something has to give. Either she must have a nanny, a maid, or a stay-at-home dad; she cannot face these chores on her own.

But changes are occurring in societal gender roles, and new patterns are emerging as a result. The woman entrepreneur adapts her work hours around the demands of her children's schedules. The service professional markets his or her skills to a variety of firms. Information technology free agents, both men and women, mold a patchwork of jobs into a consistent paycheck. Recyclers reexamine their careers at midlife and completely change their occupations. The opt-out mom or the stay-at-home dad works part-time from home or does not work at all.

As researchers in the field of executive careers, midlife issues, and women, we felt it was time to examine modern-day careers through the lens of gender issues and cultural norms. We started this research as a means of understanding how men and women navigate their careers and *balance* their work and home lives. But we found that in addition to balance people also had strong needs for *authenticity* and *challenge*—and that the interplay of these three needs greatly affected career decisions. We discovered a new way to think about careers, a more holistic approach that does not divorce the concept of "career" from the rest of the person's life. We came to this conclusion as a result of studying women's careers and, later, the changing careers of men.

Our aim as researchers was first to examine women's careers: to understand the meaning, hopes, and dreams women attached to them and the transitions that occurred at different stages of life. For our research, we took a multipronged five-study approach. First, we conducted an online survey of more than 100 high-achieving women from across the United States who belonged to a national professional association. We asked these women, primarily managers and business entrepreneurs, to describe the transitions they had made in their careers and the reasons they had made them. Although we began our research with a focus on women, we kept wondering, "Is it the same for men?" Therefore, second, we conducted a larger, more detailed online survey of professionals (837 men and 810 women) to compare differences in career motivations and transitions between men and women.[11] This large survey offered us the opportunity to compare men and women at different stages in their lives. Third, we conducted a survey on benefits in the workplace and ways in which the workplace can become more flexible.

In addition to the results of these three surveys, we wanted to gain insights into some of the transitions and setbacks associated with women's and men's careers. Therefore, we orchestrated a series of lengthy online "conversations" with 27 men and women about their careers as our fourth research endeavor. Fifth, we also conducted a series of interviews with men and women in different stages of their careers to understand the reasons behind their transitions (see Appendix A for further information on the research).

The three major surveys, the interviews, and the online conversations represent a five-year research effort in which we have documented in great detail the transitions associated with women's and men's careers. We found that careers in the twenty-first-century information age are marked by several unique features that did not apply to careers in corporations during the manufacturing age of the twentieth century. Our research led us to a new model—an information age model—that addresses not only women's careers but the changes wrought in men's careers as well.

THE IMPACT OF THE INFORMATION AGE

We now live in a global information economy. *New York Times* columnist and Pulitzer Prize–winning author Thomas L. Friedman argues that the defining feature of the new global business landscape is not necessarily how goods are traded across country boundaries but how information flows across those boundaries.[12] India and China are becoming world leaders in outsourcing information systems and in the cheap production of goods. This worldwide trend is removing key professional and knowledge jobs from workers in the more affluent United States. Information is quickly replacing tangible "things" as the object of trade. The growth of e-commerce over the past five years is only the leading edge of a much more prolific global phenomenon. Remote medical diagnoses can now be made from far-flung locations. CNN can now broadcast war events in real time—as they happen—in our living rooms.

According to strategic management expert Rosabeth Moss Kanter, companies are seeking products or service concepts that travel easily over world communication channels.[13] The global information economy offers faster information, fewer geographic constraints, and greater access to products and services around the world. For businesses, that translates to more competition, faster product obsolescence, higher standards, and the need to juggle global scope and local responsiveness. Business leaders must think across boundaries, demonstrate mental agility, and use creativity in the new information age to stay ahead.

Dr. Kanter tells a story about a corporate CEO who offered his advice to a roomful of officials and executives about what was needed for success in the new economy. "Brains," he said. "You need brains." And he sat down. Brainpower is to the global information economy what oil was to the industrial economy. Intangible assets and human capital are becoming the most important sources of a firm's information age value. In her book *Evolve! Succeeding in the Digital Culture of Tomorrow*, Kanter names the three c's—three intangible assets that are important in examining the strategies and cultures of world-class companies.

- **Concepts:** the best and latest ideas and technologies, the result of continuous innovation

- **Competence:** the ability to execute flawlessly and to deliver value to customers with ever higher standards, as people learn and then teach others their best practices

- **Connections:** strong partners that leverage a company's offerings, link the company to new markets, and provide access to innovations and opportunities that fuel the imagination to innovate[14]

She calls this new paradigm of finding creative new approaches to standard business problems "kaleidoscope thinking," because a kaleidoscope suggests that there are many ways to shake the fragments of ideas into new patterns.[15] Business leaders need to see the endless patterns that can be created from the same set of business information fragments. Those business leaders that develop the three c's—concepts, competence, and connections—are more likely to succeed in the new information age than those that follow old-line manufacturing thinking.

We agree wholeheartedly with Dr. Kanter's approach. While her focus is on corporate strategy and our research focuses on aspects of kaleidoscope thinking internal to the organization and specific to career development, we have found that corporate strategy applies to the new career model for both women and men. It is well known that corporate strategy has a spillover effect on career development. As corporate strategy shifts, internal aspects of the firm, including the employees, are affected. Employees may be downsized and the firm reshaped to better address its new strategic goals and markets. Careers may be made and broken in response to changes in corporate strategy. As the economy has become more global and information driven, career patterns have changed as well. Gone is the old-line manufacturing-age model of thirty years in the same firm. In its place is a model that rejects the standard corporate contract and defines success on employees' own terms.

Changes in corporate strategy in response to evolving environmental conditions have contributed to the demise of the traditional employment contract.[16] In the past, long-term employment relationships and systems of internal employee development, including promotions, served several key purposes. One was to foster investment in training, because the cost could be recouped by the employer over time as the employee's performance improved. Training in turn led to long-term benefits, such as an employee's intimate understanding of the firm's clients, customers, and market needs. Another was to foster loyalty, because employee job security and commitment to the organization went hand in hand. Finally, the possibility of moving up the ladder in a linear career provided powerful motivation at relatively little cost, because few employees would ever make it to the top to become, say, a Jack Welch of GE.

But now, as corporate strategy is changing in response to the global economy and the challenges of the information age, all bets are off. Career patterns are responding to this new set of changes wrought by the information age. Long-term employment relationships are increasingly rare. Training is a short-term benefit that builds a résumé. Employees feel lucky when they are employed for more than three years at the same firm. The information age represents a very different environment in which to build a career, and career patterns for both women and men are changing rapidly in response.

PROJECT-BASED CAREERS, FREE AGENCY, AND THE HOLLYWOOD MODEL

Given the rapid changes wrought by the information age, many employees have found that they prefer to be "free agents." Free agents are independent from the bonds of a large institution, or perhaps are connected only remotely.[17] For free agents, work is defined more on a project basis than an hourly basis. Free agents define their success laterally rather than in the traditional up-wardly mobile manner. They say "I'm successful because I have six active clients" rather than "I'm successful because I have been pro-moted to level X." They use services from local copy and printing shops, Starbucks, bookstores, cyber cafés, executive suites for rent, office supply superstores, the Internet, and postal service centers. The entrepreneurial spirit has overtaken the physical necessity of being in an office, so that individuals can work as free agents, sell-ing their services and solutions to a variety of firms.

In the economy of the manufacturing age, time was fundamen-tal to the concept of work. People were paid by the clock, an approach to time that fundamentally shaped the American busi-ness ethic. Beginning with Frederick Taylor's early-twentieth-cen-tury time and motion studies, the hourly wage system generated tremendous productivity gains and made America the king of mass production.[18] But as production systems moved offshore with the new global economy, the need for time as a unit of measure was diminished. In the new workplace, most workers—whether free agents or employees—are looked upon not merely as bushels of hours. Workers in the information age are selling insight, talent, expertise, ideas, creativity, and solutions, all of which are hard to measure. For this reason many free agents charge by the task instead of the hour.

The Hollywood filmmaking industry is a perfect example of the free agent model.[19] Large permanent organizations with fixed ros-ters of individuals have given way to small flexible networks with ever-changing collections of talent. Talent assembles in a specific place for a specific purpose, and when that mission is complete, the team disperses and workers move to the next project. In Holly-wood, talented people (actors, directors, writers, camera operators, key grips) receive high levels of pay for a particular, finite project, forming a coherent work team. When the project is completed, the team disbands, each participant having learned new skills, forged new connections, deepened relationships, enhanced a reputation, and earned a credit that can be added to the résumé. A different group of people will gather for a new project. When that project wraps, the free agents may take some time off until a new project is on the horizon.

Take the career of award-winning actor Tom Hanks. While in college, Hanks was involved with Cleveland's Great Lakes Shakespeare Festival. He then obtained television roles, costarring in the sitcom *Bosom Buddies* and doing guest roles on a number of popular TV series, including *Taxi, The Love Boat,* and *Family Ties.* While guest starring on the TV show *Happy Days,* he met director Ron Howard, who later cast Hanks in the movie *Splash.* He then landed a number of roles in films such as *Philadelphia, Forrest Gump,* and *Apollo 13.* With each project, he enhanced his reputation and learned new skills, which led him to write and direct the movie *The Thing That You Do!* as well as direct and produce HBO's *Earth to the Moon* series. Tom Hanks's career exemplifies the Hollywood model. He moves from project to project, working with a variety of people, honing his craft, and establishing a network of connections. There is no "career" in the sense of moving up the corporate ladder; instead, his reputation has been established through a series of well-respected projects that, taken in combination, constitute a "career."

The Hollywood model has become an increasingly common arrangement for workers in many different industries. To craft a new piece of software, high-tech companies enlist coders who work, under tight deadlines and intense pressure, on teams with a few traditional employees. Book publishers solicit manuscripts and send them out to be edited remotely, on a project-by-project basis, with workers and authors spread out all over the globe. Producers or service providers that depend on the key ingredients of the brainpower, creativity, skill, and commitment of the people involved—rather than those that are location based—can operate this way. The Hollywood free agency model puts power back in the hands of the individual and provides contract workers with enormous flexibility, which can produce a corresponding and equally profound change for workers. Workers may have some days that run from eleven o'clock in the morning to eight at night and other days that run from nine to five. As long as clients are served and money changes hands, why does it matter where or at what hours the work is being done?

THE NEW WORKPLACE REALITIES FOR MEN AND FOR WOMEN

The free agency model requires a new approach to career development. Rather than focus on careers within corporations, workers build careers across corporations or through technology-enabled free enterprise. As the respected management consultant Peter Drucker said about the new career, "There is no longer any corporate ladder. There isn't even a rope ladder. It's more like a jungle and you bring your own machete."[20] The new technology-driven workplace is unlike anything we have seen in the past. But what is surprising is that women may be better prepared than men for a modern career of twists, turns, and zigzags. In fact, women may be ahead of the curve. Our research shows that women and men are using innovative approaches to their careers like never before. Gender has a major impact on the career decisions people make at different points in their career and life cycles.

Instead of focusing on the barriers women may face as they aspire to the executive suite, the research reported in this book illuminates innovative new approaches and creative thinking. Some women are still climbing the corporate ladder. Others don't aspire to the executive suite for reasons of their own. Many have developed a lateral career, working for a multitude of businesses outside the confines of a large corporation. Some women have developed entirely entrepreneurial or project-based approaches to their careers. Still others have forged a corporate path but are doing so on their own terms. Similarly, men's careers have evolved away from the traditional manufacturing-age model, with some men adopting very nontraditional career paths and roles. Our aim is to examine modern-day careers—what women are doing, what meaning "career" has for them, how men make career decisions, and which factors are salient in the transitions both men and women make in their careers. This book captures many of these changing patterns and shows how men and women are forging careers in the new information age.

Counter to the writings of those in the media who denounce women for leaving high-powered jobs in Fortune 500 firms, we do not believe that the opt-out revolt means that feminism has failed. Women aren't failing, nor has feminism failed. What we have found instead is a new gender-based model of career choices intended to give women, and also men, more freedom to create a personal definition of career and life success. The opt-out revolt is flourishing as a result of several new trends about attitudes regarding work that are cascading against corporate life. Because this book is based on extensive research, we have been able to examine how men and women are actually fitting together all the aspects of their lives—work, family, and friends—into a coherent whole.

This book details why a career is no longer a "career" in the traditional sense. It illustrates journeys of change and discovery by using the voices of women and men who have come to terms with the new workplace realities. However, it goes beyond just providing a new way of thinking about the changing nature of careers. It also explores how an individual's attempts to satisfy deep-felt needs for authenticity, balance, and challenge—what we will refer to as "the ABCs"—affect his or her career and life decisions. This book introduces and explains the ABCs of the new Kaleidoscope Career.

Business leaders, human resources managers, and other individuals can use this new model to transform their workplaces so that they can more effectively compete—and win—in today's technology-driven global marketplace. Regardless of advances in computer technology, Internet and communications systems, methods of production, quality control, and other functions, the bottom line—and competitive advantage—still comes down to the heart, the mind, and the soul of the individual worker. By understanding how individuals can better blend, alter, and enrich the work and nonwork aspects of their lives, organizations can create cultures and change organizational policies to support workers' choices—thus freeing workers to contribute their best efforts and to perform at their highest levels.

CHAPTER 2

WHY WOMEN WALK AWAY

Kate Reddy is a high-powered, resourceful overachiever who works for a staid investment bank in a plum position as an investment portfolio analyst. Accustomed to dealing with clients at all hours, checking the stock exchange prices in Tokyo and Hong Kong, Kate is a go-getter par excellence who knows how to cut financial deals and handhold clients. At work, Kate is the epitome of the successful career woman. But at home she is conflicted, exhausted, and stressed. Returning from a cross-country flight at 1:30 a.m., she panics when she discovers a note from her young daughter's teacher telling her she's supposed to bring something homemade, of all things, to her daughter's school Christmas party the next day. So while her husband and children sleep, she grabs a rolling pin and beats store-bought mince pies to pieces in hopes of making them look homemade, feeling guilty all the while about her lack of attention to her daughter's schooling.

Kate is a fictional character, the heroine of the runaway best seller *I Don't Know How She Does It* by Alison Pearson.[1] The book details the life of a superwoman, trying to be the greatest mother and a financial whiz all at the same time. This book has resonated with working women, especially mothers, because Kate's crazy multitasking lifestyle is their lifestyle. Most women who work live a life similar to Kate's, a life that is a blurred collection of seemingly never-ending activities: getting children off to school while simultaneously checking e-mail, negotiating million-dollar contracts while having the sudden realization that gym shoes must be purchased *today*, attending a soccer practice while taking a cell phone conference call, and then returning home after grocery shopping for the second shift of cooking, household chores, and child rearing—only to do it all over again the next day.

Twenty years ago, the picture looked rosy. A woman would bring home the bacon and fry it up in a pan while splitting child care with her sensitive, understanding, feminist husband, who awaited her with a relaxing glass of wine at the end of the day. But the new reality suggests the complications of balancing the demands of work with those at home are causing some women to opt out of the corporate rat race. For example, meet a real-life Kate Reddy: Maureen Smith—successful career woman, devoted wife, and loving mom.

Maureen Smith, executive vice president and general manager of Discovery Channel's Animal Planet network, has built an exciting and productive career in the entertainment field. In December 2001, the *Hollywood Reporter* named Smith one of the "100 Most Powerful Women in Entertainment."[2] She became president of the Fox Family Channel and the Fox Kids Network after fifteen years of service in television programming. As a young girl, Maureen never imagined she would end up in a Hollywood entertainment career: "When I was young, I dreamed of being the Jane Goodall of the marine biology world, working with dolphins. I would ask my parents to drop me off at the local Marineland nearby, and I would spend as much time as I could." She went to college and found an internship working for a local television affiliate. There she worked in the research division, getting up at 5:30 a.m. to distribute the overnight ratings to the executives. When she graduated, there were no openings for a full-time position, but later she got a phone call from a friend, a former boss who said Rupert Murdoch was forming the Fox network and they needed a temp for two weeks who had a research background. "He said, 'There's this new network that is starting. Nobody thinks the network will last very long, but why not send them your résumé?'"

We know today that the Fox network did last, and thus began an exciting fifteen-year career at Fox Broadcasting and News Corporation, where Maureen built a highly regarded career in programming. She thought she had it all: "The place was really fantastic. It was a small entrepreneurial start-up, and I was in on the ground floor as one of the first thirty employees. I was in weekly meetings with CEO Barry Diller and owner Rupert Murdoch right at the start. They were brilliant men, and in just a few short years the network took off."

Maureen moved over to Fox Kids Network while still part of the Fox Broadcasting division to follow her respected mentor, Margaret Loesh, who was heading up that division. "I was interested in family-oriented programming, and it was an honor to work with her." There she became senior vice president of planning, scheduling, and station relations. A year later, when new management bought into the network and subsequently purchased the Family Channel, Maureen's mentor left the company, and Maureen had to step up to a role that involved a lot more responsibility. In June 2000 she was appointed the president of the Fox Family Channel and the Fox Kids Network, and found herself working endless but productive hours.

> *Our hard work paid off, and we turned those two entities into very profitable businesses. Then, in late 2001, the companies were sold to Disney. So I took advantage of the shift. At that time, I had two children, I was working countless hours, and had to be on call twenty-four hours a day. On top of all of that, I had a long commute that was one and a half hours each way in traffic (even at 6:30 a.m.!). I rarely had time for myself, and I never saw my husband, family, or closest friends. I managed to get to parent-teacher conferences, but quality time didn't really exist. And when we were together as a family, I was just too tired to enjoy it. So the sale of our company forced me to ask myself, "What do I really want to do? What are my priorities?"*

She had enjoyed every aspect of her challenging career, from developing programming to making creative decisions and seeing how these decisions played out in the Nielsen ratings. But in March of 2002, Maureen decided to take a career interruption.

> *I took some vacation time, attended every school function, and became involved in the PTA like never before. I was able to do all the fun things I had missed out on and go to Little League games and school picnics. I decided to clear all that clutter in my life that I never had time for before. I made all kinds of plans to paint rooms in the house, organize all my closets, and cook wonderful meals. OK, so I never did get all of the closets organized, at least I could have if I really tried! The funny thing was that it took me several weeks before I could break my habit of jumping out of bed and checking my e-mails the second I woke up. My husband would tease me because there suddenly was nothing there—other than the usual advertisements and an occasional joke from a friend.*

After six months of relaxing and reconnecting with her husband and her two sons, Maureen received an offer, out of the blue, from two former producers who had previously run her preschool programming block at Fox Family Channel. She accepted an offer to join TLC Entertainment, an independent production company, as a partner. At Fox, Maureen had enjoyed some of the trappings of Hollywood success—a penthouse office, her own conference room with six televisions, and a personal limo driver. At her new venture, she shared a common, very unglamorous production office with her two partners. Commenting on her change in status, Maureen said, "My family took a financial hit, and we simplified our lifestyle—but it was worth it. We realized it's not about the money or 'things'—instead, you gotta love what you're doing and have the energy left over to enjoy *life*. It's not about making a living, it's about *living*."

A few years before Maureen made this career change, her husband had quit his high-level position in the entertainment industry to become an elementary school teacher—something he had always wanted to do. Plus, it was a job that would allow him to spend more time with their children. Maureen and her husband made changes to their careers to align their priorities, follow their dreams, and above all spend quality time with their sons.[3]

Maureen Smith is not alone in her decision to "rightsize" her career. Consider the recent headlines when Karen Hughes, special White House aide and chief policy adviser to President George W. Bush, and Mary Matalin, chief strategist for Vice President Dick Cheney, announced they were leaving their high-powered jobs to spend more time with their families. Both women took pains to state that their resignations were personal, not political, and that they enjoyed working for their respective high-profile bosses. Though their resignations were six months apart, both women commented on how it was time to take a career interruption, leave the hustle and bustle of Washington, D.C., revisit their lives, and return to normalcy with their families.

THE OPT-OUT REVOLUTION

Many executives and human resources professionals find it puzzling when competent, talented women—like Smith, Matalin, and Hughes—groomed for the executive suite, back out of high-powered, high-achieving careers. Why are women walking away at the top of their games, after years of struggle, when their careers seem to be going so well?

New York Times reporter Lisa Belkin argues that there is a new trend afoot—highly educated women, primed for ascension to the top of their firms, are leaving their posts prematurely. The 2003 article introduced the term "the opt-out revolution" and set off a firestorm of response.[4] Questions about the role of feminism, the present restrictions of the workplace, the rights and privileges of social class, work-family balance, and the morality of the decision to leave work ensued.

Women are tired of trying to do it all while working in organizations that claim to be family friendly—but really aren't. Every day, in little ways (such as deciding whether to attend that 4:30 p.m. meeting or a child's softball game) and in not so little ways (such as making a painful choice between the so-so job offer that requires no travel and the challenging job with the great salary, great benefits, longer hours, and a lot of travel) women feel they are being forced to choose between their careers and their families and children.

THE AGE-OLD STRUGGLE:
MOTHERHOOD VERSUS WORK

There is a surprise waiting in store for those women who bought the supermom fantasy and thought they could do it all—have a high-powered career, run a household, and be a soccer mom—and that surprise is waiting in the sad and plaintive eyes of a child who wants only mommy. The primary reason why women are bailing out of corporations at increasing rates is that women find the roles of mother, worker, sister, lover, caregiver, nurturer, and corporate achiever discordant. There just aren't enough hours in the day to do it all.

Some women, recognizing the time crunch between their work and nonwork roles, opt out and become stay-at-home moms. Kim Vasquez is one of these women. A flight attendant with Delta for almost five years, she saw other women who continued to work and rear a family but realized that was not for her. "Delta was fantastic—the benefits were great, and we could travel anywhere on standby for amazingly cheap rates," said Kim. "And because I spoke French fluently, I was hired immediately." Kim enjoyed the work but knew that when she and her husband were ready to have a family, there was a decision to be made.

> *But it was not a job where I saw myself working, with children. I made a decision back when we were engaged that when we were ready to start a family, I would stay home. The job was physically very demanding, and I just didn't see myself flying all over the country with young children to raise.*

Kim weighed the costs and benefits, and decided that the demands of her job weren't compatible with the needs of her family. So she opted out. She took a career interruption while her sons were young but then ventured into part-time work as a figure skating coach when her boys grew older.

> *I love, love, love what I do now. This is the job for me. Teaching figure skating fell into my lap. I can work part-time and make my own hours. I just love it when I am coaching and my*

students perform well. My favorite time is when I am on the ice. With this job, I can work part-time, be home for my boys when I need to be, and still pursue my passion for skating.

When her children were older, working part-time became a viable option. Like Kim, many women take this route. They opt out of a full-time job when their children are young and return to work part-time when the kids are older. And, like Kim, many women find a job with the flexibility they need—one where they can choose their own hours and fit work around their family lives.

But others try to do it all. They work full-time, and, like Kate Reddy, are desperately trying to hold it all together. Doing it all isn't easy, especially when the boss is asking everyone to put in more and more hours. Americans are working more hours—per week and per year—than at any time since the Second World War.[5] Data from the Cornell Employment and Family Careers Institute indicate that in recent years employer demands have increased, and the forty-hour workweek is indeed a thing of the past, particularly for salaried workers. The combined workweek of dual earner couples has increased by ten hours per week. Couples in which one or both partners are professionals are 50 to 90 percent more likely to be overworked, and single parents are not only overworked but enjoy far less free time.[6]

A rarely recognized but important fact is that jobs requiring extensive overtime exclude virtually all mothers (93 percent).[7] Having children has a strong negative effect on women's income. Mothers who work full-time earn only sixty cents for every dollar earned by fathers who work full-time. Single mothers are most severely affected, earning the lowest percentage of men's average pay. There are large and often hidden costs to women who take time off to rear children.[8] The "mommy tax," or the forgone income of a college-educated woman, is usually greater than a million dollars, producing a bigger wage gap between mothers and women without children than the wage gap between women and young men. But not only mothers pay the price. One in four families provide care for an elderly relative, with women usually assuming the caregiver role. Women who perform caregiving pay a severe penalty of over $650,000 in lost wages, Social Security, and pension benefits over their lifetimes. Surprisingly, even though women are getting more education and experience than ever before, the wage gap is not closing. In 2004, women who worked full-time earned 76.5 percent as much as men, a slight increase from 75.5 percent in 2003 but a slight decrease from 76.6 percent in 2002.[9]

The ideal of a worker devoted to a linear career juxtaposed against the domestic roles expected by society creates an incongruity for women. Despite the fact that the education gap between women and men has all but disappeared, women in most families are still expected to shoulder the lion's share of caring for children, caring for elderly parents, and even keeping a clean house and getting dinner on the table for spouses. Women report that they spend 37 hours a week on household chores and child care, whereas working men report that they spend 20 hours a week, a gender gap of 17 hours.[10] Forty percent of high-achieving wives think their husbands create more work for them around the house than they contribute to getting it done.[11] Even today, female domesticity remains the entrenched, almost unquestioned American norm and practice.[12] As a gender system, it has two defining characteristics. The first is its organization of work around the ideal of a full-time worker who remains committed to the office. The second is its moral opposite: those who have caregiver responsibilities cannot perform as ideal workers. Caregivers become marginalized and cut off from responsible "work" roles, even though their caregiving work is highly valuable to society. The gender system supported by society frames the options women and men have in creating a balance between career and family.

Arlie Russell Hochschild writes profoundly about the double duty working women face in her book *The Second Shift*.[13] Hochschild suggests that there is a cultural cover-up that promotes the myth of the supermom, while hiding the hectic life of real working women.

> *There is no trace of stress, no suggestion that the mother needs help from others. She isn't harassed. She's busy, and it's glamorous to be busy. Indeed, the image of the on-the-go working mother is very like the glamorous image of the busy top executive. The scarcity of the working woman's time*

seems like the scarcity of the top executive's time. Yet their situation is totally different. . . . The imagistic analogy between the busy working mother and the busy top executive obscures the wage gap between them at work, and their different amounts of backstage support at home.[14]

Female domesticity takes a toll not only on the career patterns of women but on the family involvement of men. If child rearing is perceived as "mother's work," then men are excluded from this important life dimension. Bureau of Labor Statistics data from 2004 suggest that little has changed in the last twenty years. For instance, in households with children under the age of six, women spent 2.7 hours per day caring for children compared to the 1.2 hours spent by men.[15] There remains an imbalance between what women do at home, and the caregiving they provide, and what men do. Even though it may not be politically correct to say, this imbalance has a major effect on the career patterns of men and women.

Female domesticity also divides women against themselves. Mothers who stay home have a substantial investment in the notion that working mothers take on too much and ultimately fail to meet their children's needs. Working moms fight gender wars every day and are disconcerted to discover their female comrades sniping at them too. Such a scenario is described in Joan Williams's book *Unbending Gender:*

> *"How* nice *that you can walk little Bobby to school every morning,"* gushes a stay-at-home mother to a harried working mom as she arrives at her son's school. *"Otherwise, you'd never* see *him." (Opening salvo)*

> *"Listen, Sophie really needs some fake fur for her princess costume,"* wheedles a working mom talking to her next door neighbor. *"Since you're home with* so much time, *would you mind picking up some at the store for me?" (Direct hit)*

> *"Oh, so you're a lawyer. How exciting. It must be* so much fun *to get dressed up and go to an office all day. And I'm sure Joey does* just fine *at the day care center." (Heavy artillery)*[16]

Working moms feel embattled on both sides—passed over for promotions at work because they are female and disparaged by other women because they do not spend every moment with their children. Women earn seventy-six cents for every dollar earned by men, meaning the average woman earns approximately four hundred thousand dollars less over her work life and has less than half of the retirement income of her male counterparts.[17] Caught between the pressures of work and home, women must ask: "Why *am* I trying to do it all anyway?"

THE MYTH OF THE SUPERMOM

Roslinda "Rosie" Dunlap is a supermom. Since her husband's death at the age of 36 when her two children were just 13 and 11, she has been both mother and father, trying to do it all. She works many jobs to keep the household financially sound; she is general manager of a service company, director of human resources for a preferred employer organization, adjunct instructor at the local community college, and a life coach. What's a typical day like for Rosie?

> *I'm up at 6:15 a.m. Put on a pot of coffee. Jump in the shower. Turn on* Good Morning America *so I know what's going on. Leave the house about 7–7:15 a.m. First it's into the service company to see what's going on there. As GM, I usually deal with a lot of employees who have problems. Like today, in walks this employee who is always in a good mood and has a great marriage—or so I thought. He asks to talk to me and soon breaks down crying. He's having problems in his marriage. He's embarrassed and doesn't want anyone to see him crying. So I take him next door to a diner and buy him some breakfast. After he tells me all about his situation I ask him what I can do to help. He says I've done enough—that no one ever listens to him but that today I did. I recommend counseling to him and he agrees to go. [Then] it's back to the office where I handle more employee problems and even customer problems.*

But Rosie's day has just started:

Then I'm off to one of the firms that belong to the preferred employee provider group—I'm their HR director. I meet with their VP and administrative person to discuss what's going to happen tomorrow with their EEOC [Equal Employment Opportunity Commission] audit. They were awarded a government contract, and this is the first time they've gone through one of these audits. I'm there all afternoon walking them through the process.

Her exhausting day isn't over yet. Next, she jumps in her car and races to teach her 4:30 p.m. class at the local community college:

Right now I have three classes, back-to-back, from 4:30 to 10 p.m. First, I teach two sections of business communication. Then I teach the supervision class until 10 p.m. The supervision class not only has the students on the main campus site, right in the room with me, but also a video link to our remote site. I'm exhausted, but I really have to be on, you know what I mean, because you really have to work to keep the attention of the students who aren't with you physically in the same room. I finish classes, get home at about 10:30 p.m., eat some dinner, talk with my daughter—I want to catch up on her day—and then in bed.

But Rosie's day isn't over yet:

I'm in bed, almost asleep, and then my daughter Rachel comes into the room. She sits down on the end of the bed and starts crying. She's a college junior and has a paper due tomorrow. The paper's worth 50 percent of her grade—and she hasn't even started. I ask her why she waited, and she says something about how busy she's been. I think there's no point getting angry; instead I get up and offer to help. She has five books on the topic but hasn't read any of them. I skim the books, and we sit down at the computer and work. It's

4:15 a.m. when I finally get back in bed. I have the EEOC audit the next day—well, today—and the auditors are from the state so I really have to be ready for them even though I only get about three hours of sleep that night.[18]

Rosie, in the supermom role, also squeezes in community service.

I'm a member of the Business Advisory Board and Workplace Regulation Board for the chamber of commerce. I volunteer for the employer panel for the business job fair. I do charity work through my church. If my students need me to come speak for one of their organizations, I do that too.

Reading Rosie's comments about her typical day in a typical week is enough to make anyone want to catch his or her breath. But such is the reality of many working women's lives. Her schedule is jam-packed—four jobs, two kids, doctor appointments, college classes, housework, planning her son's wedding, and dating. She is constantly on overdrive and overload. Rosie wants to have it all—a fulfilling life and an exciting career for herself while supporting her children's college education and dreams. The work-family literature often describes women professionals as constantly torn between managerial and personal roles, chronically feeling both guilty and exhausted. How does she do it all and maintain her sanity?

When my husband was sick, the doctor told me: "Rosie you always have to keep the environment in your home absolutely stress free and extremely positive at all times, no matter how bad things may get because David's [my husband's] health can take no less than a stress-free environment." We always tried to stay positive and happy and save our worries for when we really knew we had them. And you know, that positive attitude we kept in our home really helped us see the positive in everything and everyone around us. That definitely made a significant difference in our lives then and who my

*children, Jason and Rachel, and I are now. . . . They are great
kids, and it was they that got me through the death of David,
along with my family, friends, and faith.*

The combination of Rosie's faith, family, and friends is her rock
that gets her through the difficult times and pushes her to do her
personal best. Rosie is a supermom. She, like many other working
moms, is constantly trying to juggle career, family, and her own
needs. She made the decision early on that her children would have
a stable, caring home life as well as the best future possible by getting their college degrees now rather than waiting, as she did. She
is a bundle of enthusiastic energy, always wanting to go the extra
mile for those around her, whether it be her children, her students,
or her employees. She often overpacks her schedule, taking on
additional work to earn extra money or to develop new skills or
take on a new challenge. The time demands and stress have taken
their toll on her health. But her children have always come first—
before her own needs and goals.

THE TALENT DRAIN

Rosie is trying to do it all. She is caught in a constant bind between
work and family responsibilities. For some women, the struggle
between work and family responsibilities is simply too draining to
manage in the long term. Women who find they can't do it all are
opting out of the workforce because they find the struggle between
work and family responsibilities to be difficult, if not impossible, to
manage, given the way work and societal roles are structured.
There is a tremendous brain drain occurring among working mothers that is harmful to our society. This drop-off in workforce participation seems especially acute among highly educated,
professional women. Consider these facts:

- According to the Center for Work-life Policy, high-achieving
  women who were expected to now be at the top of corporations are instead out of the workforce or working part-time.
  Of Harvard MBA graduates, only 38 percent of the women

who graduated in 1981, 1985, and 1991 work full-time, and of Stanford University graduates, 57 percent of the women who graduated in 1981 have left the workforce.[19]

• Married mothers are increasingly turning to part-time employment. A recent survey of Yale University women found that 60 percent of female undergraduates intend to cut back on their work or stop work entirely when they have children.[20]

• Researchers at the Simmons School of Management found that while 89 percent of the 571 women surveyed reported that they believed advancement opportunities for women had improved in the last ten years, only 58 percent were satisfied with their own advancement opportunities and only 30 percent believed that women and men have equal advancement opportunities.[21]

But it is more than the siren call of motherhood that is causing well-educated women to exit well-paid, career-directed positions prematurely—before they get to the top of their firms. The demands of the workplace—long hours, sudden travel commitments, and client crises—require an all-out effort that excludes, by necessity, spending time with children. Research on work and family issues is not clear on the precise nature of the relationship between work, family, and stress. Some researchers believe that work and nonwork domains are positively related; this is called the "positive spillover or enrichment effect." Other research suggests that work and family life demands are incompatible. However, there is a general consensus that work interferes with family life more often than family life interferes with work.[22] The demands of today's still family-unfriendly workplaces require an impossible choice: career or family—and many women (and men) are choosing family, thereby opting out. The opt-out phenomenon takes many forms. Some women opt out and leave the workforce for good. Others opt out and return once their children are older. And many opt out of full-time jobs and work part-time instead.

FROM FAST-TRACKER TO
STAY-AT-HOME MOM

Ann Storm had worked at a personal products company as a sales rep for household products, and later she crossed over to personal care products. She has an MBA and was given a promotion to the prestigious marketing training program at the company, where she would be groomed to take over a product management position. Product managers at the company are fast-tracked to the top of the firm. Said Ann: "It was an amazing program. They rotated you to various locations—to Atlanta, to New York, and you spent a few months in a finance area, a marketing area, perhaps working in advertising, and then you would settle in as a product manager." But the competitiveness of the firm's culture eventually wore her down. "I am a smiley person, and there were no smiley people— just serious, hard-driving people who wanted to do nothing but work," said Ann. "I was looking for something more."

One day she decided that the cutthroat competition—and the commute into the city—were not for her. She took a job at a small mental health care company instead. "I called them up from work, and they were advertising a position, and I said I was exploring my options," reports Ann. "When I went for an interview, the boss said, 'As soon as you smiled, I knew I wanted to hire you.'"

Ann then spent a year working on packaging, graphics, and the organization of the business. With her husband, she bought a house and was ready to start a family. The company was bought out, and she was invited to work on a small subsidiary project that was being spun off as an entrepreneurial business. But she knew it wasn't for her.

I decided to take another position working for a small firm in the mental health care industry. After working there for one year, I became pregnant with my first daughter. When she was born, I looked at her and knew I wanted to stay home with her. Here we had bought this home based on two incomes, and I didn't think I wanted to stay home after she was born, but one look at her and that's all it took.

Ann hadn't planned on being a stay-at-home mom. But things change. Ann now has four children and has never regretted the decision to stay home. She remains active in her children's school, working in the library and volunteering in the classroom. Some women, like Ann, find that opting out of the workforce completely is the best solution to the work-family dilemma.

FROM FULL-TIME WORKER TO STAY-AT-HOME MOM TO PART-TIME WORKER

Confronted with the choice between the demands of work and family, many women feel it is better to choose part-time employment or adopt a more flexible schedule—even at the loss of career advancement—than not to spend time with their children. Barbara Pasternack made the decision early to give her daughter priority over her career. Before she had her daughter, Hillary, she worked full-time, first as a sales representative for Tura, an eyewear company.

> *I was a very successful salesperson, and the reason I did well was because I built relationships. I never cold-called on a customer. I always called in advance and asked for an appointment. And I sent thank-you notes. I was one of the only female sales representatives, but I did the work by building relationships rather than the charge-ahead mentality some of the men had in the job.*

With a BS degree in health science and a minor in theater and music, she became a health care administrator for a successful endodontics practice for several years, then moved to the Harvard Community Health Plan as a supervisor for the Boston division. But then fate intervened. She met her husband, David, got married, and before their daughter arrived, she worked in a periodontal practice for five years.

> *When our daughter arrived, I stopped working. But I remained active in the community. I did a lot of volunteering,*

became active in the Junior League, and I worked on the Asheville, North Carolina, Film Development Commission. I also served on several fund-raising committees for the Jewish Community Center. But time with my daughter came first.

Barbara has a beautiful singing voice, so she decided to use her talents professionally on a part-time basis, creating a schedule that still permits her to be with her daughter.

I taught vocal technique lessons in a dance school, and then I gave private lessons in vocal technique to several students. I became a cantorial soloist in my congregation. I have always wanted to sing professionally, and now I am starting to follow that dream. I have cut a demo CD, and I have had the opportunity to sing on Broadway at the Marriott Marquis Hotel in Times Square. But I always put my daughter first.

Barbara also works part-time at a retail store and is a top-selling salesperson there, while still working as a voice coach part-time. She does not want to move into a management position at the retail chain. Rather, she makes sure her work schedule as a floor salesperson matches her daughter's school hours. Recently, she has developed a part-time career as an online entertainment writer critiquing the vocal performances of American Idol contestants.[23]

Would I have liked to have had a career in music on Broadway? Definitely. But my daughter was more important. Ultimately I would like to work in radio or be a television talk show host full-time, but that will have to wait. For now, working part-time as a Web entertainment critic and retail salesperson suits my schedule, and hers.

Barbara has reached a solution that works for her. She is a part-time voice coach, a part-time retail salesperson, and a part-time entertainment critic. Ironically, these three part-time jobs permit her the flexibility to spend time with her daughter that one full-time job wouldn't allow.

Family issues may be a component in the decision to leave the workforce, but work-family conflict doesn't tell the whole story. Women also opt out of the workforce for other reasons as well—reasons that include the need for meaning, frustration with workplace discrimination, and the lure of entrepreneurship.

THE SEARCH FOR MEANING

Many women get off the fast track when work doesn't provide the fulfillment they expected. A recent survey showed that 17 percent of women left the workforce because their jobs were not satisfying or meaningful. Only 6 percent of women stopped work because the work itself was too demanding. Overall, understimulation and a lack of opportunity were most often cited as the reasons women left the workforce.[24]

The reasons women leave the workforce are not always due to family needs. In our own survey, women mentioned a wide variety of reasons for opting out:

- A medical crisis

- Corporate downsizing

- Services no longer required

- Lack of challenge

- Gender discrimination

- Need to increase education

- Desire to travel and seek adventure

A *Fortune*-Yankelovich survey of three hundred career women, ages thirty-five to forty-nine, echoed these reasons. This survey uncovered a variety of additional reasons why women were considering leaving the corporate grind (some were considering more than one option).

- 45 percent were considering starting their own businesses

- 44 percent were thinking of changing their jobs in the same career field

- 35 percent were considering the possibility of changing their careers altogether

- 38 percent were contemplating going back to school

- 37 percent indicated the need for a sabbatical

- 33 percent were considering making a major change in their personal lives

- 31 percent were thinking of simply leaving their jobs and not working[25]

For many women, therefore, this exodus may not be about motherhood but about a sense of dissatisfaction at work. Boredom may be the cause. A recent *New York Times* article highlighted the fact that many women opt out of corporations because they do not receive the intellectual stimulation they need. Many women, especially those at midlife, opt out because they do not feel valued.[26] A recent study of ten high-achieving women at midlife found that these women were interested in reevaluating their lives during the age forty and age fifty transitions.[27] The women indicated that they were searching for greater meaning as well as balance in their lives.

Single women and women at midlife have joined the exodus of working mothers who are opting out of the workforce. Perhaps the greatest indicator of workforce movement is from single women: while single women may have more freedom to pursue their career ambitions, they are not any more satisfied with their work situations than are married mothers. Among married mothers, however, having a baby may offer a graceful escape from a boring job into a new, more complex life pattern. Beaten down by the system, dissatisfied by your career options, a baby is placed in your arms. If your work has become a grind, quality child care isn't available, and the baby's needs are great, opting out of the workforce seems a compelling course of action. Having a baby may be used as an excuse more than as the real reason or the only reason for leaving an unsatisfying job.

THE PERSISTENCE OF DISCRIMINATION

A large segment of the women we spoke with admitted that gender discrimination was a reason for leaving the workforce. Although it may be true that many women leave work to care for family, not all women are leaving corporations for that reason alone. Discrimination against women, while decreasing in frequency, still exists. According to Catalyst, Inc., an organization that supports the advancement of women, the glass ceiling has grown more permeable in recent years, but only to a select cadre of professional women. Women are still overrepresented in stereotypically female occupations (e.g., secretaries, nurses) and underrepresented in the upper echelons of management across Fortune 500 companies, although their numbers are slowly increasing. Although the percentage of women managers has increased from 16 percent in 1970 to 46 percent in 2000, women hold only 16 percent of the corporate officer positions for Fortune 500 companies.[28] Ironically, the salary gap between women and men widens the further up the pay scale you go and the higher the education level you have. Women are paid less, even in traditional female industries and jobs; women secretaries, for instance, earn eighty-four cents to the dollar earned by male secretaries. Although women own 26 percent of the businesses in the United States, only $1.8 billion of the $35.6 billion in venture-capital investments in 1999 went to women-owned businesses.[29] A majority of upper management positions in most industries, including higher education, are still filled by men. Only 47 percent of women faculty have tenure as compared to 65 percent of men; only 18 percent of full professors at doctoral universities are women.[30]

There is no question that women have made great strides in gaining entrance to firms and shattering the glass ceiling.[31] Unfortunately, many women now find themselves stuck in middle management positions, unable to unlock the door that leads to the executive suite. Considerable scholarly research shows that

Some Facts about Gender Discrimination

- Only 47 percent of women faculty have tenure compared to 65 percent of men.
- Women hold less than 10 percent of the profit-and-loss jobs that lead to executive positions.
- Women hold only 16 percent of Fortune 500 corporate officer positions.

women's advancement is still hampered by discrimination in regard to advancement opportunities as well as salaries.[32] Catalyst reports that women in the largest U.S. firms hold less than 10 percent of the profit-and-loss line jobs that eventually lead to the top organizational positions.[33] Female executives cite the following as the reasons more women don't advance to executive levels.

- Lack of general management or line experience (79 percent agreement)

- Exclusion from informal networks (77 percent agreement)

- Stereotypes about women's roles and abilities (72 percent agreement)

- Failure of top leaders to assume accountability for women's advancement (68 percent agreement)[34]

Women leave the workforce because they hit the glass ceiling. Long work hours coupled with the demands of family to create push and pull factors that cause women to leave the workforce.[35] The lack of advancement prospects for women may in fact be a stronger predictor of women's turnover than the ticking of their biological clocks and the demands placed on them by their children. In a study that examined turnover intentions of women, researchers found that women's intentions to leave were not necessarily the result of "family structure" in the sense of the number of children they had at home. Instead, women indicated that they were leaving for the same reasons male managers have traditionally left: lack of career opportunities in their current company, job dissatisfaction, and low organizational commitment.[36]

The glass ceiling may have a profound effect on women's willingness to put in the hours at work. If a woman thinks there is no possible way she will be promoted, why stay late? Studies of promotion experiences show that promoted managers are generally less likely to resign than nonpromoted managers, and promoted women are less likely to resign than promoted men.[37] If a woman feels her career is being derailed, or that she has no chance to succeed at the upper levels, she is likely to leave the company prematurely. Studies of derailment show that managers become blocked in their careers for a variety of reasons, including a lack of interpersonal skills, personality flaws, and an inability to adapt to a changing organization.[38]

For women, charges of discrimination and outright sexism cloud the waters of career decision making. Tina Heinzmann, an attorney who left a well-respected Manhattan law firm, described the discrimination she experienced in her law career.

> *In a male-dominated field, in a male-dominated culture, I got tired of all the work hours. I saw people having kids but working part-time—and in a big law firm part-time is really 60–70–80 hours a week. There were no reasonable part-time hours. Clients are calling all the time—weekends, late at night, expecting you to be at their beck and call. And law firms (at least fifteen years ago) in general have very little respect for employees, especially women who are mothers. I found it very hard to switch between being a mom to being a top-notch attorney and back. How can you do that and make partner and deal with the men in the firm and still be a mom? It was an impossible choice.*

Tina soon realized that the demands of working at a law firm in the city were incompatible with the values she held about rearing her children. She was disillusioned with a culture that she felt did not respect people, with the law in general, and with her work hours.

> *There I was, working all these hours, and I started to realize the brass ring was just that—all brass and no gold. What I wanted to do was be with my children. After some deep soul*

searching, I took myself off partnership track, moved away
from the big city, and now I really enjoy what I do.

Instead of continuing to practice law, she decided to take a job
in her community, and get involved locally.

I took a job that was a pay cut, serving as office manager for
the town youth orchestra, which is a wonderful organization.
I also was very involved in the PTA as a member of the Coun-
cil of PTAs, a PTA president of one of the elementary school
PTAs, and served on the advisory panel for the development
of a new school in town, and then I became the president of
that PTA. Would I go back to the law and all that masculine-
driven culture? No. Law firms have a culture that does not
respect employees. I stood up for a case in my husband's law
firm and found the kind of law I do, which concerns ERISA
[Employee Retirement Income Security Act] benefits, had
changed greatly. I would rather do work in my community
than return to that grind.

Other women in law firms second Tina's comments. Another
woman attorney, who preferred not to be identified, described her
career in the law today.

I started out as an attorney in New York City working for one
of the big law firms, working to midnight every day. To get to
partner you had to work, work, work; eventually you get to be
a partner, but you have no life. So I gave up the high-power
job to work in the DA's office for a quarter of the salary. I
loved it. I was in trial a lot, and it was very interesting work.
But eventually I switched jobs and went back to work for a
higher salary—my husband was starting his own business,
and we needed the extra income, so I took a job at a smaller
law firm outside of New York. I'm not going to make partner
there, either, even though I am a team player and I have been
there four years. The culture is work, work, work; clients
expect you to be at their beck and call, and the male partners
all wonder why women have such difficulty putting in all

those hours until midnight. I love my work, and being a lawyer is a part of who I am. I had such big dreams when I came out of law school. But when you have to work such long hours, day after day, including weekends, you really have to wonder, at what cost? This is how the men in the firm run the place.

A LACK OF AMBITION?

Do women lack ambition? Some have suggested that perhaps one reason why many women are not willing to put in the hours to ascend to the upper management ranks has to do with women's ambition rather than with outright discrimination. For women, the decision to pursue a career goal is reconsidered repeatedly and is often abandoned. Anna Fels, a psychiatrist who has examined women's ambition, says that women and men create, reconfigure, and realize (or abandon) their goals for different reasons.[39] She suspects that a lack of recognition affects women in the workplace. According to Fels, if women do not feel recognized for a job well done, they are less likely to pursue their goals. Women more openly seek and compete for affirmation when they are with other women. For women's ambition to thrive in corporations, both the development of expertise and the recognition of accomplishments are required.

However, there is no reason to believe that men's ambition is more powerful than women's ambition. A recent survey conducted by the Center for Gender and Organizations at Simmons College of Management showed that women continue to desire leadership positions and are comfortable with power.[40] Strong work commitments are fueled by powerful ambitions; this is true for women and for men, especially those who adopt a more masculine self-identity.[41] Research shows that few, if any, gender differences in aspiration exist from the ages of young child to adult.[42] However, differences in ambition do appear in stereotyped, role-defined activities: boys' attainment standards are higher in athletic and mechanical skills, while girls' standards are higher in artistic, verbal, and social skills. As adults and members of traditional, male-dominated corporations, women are persistently excluded from the social decision-making networks, making it difficult, if not impossible, for them to be considered as major players in the work-place.[43] Women play the game by different rules, and in a culture that is defined by masculine norms of self-aggrandizement and self-promotion, women may realize, too late, that they are losing out. Thus they shift their ambitions to other challenges—such as more entrepreneurial prospects—that might allow them to balance work and family.

THE ENTREPRENEURIAL LINK

As advancement is often blocked for women in traditional corpo-rations, many women turn to entrepreneurial endeavors. The Cen-ter for Women's Business Research estimates that women own 50 percent or more of almost half of all privately held U.S. businesses. Of these 10.6 million organizations, women are the majority owner of 6.7 million firms. Since 1997, the growth rate of women-owned firms is almost twice the rate of all other firms.[44] Dorothy P. Moore, a scholar who studied women entrepreneurs and reports the results in her book *Careerpreneurs,* found that many female busi-ness owners delve into entrepreneurial endeavors as an escape from the corporate grind.[45] Moore's work is notable because she identifies a variety of different types of women entrepreneurs, including (1) *intentional entrepreneurs,* who knew from childhood that they wanted to own their own business; (2) *latent entrepre-neurs,* who came to the realization that they wanted to own their own businesses later in life; (3) *family business owners,* who inher-ited a business; (4) *co-preneurs,* who jointly own a business with their spouses; and (5) *franchisers* or *market expanders,* who create many different businesses.

Although some women become entrepreneurs because they had always intended to do so, many women entrepreneurs delay realizing their entrepreneurial dreams until they have a family. For those women who have jumped off the corporate track, entrepre-neurial endeavors allow for a graceful return to the workforce on their own terms. Most entrepreneurial women believe that running their own business will allow for more flexibility and control over their lives, as well as provide a greater sense of challenge and contentment with work. Often they are surprised when this is not the case.

Madolyn Johnson is a proud entrepreneur.[46] Founder of her own highly successful enterprise, Signature Homestyles,[47] she began her career as a teacher. But when her daughter Cari was born, she realized that she did not want to go back to the commitment of the classroom, although she loved teaching.

> *I started the business with $1,500 from my teacher's retirement. I was so naive, I thought I could collect some money from customers, and the business would be off and running. But it doesn't work like that. Within two weeks the vendor wanted to be paid right away at pickup time. I thought of going to a bank, but I had nothing for collateral. So I went to my neighbor, who had been doing some babysitting for me with Cari, and I said to her, "Well, I guess I'm done. That's that." But Mildred went into the back bedroom and brought out a shoebox where she kept the money I gave her for babysitting. She counted out $600 and said, "Don't worry, take this." I was speechless. She said, "I'll get my money back someday." And she did. I have the business that was saved by a shoebox! Mildred became my first employee and worked for me for twenty years. When she retired, I handed her a shoebox with tickets to Hawaii inside, and now that she has passed, I established a scholarship in her name. I couldn't have done it all—business or with my girls—without Mildred by my side.*

She developed her business slowly, with a few contacts.

> *In the beginning I created a model that is still used by our sales force today. I started out on my own with friends and family to get the business going. This business was blessed—I believed in it, I lived it, and others around me believed in it and lived it, too. I had to drive the growth through initial contacts. When I was pregnant with my second daughter I would go to the bank, as I did routinely each year. All my bills were*

*paid, I was debt free, and my business was growing, but the
banker asked me what I was going to do with my business
after the baby was born. I responded that I would continue to
grow it as I had done for the past five years. The banker
informed me that they thought that would be very difficult
and that I should find another bank. I turned on my heel and
knew exactly what to do. That was one of my "Oh my God"
moments. By the end of the day I had a new banker and a new
bank.*

Asked about the risk of owning her own business and balancing
work and family, she smiled knowingly.

*In the beginning I was scared. But over time you learn that
you can get through the little hurdles and gain confidence and
you can make it through any bump in the road. As you add
people to the team, you are no longer on the journey by yourself. You develop relationships that work. Eventually you can
turn to those people for help. I had a purpose when I started
this business—I wanted to be with my family, and I wanted to
earn some money. When I had my first daughter I realized it
was great to have her, but it wasn't great to be broke. So I
found a way to integrate it all.*

Another pattern, perhaps a less risky one, is to become intrapreneurial, within the confines of a corporate structure. In the
entertainment industry, for example, careers are not characterized
by an uninterrupted ascent up the corporate ladder.[48] Instead,
women's careers in that industry can seem more like a game of
hopscotch. If an individual develops a project into a hit, she might
skip ranks regardless of age or experience or education. If an individual wants to try something different, she might move from the
production end of the business to writing. If an individual has
backed a flop, she can quickly fall from her position of power.

Some of the women in this industry have even left a major company for a while, freelanced or started their own businesses, and
later returned to another major company in the industry. Their
entrepreneurial endeavors have paid large dividends. For example,

Lucy Fisher, a prominent Hollywood producer of *Stuart Little* and *Bewitched* fame, became vice chair of Columbia Pictures during the 1990s before becoming an independent producer. Numerous women are now included in Hollywood's "New Girls network," running major film production studios, such as Ann Pascal, chair of Sony Pictures, Nina Jacobsen, president of Buena Vista Motion Pictures Group, and Gail Berman, who heads up Paramount's creative team. Many of these women have been independent producers before reaching the top of these firms.[49] These women have shown what they could accomplish on their own, and the larger companies have been eager to hire that type of talent.

Other industries besides entertainment have exhibited striking career pathing anomalies. For example, during the boom period of Silicon Valley, individuals would devote massive amounts of time and energy to their IT start-ups, hoping that they could sell their shares at the right time and become millionaires before the age of thirty. These "gambler careerists" would either strike it rich or lose big and start over at another firm, hoping this time the hard work and long hours would lead to the big payoff.[50]

So entrepreneurial efforts can be a means to leave the corporate grind, to showcase abilities and move back into a corporation at a higher level, or as a gamble that if won, could open the door to many different life choices. The numbers are staggering; many women are opting out of corporations to try to do business on their own. For women who may be blocked by the corporate glass ceiling, becoming an entrepreneur may be the ideal choice.

ONE CAREER MODEL DOES NOT FIT ALL

Women's careers, unlike those of men, have been affected by a number of complex factors—discrimination, sexual harassment, industry culture (e.g., "You're only as good as your last hit"), career pathing anomalies, trailing spouse issues, and family demands. Early career models, which were based on the work life of the typical 1950s professional, have been at a loss to explain the disparate, nonlinear, and interrupted careers of women, or the reasons why women are opting out of corporate America. In the 1950s, a husband focused on climbing the corporate ladder while his wife tended to their children and home. According to these models, men worked for one or two firms over their work lives, often starting with the company right out of high school or college and staying with the firm until retirement. The central assumption behind these career development models was that employees wanted to get ahead. External measures of success such as high salaries, company cars, expense accounts, glamorous travel, bonuses, and other perks were used to motivate them. Some men hoped to break away from their working class, union backgrounds and move into management positions. Men were expected to be the breadwinners, and women were expected to remain under their fathers' protection or engage in what was considered "women's work" (e.g., secretary, teacher, nurse) until they married.

As times changed, more and more women entered the labor force, earned university degrees, and moved from "women's work" into professional positions and male-dominated industries. Although women's place in the labor force altered, organizational policies seemed to be stuck in a 1950s time warp. Emphasis was still on extrinsic rewards. Firms assumed family matters belonged at home—and were the sole responsibility of the employee. Work and home were viewed as two different, divergent worlds. Firms assumed that women fit into the same linear model that was used to describe the careers of men.

Attempts to explain the actual lives of working women using such linear up-the-corporate-ladder male career models have been unsuccessful.[51] There is *no* overarching pattern to women's careers as a group. Instead, women's careers are marked by shifts, changes, transitions, compromises, and sharp bifurcations much too complex to compress into any existing linear career model. For example, psychologist Daniel Levinson examined men over the course of their lives through age sixty. His research documented how the life structure for men evolves over time, and he developed a stage theory that describes how men move through alternating periods of crisis and stability. Later, he tried to apply his model to the lives of women.[52] While he did find some similarities, he had to divide his sample of women into "homemakers" and "career women." Although homemakers and career women went through the same sequence of life stages, he found great differences between and within the two groups.

> *The difficulties of these women must be placed in social-historical context. We live in a time when the Traditional Marriage Enterprise, and the gender meanings, values, and social structures that support it, are undergoing major change. The homemakers' lives give evidence that the traditional pattern is difficult to sustain. Most women who tried to maintain this pattern formed life structures that were relatively unsatisfactory—not viable in the world, not suitable for the self. The few who were more or less contented paid a considerable price in restriction of self-development. The career women tried to anticipate the future: to reduce the gender splitting, to enter formerly "male" occupations, to work on equal terms with men, and to establish a family life in which homemaking and provisioning were more equally divided. Their lives attest to the pleasures and problems of innovation, of attempting to realize values not well supported by the current culture and institutions.[53]*

Levinson found considerable variability in the ways in which career women, in particular, handled issues of discrimination, sexism, and household overwork. He reported that many women experienced conflict between the traditional role of homemaker and the nontraditional role of the career woman.

Psychologist Judy Bardwick independently examined Levinson's concepts on a sample of women and found some interesting and significant differences.[54] Bardwick found that during the early adult transition years (ages 17 to 28), women focus on formulating adult commitments while men attempt to keep their career and life options open. During the settling down period (ages 30 to 40), women's biological clock and decisions about parenthood frame women's life choices. Finally, middle adulthood (ages 40 to 50) is a time of great promise for women. Women who have sacrificed their needs earlier typically become more independent, concentrating on their careers and self-identities.

Bardwick's conceptualization of Levinson's work offers a fresh perspective on issues that affect women over the course of their lives. She suggests that women value relationships as a means of development, and that, unlike men, women's biological clock frames their life decisions. Finally, she affirms what has been called the "golden middle age" for women, that time in middle age of free-dom, self-searching, and a release from serving others. Like Bard-wick, other researchers have also noted the effect of the biological clock on women's career choices, women's sequencing of caregiv-ing and achievement roles, and women's attempts to be both care-givers and achievers at the same time.[55]

Developing a coherent model for women's careers is quixotic, because biology frames women's life and career choices to a greater extent than it does men's, and women often take a secondary path to their careers. This does not mean that women are not ambitious; nor does it mean they do not desire high-powered careers, as many men do. But some women, by opting out, may relinquish their own high-powered career ambitions. At first blush, it may appear that feminism has failed and that women are resorting to sexist roles of the past. But there may be other reasons—deeper, more complex reasons related to the female psyche—that might explain why women choose the opt-out path.

THE IMPORTANCE OF RELATIONSHIPS TO WOMEN'S CAREER CHOICES

In her groundbreaking book *In a Different Voice,* Carol Gilligan suggests that women and men operate in different worlds; women see themselves amid a network of connections while men view their world from the perspective of an individual in a hierarchical social order.[56] Gilligan posits that women are entwined within the relationships they sustain, and make connections in their social context. Women socialize within a web of connections, nurture those connections, and act to preserve those connections. Men, on the other hand, see themselves as operating autonomously, individ-ually, and independently within their social worlds. For women, connecting with and taking care of others is reinforced by society. For men, separating from others and becoming an individual entity, "one's own man" who is independent from others, is reinforced.

Gilligan, who was actually studying the stages of moral de-velopment, not career development, found that women's moral development is the mirror image of men's. For men, development begins with the premise of separation and the importance of increasing individual autonomy. Male developmental patterns center on the acceptance of universal principles to define hierarchy, justice, and fairness. Men chart a developmental sequence that begins with the acknowledgment of individuality, the development of self, and individual workplace accomplishments. Eventually the developmental sequence for men moves in the direction of intimacy and connections with others, and it finally concludes with the recognition of others as equally important to the self.

For women, the developmental process is reversed. Women start from an assumption of connection, gradually explore ways of managing and tolerating separation, and finally move along a developmental path that permits them to see the self as equal to others. Attachment, connectedness, relationships, sacrificing one's needs for others, and working within a framework of other relationships are distinct parts of women's development.

Scholar Joan Gallos closely examined Gilligan's model and noted that the two basic tensions of human development—attachment and separation—are resolved differently by women and by men. Development for men often suggests increased autonomy and separation from others as a means of strengthening identity, empowering oneself, and developing a life action plan. For women, development is relational. A woman's development is tied to her understanding of and her strengthening of herself in relation to others.[57] Theories of careers that don't include attention to relational aspects lose sight of the potential of growth-in-connection aspects of career development so important to women and cannot explain how women's careers actually unfold.[58]

THE NEW NEUROSCIENCE AND RELATIONALISM

Studies on the neuroscience of the brain supports this theme of "relationalism" (connectedness, nurturing, and interdependence) on the part of women. Table 1 compares relationalism for women with men's views. It is possible that relationalism could be hard-

TABLE 1
Women's and Men's Worldviews

	Women	Men
Decisions guided by	Relationships	Hierarchical social order
Traditional role	Nurturer	Breadwinner
Goal	Attachment	Separation
Needs	Sacrifice of own needs for needs of others	Development of self-identity
Sequence of moral development	Putting others' needs first to putting one's own needs on an equal footing to those of others	Individuality to intimacy

wired into the female psyche. Neuroimaging techniques that allow scientists to study brains as they think, feel, or remember have revealed that there are more synaptic connections and greater thickening across the corpus callosum (the dividing midline of the brain) in women's brains than in men's. Scientists have also found evidence that blood flow across the two hemispheres of the brain is almost 20 percent higher in women than in men.[59] Whatever women do, more neurons are activated in their brains. These observations support the theory that the male brain divides tasks between the two hemispheres, while the female brain connects information across both sides.

The compartmentalization of the male brain, researchers theorize, may enhance the necessary ability to focus in male brains—an artifact of evolution from the days when it was the male's role to find territory, food, and a female with whom to mate. Females need to be simultaneous, multitasking, and ready to go in all directions to protect their young. Male and female brains may have evolved differently to allow greater adaptability to the tasks at hand, with the male's survival instinct creating an independent, action-oriented brain pathway and the female's protection reflex for her young causing a more connected, nurturing set of brain elements and synapses.

The connectivity of the female brain may also translate into an edge in verbal skills. Girls usually speak sooner, learn to read more easily, are less prone to learning disorders, have larger vocabularies than boys, and are absolutely more verbally adept than boys.[60] Men excel in spatial reasoning, mapping, and three-dimensional tasks. The ways in which brains process information show up in behavioral differences by gender. Women have an easier time evaluating emotions accurately, while men's brains work harder at evaluating which emotion is displayed. Men's lack of literacy in emotional expression may result from a tuning out process that occurs in childhood and adolescence that allows them to lose touch with their feelings. The opposite occurs for women: young girls are recognized, supported, and applauded for their intense acuity with emotions. Women and men may also experience emotion differently: while happiness is a unisex brain experience, sadness saturates an area eight times larger in women's brains than in men's.[61] Recently, researchers have discovered a biobehavioral stress response in females that amounts to a "tend and befriend" response rather than the typical male "fight or flight" response; this response demonstrates how ingrained attachments and caregiving may be in women.[62] The "tend and befriend" response on the part of women may suggest an inherent tendency toward relationalism that helps women cope during times of stress.[63]

CONNECTION AND RELATIONALISM AT WORK

Because the workplace has been a man's world, the behaviors valued by men—a command and control leadership style, attention to hierarchy, quick action and response—have dominated and been rewarded. Women—who value connection, attachment, caregiving, and process—find they are odd ducks in a sea of masculine corporate values. An outstanding book about the culture clash between men and women in corporations is *Disappearing Acts: Gender, Power, and Relational Practice at Work* by researcher Joyce Fletcher. Fletcher identifies several actual "relational practices" that women pursue at work that are discounted, or ignored, by men.[64]

- Mutual empowering through sharing information, facilitating connections, and protecting others from the consequences of their relative ineptitude

- Affirming team members' individual uniqueness through listening, respecting, and responding to them

- Focusing on the team's task by placing project needs ahead of individual career concerns, resolving conflict, and anticipating and taking action to prevent further problems

- Recognizing and accepting responsibility for breaks in relationships that could impede achievement, and reconnecting after such breaks

- Using feelings as a source of data to understand and anticipate reactions and consequences

- Responding to emotional data to understand situations and strategize appropriate responses

Fletcher makes the point that these valuable relational acts "are disappeared," or, in other words, were devalued or unrecognized in the larger social (male) context of the organization. Women's relational contributions to the *process* of running a department, and their attention to the relations and interdependencies of departmental units were not formally recognized or rewarded.

Studies of women's leadership styles also suggest evidence for the relational perspective. Women may be more transformational and team oriented in their leadership style, and may focus more on empowering others.[65] Women tend to adopt a more interactive leadership style—a style that includes participation, power sharing, and information sharing—that is distinctly relational.[66] Women focus on making people feel important, included, and energized. "Participation" and "empowerment" are keywords that women use to describe how they lead and manage others. Research has found that there is a belief among women that sharing power and information accomplishes several things. Sharing power and information creates loyalty by signaling to employees that they are trusted and their ideas are respected. It also gives employees the ability to reach conclusions on their own, solve problems, and reach similar benchmarks. Such aspects of management are valued by women in ways that are not traditionally valued by men. Many best-selling business books, however, have suggested that managers who readily share information, empower employees, and use a democratic rather than traditional command and control management style— all the behaviors that are more likely to be displayed by women than men—are the leaders who will guide their organizations to future success.[67]

In sum, women's styles of relating to others in the workplace

- Are more contextual, connected, and interdependent than men's

- Focus on the team first rather than "me first"

- Maintain balance in life activities and relationships

- Develop a sense of "knowing" through wholehearted identification with others

- Exercise an ethic of caring and connection

- Attempt to create synergism, collaboration, and compromise

RELATIONALISM: AN EXPLANATION FOR THE OPT-OUT PHENOMENON

These recent developments in neuroscience, psychology, and behavioral studies lend credence to our thesis that relationships, connections, interdependence, empowerment, and the nurturance of others may be a feature of women's development that may have an impact on their career choices and aspirations. Most traditional career models—defined by men for men and similar to leadership models defined by men for men in corporations—view this relational proclivity on the part of women as a shortcoming. We disagree. From our conversations with women, we have found that relationalism is *not* a shortcoming of women's lives but a *feature* of women's career development—the starting point to understanding women's career choices and transitions.

The "river of time" model, developed by Gary N. Powell and Lisa Mainiero, suggests that women place themselves somewhere on a continuum between an emphasis on their careers, their relationships, or a balance of both.[68] Career-stage models for women are not applicable, because women emphasize one aspect of their lives or careers over another at different times. Women continually shift focus between career and relationships, trying to find the right balance between the two at any given time.

The "river of time" model suggests that women's lives run like crosscurrents in a river, where at certain stages in life, relationship and balance issues will predominate, while at others, career aspirations and achievements will take precedence. This river metaphor is different from the life-stage models that summarized men's corporate careers in the twentieth century. Each woman makes her choices about which aspects to prioritize in her life at a given time for her own personal reasons.[69]

In our research for this book—the three major surveys, online dialogues, and interviews with men and women—we have been struck by the continual and pervasive theme on the part of women that their career decisions were made as a result of awareness of the larger network of relationships around them. We found that for women the concept of "career" is not divorced from family or lifestyle considerations. Career is part of the gestalt of a woman's life, which includes family, friends, children, community, caregiving responsibilities, and nurturing others. For women, the concept of "career" cannot be summarily separated out from a larger understanding of context. Women often sacrifice their own needs and make adjustments in their careers in service of the needs of others. The women we surveyed and spoke with made career decisions from a lens of relationalism—factoring in the needs of their children, spouses, aging parents, friends, and even coworkers and clients—as part of the gestalt of their careers.

The theme of relationalism was so pervasive as we talked to women that it seemed obvious that it ran deep in women's hearts and minds. Women put their families *first* as a component of their career plans, sometimes to the point of opting out to accommodate family needs. Forced to choose between her relationships—regardless of whether these relationships are with her children, spouse, parents, siblings, elderly relatives, or friends—and career advancement, a woman adjusts her career ambitions to suit the needs of those with whom she is connected. For example, the women we talked to made comments such as the following.

> *I do make my career decisions based on being able to spend time with my family. I currently work from home from 5:00 a.m. to 7:00 a.m., then I get my son ready for school and on the bus and go to work from 9:00 a.m. to 3:30 p.m., and am home when he gets off the school bus at 4:00 p.m. I chose the career I did so that I could have these flexible hours in order to be with my son during those special times before and after school.*

> *I turned down a number of promotions over a period of seven years while I started a marriage and a stepfamily. My employer was patient and continued to offer me promotions, one of which I recently took when I felt our family was stable enough for it to work for all of us.*

> *I limited my career to firms less than five miles from home so I could quickly be available to handle family or household situations, for example, picking up sick children from school; taking an elderly parent for medical treatment; meeting delivery, installation and repair people; etc.*

> *Until my boys started school, it was not an issue. Now that they are in school I have turned down several interviews for positions which would involve a move to a different state.*

The changes I made were all due to family obligations that I chose to put first. My whole career has been based on working around my family responsibilities.

The work-family literature shows that gender is deeply ingrained in work-family relations. Women experience more work-family conflict than do men, and they may be subject to unique stressors that do not apply to men.[70] Women also identify more with their family roles than do men.[71] Our research revealed that women's family values were clear and direct. Many of the women we surveyed stated clearly that their families were more important to them than their work. Women said, "Work is meaningless if there is not time for family," and "My children are my legacy, and I want to rear them well." Further, the regrets women had about their careers suggested a relationalism theme: "I wish I could have worked harder than I did, but it was not worth compromising my family or personal needs to work so many hours on the job" and "I wish I had taken a career interruption and/or moved out of the

Women's Comments on Why They Left the Workforce

About career interruptions and why they left the workforce:

- Nothing is more important to me than my family, so I arrange my work around my family's needs. My job changes have happened because of family needs that have involuntarily interrupted my career.
- Family needs necessitated that I change jobs or careers so that I could achieve a better balance for my work and family.
- I took a break from work/career to care for family, children, and/or elders.
- My career has constantly been about transitions and change. I enjoy experimenting with job assignments in different industries, firms, or professions. I enjoy doing new things, practicing new skills, and seeking out new experiences in my career.

About the value they place on family:

- My family is more important to me than my work.
- Work is meaningless if there is not time for family.
- My children are my legacy, and I want to rear them well.

workforce for a period of time to better serve the needs of my family." But not all regrets were family related; some women admitted that they wished they had gone back to school and restarted another career path that was better suited to them.

Women who opted out of the workforce by stating, "My family needs necessitated a job change" or "I took a work break to care for family" were likely to have more than one child in their households. Many of these women also indicated that they had caregiving responsibilities for an elderly parent or relative. Furthermore, women who left the workforce were busy people—they did more of the household chores and handled more of the family responsibilities than those women who remained in the workforce.

But what about single women or women without children? Do they react the same way as working mothers do? Although single women without children did not take career interruptions at the same rate as those who were mothers, surprisingly women without children who remained in the workforce reported that they also "do not have a traditional career." Single and childfree women reported that "I need a variety of challenges in my career" and "I have developed expertise." Single and childfree women acknowledged the relationalism theme in their lives by stating "My family is most important to me"; often they were in the position of caring for an elderly family member or relative. Reported one single woman who was without children,

> *Yes, I have certainly passed up opportunities for much more desirable work in order to benefit people I care about. And rather than taking real pleasure and relaxation holidays I generally go visit my folks, which though dearly loved is not relaxation. It is strongly integrated in women to put others first.*

Even those women who are single and childfree and who have made it in the masculine corporate world, as the statement above suggests, still echo the themes of connection and attachment. Relationalism may be ingrained in women's brains and activated in social relationships, in predispositions toward leadership styles, through coping with stress, and in the ways in which women make decisions about career choices. For women, career choices may not be simple, based only on the merits of a job. A woman's career choices are relational, a part of the whole—her relationships with family, friends, her home, her husband or partner, her community—that form the gestalt of her life.

A TYPOLOGY OF WOMEN'S CAREER PATTERNS

Career development for women is undergoing change. The linear models used to describe men's careers cannot be bent to fit women's lives. Similarly, the simple patterns of the past—women who have a family first, then a career, for example—do not capture the complexities of women's lives today. We found that the career patterns of women are varied and complex. Instead of two mirror-image patterns, we found that women follow one of five patterns, and that clear distinctions between work and home lives are rarely found. The following are the five patterns:

1. The supermom heroine

2. The opt-out prioritizer

3. The late-blooming careerist

4. The traditionalist

5. The nonconformist

The Supermom Heroine

The "supermom heroine" is the woman who is trying to do it all. She's been on fast-forward ever since she became a mother. Running to the mall after work to pick up forgotten basketball shoes for her daughter, calling the PTA chairperson during a break in a business meeting, and missing a soccer game due to travel commitments—all these activities are bound to fatigue anyone, and this woman deserves a medal for holding it together. But after a while she realizes that reading a book to her son over the phone from a remote location is far less satisfying than being there in person.

This is the woman who has been trying for years to fit her family and career demands together in a way that does not compromise both. She is run ragged, and issues emerge in her family life and her career that suggest that compromises are being made in all the wrong directions.

The Opt-Out Prioritizer

The "opt-out prioritizer" is the woman who followed her career ambitions in her twenties and thirties yet heard the siren call of motherhood around age thirty or thirty-five. She excelled in her career early in life but dropped out when the demands of rearing a family became too complicated. Tired, stressed out, and beaten, she retreats from her high-powered career to find fulfillment in a more flexible balance between career and home life. Railing against how unfair the demands of corporations can be, she realizes that she must make a choice between her career and her family. Because she is relational, she prioritizes family over career. She may leave work altogether for a while and return to the workforce at a later date when her family is more capable of caring for themselves. Or she may take a job closer to home to better address the needs of family. But uppermost in her mind is her need to serve her family, and she adjusts her career to suit their needs. She may become an entrepreneur so that she'll have the flexibility of schedule to be home to greet the kids as they get off the school bus. Or she may settle down to a small, focused job in her hometown, one that doesn't require the long hours and travel. Somehow she down-scales her career and believes she now has a more reasonable chance at work-family balance.

The Late-Blooming Careerist

"Late-blooming careerists" are women who had family demands placed upon them early in life but in their forties decided to pursue their own dreams. These women have been lying in wait, serving the needs of others around them, until it became "their time." Several of the entrepreneurs in our sample were late bloomers. "I bided my time all those years," said one woman entrepreneur. "I may have been home, but I was really working out in my mind what it was going to take for me to launch this business." When the demands of child rearing are complete, or perhaps when her marriage fails, this woman decides to find her own way, develop her own career path. But, often because corporations see her as unskilled, she chooses an entrepreneurial path.

The Traditionalist

The "traditionalist" is the woman who may have worked at one or two jobs in her twenties prior to having a family but made a choice to stay home permanently and rear her family. She may have no aspirations to return to the workforce at all, or she may take a part-time job in her hometown. This woman decides that a job is just a job; she is not interested in having a career. Instead, she may find work to put food on the table while doing something that doesn't make her crazy. Or she may stop working while her children are young, settling into a comfortable, reduced lifestyle with her children and family at home. Perhaps she intends to return to the workforce when her children are older and her salary is needed to help meet tuition payments.

The Nonconformist

The "nonconformist" is often characterized for what she is not: she's not a wife, she's not a mother. She has broken one of the unwritten rules of our society—she isn't married. Although the numbers of single women and men have increased in recent years, it is still a societal norm that women of a certain age will be married. Those who aren't married by that age are seen as nonconformist. She may be single by choice; perhaps she didn't marry or have children, figuring that forgoing a family was the price of success. Or she may be single by default, never having found the right partner with whom to share her life or never having had the time in her hectic work schedule to even look. Although neither wife nor mother, she still sees the world from a relational perspective. She still has connections and ties—parents, siblings, friends, and a host of others who depend upon her.

Perhaps burdened by the health care crisis of a parent or a health scare of her own, this woman finds that the degree of travel and political machination in her corporation is simply not worth the effort anymore. She has worked hard and developed her career ambitions over the years—yet even if that success has come, she's wondering if her choices were the best ones. "So I have had this golden career, but what does it all mean?" asked one highly successful executive female. Or she may realize that her talents and skills can be better applied elsewhere, perhaps in pro bono community service work that can make a real difference in the lives of others. This woman may opt out later in life, deciding to get her priorities in order. Maybe she wants to travel the world, or stay home and do gardening. Maybe she just wants to take a break, really examine what she wants out of life, and then return to the workforce at a later time when things are in focus. For her, the motivation to walk away is much more personal. It is about herself—her decisions, her priorities, her values—that may be inconsistent with the corporate model. She craves relationships to create meaning in her life. The only way she can gain clarity and control over her priorities and values is simply to walk away and find more congruent challenges elsewhere—and perhaps less stressful and more meaningful ones.

THE GESTALT OF WOMEN'S CAREERS

Although the idea of relationalism is not new, the extent of its impact on women's career decisions was a surprise to us. In this day and age of women socialized to compete against men in the workforce, it is astonishing to see the level of adjustment to family that women make in their careers. The opting-out phenomenon may be the result of the dual realizations that discrimination in the workplace may mean that promotions will be minimal and that there needs to be a career adjustment to family needs.

The relational model, therefore, puts a new spin on the opting-out phenomenon. Opting out of the workforce may be a natural response from a woman's perspective to the nonwork demands on her life. Rather than decrying those women who leave their posts in midcareer, we may need to have a greater understanding of how women must balance and prioritize different aspects of their lives.

This dimension of women's lives—that nonwork demands intercede with work demands—is wholly different from how men view their careers. In the next chapter, we explore men's careers and examine the absence of relationalism for men in early career.

CHAPTER 3

OFF WITH THE MALE STRAITJACKET

Being a man used to be so easy. In true *Mary Poppins* fashion, the average male led a charmed and well-defined existence. He'd rise in the morning, grab his coffee, and take the train into the office. He'd spend a long and productive day at work, say yes to his boss a lot, and collect his check at the end of the week. When he returned to his home after 6 p.m., he would have dinner, catch up on the day's events, and then give each child a quick kiss on the cheek before settling down in front of the television for the night. Ah! Domestic bliss. His wife took care of the mothering and household duties while he was at work, and everything was right in his corner of the world.

But times have changed. Ozzie Nelson and Ward Cleaver are no longer the models of the perfect father. Instead, dads like Suma Chakrabati are the unlikely heroes for the new form of career. Chakrabati is employed by the United Kingdom's Department of International Development. Like all British civil servants he was expected to be in his office the requisite eight to ten hours a day. But Chakrabati saw things a bit differently. He made headlines when it was revealed he had negotiated a child-friendly employment contract with his boss that stipulated that he would be allowed to have daily breakfasts with his six-year-old daughter and attend his daughter's biweekly school assemblies. When asked for comment, the prime minister's official spokesperson said, "I don't think the indicator of performance is necessarily the amount of time you spend in your office with your jacket over the back of the chair—it's about what you deliver."[1]

The twenty-first-century dad is staring us in the face, and not everyone likes what he sees. Caught between changing mores and expectations for parenthood, working dads are standing up for their rights. As their wives go off to work, men are changing their expectations about the meaning of work-family conflict. Being released from the sole family provider role allows men to value work-family balance.

TRADITIONAL MEN AND THE LINEAR CAREER

In the 1950s the roles of men and women were separate and distinct. Men were socialized to be the sole breadwinners for their families. Their role was clear: earn money to put food on the table. "Be a man," said a father to his son, "and go out and provide for your family." Caught in the Leave-It-to-Beaver, Ozzie-and-Harriet mentality that was so pervasive at that time, women stayed home and did women's work, while men's worth was measured by their ability to provide for their families.

Therefore, earning money (more and more of it for validation purposes) and career advancement (the means of getting more money) became one and the same, and the linear career was born. Taught to covet that next promotion, men worked long hours, typically in manufacturing or the financial services industry, in the hopes of increasing the size of their paychecks. In the twentieth-century mind-set, men went to work for a firm and stayed for the duration of their careers until retirement. Men viewed career development as an uninterrupted ascent up the corporate ladder, or, barring that, long-term full-time employment with the same firm. The reward at the end of the line was a gold watch and a retirement fund.

Traditional career models were built on the experiences of these male employees, who were at their desks from 9 a.m. to 5 p.m. The belief in the hierarchical, linear career path was supported by educational systems that focused on preparing individuals for lifetime employment in a secure profession that was often chosen by parents for the young adults. These corporate career paths were created as a result of the enmeshing of workers returning from World War II who needed employment with the hard-driving mentality that existed at that time. Men returning from the war took pride in the American manufacturing that employed them. Their wives, including many former Rosie the Riveters, were home with their children, tending to hearth and household. Corporations developed policies that suited the times. Other than health insurance, no child care policies addressed children's needs, as children were well cared for by their mothers. The big issue was life insurance. After all, what would happen to the family if the sole provider dropped dead?

EARLY CAREER MODELS

Career models of the twentieth-century were based on moving up the corporate ladder. The central assumption behind career development was that employees desired advancement in their firms and the higher salaries and perks that went with it. Early models of careers discussed specific tasks individuals needed to complete in order to develop and successfully move on to the next stage. For example, Donald Super's theory divides careers into four stages.

- **Exploration:** engaging in self-examination, schooling, and the study of different career options

- **Establishment:** becoming employed and finding a niche

- **Maintenance:** holding on to one's position and updating skills

- **Disengagement:** phasing into retirement[2]

Early career-stage models assumed a linear, upward progression. Super's model, for example, implies long-term employment with one or two firms. Although that may have described the typical 1950s worker, it is no longer true that employees stay with the same firm for the duration of their careers. Today, most workers change jobs every four and one-half years.[3] Super's theory, an artifact of its time, defined success as moving up the corporate ladder and making money. But for today's workers this assumption may no longer reflect reality.[4]

During the 1980s, there were numerous corporate restructurings and downsizings that ended the upward corporate climb for many white-collar workers.[5] Organizations restructured their units from tall and multilayered to flat and lean. To become more flexible in response to rapid technological advancements and increased global competition, firms downsized, eliminating many jobs. There just wasn't room at the upper layers of management for everyone to climb the corporate ladder anymore. Men in their forties and fifties—many with high-powered jobs—were suddenly unemployed with little hope of finding a new position comparable to the old one. Workers who thought they had job security for life found out the hard way that they didn't have that after all. Working hard no longer led to a promotion; instead, it led to a pink slip and a severance package, if you were lucky. Corporate loyalty was reserved for those who were too foolish or too naive to read the warning signs.

Nonetheless, until recently career development experts have held onto Super's theory as the gold standard of the successful career—one that is well-paid, with the worker flush from advancement to the coveted top of the corporate pyramid. As times changed, scholars began to question whether the stage models truly captured workplace realities.[6] While people may progress across stages in the development of their careers, the intersection of family and work complicates career decisions. Distilling career development to a series of stages does not address the complexities of life, career, and balance issues. However, many men, even today, remain entrenched in the idea of the linear career, or at least wish for the fruits of such a linear career path. See Table 2 for a comparison between linear and new careers.

TABLE 2
Linear Careers versus the New Careers

The Old Deal	The New Reality
Work for one or two organizations	Work in many jobs, firms, industries, fields, or even countries
Multilayered hierarchical organizations	Flat, lean organizations
Success measured by salary, promotion, and perks (e.g., the corner office)	Success defined by the individual, with a focus on intrinsic rewards
Employees expected to be in the workplace physically at least from nine to five, and travel required	Because of technology, more flexibility permitted in where employees do their work, and reduced travel requirements
Face time used as a proxy for performance and ambition	Focus on performance outcomes over being physically in the workplace
Employees predominantly white males	Diversified workplace with increased numbers of women and minorities
Man as sole breadwinner	Dual-career couples common
Wife at home to support husband's career and take care of children	Wife still responsible for most of the housework and child care, but husband expected to share some of the load
Man involved in children's lives as work schedule permitted	Man more active in children's lives and willing to trade some extrinsic rewards for more time with his children

THE CLASSIC MALE
LINEAR CAREER PATTERN

A. Thomas Kelly had a linear career. Brought up in the 1950s, he expected that he would work for the same firm all his life. He began his career at Southern New England Telephone (SNET) after serving in the armed forces. His wife, Ginny, already worked there, so he followed her, he thought for a short while.

> *SNET had the reputation as a good company to work for. As a fresh-out-of-college electrical engineer from Rensselaer Polytechnic Institute, I started my career at SNET in the IMDP [Initial Management Development Program], and took a radio engineering job and then moved to Central Office Engineering. After a year on the job, I left SNET to report for army officer basic training, attended the U.S. Army's Guided Missile School, and then studied, analyzed, and assessed the capabilities of the Soviet antiballistic missile (ABM) program. After my three-year obligation was completed, I returned to SNET in a plant extension engineering job, and then my next job was a lateral move to circuit design engineer in the Transmission Engineering Group. In this position I supervised a team of about twelve engineers and support staff; this was a production job, and I interacted with the sales and marketing personnel who dealt with customers and field technicians who performed the work. After twelve months, I was promoted to customer equipment engineer, and, later, to switching supervisor in the Transmission Services Group. This was my first job assignment outside of the engineering organization, and all my previous job assignments were considered staff or headquarters type work. The emphasis of this job was managing a line organization and dealing with operations. After a year on this job, I was promoted to a very visible field job as district switching systems manager. Here I supervised 150 people and managed twelve switching offices.*

Tom Kelly's career developed on a clearly upward, linear career path.

After nearly three years, I was promoted to the position of general operations supervisor, and I supervised a headquarters group of one hundred management employees who provided staff support and direction to the eight field switching districts. At this point in time in the late 1970s, the Bell System was being impacted by market changes. The Justice Department's breakup of AT&T was a factor. At the time of divestiture, AT&T was testing a new mobile radio technology which had been developed at Bell Labs: cellular phone service. I was asked if I would be interested in leading the effort to evaluate the feasibility of deploying the service in Connecticut and, if approved, developing and implementing the business plan for cellular/wireless. I was excited about the prospect of having my own business within the larger company with total responsibility for its creation and results, so after thinking about it for a day, I accepted the offer. We prepared the business case, obtained funding from SNET's board of directors, secured the FCC [Federal Communications Commission] licenses, received Connecticut regulatory approvals, constructed antennas, and built the organizational infrastructure to operate the business. Within three years we went "on air" and launched cellular telephone service. The business start-up was a success, on time and on budget.

Tom Kelly's business success with the cellular organization led him to an opportunity to run yet another, larger business within SNET.

Upon becoming president of the cellular subsidiary, I was promoted to general manager (officer level). While I enjoyed leading the cellular subsidiary and did not lobby for my next job, I was dedicated to the company and would go where I was needed. So I became president of Sonecor Systems, a subsidiary which marketed, installed, and serviced customer premises equipment (CPE). There I was to lead a large organization of one thousand employees. The focus of my attention was on streamlining the business, growing revenue, and reducing costs while keeping employees motivated. After six years on this job, SNET decided to exit the CPE business and sell off the installed customer base. The subsidiary became the SNET Custom Business Group, a much smaller organization which focused on providing network solutions to large business customers. Although accomplishing this transformation was challenging, it was far from enjoyable. I took pleasure in working with my management team to build and grow the organization. However, the task of downsizing, doing more work with less people, and meeting arbitrary budget targets were far less satisfying. For the first time in my career, it was no longer fun to go to work.

He made the decision to retire, at age fifty-five.

I always had desired to be in a position to retire at age fifty-five, even though I never actually planned on it. After doing the financial math, I concluded that I could retire and announced my decision to do so. At the time, we were expecting our first grandchild (a child for Tom, our oldest son); our middle daughter, Lisa, was getting married; and our youngest daughter, Debra, was starting law school.

When Tom was asked about his wife and children, he proudly responded:

I can't complete a reflection on my work career without addressing a major influence—my wife, Ginny. From the beginning when she suggested I seek a summer job at SNET, she was by my side. When our first child, Tom, was born, she gave up her paying job at SNET and took on the more important roles as mother, child raiser, housekeeper, and designated worrier. She was my confidant, sounding board, fashion advisor, seamstress, and launderer, who made sure there was a freshly ironed shirt to wear every day. On those occasions when she socialized with my business associates, she proved to be a good observer and judge of character. In short, she supported me, was my cheerleader, and the rock that held the family together.

Talk to most men whose careers took place in the twentieth century and they will describe climbs similar to A. Thomas Kelly's up the corporate ladder. After living through the Great Depression and losing neighbors and friends during the attack on Pearl Harbor as well as on battlefields in Korea far away from home, these men were willing to work hard in exchange for job security and a chance at the American dream. Tom Kelly was one of the sons of the Greatest Generation, and he and many of his generation followed the same path.

In sum, the typical linear career progresses as follows.

- Work for the same firm, or same industry, for twenty-plus years

- Prioritize work hours

- Climb the corporate ladder as a means to increase salary

- Follow company norms of making family invisible

- Retire when financial goals are reached

THROWBACK TO THE 1950s: THE MALE LINEAR CAREER LIVES ON

Would it come as a surprise that the typical 1950s pattern, as we've seen in the profile of Tom Kelly's career, still exists? Despite the great social and technological changes that have occurred in the past forty-plus years, our research found that men still followed the climb-the-corporate-ladder linear career pattern. We found that most of the men—sons reared by the Greatest Generation—had enacted a typical linear career pattern, working for one industry, if not one firm, for the duration of their careers. Our statistical analyses show a distinctly linear, orderly, upward-trending career pattern for men. Out of 1,630 men and women we surveyed, men consistently produced a pattern that was more indicative of upward movement within a single firm or a set of firms within the same industry. This was a distinct difference from how women described their careers. The majority of the men we studied described a clear linear career path, similar to that of John, who describes his career as a banker:

> *I started with my bank over twenty-five years ago as a part-time teller. I have had the opportunity, over the course of my career with the bank, to be involved in various areas of the organization. These areas include branch management, management of the accounting and proof areas, director of deposit operations, management of consumer loan operations, management of the mortgage field representative team, direction of project management, and my current position as a first vice president as division head of delivery and distribution, where I am responsible for the bank's fifty-branch network and the growth of our deposit portfolio, the alternative financial services area, the trust department portfolio, as well as departments that support branch operations and sales management. I serve as a member of the executive management team of the bank with responsibilities for the development and implementation of the organization's strategic and business plans. I have had the pleasure of a one-bank career. I grew up in the organization, similar to many at our bank. Having been given the opportunity to work in various areas of the organization, I feel that I have a broad view of the organization and have interacted with a vast majority of the people who work here.*

Another classic linear example comes from Tony, who started out in agriculture but moved into a financial/regulatory career for the majority of his career:

> *I graduated college in 1981 with a BS in agriculture and joined the USDA [U.S. Department of Agriculture] as a loan officer. After four years at the USDA working in three locations, I transferred to the Farm Credit Administration [FCA] and moved to Albany, New York, in 1986. At the FCA, I moved to the "other side of the desk" as a bank examiner for the various institutions comprising the Farm Credit System. After fourteen years at the FCA I needed a change of scenery as*

well as a promotion. Therefore, I transferred to the Federal Housing Finance Board [FHFB]. The FHFB is the federal regulator for the twelve Federal Home Loan Banks, a major source of credit and liquidity for most commercial banks, thrifts, credit unions, and some insurance companies. An examiner for sixteen years and a few promotions later, I travel between 35 and 45 percent of the time. On the one hand, this appeals to me, as I am not one to ride a desk five days a week. On the other hand, being away from home gets old [quickly].

Many of the men we surveyed were unequivocal about their linear career paths, as if there were no other choice available. Men responded affirmatively to the questions "My work describes who I am," "The number of promotions is my greatest accomplishment," and "One's salary defines one's worth." Men were far more likely than women to report, "I have pursued my career goals at several different firms all within the same industry," "I was promoted several times after working hard to achieve my goals," and "I have developed a certain level of expertise in my field."[7] A large segment of men reported that they never left the workforce, and if they did, it was because of downsizing, a medical crisis, or retirement.[8] Most men switched jobs because they found "more money offered by the new firm," "more opportunities for advancement by the new firm," or "more challenges offered by the new firm." Family-friendly reasons, such as a shorter commute, more flexibility in work hours, or children, elder care, or household issues were off the radar screen entirely for most of the men in our survey.[9]

Research has found that in dealing with work-family conflict, men are more likely to sacrifice relationships for the sake of their career ambitions in early career.[10] This is the direct opposite of what we found for women. Studies conducted by the Cornell University Work and Family Project concur that men have more linear careers even today. In their research, they found that most men follow orderly or high-geared career paths, moving up through seniority or career ladders in one firm or across several firms. Men's careers also were more likely to be characterized by long-term full-time employment. This is in direct contrast to the experience of women, whose career paths were more varied as a result of delayed entry into the workforce or intermittent or part-time work.[11]

THE CORPORATE MODEL OF MASCULINITY

Why would the linear corporate career remain the standard for men, despite changes and trends that suggest other possibilities for career development? Scholar Mark Maier writes eloquently about the paradigm of corporate masculinity and how this affects male behavior in organizations.[12] He maintains that there are gendered organizational substructures that reward masculinity. Following from the writings of Carol Gilligan, Maier believes that most men view themselves as autonomous, separate, and independent beings. Men respect authority and subordinate themselves to other men in a hierarchy. Men focus on the competition and adopt a me-first mentality that is a throwback to hunter-gatherer days. "Winning" a point in a meeting, or even better garnering a promotion, is paramount, similar to the thrill of the kill. Maier suggests that most men take a view of organizational commitment that is opposed to that of women. Men expect that other life activities and commitments will be subordinated to the priority of career advancement. Therefore, work and one's employer is expected to be a man's central life focus. One must act as though there were no competing loyalties and take the attitude "Family is invisible. I'm a player here, and I can jump as high as you make me." For men, work and family exist in two separate worlds.

Men examine career decisions from the perspective of autonomous, independent action—acting first for the benefit of career, because career advancement ultimately will benefit their families. In our research, we found that men described their careers in terms of outcomes and solutions. "I enjoy using my skills and talents to solve problems and provide solutions" reported a significant proportion of men. "Much of my career has involved being a troubleshooter—the person who goes into an area and fixes things." Reflecting the need to be independent and to take action, they reported: "I was a maverick in my career and did what suited me."

Men's Views: Self-Identity through Work

Men are likely to see themselves as . . .

- Autonomous, separate, and independent
- Concerned with "me first" rather than with teamwork
- Focused on advancement in corporations and responsive to hierarchy in the pyramid
- In competition with those at the same level to "win"
- Ready to subordinate life activities and commitments to the priority of career advancement
- Convinced that knowing occurs through dispassionate distancing of the self that "objectivity" rules

Men are likely to say . . .

- I have pursued my career goals at several different firms all within the same industry.
- I was promoted several times after working hard to achieve my goals.
- I have developed a certain level of expertise in my field.
- I enjoy using my skills and talents to solve problems and provide solutions.
- Much of my career has involved being a troubleshooter—the person who goes into an area and fixes things.
- I was a maverick in my career and did what suited me.

As discussed in Chapter 2, relationalism causes women to find ways to *integrate* work and family. By contrast, the men in our research *compartmentalized* their worlds of work and family. Men's work identity tends to be independent of their family identity.[13] Throughout the surveys and interviews, we learned that men keep their work and home lives separate—and often could do that because the women in their lives help them manage the issues that arise. As one typical male, a banker, said rather proudly, "I have managed to keep life issues completely separate from work issues. I don't bring my work problems home, and I don't take my personal problems to work."

Most men checked off a simple "Not applicable" to the question in the survey that asked, "Was family life ever a reason for a career transition? If so, please describe what happened." For most men, this was simply not an issue. Reported one man in the survey, "I am married and have a child, but those things don't impact my career transitions beyond the need to pay the bills and strive for enough money to live comfortably and provide what they need."

These comments were a distinct and compelling contrast to the voices of the women in our sample. While women discussed leaving work for the benefit of family, men reported that they stayed at work for the benefit of their families, with the overriding philosophy, "If I do well in my career, then my family will prosper." That was Terence's attitude when he described his life and career.

> *The deal was, I was the provider with the career, and my wife took care of the house and home. If I did well in my career, then there was more money to go around. We had to pay for our children's college educations and the house we built, plus salt money away for retirement. That was my job, being the provider.*

It is important to recognize that while men may view work and family as separate spheres, there is a connection between being a provider and a man's family role. To the extent that they view their family role as being the provider, men demonstrate their commitment (and love) for their families by going to work. The good-provider model causes men to demonstrate their commitment to their families by being responsible workers and bringing home an acceptable income. But that leads to an unfortunate nexus between career and identity for men: the male straitjacket.

THE MALE STRAITJACKET

The pressures of being the sole family provider actively pursuing a linear, upward-climbing career for greater financial rewards has produced a "male straitjacket" that few men have escaped. The typical portrait of manhood/masculinity includes a command-and-control leadership style—and a desire to win at all costs. According to the stereotype of what it means to be male, men are supposed to exert dominance, be independent, raise the bar for competition, and show a hardball mentality, largely couched in sports metaphors. Men value logic, numbers, analysis, rules, and hierarchy. In the workplace, men adhere to a rigid structure of command and control. Men show respect for authority and defer to the hierarchy above them.

This stereotype, played out as part of the definition of masculinity in the workplace and reinforced through social norms, has led to a uniform definition of "success" for many men.[14] According to social psychologist Joseph Pleck, "As [men's] paid work role has evolved in modern society, it has come to call for full-time, continuous work from the end of one's education to retirement, desire to actualize one's potential to the fullest, and subordination of other roles to work."[15] By "other roles" we presume that he means the roles associated with housework and rearing children. In other words, if you are a man, you provide for your family and earn as much money as possible—that is your role in life and nothing more.

This rigid definition of masculine success has led to a common occurrence of the male midlife crisis. Daniel Levinson, a psychologist who studied the intimate details of men's development over the life cycle, describes the midlife crisis as a time when there is a contradiction between a man's initial dreams of success and the reality he has achieved.[16] Midlife crisis has been portrayed in countless novels and plays. It is a recurrent theme in the works of writers such as Chekhov, Ibsen, Strindberg, and O'Neill. The Willie Loman character in the play *Death of a Salesman,* by Arthur Miller, is perhaps the most famous and profound portrait of a man in midlife crisis. Caught between his dreams of material success and reality, he lashes out at his wife, drinks too much, and fails miserably as a man because he has not fulfilled the rigid societal definition of masculine success.

The cultlike adherence to male norms and the male tribe has influenced (1) how work gets done in the workplace, and (2) the system of career succession that is in place in many corporations. A man's identity is often inextricably tied up with his work identity. A successful man is a successful careerist. He has achieved a position of prominence in his career, advancing up the hierarchy through a series of career moves. He is thus able to provide amply for his family's needs and to serve as a role model for other men, including his own sons. Men like Willie Loman who adhere to this narrow definition of male success but fail to grasp the brass ring suffer reprisals from family and society at large. And when corporate layoffs hit, men feel the pain of being unemployed and out of work.

WHY DOWNSIZING HURTS SO MUCH

The statistics are alarming. These days, getting downsized is part of the corporate lifestyle. It used to be that working for a major company like IBM, GE, or PepsiCo was a guarantee of long-term employment, but not anymore. To remain profitable, companies are outsourcing jobs to workers in India and China. The need to supervise a vast cadre of underlings has been left to the managers in these countries, where employment is booming. So what's left? A growing unemployment problem.

Jobs are going to Bangalore, India, and Dalian, China, like never before.[17] Call centers, IT (information technology) shops, and engineering and production facilities abound there, and workers in these countries are being paid cents on the dollar compared to workers in this country. For the United States this translates into hundreds of thousands of largely successful, competent, employable professionals who can't find work. Many of these people are living off their retirement savings fifteen years before they were supposed to retire.

Being hit by downsizing hurts. And it hurts mostly those between ages 40 and 65 who have already established themselves as seasoned, competent professionals. Bruce Tulgan, a consultant on generational workplace issues, estimates that 3.5 million people between the ages of 40 and 58 vanished from the American workplace from 2001 to 2004.[18] The Bureau of Labor Statistics survey of displaced workers shows that 55- to 64-year-old displaced workers were less likely to find new jobs than 25- to 54-year-olds and were more likely to drop out of the workforce altogether.[19] Formerly inconceivable career stories like the following put a human face on the statistics.

- A graduate of the Ivy League—educated at Hotchkiss, Princeton, and Harvard Business School—making more than two hundred thousand dollars a year at a New York bank, reached age fifty and was laid off. He tried working for a nonprofit organization, but they laid him off as well.

- An executive vice president and director of interactive marketing, who had published his own computer guides that were widely respected in the IT industry, was laid off for two years. He went from a high-level IT position to working at the local Gap retail store in order to make ends meet.

- A senior vice president of Philips Electronics was laid off at age fifty-one and could not find any other company to hire him, despite his multiple skills in marketing, strategic planning, and the production of technology. Using the skills acquired during his days at Philips, he ended up developing his own "involuntary consulting" practice, working on short-term projects for a few firms he connects with via trade shows.

- A financial services marketer with twenty years of experience and a Rolodex overflowing with the names of insurance agents and financial planners was given a pink slip. Despite his extensive network of contacts, after more than a year he remains unemployed.[20]

These days, many jobs that used to be part of the American economy are gone and are simply not coming back. For men who have been used to the linear approach to career development, who are still looking for the old implied employment agreement that the company would take care of you, being laid off is a double blow that hits the psyche and the pocketbook.

Studies on organizational layoffs and corporate downsizing show that women and men experience unemployment differently. For women, survival trumps ego; they simply adapt and find a new job.[21] For men, their career is so intimately tied into their core identity that unemployment changes them as a person. "I'm a software

What Men Say about Work

On reasons for making career changes . . .

- An opportunity presented itself for more money, greater flexibility, greater security.
- A risky opportunity presented itself that had a greater long-term payoff.
- My firm made the decision for me.
- I left because of downsizing.
- I left due to a medical crisis.
- It was time for retirement.
- I never left the workforce.

On reasons for switching jobs . . .

- Offered more money by new firm.
- Given better opportunities for advancement.
- Offered more challenges by the new firm.

On values held about work . . .

- My work describes who I am.
- The number of promotions I have achieved is my greatest accomplishment.
- One's salary defines one's worth.

specialist" or "I am a division manager" is how men describe themselves. With their work identities stripped from them, they are left puzzled and bereft. When unemployed, men surrender their work identities. When that is stripped from them via a pink slip, feelings of inadequacy, guilt, and shame complicate their recovery.

Men who are unemployed feel a sense of loss and isolation. Common responses we heard from unemployed men were: "I felt cut off from the working world," "I felt ashamed and upset all the time," "I felt isolated and alone," "I felt angry and confused," "I felt my unemployment was a hardship," and "I felt I made a negative impact on my family." Contrast the negative emotions of the men to the positive feelings expressed by the women who had lost jobs: "I felt free to be released from the working world," "I rediscovered myself and who I am," and "I felt I made a positive impact on my family."[22]

We also found that men were significantly more likely than women to report that "I have leveled off somewhat, and there are fewer opportunities for promotion in my firm." "Leveling off" is a function of a linear career path mentality. Men who buy in to the linear mentality discover too late that the realities of the corporate pyramid may not be in their favor. Derailed men experience a punch to the gut. Because so much of their identity is drawn from being the family breadwinner, when career advancement is no longer a possibility, most men question their self-worth.

Some men in our research talked about the cost to their families of the linear career. For example, one survey respondent said, "I lost two families as a result of my career ambitions." Another remarked, "I did not know that the price of working all the time could cost you your wife and kids. I did not know that I would have to change jobs because the economy would go to hell. These are the things I wish someone told me [up front]."

Men who were downsized were more likely than women to wish that they had been "more of a strong corporate player," had "paid attention to corporate signals and political changes," and had "chosen friends and allies more carefully." Men also said that they wished they had been "more successful at networking in general."[23]

CHOICE OR CIRCUMSTANCE?

One intriguing difference between men and women is that often men change jobs as a result of circumstances, while for women it is by choice. This is the underpinning of the opt-out phenomenon for women. The fact that many women perceive that they have a choice to leave the workforce to care for small children—often because they have a husband who can continue to be the main breadwinner of the household—is supported by socially accepted norms that dictate women are the primary caregivers for their children. For men, however, there are fewer socially acceptable choices available. The male straitjacket dictates that being a provider rules men's lives. Leaving work, therefore, is often a function of circumstance and layoffs, not of free choice.

For those men who were brought up with the breadwinner mentality, the harsh reality of the "downsizing" age of mergers, acquisitions, and leaner and meaner company staffing has been a difficult pill to swallow. These men have discovered the hard way that promises made are not always kept. They had been promised that if they applied themselves and worked hard, their performance would be rewarded with upward mobility. Despite stellar performance records, many men have found themselves laid off because of circumstances beyond their control. Men today must contend with a shaky economy, buyouts, layoffs, mergers and acquisitions, as well as rapidly changing technology and increased globalization.

While A. Thomas Kelly and Dick Kleine (profiled in Chapter 1) remained with the same firms for the duration of their careers, we surveyed several men who changed their jobs and moved across firms. Was this the male version of opting out, we wondered? Not exactly. Men change jobs for improved opportunities or career challenges or for the possibility of earning more money and achieving greater financial security.[24] Generally, the reason for changing jobs had to do with pay increases or, less fortuitously, layoffs. Surprisingly, corporate politics was equally to blame for job loss for both men and women; there was no difference by gender when corporate politics was named as the reason for career transitions.

ADAPTING TO NEW CAREER REALITIES

We found that a new career pattern is being created for men—one born of circumstance, not choice. Tucker O'Connell is one of the men who has learned the hard realities of the new workplace. During our interview, he described his career as a complex assortment of jobs taken on while trying to find his true career path. He graduated from Fairfield University in 1984 as a management major and found a job working for Eagle Snacks as a "regional manager," a job that turned out to be nothing more than driving a delivery truck. He was just starting his career and felt that he deserved something more: "I moved to ADP for a while and sold payroll systems. That was a hard-driving business. Every week, they did 'roll call' to see how much business you brought in that week. . . . If you didn't make their numbers, you were out on your ear."

In the 1980s he moved through a series of jobs in information systems and computer support, at the Bank of New England, the Bank of Boston, Northeast Systems, and Management Solutions. He then took a job with XL/Datacomp, which was acquired by Storagetek a year later, and landed at AT&T Capital in the mid-1990s when AT&T Capital bought a business unit from Storagetek. He explained the reasons behind his frequent job changes:

> *All my early job changes were voluntary. The motivation was generally money, although looking back, the changes weren't terribly significant on a gross dollar basis. Each time I changed jobs, however, it wasn't something I was looking for—the job found me, so to speak.*

As with many of the men we interviewed, Tucker changed jobs to get a higher salary or advancement. With each change, his salary went a little higher. Then he thought he had finally hit it big with XL/Datacomp. There he "learned how to sell a solution—that's my skill set." He continued doing computer support and learned the leasing business. However, XL/Datacomp was bought out by AT&T Capital's systems leasing unit. A series of acquisitions followed over the next five years for the systems leasing unit that included three companies and then Tyco. Tyco then sold off its interest in the company he was working for. Despite the fact that his performance record was highly rated, he was let go.

> *The move in which I was let go by the company after they were spun back off from Tyco was one in which there were plenty of warning signs. After being in the organization for six years, I had a sense that the people that would be retained to work down the portfolio would not necessarily be the sales people that had been the top performers. Geographical location (headquarters in Michigan, I was in Connecticut) and out-of-the-office long-term relationships play heavily in decisions like that.*

Tucker described how he felt about being laid off.

I had five girls at home and a wife to support, so I had to do something. I didn't even take the time to be angry or despondent. I just grabbed the next opportunity after that lesson had been learned. There was an opportunity because my customers, theoretically, would not get the same support from their existing leasing relationship because the company was going to phase out of the business. So I realized there was a way I could use the opportunity to support my customers from a new organization—one in which I was a partner and decision maker.

Fed up with the corporate grind and interested in charting his own course, he became a partner in DDI Leasing, an entrepreneurial firm that provides third-party equipment leasing to commercial customers. But despite all the job changes, corporate acquisitions, and shifts to his career, providing for his family is still very much on Tucker's mind. "The situation I am in now, if I don't work, my family does not eat. Talk about direct motivation to become a good provider."

Throughout the ups and downs of his complicated career—more than twelve jobs in all—the lesson Tucker has learned is that steady, continuous employment—the kind that prevailed in the 1950s—does not exist anymore. That has been a sobering lesson for many men to learn because they were socialized in the male straitjacket mode. Having been brought up with the understanding that one's role is to provide, and with the expectation that hard work would ensure continuous employment, the downsizing wave of the 1980s and 1990s sent men into a state of confusion. Many men, like Tucker, found that they had to adapt to survive.

An unintended consequence of the downsizing wave is that men have had to call into question the old employment contract and, with it, the male definition of success. Baby boomer men (those who were born between 1946 and 1960), who began their careers under the traditional system that supported linear careers and had the rules of the game changed when they hit midcareer, often found it hard to adjust. The Gen X men (those born in the 1960s and 1970s) and Gen Y men (born in the 1980s and 1990s), however, were quicker to question why they weren't spending time with their families rather than simply spending money on them. Suddenly men who had the corporate rug pulled out from under them—Gen Xers and Gen Yers and those baby boomers who were willing to adapt to the new deal at work—started realizing that their corporate identity and their manhood did not have to be aligned quite so closely. A career path for the new age man was born.

GEN X AND GEN Y MEN: A NEW PATTERN?

As our research shows, the linear career path still predominates for many men, but a new career pattern for men is being created. Gen X and Gen Y men are singing a new tune that eschews the traditional male straitjacket and its corollary defining male financial success. A study from the Radcliffe Public Policy Center, which examined one thousand men's and women's attitudes toward work, indicates that a major social change is afoot. The study challenges a long-standing belief that women are the only ones who want a more balanced career. Eighty-two percent of young men said that their family relationships were more important than increasing salary, prestige, or power in the workplace. Men in their twenties are more likely than older men to give up a portion of their incomes to spend time with their children.[25] A similar survey by the Families and Work Institute involving 2,800 respondents found Boomers were more likely to be more work-centric, while Gen X and Gen Y respondents placed a higher value on family than on work.[26]

Why the big difference in how male baby boomers and Gen Xers and Gen Yers view careers? Baby boomers grew up embracing the American dream, and held as their mantra "work hard to reap great rewards."[27] Taught to apply themselves to achieve goals set by parents and shaped by the 1950s and early 1960s cultural mentality, this generational cohort witnessed great political, religious, and business upheavals. Boomers watched the Vietnam War, the civil rights protests, the Kennedy and King assassinations, Watergate, the advance of feminism, and the sexual revolution shape their generation. Because of parental and cultural influences, baby boomers' work ethic includes being goal oriented, using collective effort, effecting change, and mentoring others.[28]

In contrast, Gen Xers and Gen Yers grew up with financial, family, and societal insecurity; rapid change; and a lack of solid traditions.[29] Their boomer parents, trained to seek career opportunities amid a wave of feminism, placed their children in child care centers in the hopes of enriching their children's lives. The boomers put in long, hard hours in pursuit of the American dream. But they did so at a cost. Their latchkey kids saw their parents working long hours, often away from home, under constant stress—only to be downsized and abandoned later in the merger and acquisition frenzy of the 1990s.

This generational cohort was influenced greatly by cultural trends of the computer and Internet revolution, AIDS, and global competition.[30] Accustomed to receiving immediate feedback from personal computers and video games, Gen Xers and Gen Yers are technically competent and comfortable with diversity, change, multitasking, individualism, and competition. For this generation, technology is central to their lives. Immediate feedback via videogames and instant messaging is taken for granted. The ease with which Gen Xers and Gen Yers use iPods, wireless communications, personal data organizers (PDAs), and message boards is their cultural context. Ascendant technologies allowing virtual teams, video-conferencing, Internet services, and flexible work arrangements are reshaping how and where business is being accomplished. The flexibility to work from home and have time to spend with family, as well as the benefits of getting out of the corporate rat race, has become a reality. A survey by Catalyst found that 76 percent of Gen Xers do want a compressed workweek and 59 percent want to telecommute or have flexible working arrangements. In addition, Gen Xers rated personal and family goals higher than career goals.[31]

One outcome of the downsizing frenzy of the 1990s was the need for retained workers to work exceptionally long, hard hours. Gen X and Gen Y values are at odds with the corporate requirement that workers now must work what was formerly two jobs for the pay of one. While the average workweek remains around 39 hours, in financial services it is 55 hours, and for top executives it may exceed 60–70 hours.[32] Heavy work loads and worldwide travel requirements to support firms in the era of global competition have made work hours burdensome. Gen X and Gen Y workers wonder why *should* they work long hours tethered to a corporation? Better to be free of corporate shackles and independent, rather than defined by a linear career path.

THE NEW LIBERATED-BY-TECHNOLOGY WORKER

While the length of the workday may have increased, the promise of technology has also liberated workers from corporations. New technologies—Internet applications, wireless and remote technologies—have created a new breed of worker who may eschew a linear career in favor of making money a different way. This is the new entrepreneurial man, the free agent software worker, who may find that technology has liberated him from outdated definitions of masculine success. Bruce Miller, an industry researcher and librarian who had worked for many years at PricewaterhouseCoopers and IBM knows the value of hard work and the lure of a linear career. Having started his career in New York City, he spent many years commuting in and out of the city.

Knowledge workers like Bruce, who now works entirely from home, are considered the new breed of liberated-by-technology worker. We found several examples of this type of knowledge-based/free agent/technology worker—professional consultants, market analysts, software engineers, and publishing and sales professionals—who have benefited from what the new technology has to offer. Liberated from the confines of an office and the restrictions of a linear career, these men are taking advantage of the information available on the Internet, as well as the opportunity to network with others, as the bread and butter of their newfound freedoms. Bruce reflected on the ways in which technology has enabled him to work from home.

I worked full-time for many years, straight out of an office, with the daily commute in and out of the city. But as a result of technological advances, I was able to work out of the office, from home, two to three days a week, and then eventually I was able to work five full days a week at home. Because in my job due to the nature of the work I do, what matters is the ability to do the work, not the number of hours spent in an office. I am an industry researcher, and I answer questions from people all over the globe. Let's suppose someone has a research question. They send it in electronically on Lotus Notes. Then, sitting at home, I am able to research the question and provide the answer. Who cares where the answer came from—home or office?

The miracle of technology—specifically wireless data and the Internet—has created a new career path that allows men (and women) to provide for their families without necessarily leaving their homes. But in many cases they must be ready and able to respond quickly, as Bruce explains,

It is now irrelevant where you work. What matters instead is the ability to work from anywhere on the globe. You can work from a mountaintop, from the moon, on the beach in Hawaii, it doesn't matter. What does matter is the speed with which you answer a question. I have received requests in my work from people all over the globe who have a question—from Russia, from China, from Korea as well as other far-flung locations. There was this employee in Russia who had a question, and I was able to answer it quickly and efficiently, as the speed of information that travels around the globe is absolutely amazing.

Some jobs, like Bruce Miller's, provide a technological prerogative of flexibility. Knowledge workers are able to fill their days with all the work they need. Want to increase your take-home pay? Work harder through the weekends, add a few clients, and your salary rises. Want to slow down a bit? Remove a few clients from the list and free up some time. This type of work—a lateral career rather than a linear career—has gained popularity among both the Gen X and Gen Y crowd and with the laid-off crowd, spawning a new type of dad—an astute knowledge professional who has something to sell. Said Bruce,

> *What has changed is the way the work is done. The technology has been a great enabler. When I first started working at home, I welcomed the quiet. I did not miss the office politics, or the boss watching over my shoulder. This is a new mindset—the ability to work on your own, do your work, and no one will bug you if you do your share. And I have had the advantage of being able to attend my sons' soccer games and participate more in my sons' lives as a father.*

But the advent of such new technologies may enhance family relationships while at the same time complicating home life. A cell phone may ring at 3 a.m. for a global conference call, and "you've got mail" may chime urgently from the computer as your children are going to bed. Gary Vasquez, a regional property manager for Capital Senior Living, a senior-living development and management firm, is a new technology-liberated dad who has been working from home for the past nine years. His work is separated into two domains: a week of travel to the properties he manages and a week spent working at home on property management issues. He described working at home.

> *Not everyone can work out of the house. It takes a lot of discipline and self-motivation to work from home. I found that I had to develop a routine for myself, then adhere to repeating that same routine daily. When I need to focus on my work, I shut the door to my office, and that symbolizes it's time to get down to business. Early on, I taught my sons that the door closed means "do not interrupt." I also believe you have to establish a professional presence at all times. That's why, when I'm on a phone call, there is never any background noise such as dogs barking or children yelling. There are no interruptions, and establishing that constant professional decorum sends a message to both bosses and business associates alike.*

> *I never like it when I speak to someone on the phone and I can hear dogs barking and children playing in the background. To the person at the other end of the phone, those sounds do not conjure up a strong sense that work is actually getting accomplished. My family understands the closed-door policy, and although I am home, I have never had to put anyone on hold to respond to my children's questions. On the occasion that my wife absolutely must communicate with me, she will quietly enter my office and write a note to my attention.*

Gary's ability to work at home is based on the mutual trust that he has established with his boss that he will perform on his job.

> *My boss offered for me to be able to work out of my home provided that I perform in my job results. My regional properties are still required to perform and meet their budgets. I am always where I say I will be when I am traveling and do not abuse that aspect of my job. Again, it's all about trust and performance. So what if you drop off your son at a baseball game or slip out for an hour to watch your son's spring concert? What really matters is whether or not you can still deliver results in your job. As I said, working from home is not something everyone can do. It takes a special person. I know of another employee who begged to work from his home. Yet, when his boss called looking for him, he was out on the golf course and not where he said he would be. It turned out to be a disaster and viewed as a serious breach of trust. It definitely takes a sense of discipline, self-motivation, and strong organizational skills to work at home. With no other office support available, to be effective, you need strong organizational skills.*

The promise of the new remote technology is that a worker may be expected to handle it all—household demands, carpool commitments, work interruptions—on and "off" the job. One executive we spoke with commented that the Blackberry PDA is considered a liberating device, as well as an addiction and a curse. "Yes, they could reach me, anytime, anywhere," reported this executive.

"But there is never any true 'off' time. Only when I turn the thing off. And then, I get, 'Hey, why did you turn that off? I was trying to reach you.'" The constant demands of work and the need for more work time is causing many to try and make do with less and less sleep. What's the price of this high-tech new lifestyle? The National Sleep Foundation has found the following.

- Sixty-three percent of Americans don't get the recommended eight hours of sleep needed for optimum performance.

- Long-term lack of sleep has been associated with such serious health conditions as high blood pressure, heart attacks, strokes, obesity, and depression.

- Each year drowsy drivers cause 100,000 car crashes, 71,000 injuries, and 1,550 deaths.[33]

So while technology is helping both men and women manage the work shift and home shift, and provides options to men that allow them to be better fathers, there may be unrecognized physical and psychological costs for doing so. Where do we draw the line between work and family life?

THE STAY-AT-HOME DAD

As modern-day men are trashing the male straitjacket by going against societal mores that a man is the provider and a woman's place is in the home, they are embracing a new definition of masculine success. A new phenomenon can be seen in the increasing proportion of stay-at-home dads. Some men are finding the courage to go beyond attending fatherhood seminars and are deciding to leave work altogether and become stay-at-home fathers.

Jim Silver is a modern stay-at-home dad, and proud of it. But from his background you would never have believed he would end up in that role. He grew up in the Boston area as one of eight siblings. He is a 1985 graduate of the University of Notre Dame, a philosophy major, and Phi Beta Kappa. But his passion—or so he thought—was the law, so he attended Harvard Law School. After law school he took the conventional path and went to work in Washington, D.C., for one of the largest law firms in the country and pursued a career as a litigator. Jim said,

> *I soon learned that I wouldn't be getting into court any time soon. It was a fantastic law firm, filled with incredibly smart, talented, hardworking people. But it wasn't for me. I was going to work every day looking at a stack of papers. They were paying me a lot of money, and I learned a lot, but it was so boring that I wanted to shoot myself. It was clear to me from the beginning that I was not going to stay there for the long haul, but I made it through three-and-a-half long years.*

He decided to look around for something new. While he was still in Washington, D.C., he wanted more practical legal experience. He had a friend who was working at the U.S. attorney's office, so he applied for a job as one of their litigators and was appointed as an assistant United States attorney in 1992.

> *As an assistant U.S. attorney in Washington, D.C., you end up trying all kinds of cases. Street-level crimes, drugs and guns, domestic crimes, petty larceny, lots of variety in casework, and they throw you right in. I loved it—it was thinking on my feet, real law, applied to real people. Not that corporate law isn't real law, either, but this kind of law simply grabbed my attention as the kind of work where I could make a difference.*

The expectation at the U.S. attorney's office was that lawyers would stay for at least three years before they moved on to other challenges. But Jim saw it differently: "I would have stayed longer, I loved that job." As one of his coworkers had told him, "Yeah, this is the best job you'll ever have." But meanwhile he met and married his wife. She was ensconced in medical school and was starting her residency training while he was busy at the U.S. attorney's office. Both were extremely busy, embroiled in the cases of their professions on a daily basis, and it was an exciting time for their marriage. Except for one little detail. They were expecting a baby boy, their first son. Their son was born prematurely, and he required bottle feeding every four hours and careful, supervised care. With their busy work commitments, they employed a nanny every day for the first year or so. But they knew the situation was untenable for them: "My wife and I had decided, even before we had our son, that raising our children was of paramount importance. We knew that from the beginning." But at the time they were both stuck in three-year commitments—her residency, and his time at the U.S. attorney's office. They did not make any decisions right away about who would be the parent who would stay home. They realized that what they decided would depend in part on where Jim's wife found a job after her residency, as Jim felt, with thirty-five trials under his belt, he could continue law practice anywhere. His wife found a prestigious job at Harvard Medical School as an instructor, and she would also run an outpatient center for Spaulding Rehabilitation Hospital. That was a big opportunity that they could not turn down. Jim's wife had to work for a year to become board certified, so Jim volunteered to be the first one to take some time off. Jim suddenly found himself surprisingly comfortable with the role of the stay-at-home dad.

> *I was confident I could get a job in Boston at any point. At that time my son, Alex, was just turning three years old. But I stayed home for that year and found out it was great. He only went to preschool two mornings a week, and it was just the two of us. I loved hanging out with him, playing games with him on the floor. All the neighborhood kids wanted to come over and play with us. In fact, some of them asked for a playdate (with me).*

Two additional children, Emily and Anna, have been added to the Silver family since then, and Jim has remained the stay-at-home parent. "We are very family oriented. We stay home on weekends, and really felt it was the right thing to do for one of us to stay home. We don't live an extravagant lifestyle. We would be fine living on either one's salary." Although at the beginning, Jim fully expected he would go back to work, he has now been home for ten years, and he doesn't even think about the return much anymore.

I spend my days having lots of fun. We go to the park, the library, see grandma, take swimming lessons, have tea parties, and snowball fights. I don't run a business out of the house, as some stay-at-home dads do. I spend my time doing the laundry, driving the kids everywhere, getting groceries, volunteering at school, cleaning bathrooms, but mostly I am playing with my kids. My wife is a good cook—I don't bake, and I'm not a great cook—and we have lots of fun.

Jim doesn't understand why more working dads don't make his choice. He is working on a humorous book about staying home with kids.

I have no regrets. Staying home has allowed me to pick up other interests such as tae kwon do, which I couldn't have done if I was working, and I coach soccer and dabble in writing. It is so energizing to be at home, so freeing. My question is: Why don't other men do this?

Jim has achieved sort of a celebrity status in his town as a stay-at-home dad.

In the beginning I did receive some strange looks. Every new place I went to with my son, people would comment, "Oh, how nice you have a day off," and when I would explain, "No, I am a stay-at-home dad full-time" once or twice, they started to genuinely affirm my choice. People overall have been pretty supportive. Occasionally I have had a mom offer advice to me about diapering, for example, that a mom would not give to another mom, only to a dad. And sometimes when I volunteer at school I have to explain everything all over again. Men don't know what to say to me at parties. At first, my wife didn't know how to explain me either, and she kept talking about my background, Harvard Law, all that. But finally I took her aside and told her not to do it—introduce me as who I am, currently. I have a friendly personality and I don't easily get offended about these things.

Jim's wife sometimes wishes she could be the one who was staying home, but she is fully engaged in her career. Jim proudly reports, "She is a creative entrepreneurial person, has edited lots of books and created a Smithsonian exhibit, in addition to her regular work. At one point she started talking about switching roles. But now I can't imagine things any other way."

Men like Jim are still rare, but they are on the increase. According to Census Bureau statistics, in 2002 there were 105,000 stay-at-home fathers of children under fifteen who were not in the workforce, compared to 5.2 million mothers.[34] These men want to give priority to their families and explore their abilities to nurture their children. Stay-at-home dads want to avoid being "dinosaur dads"—fathers who do not know their children and who adhere to a belief in the linear career path and accompanying definition of masculine success.[35] They know what Quidditch is and who Mary Kate and Ashley are, and they can name the friends of their children, as well as the kids' most loved and most loathed foods.

For those stay-at-home dads who decide to return to the workplace, however, it can be a harsh clash of reality between the old masculine definition of success ("So, exactly what were you doing during those five years?") and modern prescriptions for egalitarian work-family balance. One returning dad decided his time at home was a job and put it right on his resume. Under the heading "Temporary Retirement," he wrote, "Devoted five years to raising my son and daughter. Responsibilities included changing diapers, preparing nutritious meals, and making boo-boos feel better."[36] Dr. Kyle Pruett, a professor of child psychiatry at the Yale School of Medicine, conducted a ten-year study of twenty stay-at-home fathers and found that they were all profoundly changed by their experiences. None were able to return to their original jobs, but ten years after the study began, about half had changed their professions.[37]

Stay-at-home dads make a courageous choice. Throwing off the straitjacket that traditionally has defined male success, they decide to chart their own course, risky though it may be. Proud of their time nurturing their children, these dads feel good about what they accomplish. Says Jim Silver,

*When I do return to work, if I do, I want it to be something
involving kids, maybe teaching, or working as an attorney
with disadvantaged kids. I want to work for someone where
it is a badge of honor to have made the choice I made, rather
than someone who sees it as an embarrassment, and I want
to give something back to kids, since that seems to be my true
calling.*

The "Generation and Gender" survey produced by the Families
and Work Institute makes the point that over the past twenty-five
years, it is *men* rather than women who have changed their minds
about their role in the home. When asked whether "it is better for
everyone involved if the man earns the money and the woman
takes care of the home and children," more men responded less
affirmatively than in years past. Men are now seeing the possibilities associated with being a stay-at-home dad or a technology-flex-
ible dad. This flexible role reversal allows men to cast off the male
straitjacket while allowing women more opportunities to pursue
full-time careers.[38]

DIFFERENT MALE CAREER PATTERNS

We have found that although career development for men is undergoing change, the traditional linear career still exists along with
other new emerging patterns.[39] Because of the changing nature of
technology, the roles of men, and their desire for a more complete
fatherhood experience, we have identified five distinct patterns
that capture the careers of men today.

1. The linear careerist

2. The tech-flex dad

3. The resilient careerist

4. The abandoned careerist

5. The stay-at-home dad

The Linear Careerist

Expected to be a provider to his family, the "traditional breadwinner careerist" views his role at work as a means of taking care of his family. He often wants to provide his children with better lives financially than he had growing up. This man compartmentalizes a bifurcation between "work" and "family." This is the traditional pattern of the successful, upward-climbing career male, who still has a stay-at-home wife to care for his children. His wife's role is to support his career, perhaps by hosting dinner parties for his boss and coworkers. She takes care of household chores and creates a haven for her weary husband to come home to after a long day in the corporate jungle.

The Tech-Flex Dad

The second pattern arose because of the experiences of professionals in the technology, knowledge, and service industries. Benefiting from the new wireless technology, the "tech-flex dad" is no longer tethered to an office. He may build his career by developing a roster of clients or by working a series of jobs as a freelancer. He adds flexibility to his repertoire through the savvy use of gadgetry, a laptop ready to go where he goes, and a fully equipped office in his home. Unlike the linear careerist, his goal is not to climb the corporate ladder. His career moves are usually lateral; he is satisfied with his career as long as these lateral moves enhance his knowledge and skills and permit him to remain marketable. He may be a consultant, an IT professional, a salesperson, or a literary agent. His work is defined by the number of clients he serves and the number of work hours he can bill. He controls his time as well as his salary. He uses the autonomy and flexibility his career style has afforded him to spend more time with his family and friends.

The Resilient Careerist

The "resilient careerist" is the man who had bought in to the linear career model; he worked long, exhausting hours in a continuing effort to move higher and higher up the corporate hierarchy. Then suddenly the ladder was knocked out from under him. He may have been laid off because of corporate restructuring or passed over for that expected promotion, causing his career to derail. Or he may have suffered a serious health problem such as a heart-attack that prevented him from returning to his stress-filled, high-powered lifestyle. He is angry and frustrated. He has worked hard and been loyal to the system yet the corporation reneged on its end of the deal. Such a betrayal may spawn a major midlife crisis, or at least a major reevaluation of the resilient careerist's life and goals. He vows to make his own choices regarding employment, some-times opting for greater control through his starting his own con-sulting firm, sometimes choosing a new corporate job, but always with a contingency plan in mind. He won't be caught without a safety net again. His follows a combination of an upward pattern and a lateral pattern, combining aspects of the traditional careerist and lateral careerist.

The Abandoned Careerist

Like the resilient careerist, the "abandoned careerist" has been betrayed by the system. He has played by all the rules, yet reaching the top of the pyramid, grabbing the brass ring has evaded him. Unlike the resilient careerist, however, the abandoned careerist can't find his footing again. He wants the money, the power, and the perks he once had, but he just can't find a comparable position. Maybe he doesn't have the technology skills to keep up with the changing environment. Maybe he's over forty, or worse, over fifty, and companies see him as too old. Maybe his industry took such an economic beating that many of his colleagues are also pounding the pavement, fighting over what few jobs come open. He may be out of work for a long period of time while his savings keep his family afloat. His wife may even take a job because his male pride won't permit him to accept any position unequal in salary or rank to his previous job. Eventually he may realize that he will never regain the power and prestige he has lost. He may end up taking a job that is many rungs lower on the corporate ladder just to support his family. He may find that the only jobs open are relatively low-pay-ing jobs such as those of a salesman in a retail chain, a taxi cab driver, or a grocery bagger at the local supermarket. The workplace changed, and he was left behind.

The Stay-at-Home Dad

This final emerging pattern is a relatively new one that describes those dads who want to nurture their children and who elect to be the full-time parent while their highly successful wives take the corporate track. This is the counterpoint to the traditional stay-at-home-mom pattern that dominated in the 1950s. The "stay-at-home dad" is often highly educated and probably always thought he would have a traditional linear career. Although often questioned about his priorities, he makes a courageous decision to go against societal norms and embrace fatherhood full-time.

These patterns are emerging in defiance of corporate norms that reinforce the male straitjacket of the twentieth-century manufacturing model. But the straitjacket still exists. One survey respondent, a vice president in the banking industry, spoke about the reality of "flexibility" for men at his bank.

> *Although I believe my workplace can finally balance family needs against one's job, for myself, taking off time continues to come at a cost, as one still has the job to get done. In addition, any requested days off seem to be always challenged. I was told verbatim that I would not be able to take all the vacation that was granted because of the needs of the organization. While there has been significant improvement in these areas, I continue to believe there is a belief by the CEO that the father's role is to [be the] provider and the mother's role is to [be the] nurturer. He has only mellowed as he approaches retirement. Each time he attempts to schedule a meeting at a time I have scheduled off he expresses his displeasure for the inconvenience.*

Men are trying to remove the male straitjacket, but corporate policies and societal norms will not change without a struggle. Someone has to be the provider.

As much as women's career ambitions are changing, men's career ambitions are changing as well. Examining the concept of careers through a gender lens allows us to look at the yin and yang, the differences in male and female existence. Women may integrate work and family, but men compartmentalize both. While women make the choice to opt out, men do so as a result of circumstance. Blindly following one's ambitions may lead to a cost to one's family relationships, for men and for women. But opting out of the workforce and not sharing one's skills with the workplace presents another cost to one's self-esteem and one's pocketbook. Moreover, in today's rapidly changing global economy, the opt-out revolt also hurts American companies, especially those that are already losing ground to international competitors. Instead of finding solutions and changing the factors contributing to this brain drain, companies continue to force men (and women) to choose between work and family. Many of these companies are under the impression that men will always put working longer hours first, ahead of their desire to spend time with their families. These firms have failed to account for both the male Baby Boomers' increased desire to spend time with their families as they age and the younger Gen X and Gen Y men's lack of desire for the traditional linear career model of advancement at all costs. In the next chapter, we will discuss a new career model—that of Kaleidoscope Careers—that allows men and women to pursue career ambitions and integrate family and life issues in a way that defies compromise.

CHAPTER 4

KALEIDOSCOPE CAREERS

Leah Bateson is a typical modern-day woman who is trying to balance work, marriage, and motherhood. After attending college and obtaining a degree in English with a minor in television production, she graduated from Florida State University, ready to conquer the world. With great excitement, she obtained work as a production assistant for PGA Tour Productions. Then, two years later, she moved to Orlando, Florida, to be a freelance writer, editor, and producer with the Golf Channel. Leah described the experience.

> *[PGA Tour Productions] was the best training ground I could have asked for: great people, meaningful work, and all that time on the golf course to boot. I was there for a year and a half, and that was a super job. I had tremendous responsibilities and was definitely on a career track with them. When I left, I had just produced my first show.*

Along the way, she met the man of her dreams. Added to her successful career, life was good. But then her man was transferred to Key West.

> *So I left the Golf Channel and followed him there. I briefly worked in sales with an Internet company there but was*

*disappointed with the unprofessionalism of the operation. I
left that firm and returned to Miami to freelance in TV again.*

She commuted back and forth to Key West, and that worked for
a while, but eventually her fiancé was transferred to Atlanta. She
packed her bags again but ran into trouble keeping her career on
track in Atlanta. Leah explained: "Due to a massive layoff at CNN, I
was only able to find sporadic work as a freelancer there." The couple stayed there two years but then moved back to Florida when
her fiancé had the opportunity to transfer back to Orlando. She was
finally able to plan her long-awaited wedding, and additional surprises were in store.

*We jumped at that [moving back to Florida] because I knew I
would be able to once again work at the Golf Channel and we
would be closer to our families and friends who are in our
hometown [St. Augustine]. My fiancé and I were finally able
to get married, and shortly after I became pregnant with our
first child.*

Her pregnancy was problematic, and it became necessary to
slow down her travel schedule.

*Our son was born very premature, forcing me to leave work
and become a stay-at-home mom until we can place our son
in school. Yes, meeting my husband and having my son have
definitely impacted my work. My work, however necessary to
me, my need for challenge, and my self-esteem . . . must adjust
to their needs.*

Contrast Leah Bateson's career history with that of Greg
Varscroft, who has worked not for corporations but for various
nonprofit agencies, specializing in global environmental issues. His
career is notable for its linear career path, even though he has not
worked for a large corporation. Greg described his career.

*I have had a rewarding and successful career in international
development, working on issues such as conservation of trop-*

ical forests and associated natural resources (biodiversity, soils, water, climate), sustainable agriculture, and global climate change in Latin America and the Middle East. After earning a B.A. in English, service in the Marine Corps, and a Master of Forestry degree from Yale, I worked for various governmental agencies associated with sustainable agriculture projects, moving up the ladder. I made major contributions to conservation of natural resources and sustainable agriculture in Ecuador, Paraguay, Costa Rica, Jamaica, Nicaragua, Panama, Lebanon, and other countries. Eventually I became a director of the U.S. Agency for International Development. Upon my retirement, I carried out numerous consulting assignments in Latin American countries, Lebanon, and Washington, D.C. I now work with the Nature Conservancy for many of these projects.[1]

His career involved considerable travel, but the long sojourns from home to complete research projects did not seem to affect his family life. He said, simply and starkly, "My career was not influenced by marriage, divorce, or children." Like many men, Greg did not discuss his family as part of his comments on his career. Instead he kept his career and family life separate.

DIFFERENCES IN CAREER PATTERNS

We were surprised to find that despite great changes in the workplace and advances in gender equality, dramatic differences persist between the career histories of men and women. Women's careers are disjointed, intermittent, and subject to the forces of change. Men's careers are more orderly, stable, and focused on advancement. When we examine the passages of women's and men's careers through a gender lens, we find that men and women respond to different priorities, life issues, and challenges. For men, the prospect of a linear career within the same firm or industry is still highly valued. For women, a "career"—often defined as a series of interrupted jobs, transitions, and shifts—cannot be separated from a larger understanding of their lifestyle priorities.

One's career and one's personal life are inexorably intertwined. Everyone has a personal life. Whether it is acknowledged or not, our personal lives have an effect on our ability to do our work. But to the extent that "work" and "personal" issues make up the totality of our lives, we discovered that the adjustments and compromises that women and men made serving their careers versus their family and personal lives were *different*. To some degree, we found men and women to be *polar opposites* in terms of the compromises they were willing to make. We found the following clear gender-based themes.

1. Men's careers remain linear, although their careers may take place in more than one firm. Men still remain the primary family breadwinners. However, the loss of job security has had an impact on men's careers, and there is change afoot with the rising phenomenon of stay-at-home dads. Some men are developing more lateral approaches to their careers via the benefits of technology.

2. Women's careers are disjointed, interrupted, and nonlinear. In sharp contrast to the career histories of men, those of women are *relational*. This is not to say that women do not value getting to the top of their firms; they do. But the long hours demanded by executive careers make it difficult, if not impossible, for women to balance work and family. Women's career decisions reflect a large and intricate web of considerations involving personal life issues that must come together in a delicately balanced package before career progression can be considered comfortably. Often women's careers are interrupted by family concerns such as having a baby or caring for an elderly relative.

3. Men *compartmentalize* work and family. This is not to say that men do not care about their families; they do. Women *integrate* both work and family to the extent it is possible. Men's careers are more *sequential*. When the conflicting demands of work and family become impossible to reconcile, women may opt out and leave the workforce. When men have problems balancing work and family, they usually

continue to pursue their career ambitions, perhaps through consulting or in other, smaller firms that permit more flexibility. Relatively few men consider voluntarily opting out of the workforce.

4. Women are leaving corporations by *choice* in record numbers for a variety of often interconnected reasons. Faced with long work hours, discrimination, the "Ole Boys' Club," and seeing no advancement prospects on the horizon, many women make a choice to be stay-at-home mothers, to pursue a more flexible work schedule, or to become entrepreneurs. Men tend to focus on a traditional linear career unless *circumstances,* such as downsizing and layoffs, cause them to consider other paths.

5. Men's self-identity and work identity are more *singular* and closely tied than are women's self-identity and work identity. If a woman has a career setback, she still has *multiple* self-identities based on her nurturing roles (e.g., mother, caregiver). A man, in contrast, is often so focused on providing for his family through his career and his salary that when a career setback occurs he is devastated. Men in general have more problems drawing validation from nonwork roles—until retirement, when society suggests it is OK to do so.

Men and women operate from very different vantage points, as Table 3 shows. This difference in perspective complicates our understanding of career models for women, models that operate on different assumptions than those of men. Most women simply don't fit the standard male definition of a corporate career.[2] They are far more interested in developing careers that suit their lives rather than ones that overtake their lives.

Acknowledging the different perspectives of men and women, Gary Powell and Lisa Mainiero recognized that women's lives are too complex to fit into a traditional career-stage sequence. Their work pointed to the need for a theory that addressed the complex choices and constraints on the part of women, examining the issues of balance, connectedness, and interdependence, in addition to

TABLE 3

Men's and Women's Approaches to Career

Men's careers are characterized by . . .	Women's careers are characterized by . . .
Linear in nature	Nonlinear in nature
Jobs held in the same industry for several years. Lateral careers are a new phenomenon due to changes in information technology.	Frequent interruptions, opt-out periods, and change
Sequential in nature	Relational in nature
Family responsibilities are separated from work responsibilities.	Family and work are integrated; if that is not possible, women opt out.
Remaining in traditional careers and leaving the workforce only if circumstances such as layoffs or downsizing require it.	Leaving the workforce and forming alternate careers by choice to achieve greater balance with family needs or to resist discrimination.

issues of achievement and individualism. Their conceptualization of "crosscurrents in a river of time" proposed a framework for looking at women's careers that takes into account nonwork issues, subjective measures of success, and the impact of personal, organizational, and societal factors on women's choices. The "river of time" metaphor suggests that at different times in their lives, women prioritize career achievements, while at other times in their lives they focus on achieving a measure of balance between family and personal commitments.[3] This conceptualization of women's careers suggests that women use a different lens concerning their career decisions than do men. Women's lives may require more adjustments between family and career, while men's careers call for more of a dedicated, singular focus on career.

The original "river of time" model and our current research show why a gender-based lens is so important for the study of careers. Men and women approach their careers from different perspectives, pursue focused objectives at different times, and make unique career and family decisions accordingly. Studying careers, especially fast-changing careers in a technology-enabled world, without a full appreciation for gender issues misses this central difference.

THE KALEIDOSCOPE CAREER MODEL

To understand the changes that are taking place in this new age of careers, we developed a new model, the *Kaleidoscope Career model,* to illustrate how women and men think about and enact their careers.[4] A Kaleidoscope Career is a career created on your own terms, defined not by a corporation but by your own values, life choices, and parameters. Like a kaleidoscope, your career is dynamic and in motion; as your life changes, you can alter your career to adjust to these changes rather than relinquishing control and letting a corporation dictate your life for you.

Consider the working of a kaleidoscope; as one part moves, the other parts change. Women understand that any decision they make in their careers creates changes in others' lives. Like a kaleidoscope that produces changing patterns when the tube is rotated and its glass chips fall into new arrangements, women shift the patterns of their careers by rotating different aspects of their lives to arrange their roles and relationships in new ways. Women evaluate the choices and options available through the lens of the kaleidoscope to determine the best fit among their many relationships and work constraints and opportunities. As one decision is made, it affects the outcome of the kaleidoscope pattern. Rather than being single-mindedly ambitious, we found women determined the set of options in that kaleidoscope that marked the best fit at the time, always considering how their decisions will affect others in their lives.

Women's careers, like kaleidoscopes, are relational. Each action taken by a woman in her career is viewed as having profound and long-lasting effects on others around her. Each career action, therefore, is evaluated in light of the impact such decisions may have on her relationships with others, rather than based on insulated actions as an independent actor on her own. In our Kaleidoscope Career model, "family" and "context" are more broadly defined as the set of connections, representing individuals who deserve consideration as a weight in the decision, each with their own needs, wants, and desires, that must be evaluated as parts of the whole.

Our research showed that men, on the other hand, compartmentalize their lives and their careers and focus on their career ambitions first, because they know that they are the family providers. As one man from our survey, a financial services analyst, said:

> *Yes, I guess you can say I was very career focused early in my career. But I was family focused as well. By doing well in my career, which required travel all over the country, I was keeping my family in the lifestyle they were accustomed to and providing for my kids' future education. So it wasn't that I didn't value family life—I did, very much. I loved coming home after all those trips. But I did it because of them. Doing well in my career meant more money, more perks, more things for the family.*

Does this mean that women's careers are relational and men's are not? Not necessarily. But there is a yin/yang aspect to men's and women's careers—while men follow a more linear corporate career path, women adapt and change their career objectives in accordance with relational needs and demands. We found that men and women respond to the same career and life issues, but often in a different order. Men are more *sequential* in how they deal with life and career issues.[5] Women are *integrators,* and this is why so many women are concerned about the issue of balance. Women are trying to do it all, at least some of the time, while men are doing what they must.

Our interviews for this book provide a window into how men and women weigh certain factors over others in their career decisions. We offer the kaleidoscope metaphor as a new way of thinking about careers emanating from gender issues, valuing gender and context rather than making it invisible in the study of careers. The Kaleidoscope Career model shows how women and men shift and move the facets of their lives around to find the mosaic that best fits their life circumstances and their own wants and needs, even if those choices defy typical definitions of career success. We think the reasons why women and even some men are leaving the workforce have more to do with actively pursuing a new career model that is available through technology rather than solely because of the inflexibility of modern-day corporations.

PARAMETERS OF THE KALEIDOSCOPE CAREER: THE ABC MODEL

We found that there were three reasons, or parameters, that led women, and also men, to take stock of their career decisions and make changes and transitions to meet their needs for their lives, families, and themselves. These parameters reflected

1. A person's need to find congruence between work and his/her own personal values, often asking the questions: "What about me?" "How can I be authentic, true to myself, and make genuine decisions for myself in my life?" juxtaposed against

2. A family's need for balance, relationships, and caregiving, intersecting with

3. An individual's need for challenge, career advancement, and self-worth

We call this the "ABC Model of Kaleidoscope Careers."[6] Just as a kaleidoscope uses three mirrors to create infinite patterns, our Kaleidoscope Career model has three parameters (authenticity, balance, and challenge) that combine in different ways throughout the lives of individuals, reflecting the unique patterns of their careers. Consider, for example, a woman's career using the metaphor of a kaleidoscope. The colors of a woman's kaleidoscope are reflected in these three parameters, shaping her decisions as one aspect, or color, of the kaleidoscope takes on greater intensity as a decision parameter at a particular point in the life cycle. Over the course of the life cycle, as a woman searches for the best fit that matches the character and context of her life, the colors of the kaleidoscope shift in response, with one color (parameter) moving to the foreground and intensifying as that parameter takes priority at that time in her life. The other two colors (parameters) lessen in intensity and recede to the background but are still present and active as all aspects are necessary to create the current pattern of her life and career.

At one point, she may delay having children to devote more energy to her career. At another point, she may subjugate career ambitions for the sake of her family's needs. Later in life, she may forge ahead, searching for meaning and spirituality in her life. Somewhere in the middle she may be most concerned about balance and relationships in her life. Her context shapes her choices. Therefore, opting out becomes a natural decision based on the fit of the colors of her kaleidoscope at that time. Her career does not dictate her life. Instead, she shapes her career to fit her life as marked by her distinct and changing personal kaleidoscope patterns over her lifetime.

Men, however, responded to a different career agenda. The male straitjacket has caused most men to be singularly focused on their career achievements. Climbing the layers of the corporate pyramid became a quest for fulfillment. For linear, career-driven men, challenge is defined as making more money, achieving new positions, and taking on more clients. Because the careers of men often do not require a career interruption to care for family, men pursued challenges in their careers well past age fifty. Authenticity, for men, was defined differently. For many men, authenticity became a drive more to become one's own man rather than to seek new passions or smell the roses. Issues of family, balance, and relationships became appreciated more in late career than in early career.

Each of these parameters, or decision-making questions, was active as a signpost throughout a person's career. Certain parameters predominated at different points in the life cycle, forcing decisions about opting out or staying in the workforce. The strength of a parameter to shape a career transition depended on what was going on in that person's life at the time. If money was needed, then career issues took priority. If family balance was needed, then adjustments were made to better serve family needs. If both these parameters were not active, then the individual could take stock and ask the big questions, such as, "Am I doing what I need to be doing with my life?" and become more centered, reflective, and spiritual in the process.

AUTHENTICITY, BALANCE, AND CHALLENGE

The ABC Model of Kaleidoscope Careers indicates that individuals have three major needs that come into play when they make decisions about their careers: for authenticity, for balance, and for challenge.

The Need for Authenticity

Many of the women and men we talked to described the need to make sense of their decisions in light of competing factors and needs. This theme or parameter is the most difficult to describe because it was often drowned out in the discussion about bad bosses, lack of advancement, bringing children to soccer games, and the continual demands of the caregiving role. But this was the voice of women and men as they reflected upon their decisions to ask, "Did I make the right decision? Does this decision make sense for me as well as for others around me?" Authenticity is a parameter that describes being genuine and true to oneself, knowing one's strengths and limitations, and acting on the best information at the time.[7] The need for authenticity is the quest to find one's true voice. Fifty-five-year-old Alice described authenticity in the following manner.

I now recognize when I am in my own way. I know the power of the universe firsthand, and I remind myself daily of what it can provide. As long as I am on the right track for me, I'm OK with myself.

And Katherine said about authenticity,

I don't define myself by my career [even though] it takes up the bulk of my time. At this point in my life, I have a different life view. I am striving to be more effective in my community and world. The last [career] change has given me the opportunity to make a difference in this world.

For some of our respondents, authenticity took the form of artistic or leisure pursuits that they followed in spite of other demands on their time. For others it took the form of being true to oneself at work, being secure in one's knowledge or style as a manager. For still others it was reflected in a long-awaited dream at the end of child rearing and salary earning that culminated in a perfect retirement. We met one woman who left work to form her own catering business. We discovered one man who gave up his accounting job to write a novel. Another developed a secondary, postretirement career selling items on eBay. Although finding authenticity is difficult to describe, we heard this theme over and over again from individuals in late career. When competing demands are eliminated from the personal regression equation, this theme was the end result.

The Need for Balance

Balance, defined as a state of equilibrium, was the holy grail for most of the women we spoke with. Although women want successful and challenging work lives, the need for balance often overwhelms one's wishes for a more directed, upward-driven set of career accomplishments. Seeking a job closer to home to better suit the needs of children was often viewed as a means of achieving a better equilibrium while adjusting to the needs of others. Prioritizing one's children as a reason to leave the workforce was another means of achieving balance. As Stacey commented,

The paths that I have chosen over the last twenty-five years have been directly related to my family. I chose to be home when the children were small and increased my hours as they got older. I sacrificed benefits and advancements but received the greatest reward—I have two fabulous kids!

Added Carley,

All my career decisions have factored in the needs of my children, my elderly parents, and my family in general. I have had five different part-time jobs since I left my full-time position as a director of marketing, and I would not go back to the corporate grind even now. My family needs me, and I needed to adjust my career to handle all their issues.

Even for those women who were single or had no children, we found that they discussed the absence of balance—relationships—as a factor in their lives. Reported Bridget, a real estate agent, "I spent so much time on my career that I forgot relationships were important, too. Now I have all this money and no one to share it with."

Balance is a nexus issue for people as the demands of their work outstrip the time available to spend with family, or to take time for themselves. Unfortunately for many, imbalance is a constant. We heard all kinds of stories about women running to meetings from a teacher conference with pantyhose slipping; dashing home to attend a child's soccer game while discovering there was a crisis at the office that required rushing back there with child in tow; devoting lunch breaks to bringing an elderly family member to a doctor's appointment but getting delayed for the important worldwide 2 p.m. conference call; and traveling between airports miles away from home but catching time to read a book to a child over the phone to put her to sleep.

For most people, there just aren't enough hours in the day to do it all. Opting out of work is sometimes the only hope of regaining sanity lost while in the corporate rat race. The need for greater balance—fewer work demands, more family time—often was used as a reason for a career transition in midcareer, when the demands of child rearing and work accomplishments peaked.

The Need for Challenge

This parameter reflects a worker's need to learn, to develop as a person, and to find stimulating, exciting work. Both men and women want challenging work. Boredom is not an option for most. The challenge of innovating a new product, defining a new entrepreneurial enterprise, or taking part in a stretch work assignment is a key motivation, or need for achievement, that many survey participants and interviewees mentioned as a driving force in their careers. Pila, a manager for a large-scale computer manufacturer said,

> *I like to make things happen. Connecting with people to bring them into a work situation to solve a problem, develop the business, or create new ideas. I love to motivate, orchestrate, and congregate.*

Another respondent, Morgan, said,

> *What excites me most is having an impact on people. In the bank where I work, I am the person who can make it all come together. It is exhilarating sometimes at the end of a really good day at work to feel like I have accomplished something meaningful for a customer. I live for the challenge to do so.*

Some people are incredibly productive. They drive change in their companies and in their businesses. They hold themselves to a higher standard. One woman known to one of the authors of this book works nonstop. A single mother, she often works until 8 or 9 p.m., then returns home with her laptop, PDA, and cell phone and continues to update her e-mail until midnight. On other days she travels to business locations as a sales representative for a major technology company. When asked why she works so hard, she replied, "I just can't stop. I can't help myself. I couldn't stop working if I tried."

Challenge is the engine of work achievement. When people are given a stretch assignment and are challenged in their work, they don't mind putting in the extra hours that are required to get the job done. Challenge springs from the underlying source of creativity and drive that exists within each individual and spurs the accomplishment of great things. Challenge can be a powerful motivator. For some people it is a validation of who they are. For others it is a way to learn and grow and develop a base of expertise. For still others it manifests a need to help others.

Timing of the ABCs Across the Life Span

Our research showed that the three ABC parameters—authenticity, balance, and challenge—ebb and flow in intensity over the course of a lifetime. Early career is the promised land of possibilities, not probabilities. In early career, men and women equally pursue the thrill of the hunt, the quest for the brass ring, the desire to achieve in their work most profoundly. Among our survey participants, this was the time when the flame of challenge burned most brightly. Both men and women were motivated to make their respective marks on their firms, show what they could accomplish, and define a work identity for themselves. Some moved to different firms to accomplish their goals. Others took on additional responsibilities in the jobs they held. Still others developed new ideas and processes, using creative thinking, as a means to accomplish their goals.

As people grow older, their priorities shift. For most women, the desire for challenge remains but is pushed into the background to be replaced by a new parameter—the need for balance. For men, the need for challenge remains for a longer time, and arguably in stronger intensity, but eventually the quest for authenticity shares center stage. Whereas women worry about whether they should start a new business to achieve flexibility and balance, most men are concerned about developing a style that is all their own. Men continue to seek work challenges while the more prominent pattern for married mothers is to request reduced work schedules and direct their needs for challenge elsewhere. By restricting their work hours, these married mothers are usually removed from consideration for more challenging work assignments that might require travel to adventurous locations away from their families or that require more face time at night or on weekends.

When they reach their thirties, and even into their forties, men's and women's paths diverge. Men continue to pursue work challenges, while most women back off to make room for the more relational aspects of their lives. The kaleidoscope shifts for women, while the pattern remains linear for most men who are in the breadwinner's role. Some women do continue to pursue career challenges if they have a stable life structure in place—such as that provided by a competent and treasured nanny or a grandparent or a stay-at-home husband—to whom they can delegate the daily demands of child rearing. For those in more egalitarian, shared provider families, there is more give and take and both partners may have a Kaleidoscope Career pattern.

Among our survey participants, women and men were concerned with their career challenges in early career, but for women, the point at which they slowed down was a function of their child-raising years—beginning at age 25, 30, 35, 40, or whatever age at which they chose to have their children. The timing of children and family issues affected the timing of women's kaleidoscope career pattern. Women, especially those who reentered the workforce, were concerned with the balance of family and work throughout their lives, at least until their children left the nest. Therefore, most women did not feel free to pursue their career ambitions until their nurturing duties were handled by someone else, or were completed by virtue of the ages and needs of their children. This meant that women had ups and downs in their career trajectories, often peaking early but not reaching their strides until midforties or beyond.

Men had a longer, more fruitful period of securing challenge for the most part, usually well into their forties and beyond. Most men had the luxury of pursuing their career ambitions, considering their management style and options, and pursuing career advancement for a longer period without interruption than that experienced by women. But other options became more attractive once they became plateaued in midcareer. This was a difficult transition period for most men, and it usually hit in their late forties and fifties. The realization of "Is that all there is?" opened the door for most men to reconnect with and consider family issues late in their careers.

When the primary obligations were complete, the picture changed again for men and for women. When his duties of providing for his family were completed, a man could then relish his free time and family relationships. When a woman's duties of nurturing her family were discharged, she could then concentrate more on being authentic, being true to herself, and perhaps even on exploring new challenges by returning to the workforce. In short, the timing of men's and women's kaleidoscopes mirror one another and shift again in the dance of their lifetime demands.

KALEIDOSCOPE CAREER PORTFOLIOS FOR WOMEN

Because the kaleidoscope metaphor cannot be easily categorized, we offer the concept of "portfolio" as a means of understanding how ABC parameters intersect and shape the transitions of a woman's career. For most women in our sample, we found a certain rhythm to their careers that reflected the demands of their families versus their own needs for challenge, balance, and authenticity. In the words of fifty-year-old Marge,

> *The first twenty years of my career I had to strike a balance between work and family, first work and family second, then family first, giving up a particular opportunity that would have changed my direction. In retrospect it was for the best and now has come back around.*

What do women's Kaleidoscope Career portfolios look like? Following are three stories of women who developed a C-B-A pattern.

From Law to Chocolates: Deborah Ann's Story

Deborah Ann's career encompassed a fascinating set of career transitions. A graduate of Drew University, she had considered majoring in the sciences. After taking a series of interdisciplinary courses in psychology, sociology, and anthropology, she decided to go to Yale Law School, where her initial focus was on mental health law. Her career story represents the common C-B-A (challenge first, then balance predominates, then later authenticity) portfolio.

In college, I was lucky enough to be part of a project where, with professors, we were researching the law associated with children, specifically how children act as eyewitnesses. As part of a course I took, I spent a whole summer interviewing kids for that project, and it was amazing how easy it is to manipulate what kids say on the witness stand. It was a real eye-opening project. I enjoyed law school, and I was very into it back then. My focus was on mental health law.

After graduating from law school, she landed a job with a major New York law firm. She intended to pursue litigation, but after a few months realized that she had an interest in tax law. Because this firm primarily represented insurance cases, she accepted a position at an even more prestigious firm where there was plenty of tax work.

I liked the work, but I didn't want to do it forever. I liked the people I worked with, though. But I could see if I went that route the law firm would become my whole life. Although I found it interesting, I wondered if this was what I wanted to do with my life.

Deborah Ann started to wonder about the career she had chosen. She was concerned about the lack of meaning in her work and desired more challenge. At Yale Law School, she had met her future husband, Michael Grissmer, who was having similar misgivings about the law.

My husband decided not to practice law; instead, he worked for a talent agency. The talent field is very irregular. He did not like it. I knew I didn't want to make partner, so I wondered, why was I doing all of this? I needed to find something that had some meaning, like the original law work I had gotten involved in. With tax, there isn't always an answer, it's often a judgment call, and people are calling wanting instant answers. It wasn't that I couldn't do the work, it was instead that I didn't want to do the work. Lots of people leave law firms by the droves, and the common thing they say is,

"You're getting out? Wish I was, too." For me, I wasn't turned off by the work, but I wasn't helping anybody either.

While working, she became pregnant with their first child. The couple started brainstorming about businesses they could run. They thought it would be ideal to set up shop on the streets of New York, to live within a stone's throw of their business. But what business? Deborah Ann's mother made chocolate when she was a child, and it occurred to her that they could develop a storefront business making chocolates. Intrigued by the idea, Michael quit his job, took some courses in candy making, and soon they were on their way to owning their own business.

We set a goal to open the business by Easter, 1998. But we found the New York rentals were impossible and unavailable. So we thought about finding a spot outside of the city where we could set up shop. Mike's parents lived in a lovely, family-oriented Connecticut town, so we thought, why not?

They didn't make their Easter goal. Their son arrived four days before Easter, and the shop wasn't ready until September, but that was OK. The baby became a fixture in the playpen at the back of the store, and mom, dad, and son started the business together.

Now that the business has taken off as a successful retail chocolate-making business, the couple has developed a Web site, opened a production facility nearby, and is considering selling their chocolates wholesale as part of a larger strategic plan.[8] Meanwhile, life is full of daily tasks such as juggling doctors' appointments, trips to the vet, school volunteer work, and meetings with the downtown business association. A second child, a daughter, arrived on the scene three years ago, making their family lives rich and full. When asked if she had any regrets about leaving her law career behind, Deborah Ann responded,

I have not really regretted changing my career. I may be busy, and the business may be overwhelming, but I have a great business. The holidays are tough, but as a family we vacation for a week right after the holiday rush and in the summer. I enjoy the creativity and love being part of a great town.

Deborah Ann's career and life history represent a common Kaleidoscope Career portfolio, that of C-B-A. Deborah Ann leads a busy life, but now that her business is in order, she is starting to take some time to relax and enjoy the creative aspects of it. Her business is making an impact on her town, and she is now considering issues of authenticity in her life. Our survey research showed this pattern to be the most common among women: the desire to accomplish career goals and challenges was prominent in early career, issues of balance predominated later in early career and in midcareer, and issues of authenticity arose in midcareer and late career.[9]

From Medical School to Part-Time Professional: Karen's Story

Karen Nordberg had always wanted to be a doctor. She said, "If you even ask my childhood friends, I've been saying it since I was old enough to know what it was. In first grade I knew I wanted to be a doctor." A native of Long Island, she attended Bucknell University. Karen's dedication to science required her to develop a research project while an undergraduate premed student. Her research took her to a lab at Temple Medical, where she met her husband.

> I set it out for myself, and there was a lot of reaching for goals, but I kept myself on that path knowing what I needed to do to get here, to be a doctor of pediatrics. My husband was doing research in the same lab at Temple. He was in medical school at Temple, two years ahead. Needless to say, I applied to Temple for medical school, and I was accepted.

After long hours of study, she completed medical school at Temple University and did her residency at St. Christopher's Hospital for Children. While there, she found herself challenged by casework in pediatrics. She recalled one of her cases:

> I had one case when I was the ICU [intensive care unit] chief at St. Christopher's, where a two-year-old girl was transferred down from the floor due to diarrhea, dehydration, and her kidney function was declining. My mentor, a wonderful,

dedicated woman physician and infectious disease specialist, taught me that sometimes the most important thing you can do is get really good case histories. She would perform these long and thorough histories, asking all kinds of questions. So I sat down with the parents and asked a lot of questions about where the two-year-old had gone, what she had eaten. The first interview the parents were worried, and I didn't get anything out of them. But I persisted for a second interview, and one of the parents happened to mention a petting zoo outside of Philadelphia. I started investigating, and there was another child who had been at the petting zoo with similar symptoms. I called that family, got a full picture, and realized my suspicions were on target—it was a type of E. coli that can cause kidney damage in small children.

With her schooling and residency completed, she was free to pursue her dream of being a practicing pediatrician. She relished doing her share of challenging diagnoses while she practiced medicine for two years as a qualified pediatrician in North Carolina. She found herself immersed in daily casework, supporting the needs of the children under her care. She found she had finally fulfilled her dream to become a practicing pediatrician.

I never really wavered from pediatrics. There was one point where I was thinking of ob-gyn, but that only lasted a short time. I realized what I was really interested in was not the mom but the baby, so I remained solidly interested in pediatrics for my entire medical career.

Medicine is certainly a challenging profession, where there are daily problems to be solved and critical diagnoses to be made. Dr. Karen Nordberg is, in every way, the picture of the caring and dedicated physician. Her career is typical of the C-B-A portfolio shared by so many women, in which challenge underlay her early career decisions.

My early career was full-force pediatrics, and I even contemplated doing academic pediatrics, which can be really intense.

I love the field of medicine, and all my leadership roles felt comfortable up to that point, like I had found a good fit with my profession. I always thought I would be just like my mentors—totally dedicated, on call a lot, making amazing diagnoses and saving the day. I had one mentor who worked only three days a week to raise her children, and I thought, "Well, that's nice for her," but I never imagined I would follow in her path.

Dr. Nordberg practiced medicine full-time while she was in North Carolina, and at the end of her residency, her son was born. Suddenly balance became an important parameter for her.

For the first year of his life, for eighteen months, I was basically supporting the family because my husband was still a fellow at the hospital. But once I had my son, and with a daughter on the way, the desire to work part-time in medicine came from within. When the baby is placed in your arms you realize that no one can do a better job caring for him than you can. Although certainly there are people who can care for your child, it is the bond between mother and child that is so important. I decided that going to work part-time would make everything work.

When her husband's fellowship was completed, he received a good offer at a hospital in Connecticut, and she followed, looking for a part-time position.

I love what I do. Working part-time is a good balance for me personally. I am satisfied intellectually, and I love being here and interacting with patients. Then I go home and be a mom. I am Dr. Mom at home, but I am able to spend much more time with my children.

Now she works three days a week, which satisfies her craving to be active in medicine while still being available to her children. When asked about time for herself, she smiles.

Time for myself is minimal at this point. There used to be time to get my hair done, that sort of thing. Having children focused my priorities. Whereas my husband still thinks about taking time for himself, to play golf, whatever, when I have free time I make a choice to spend it with my children. Whether it is taking them to the park or reading to them, it is my wish to spend as much time as I can with them. I think women need to define what makes them happy and what time for themselves really means. For me, it is all about my children.

Karen has made a values-driven choice between her family and her career. As committed as ever to the practice of medicine, she is nonetheless passionate about her children's upbringing and her dedication to them. Because Karen is in midcareer, the authenticity parameter has not yet begun to shape her choices. Instead, challenge and balance predominate. She laughs, saying, "All I can do is two things right now, not three. Between medicine and being a mother, I have a full and very rich plate."

A Corporate Career, with Interruptions: Pat's Story

Pat Gaglione, a corporate professional and mother of three, has already had a productive and fulfilling career, despite having taken two career interruptions to be with her children. A graduate of SUNY Buffalo as a chemical engineer, she pursued her studies at the California Institute of Technology and landed a job at Unisys, where she learned the ropes of management.

My first job was at Unisys, and they had a great training program. I worked there ten years. At Unisys I had the good fortune of being promoted frequently, and I worked my way up from section manager to manager and then to director level. I enjoyed the challenge of the work. I loved working towards a goal with a team of people. I learned a lot at that company, a lot about change management also. But they were downsizing, so I put my name out there, and figured I would find another job in California at one of the high-tech companies.

*By the end of my run there, I had had my two sons, so I was
ready for a change.*

Pat enjoyed the challenge of her work and wanted to continue
working. For practice, Pat went on an interview with Philips Electronics. They offered her a position in New York, which was closer
to her family. After several discussions with her husband, they
decided it was time for a move back east to raise their children near
family.

*The job was an opportunity to run a business unit for Philips
Electronics. It was a very challenging and exciting opportunity, and I was ready for the change. I learned a lot on that
job as well, and enjoyed having responsibility for the entire
business unit. The division did well, and after several years
there, I was asked to move to Singapore and manage a business unit there. But I was pregnant with my third child, and a
move was not right for us at that time. Later, I was offered
positions in Sunnyvale and Paris, but decided against those
moves as well.*

In making her choices, balancing family life with her challenging work responsibilities was important to Pat.

*I love working. I love using my brain. I love the problem solv-
ing of work, the creativity, the pulling together of the team
toward a goal. But being a mom is a massive responsibility. It
took me a year to realize what I wanted and needed in my life.
I needed more balance in my life to resolve some of the feelings of internal conflict I had about not having enough time
with my children and also working.*

Pat decided to take a career interruption for a while and left
Philips Electronics. She had stayed home with her new baby girl
for eight months when she thought about going back to work.

*One day, I woke up, looked at my daughter, and said, I gotta
go back to work. With my first child I cried to go back to
work, but my boys are one and a half years apart, so when the*

second one arrived I was more ready to return to the work-
force. When I had been home with my daughter for a while, it
was time to go back.

She did not want to return to work over the summer while her
children were home, but she put out feelers for a new position. She
took a position that would be a new challenge.

I took a job with Moore, a company that needed a major turn-
around effort. This was a small team but an exciting opportu-
nity, and there was no guarantee that we would be successful.
It was a unique opportunity. I took the job at a lower level of
responsibility. The company culture was all about face time,
very conservative environment, and face time was king. I was
working with all men and the only other woman was the chief
counsel. I told them, "It's not about the money, it's about the
flexibility in the job." They said, "We hear you saying that, but
we don't believe you." I made it clear that I would work from
8 to 5 p.m., and I really didn't take home a lot of work at
night. The experience was a phenomenal ride—we turned it
around, acquired at first another firm and then, as the classic
case of the small fish gobbling up the big fish, we acquired a
company many times our size.

When the acquisition was complete, Pat was ready for another
change. "They said, 'We really like you; how about you take this
position in Chicago?' There were good reasons to take the position,
but ultimately my husband and I decided to remain here. So I took
the severance package and stayed home for a while." Pat was content at home, and enjoyed spending time with her children. But a
former colleague came calling with yet another opportunity.

He told me about this new company, Jarden, which owns sev-
eral underperforming but huge market share brands in the
consumer product business. All the management staff have
young children, and they have a culture of flexibility in their
work hours. He made a convincing argument that this might
be the right opportunity for me. I am now the VP for the glo-
bal business.

Pat is enjoying her new position and feels she might have found the right balance between her need for challenge and for time with her family. Pat represents the classic C-B-A profile we found for so many women—challenge first as a career driver, then balance, and finally authenticity. When asked about herself, Pat responded,

> *I do fund-raising for the Leukemia and Lymphoma Society, and when I can, I participate in their bike races, triathlons, and hold charity events for them. I enjoy the physical challenges of working out, and I find it clears my mind and relieves stress. So when I get a chance to work out and train for an event, that is what I do for me. But other than my physical activities, what is missing in my life right now is more time. More time to spend with my mother, whom I consider to be my best friend, and also more time with my children and husband and family.*

THE BETA KALEIDOSCOPE CAREER PATTERN

According to the Kaleidoscope Career model, each of the parameters—authenticity, balance, and challenge—is active as a signpost throughout a woman's career. We found that certain issues took precedence at different stages in life, becoming the parameters about which women's decision making about their careers pivoted. The remaining issues, while still worthy of consideration, took on a secondary role at that time.

As Pat's, Karen's, and Deborah Ann's careers suggest, most women felt the need for challenge in the early part of their careers. This was the point at which the desire to be ambitious, to make a mark, to develop expertise, or to demonstrate skills was most pronounced. In early career, issues of balance and authenticity were of secondary concern, although they would be important later. For instance, a woman may make a career decision to take a position offering more responsibility, because challenge is the key parameter at that time; the remaining issues (balance, authenticity) become secondary for the moment.

In midcareer, we found that most women were concerned about the issue of balance. It did not matter whether the woman had a husband and children or was single. Pat, Karen, and Deborah Ann were concerned about creating balance with family needs as a priority; in the case of single women, the priority might be soliciting elder care for aging parents, aiding the concerns and interests of nephews and nieces, or searching for a companion with whom she could share her life. Women may make adjustments to their career ambitions at that point to take on more flexible schedules.

In late career, most women we interviewed were asking the question, "Is that all there is?" Desire for authenticity, being true to oneself, and making decisions that suited oneself above others predominated in career and life decisions. We found that late in the career cycle, most women were interested in challenge, but on their own terms, making decisions in an authentic, meaningful way. The issue of balance, while still active, had receded into the background.[10]

For most women, issues of challenge, ambition, and advancement were most easily addressed in early career. But then other aspects of life intervened, with marriage, children, and other responsibilities. Issues of balance became prominent later in early career and in midcareer, which was just as promotions and opportunities for greater responsibility would start to become available. As we have seen in the case of Pat, in late career women pondered the choices they had made, and feeling freer from their responsibilities, started to consider their own needs. Issues of authenticity—such as following leisure or spiritual pursuits, starting a business because of a long-standing desire, or finding ways to have their own voice heard—would crop up.[11] This is what we call the *"Beta* pattern," a pattern driven by flexibility yet allowing for simultaneous active kaleidoscope parameters. It is a pattern that characterized the rhythm of most women's lives. Figure 1 summarizes the characteristics of the *Beta* Kaleidoscope Career pattern.

The *Beta* Kaleidoscope Career pattern prioritizes the quest for challenge in early career. In midcareer, "push and pull" factors simultaneously exert pressure on women's careers; when family and balance concerns become off-kilter, women may want to pull away from their careers for a while to better manage the relational aspects of their lives. Finally, in late career, women are freed from balance issues and able to define identities of their own, so issues of authenticity arise.

FIGURE 1

Kaleidoscope Career Patterns for Women: The Beta Profile

For most women, especially those married with children:

- In **early career,** one predominant life/career pattern for women is to be concerned with goal achievement and challenge in their careers.
- Issues of balance and authenticity remain active, but recede to the background, while the woman pursues her career interests.

- In **midcareer,** women must cope with issues of balance and family/relational demands. This ssue moves to the forefront.
- Women also wish for challenge and authenticity, but these issues take on a secondary role as compromises are made for balance issues.

- In **late career,** women have been freed from balance issues, so questions of authenticity arise. This issue moves to the forefront.
- Women may find new ways to be challenged and remain concerned about balance, but the kaleidoscope shifts according to the woman's choices and desires in each arena as dictated by her life pattern(s).

| | authencity | | balance | | challenge |

For those women who are career-centric:

- Similar to the (male) *Alpha* Kaleidoscope Career pattern

WOMEN'S KALEIDOSCOPE CAREERS

The *Beta* Kaleidoscope Career portfolio we found for women—challenge, balance, then authenticity—was born from the adjustments and compromises these women made while integrating their relationships with their careers. Most often these issues played out over the course of the life cycle, creating a constantly changing, shifting panorama within the dimensions of their kaleidoscopes. Other times these parameters peaked and ebbed at different points in the life cycle. All three issues remained active; it was simply that one particular parameter took precedence over the others for a while, then receded into the background while another parameter came into focus. Other researchers who have categorized women's careers have found similar themes.[12]

Research completed by other scholars supports our Kaleidoscope Career model for women. For example, consider the research conducted by the Center for Creative Leadership (CCL). The CCL team studied sixty-one high-achieving women and found that women in their late twenties and early thirties identified the developmental theme of "agency," or taking action. From age 34 to 40, the women focused on issues of wholeness and connection. The concept of authenticity predominated in these women's lives from age 41 to 45. A combination of agency and authenticity dominated ages 45 to 50, with a search for clarity emerging when the women were in their fifties.[13]

Another study, this one of thirty-eight successful professional women in midlife, showed that these women, looking back on their careers, reassessed their work and family priorities. They acknowledged that they needed to prepare for different family, career, and personal challenges in the next decade. In midlife, these women accepted the need to put themselves first, having spent several years meeting the needs of coworkers, bosses, subordinates, spouses, and children.[14]

Research stemming from the work-family literature also supports the transitions and shifts as indicated by the Kaleidoscope Career model.[15] As people age, men and women are less willing to endure work-family conflict for the sake of their careers, and women's careers are generally adversely affected by work-family conflict. In early career women are more inclined to emphasize relationships while men are more likely to sacrifice relationships for the sake of their work. One study in particular showed that for men the relationship between work involvement and family was generally positive. But for women the results showed that there was a negative relationship between family and work involvement that could not be denied.

As women go through changes, accommodate others, and finally come into their own over their lifetimes, their career decisions shift according to the parameters that are most salient at that time. Challenge appears in early career before most women are weighed down by nurturing responsibilities. Balance becomes the predominant issue once she has a family, with other aspects receding into the background. Finally, she finds authenticity at the end of her career when her nurturing role is complete.

THE ALPHA KALEIDOSCOPE PATTERN

While the *Beta* Kaleidoscope Career pattern is more personal values–driven, subject to shifting life style changes, and family-centric, the *Alpha* Kaleidoscope Career pattern is more linear and career-centric. This pattern described most of the men's careers in our samples. However, although previous research based on gender archetypes has focused on hierarchy, independent action, and goal orientation for men, we do not believe such distinctions are quite that clear-cut. Our research showed that men came to value relationships more once they had made progress in their careers. Their Kaleidoscope Career portfolios took on a different pattern from those of women.

Men's careers had a linear, or sequential, pattern—challenges first, concerns about the self, then a later focus on balance and others—that was more straightforward than the complex kaleidoscope patterns and career-family decision making of women. Generally, men actively pursued career challenges as a significant, all-encompassing parameter of their lives. For those men who served as the family breadwinners, their career advancement became their barometer of success and their means of providing for their families. At some point in their careers, however, most men become plateaued. The linear career has its shortcomings, and all are not anointed for success. In midcareer, men would ask themselves the question, Is this all there is? Authenticity became a spur to find recognition and respect, to make a contribution, and to have an impact on others. Once accomplished, men most commonly would then, at the end of their career cycles, openly value the luxury of time with family. We call this Kaleidoscope Career portfolio C-A-B, or the "*Alpha* kaleidoscope pattern." However, unlike women's portfolios, this portfolio is more sequential rather than simultaneous. See Figure 2 on the following page for characteristics of the *Alpha* kaleidoscope pattern.

A Linear Banking Career: John's Story

John, a vice president for a prominent banking institution, has followed a typical male linear career path: he has demonstrated his love for his family through being a good provider. This is how he describes his early career:

> *In my early years I was guided by values instilled by my family. I am the first generation of my family to be born in the United States. My parents are of European descent. While it is easier to admit now than it was when I was twenty-one, my family influenced me. Work hard, save your money, be respectful, and you will be successful for your family. Family is, and was, a very important motivator.*

John has had special challenges stemming from an early marriage.

> *My wife and I married young—at twenty-two—and had our first son just about a year later. My motivation was to do whatever I needed to do to be successful to support my family. Long hours, following the rules, facilitated success. Once I tasted success (my first promotion), my motivation continued to be family support and a need for recognition for hard work. As my career developed, I earned the opportunity to become involved in the managerial and directional functions of the*

FIGURE 2

Kaleidoscope Career Patterns for Men: The Alpha Profile

For most men who typify the linear career pattern:

Challenge

- In **early to midcareer,** one predominant life/career pattern for men is to focus on their careers and pursue challenges. Many men are driven to make headway in their careers at this time. The challenge parameter remains strong for several years.

Authenticity

- In **mid- to late career,** career-driven men must cope with issues of possible layoffs, downsizing, and less rapid upward movement. Their careers may plateau. Many men search for authenticity at this time, asking themselves if they have chosen the right career path.

Balance

- In **late career,** issues of balance rise to the forefront as some men look toward retirement. Men who have been focused on challenge and authenticity now turn to issues of balance and relationships in their lives.

For stay-at-home dads and Gen X family-centric men:

- Similar to the (female) *Beta* Kaleidoscope Career pattern

bank. While my earlier motivations never went away, an additional motivation of being part of the group that shaped the direction and future of the organization became stronger.

In midcareer, John took on large responsibilities for the bank, managing large work teams, and developing strategy.

Taking part in projects and seeing how they changed the organization have become very rewarding. Recognition was a by-product of achieving a desired goal. A real motivator for me now is developing others. I get a charge out of conveying the vision, mission, and strategies of the bank to our personnel and working with our up-and-coming starts to keep them motivated. I feel like I have finally hit my stride when I am managing team meetings. In my forties, I am learning that success is attained not by myself but through the contribution of all. This is what I was meant to do, I have found.

We found that for many men authenticity became apparent as part of their need to make a mark, or leave a contribution behind, in their careers. In John's case, authenticity is shown by his developing his management talents and finding his "calling" by helping others realize their true potential.

We found that most men had to be directly asked about balance issues, while for women the balance parameter was in the forefront of their careers and their discussions with us. When asked about issues of balance, John replied:

Over the last seven-plus years, creating a balance between work and family became a motivation. It was difficult to balance the work issues (dedication to the company and a desire to climb the corporate ladder) with my responsibilities to my family (the ones that didn't have to do with how much I earned and my status at work). It's been a learning process.

From Wall Street to a Culinary Career: Paul's Story

Paul Robert is a successful entrepreneur. He has a retail kitchen product business that boasts a well-known cooking school. But before he followed his passion for cooking, he worked on Wall Street for American Express and MasterCard International in a full-fledged corporate sales career. Paul explained why he made so many career transitions and how his career unfolded.

I graduated in 1980 from Boston University, and during the summers I worked for a limousine service that was run by two music executives who had a celebrity clientele. I loved the limousine business, and enjoyed the work immensely. In my early twenties, I had the idea, "Why do this for someone else?" So I started my own limousine service with two stretch limos, a town car, and a dispatcher from my former summer job. Unfortunately, I housed the business a few doors down the street from the original limousine service, which, as you would predict, meant that my relationship with my former employer ended badly. I'll never forget the look on my boss's face when I said I was going to be starting my own business and moving down the street. I was still very young—twenty-one or twenty-two—and I did quite well with it, but I was young and naive. Unfortunately, the business was started as a partnership and eventually it went sour.

His early business experiences made him realize that he needed to get a solid foundation in sales.

In the early 1980s I went to work for New York Business Products, a firm that sold copiers and fax machines. I worked my way up the ladder, and found I loved it. My relationship with that boss was great. Then I moved to Charette Art Supplies as a sales manager, and from there to General Building Corporation also as a sales manager. All the while I built a strong support base in sales.

In 1987 he married his wife, Corinna, and bought a house. This prompted another transition.

I decided to take a year off because I wanted the challenge of working on my own house. So I did—for about a year. When the year was over and money was running out, I decided to get back in the game. I interviewed for sales positions at some of the large, blue chip firms and landed a job at American Express in their Travel Related Services Division. My territory was right in downtown Manhattan, where I walked by the World Trade Center buildings every day. Because my territory was the financial district I did quite well.

While at American Express, Paul had four different bosses, but the third boss and Paul just didn't get along.

He wanted me out. So I wrote out my resignation, put it in my pocket, and walked to my boss's superior's office. I told her that my boss wanted me out and they were making a mistake. She listened and gave me responsibility for the liability-free card that American Express put out at the time that was a huge seller. She switched my territory to Fairfield County, Connecticut, and by the time I left American Express, I was at the top in terms of sales, a member of the Presidential Club and the Centurion Club, and I had a top-notch, financially rewarding sales career.

Then Paul went to work for MasterCard International.

There were some people I knew and trusted who had moved over to MasterCard International. So, after some prodding, I relented and took a job as the director of corporate products, but the job was poorly conceived. I was able to grow their sales card portfolio substantially, but I was placed in a difficult position, where I was telling bank executives how to sell, which was not a good position to be in. So I left in September 1997. I've never been one to panic, so I took some time off and used the severance wisely. I found I was in a position to do what I wanted until the money ran out.

It struck Paul one day that he had always loved to cook.

Cooking is art; cooking is therapy; cooking is creative. It is everything I have ever been passionate about. Cooking provides a satisfaction like no other when someone else eats and enjoys your food. I had started cooking early in life—since childhood—but I had never really considered the possibilities of a cooking career. I found a kitchen store that was a franchise called The Complete Kitchen. So I made a deal and in September of 1998 opened one store in Greenwich, then another store in Ridgefield, Connecticut.

Owning the cooking stores has allowed Paul to surface his drive for authenticity as well as discover newfound challenges. The stores have flourished, and his hands-on cooking classes have been a raging success. He has appeared on the Food Channel and has received widespread recognition for establishing a serious gourmet cooking school as well as a popular gourmet cooking camp for children. His cooking school showcases locally known chefs and their signature dishes.

Paul's drive for success as an entrepreneur has allowed his passion for cooking to fulfill his needs for authenticity, and he has had a major impact on the business community as well: "Now I am growing the business by identifying new corporate markets. My latest venture has been bringing executives in to cook at the cooking school as a team-building experience. So far I have done business with General Electric and Pfizer, among other firms."

Like so many men in our sample, when asked to what extent did balance and family issues affect his decision to get out of the corporate world and follow his passion, Paul responded unequivocally:

Not at all. In fact, it was just the opposite. In the beginning, I was working a hundred hours a week, and sometimes I did not go home at night. Instead, I slept in the store many nights. The decision to change career paths and become a full-time entrepreneur actually led to working harder and working longer hours. Balancing my family was not a factor; getting the business off the ground was the primary objective during those years.

Paul is now in a position to enjoy the fruits of his labors and his family. His Kaleidoscope Career portfolio—a classic C (*challenge*), A (*authenticity*), and later B (*balance*)—was marked by pursuing challenges in early career through his sales jobs, then finding authenticity in his life by following his passion. What advice would he give to new, struggling entrepreneurs who want to launch a successful business? "Hire an excellent staff. Training a staff is so very important. I'm lucky I have an excellent staff so I can follow my passion, develop the business, and cook."

From Business to Academe to Theater: Keith's Story

So far R. Keith Martin has had two careers: a very meaningful and illustrious career in business and an equally successful career in academia. His career portfolio represents the typical alpha (C-A-B) cycle of most men—but with a twist. Now, at the end of his academic career, he has rediscovered his love of acting and singing—and is preparing for act three.

Keith's first career in business represents the traditional linear model: he graduated from college, went to work as division manager for a national marketing firm, turned down a promotion to take a job as a marketing representative with IBM, and then resigned and joined Price Waterhouse (now Pricewaterhouse-Coopers) Consulting. Keith explained:

In my first job I felt constrained; representing an equipment manufacturer means that "business solutions" must always involve the use of the manufacturer's equipment—which certainly is not the panacea for all corporate problems. Wanting to be in an environment where the most appropriate solution might be recommended, I resigned and joined Price Water-house's consulting group. Soon after joining the firm's staff, and due to some lucky timing, I became its specialist to the securities and brokerage industry. And another staff member and I were assigned to design, develop, and install the firm's first computer-based information system (which was operational for over twenty-five years). When the firm decided to reestablish its consulting practice in the Seattle office, which was responsible for the firm's practice throughout the Pacific Northwest and Alaska, I was offered a transfer to lead that effort, which I readily accepted. In two years the consulting practice in the Seattle office supported twelve staff professionals.

However, an academic opportunity presented a new challenge. Keith had to make an important decision: to stay in the business world or begin a new career in academe.

I was asked to join the administrative staff of the University of Washington as director of a newly established department that would be responsible for university-wide systems development, administrative computing activities, some research computing facilities, records retention programs, and specified long-range planning activities. I saw this as a professional challenge—to build a department within a major university that would provide the wherewithal for the development and implementation of decision-based, technically grounded systems to facilitate the institution's operations. While director, I took advantage of the university's staff-tuition-free policy and completed a doctoral program.

With his doctorate in hand, a position in New York lured him to the East Coast, where he took a teaching position at Baruch College of the City University of New York to establish a program in information systems. He was then offered a position at Fairfield University, where he was quickly appointed associate dean and then dean. Keith explained how each job opened up new opportunities for challenge.

At Baruch I worked closely with the dean of Graduate Faculties, who left Baruch when invited by Fairfield University to establish a School of Business. He, in turn, enticed me to join him [at Fairfield] a couple of years later. My appointment was as a professor of accounting, although during that first year I was appointed associate dean, a faculty position with administrative responsibilities. When the dean retired, and following a nationwide search, I was appointed dean, serving in that position for eleven years.

A major challenge of his tenure as dean was providing the vision and leadership to build a school, basically from scratch, that ultimately would obtain American Association of Collegiate Schools of Business (AACSB) accreditation.

Perhaps the most important curriculum innovation during my tenure as dean was the development of an integrated program as part of the school's core requirements. Eventually, AACSB gave the innovative, integrated curriculum national exposure, providing testimony to its educational impact. I take a great deal of satisfaction in several programmatic accomplishments, including the establishment of the graduate program, the creation of a major in information systems, and the development of the international dimension of the curriculum.

Despite this long list of accomplishments, Keith felt that there was something missing in his life. He wanted to remain in academe, but on his own terms. Authenticity became a career pivot when he realized that the trials and tribulations of the politics of the university were getting in the way of his true mission—teaching.

I had entered academe primarily to teach, and had continued to teach one course each semester during much of the time I was dean. So with exciting things happening in the curriculum, a stable and vibrant faculty in place, I felt it was time to return to full-time faculty status. I was named to the Stephen and Camille Schramm Chair in Business, the first endowed chair within the school.

Keith's drive for challenge and authenticity was consumed in this desire to make a solid contribution by building a respected academic unit. Reflecting on his career and the transitions he had made over time, Keith spoke eloquently about the issue of balance, which became more prominent later in his career.

Without question, my family is the foundation for all that I have done these many years. First my parents, and then my wife and children, have encouraged me throughout my career. They agreed with my rationale for each career move and encouraged me to make the transition. My wife, four children, and seven grandchildren—they're what my life's all about. My joining the university may not have been the most logical financial decision I've ever made, but it was unquestionably one of my best family decisions. I would have more control over my life and be able to spend more quality time with my family. How many people have coached Little League–type teams for fourteen years? I have four children, two boys and two girls, all catchers, and did just that! I would often hold practices when the players got out of school, usually about 3:00 p.m., and then return to the university to teach an evening class. I attended virtually every performance and athletic event they were in from kindergarten through high school—priceless experiences for a parent.

Now retired from university life, R. Keith Martin is developing yet another career as a member of a theatrical group and is a member of a barbershop quartet that competes at the national level.

So there it is—a professional career of fifty years that has been challenging, exciting, and satisfying. Although I'm retiring from academe, there's much ahead. Acting and singing, of course, and, most important, more time with the family!

For many men, like Keith, being the family provider means seeking out a long and satisfying career path. We found that most men's careers were linear and sequential. Keith's pattern represents a long series of challenges through business and academe, then later a reflection on what was authentic in his life (returning to teaching and then to his roots in the theater) and achieving greater balance with his family life. This is the typical pattern we found for many men.

HOW MEN DEFINE BALANCE

Even though the careers of men were more sequential than those of women, men are still concerned with issues of balance. For those men who serve in the role of the family provider, the pressure of earning a continuous salary weighs heavily on their shoulders. Fred, a professional financial services vice president who also followed an *Alpha* Kaleidoscope Career pattern, shared these insights.

Along with the obvious financial needs, during my early career I looked to be recognized for doing a job well. I was motivated to work hard to achieve these goals and frequently accepted challenging assignments and worked long hours to ensure success. At the midstage of my career I know what I contribute, and need far less reinforcement from a boss or the company to feel good about what I do. However, I still need the money, and because of the environment we live in today, I feel far less secure in my career. I find that I still put in the hours necessary to get the job done, but I find myself resent-ing the fact that I do when the weeks stretch well beyond forty hours. I find myself thinking there is a lot more that is interesting in life than work, and that work is too daily. I fre-quently imagine doing something else, but I struggle with giv-ing up the income from a job I can do well [that] compensates me adequately in meeting the lifestyle trap we have settled into. My struggle is more about keeping those in my family content with their lifestyle than myself. I often kid about sim-ply quitting and driving a beer truck and focusing on my painting, but in that kidding there is an element of truth.

Other men expressed similar comments about realizing the need for balance late in their careers. Here's what Joe, a sixty-two-year-old banking executive, said:

I have made many personal sacrifices for success. While I was a good provider, the time and dedication to my job left lit-tle time and energy to enjoy my family. This really hit home seven years ago when my mother passed away and I realized that certain things, like one's success and accomplishments, are not as important as one's family. [Since then] I have made conscious efforts to form relationships with my own family.

Likewise, Edward, a fifty-year-old VP, discussed trade-offs and how balance became more of an issue to him as he aged.

My wife chose the harder career and stayed home with our three sons while I went to work. Having worked for one firm my entire career, I grew up with the company and found the company has been very supportive when I needed time. The real issue was me. I did not ask for much time. We needed the money, and I worked a lot of overtime in the early years. As time passed, [balance] became more of an issue. I knew there had to be tradeoffs. Supporting my family meant working hard, getting the promotions, and increasing my pay. I found that balance means making choices. [So] I picked a few things I would participate in (soccer, scouts, vacation).

Matt, a mortgage banker, had comments along the same lines.

Several years ago, balance was a challenge [that] we all are guilty of from time to time. But without the balance, everything goes to hell quickly on all fronts. I almost was guilty of losing sight of what is truly important and almost not realizing it in time.

Men focus on their career ambitions first but come to value personal relationships more over time. We found that the importance of balance began to be highlighted in midcareer for most men and grew stronger, often wistfully so, in late career. This difference in perspective, and the timing of giving importance to family relationships versus career, marks a profound contrast between women and men. It's not that men do not value family. It is more that men value family sufficiently to sacrifice themselves in the male linear career straitjacket so that their families are well provided for.

This theme has been seconded by other researchers who study work-family conflict. A number of studies show that women and men prioritize their work and family roles differently.[17] While married women employed outside the home tend to give precedence to family in balancing work and family identities, married men have the discretion to build identification with work and family roles without trading one off against the other.[18] Men compartmentalize work and family so that family issues tend not to interfere with their work. But women's work-family conflict suggests interference between both areas.[19] Women may be negatively affected by work-family conflict throughout their lives. Men, however, feel the adverse effects only in late career when they are forty and older.[20] In late career, working long hours or traveling extensively seems hardly worth the harm it does to relationships.[21] So men do value family and flexibility but at different times over their lifetimes than do women.

GENDER AND THE ALPHA AND BETA KALEIDOSCOPE PATTERNS

The *Alpha* Kaleidoscope Career pattern—challenge, authenticity, then balance—represents the career of someone who is more career-centric. Because of the male straitjacket and the linear career, most men discovered the benefits of their families and friendships later in life. For this reason, men are more commonly associated with the *Alpha* pattern.

The *Beta* Kaleidoscope Career pattern—challenge, balance, then authenticity—represents the career of someone who values family and makes adjustments to career for the sake of balance. Because women's relationalism leads women to the conclusion that they should be the ones who can be more flexible in attending to the needs of their families, this pattern represents most women. But gender, while correlated with these patterns, does not control them. We also found evidence of other Kaleidoscope Career portfolios that didn't fit the typical profile.

OTHER KALEIDOSCOPE PATTERNS

Although most of the women in our study exhibited some variation of the *Beta* kaleidoscope portfolio, and most of the men exhibited the *Alpha* kaleidoscope portfolio, two atypical patterns did emerge in our research: (1) women who pursue linear careers, or "*Alpha* women," and (2) stay-at-home Gen X and Gen Y men, or "*Beta* men." See Table 4 for a summary of these patterns.

TABLE 4

Alpha and Beta Kaleidoscope Patterns

	Typical of ...	Pattern
The Alpha Pattern	Most men Single, career-driven women	Challenge- Authenticity- Balance
The Beta Pattern	Most women Stay-at-home dads Gen X and Gen Y men	Challenge- Balance- Authenticity

Alpha Women: Scaling the Career Ladder

Alpha women are atypical because they are career-centric. These women choose to pursue a more traditional, linear career pattern similar to that of most career-driven men. While in our research the number of *Alpha* career-centric Kaleidoscope Career women paled in comparison to the family-centric *Beta* Kaleidoscope Career women, we did find some career-driven women who crafted a kaleidoscope portfolio focused on challenge and authenticity, rather than on balance.

Career-driven *Alpha* women seek power and are fully intent on pursuing their career goals to reach the top of their corporations. Research on executive women profiles hard-driving, performance savvy, achievement-driven careerists who fought their way to the top.[22] Women who have made *Fortune* magazine's annual list of "Top Fifty Women" usually fit this category.[23] These women are determined, persistent, and in relentless pursuit of challenging career goals. But behind a high-level *Alpha* woman at work, there is often an off-the-career-track *Beta* man at home. Many of these high-level executive women have what has been called in the popular press "trophy husbands," who often handle the responsibilities of the traditional "corporate wife." Such successful executive women as Dawn Lepore, vice chairman of Charles Schwab; Dina Dublon, CFO of J. P. Morgan Chase; and Madeline Hamill, vice president of worldwide strategic planning at Coca-Cola, all have husbands who stay at home with their children and are proud of that fact. Reported in the article was the statistic that of the 187 participants at Fortune's 2002 Most Powerful Women in Business Summit, 30 percent had househusbands. Many of these men, however, became "trophy husbands" only after they had already pursued their own challenging careers.[24]

More and more, women and their husbands are wrestling with gender roles as high-powered jobs are within their reach. Something has to give. Often it is a question of which member of the couple will provide the greater financial benefits for the family. One of our interviewees who wished to remain anonymous is a stay-at-home dad who supports his wife's high-flying financial career. He explained: "My wife enjoys the challenge of her work, and her firm paid more overall, while my salary was flat (no bonuses or commissions). So we made the mutual decision that I would be the one to stay home." This stay-at home dad had already pursued a career in the accounting field before he made the decision to step out of the work world and spend time with the family's two little girls.

It seems the higher one advances in a linear, corporate career, the harder it is to keep two high-octane careers on track, especially when children enter into the equation. For many *Alpha* executive women pursuing challenge and authenticity, there had to be a bargain struck with a nanny or spouse who become their children's primary caregiver. For some of these corporate women, a decision is made to have no children at all. A sobering statistic from a nationwide survey of high-achieving women in corporate America in 2001 showed that 42 percent did not have children.[25]

The Kaleidoscope Career portfolios of high-achieving career women were similar to the *Alpha* profile we found in the linear careers of career-driven men. But we wondered how the theme of relationalism that so profoundly characterized most women affected the life choices of these career-driven women. Not surprisingly, *Alpha* women still feel the balance parameter quite acutely. Like traditional fathers, many of these women are weekend parents. And, according to the *Fortune* article that profiled many of these extremely successful women, they are grateful to their husbands or caregivers but also are a little jealous of the close relationships their husbands have with their children. While some women at the top of their firms choose to have children, others choose not to complicate their lives with the added dimension of relationships and children. For those who remained single, the absence of relationships in their lives was a profound concern. In the words of Beth,

> *I reached the pinnacle of my profession—making principal (aka "partner") with a large international architectural practice, having gone through highly-regarded undergraduate and graduate schools, watching the already small number of women in my male-dominated firm dwindle ever further. And much to my surprise, I realized that after a few years on top that even having achieved that measure of so-called success, that I was not happy and fulfilled. . . . I realized there is something missing in my life. I never thought I would feel this way. I am actively looking for someone, and I no longer feel guilty if I take a weekend off and don't check my e-mail every day while on vacation. I don't need to apologize for having a life even if there are no children demanding my time.*

Singles often face a catch-22. At work they are expected by supervisors to work more hours, pick up the slack for coworkers absent for child care reasons, and be free to travel and transfer. At home, they are expected by married siblings to take care of aging parents and are also seen as needing less personal time because they don't have a spouse or children.[26]

Although single workers may not have traditionally defined "families" of spouse and children, they may have families of aging relatives or disabled siblings in their care, as well as friendships, romantic relationships, and nonwork activities (e.g., volunteer organizations, attending classes) that they wish to nurture. A recent study showed that never-married women without children experience similar levels of work-life conflict as those experienced by other groups of working women.[27] The problem is that corporate human resources policies have been based on the work life and needs of the typical professional man, who usually has had a wife at home taking care of personal issues so he could focus 100 percent on his career. Single workers are often aggrieved that work life policies do not capture their particular lifestyle issues.[28]

Beta Men: "I Don't Want My Father's Career"

We also found an emerging *Beta* Kaleidoscope Career pattern for men. Not all men want to have the hard-driving corporate career anymore. Disturbed by layoffs and corporate insecurity, these men are saying, "Take this job and shove it—I'll go my own way." With the advent of technology that enables a work-at-home environment, men of Generation X and Y are welcoming the opportunity to work outside corporate boundaries. "I don't want my father's career" has become their new mantra.

One of these *Beta* men is Gary Vasquez, whose career was profiled in Chapter 3. Gary explained,

> Some years ago I had the opportunity to switch careers and work in a Wall Street financial brokerage business, but I decided against it. After much consideration, I decided that I didn't want to work long hours, commute to the train station, commute to New York City, and find my way to and from the office both ways each day. Although the money would have been better, I didn't want to sacrifice my time with my family, especially while my boys are still young. What fun would it have been to have that great retirement party, only to look back and realize I did not get to spend time with my children while they were growing up and wanted to be with me. That's not for me. Some years ago, I made a decision and sacrificed climbing the corporate ladder so I could spend time with my sons. Seeing my son pitch in a little league baseball game or attending the third-grade musical recorder concert—now that's priceless.

Not everyone can be a star player in a corporation, and many would prefer not to become one. The level of responsibility, degree of travel demands, and the unyielding nature of the business overtaking one's life are not components of the sought-after career scenario among many men in the new millennium. While many of us would appreciate earning six figures or more, we realize there is a huge price to pay in family time. More and more, Generation Y men are deciding the corporate climb is simply not worth it.

A recent article in *Harvard Business Review* championed the point that the backbone of most companies comprises the B players, or the average performers, who keep firms running strong.[29] Firms are routinely blinded to the important role B players serve in saving the bottom line of their organizations. Not only do these people make the company run, but they counterbalance the ambitions of the firm's high-flying performers and stabilize the firm. In times of crisis, B players' stability can be an organization's saving grace.

The advent of technology has created a new choice for many men. Should I prostitute myself to the vagaries of the corporation as an A player, only to be slapped down when I get close to reaching the top, losing my family and what is important in the process? Or should I elect to remain a B player—never receiving recognition for my efforts in my career, but solidly supporting and enjoying my family? Many Generation X and Y men are making a resounding choice to be more family-centric and less corporate-driven than their father's generation. Having watched their fathers work their fingers to the bone, only to have their hands cut off by an unfeeling corporate merger, these men are valuing their family and their relationships over outlandish career ambitions and goals.

Beta Kaleidoscope Career men form an emerging pattern consistent with the relaxed societal norms of today's workforce. Valuing challenge, but also prioritizing family balance, these men are saying they want to forge identities independent of a corporate lifestyle. Similar to *Beta* Kaleidoscope Career women, *Beta* men forgo their career ambitions in midcareer to follow a more relaxed, family-centric lifestyle. By doing so, they are opening up new Kaleidoscope Career patterns for their sons and daughters who follow them.

CHANGING KALEIDOSCOPES,
CHANGING LIVES

While our research showed that most women adopted the *Beta* Kaleidoscope Career pattern of challenge-balance, then authenticity, and most men followed an *Alpha* Kaleidoscope Career pattern of challenge and authenticity, then later balance, we found small but emerging opposing gender patterns as well. As researchers, we expect we have captured a new societal trend. As social mores about stay-at-home dads and career-driven moms become more relaxed, these patterns will become more socially acceptable and prominent over time. Eventually, our hope is that gender issues will no longer dominate these *Alpha* and *Beta* kaleidoscope patterns. Instead, individuals, regardless of gender, may choose the Kaleidoscope Career pattern that best suits their lives.

Part of the value of the Kaleidoscope Career model is that kaleidoscope patterns are like snowflakes, with a multiplicity of patterns that could emerge given the push, pull, and tug of lifestyle versus career domain issues over the life span. Both women and men operate with kaleidoscope thinking, but they do so in different ways at different points in the life cycle. Our research shows that women as well as men may prioritize different parameters— authenticity, balance, and challenge—at different points in their careers and life cycles. The parameters that are most salient at a stage in the life cycle for a woman or a man dictate the career changes that are made as a consequence.

For employers, understanding the importance of the Kaleidoscope Career is critical, because the timing of life cycle issues affects turnover. Until now, career paths and succession plans within corporations have been based on the sequential *Alpha* (challenge-authenticity-balance) Kaleidoscope Career pattern, not the simultaneous *Beta* (challenge-balance-authenticity) Kaleidoscope Career pattern that characterizes most women. Firms often fail to understand these gender-based differences. As a result, they try to force women into the cookie-cutter traditional corporate linear model of long hours, face time, and extensive travel, not realizing that inflexible corporate polices contribute to women's turnover and result in an immeasurable loss of human capital for the firm.[30] Organizations must realize that gender issues do affect career development possibilities and succession planning. Human resources policies and criteria for advancement based on the traditional linear career model work against women and some *Beta* Kaleidoscope Career men as well.

The Kaleidoscope Career model provides a reason for the opt-out revolt currently plaguing corporations. Women and men are opting out of corporations to create values-centered Kaleidoscope Careers. The drivers for Kaleidoscope Careers include the parameters of authenticity, balance, and challenge. People want to feel they have made a contribution to their careers. Men and women want to have a consistent and powerful impact on others, be it their family members or their co-workers. Everyone wants to have a higher purpose than a typical nine-to-five job allows. Workers want more from their careers than the drudgery of daily tasks.

In the next three chapters we will explore in greater detail the parameters of authenticity, balance, and challenge—the ABC of the Kaleidoscope Career model—as they play out over time in the lives of women and men. We begin with the parameter of authenticity, or the need to be true to oneself. Although much has been written about balancing work-family demands and about creating challenge through work redesign, little focus in the business literature has been directed to the inherent need of men and women to have meaningful work that is aligned with their personal values.

THE QUEST FOR AUTHENTICITY

Mim Schreck, a classic *Alpha,* made it to the top of her firm, becoming president of Easy Spirit footwear, a division of the Nine West Group, only to discover that she wanted more from life. Mim graduated from Russell Sage College with a bachelor's degree in physical education and taught high school in Peabody, Massachusetts, for four years. She grew tired of the bureaucracy associated with teaching, so she changed occupations, going to work for the Jordan Marsh Company.

> *I enjoyed working retail, and I found it interesting. I could see the effect of my performance directly on sales results; for example, if I moved things around in a department, they would fly out of the store. I liked having an impact. And I enjoyed being creative.*

Mim was on the fast track. She quickly learned the business and rotated through several departments. After only six months with the firm, she had the opportunity to participate in the executive training program. She liked the work and earned promotion after promotion, ascending the corporation's retail ranks from department manager to assistant buyer to men's dress shirt and neckwear buyer to assistant store manager to general manager of her own store, and all the way up to the vice presidential level as a divisional merchandise manager of footwear.

While Mim was climbing the corporate ladder, the retail industry was undergoing great merger and acquisition activity. Allied Department Stores, which owned Jordan Marsh, was bought out and then merged with Federated Department Stores. In January 1990, the megaconglomerate filed for bankruptcy.

In the midst of all of these mergers and acquisitions, she accepted an offer from the president of the Nine West Group, who asked her to become vice president and concept director of the Nine West brand. The job entailed convincing the major department stores to buy Nine West footwear in quantity and help the stores advertise and market the products. During her thirteen years with the Nine West Group, Mim was promoted to senior vice president of Nine West, then executive vice president of Nine West, president of Bandolino, and finally president of one of the footwear brands. As the firm grew, the business changed.

I worked with an incredible team of people who were well respected by retailers and wholesalers. We were a wonderful team. It was a great place to work. [But then] when the company was purchased by Jones Apparel Group, the company became a billion dollar firm. Suddenly it was all bureaucracy and politics. They hired someone else to run the footwear business, so I saw the light and said, "That's it."

Having worked her way to the top of a Fortune 500 corporation, Mim, at age fifty, spent time reconsidering her priorities, asking herself, "Is this all there is to life?"

At the time, I was attending all these dinners where these women, some of the most notable women of the Fortune 500, were being recognized. I was known in my company as someone who did not shirk from work, who got the job done. Yet there was this gnawing need inside of me that said, Is it worth it? Do I want the top job? Do I want to fight for it in this highly bureaucratic, very political environment? Do I want to keep traveling all over the world at the drop of a hat?

One day, Mim found it hard to get out of bed and go to the office. She had lost her zest for work. The travel required of her as an upper-level executive just wasn't fun anymore. She realized she needed to do something else. To the chagrin and surprise of many of her colleagues in the industry, Mim announced her plans to opt out.

They said, "No, not you! What will you do?" But I said, "Look, I have sweated blood for this company. I have paid my dues. I have worked into the wee hours of the morning many times. I have finally concluded there is more to life than travel and the daily grind of reports, presentations, and meetings. And I am finally realizing there is more to life than airplanes and offices. I have many interests and I intend to pursue them."

Having retired from the corporate world, Mim spends her days playing golf or tennis, practicing yoga, skiing, or taking art classes. She serves on two nonprofit boards and mentors a high school student in Bridgeport, Connecticut. Finally, to her joy and surprise, she is living in her own house rather than in a constant parade of hotels on the road. She has no regrets.

I used to really enjoy my job, but I wasn't having fun anymore. I wanted to leave while I was still young enough to play all the sports I truly like and to give something back. I love being home and enjoying the wonderful town we live in. I do not have children, as I did not get married until thirty-seven and my husband was forty. Amazingly, it was a first marriage for both of us. Having children just did not work out. I have no regrets about getting married late, and I wasn't obsessed with having children. I'm just glad I found a wonderful man to share my life with.

Now that she has been off the job for a year, Mim is ready to charge up her life again. She is consulting to nonprofits and possibly developing her own business endeavor. Mim admits,

It is great just having nothing scheduled to do in the morning. But I can't help myself. . . . I am constantly in planning

mode. I need to always have something to do. We'll see what develops.

Like many *Alpha* men and women, Mim rose quickly through the corporate ranks, loving the challenge of the job, and the chance to make a difference. But then there came a time when the job was no longer fun. The politics and the bureaucracy became too much of a hassle. It was time for something else, something new—something more.

THE SEARCH FOR AUTHENTICITY

"Needing a change" is a phrase often heard from women, and some men, when they reached a point for a career transition. They may find that the corporate environment loses its gloss after a while. Ann Fudge, recently profiled in the media as a Harvard MBA who opted out of the workforce after she had been promoted to run a $5 billion division of Kraft Foods, said she left the workplace not to be with her sons, who are grown, but more for self-fulfillment. The corporate grind got to her, so she spent two years doing things she wanted to do: bicycling around Sardinia, going to movies, enjoying meals at home, and writing in her journal.[1] And Ms. Fudge is not alone. A 2005 survey conducted by the Conference Board found that 50 percent of Americans are satisfied with their jobs, a decrease of about 10 percent since 1995. Of those who are satisfied, only 14 percent claim to be very satisfied.[2] Some of the individuals in our study agreed. One of them, Jude, said, "It was my secret. I just did not find work to be fun anymore. So I quit to do something more fulfilling." Likewise, fifty-two-year-old Kate talked about the importance of being happy: "Find work that feeds your soul. You'll be working for a long time, so you need to find something that gives you satisfaction."

After years of work and toil, people begin to ask the big questions and search for the greater meanings: Is that all there is to life? Could there be something more, something different from what I've already achieved? Does what I've done so far in life reflect who I really am—and what I want to leave behind after I'm gone?

Men who have been downsized or have plateaued from their linear careers ask these questions of themselves.[3] Other men, who lead outwardly successfully careers, begin to think about what being successful really means to them and what their legacy will be. Some women who have followed a linear career path question whether they have hidden who they truly are to fit into a male-dominated workplace.[4] Numerous women who have spent so many years balancing their work and family lives, tending and nurturing others while subjugating their own needs, question when it will be their turn.[5] All of these individuals find they are on a quest. They want to find a better alignment between what they want to achieve for themselves, what others need them to do, and what work demands of them. They want authenticity.

Authenticity is a striving to be genuine—to be one's true self, whatever that might be. It drives individuals to make the changes required so there is a healthy alignment between their inner values and their outward behaviors, both at home and at work. The women and men in our study spoke again and again about realizing the need to be true to oneself.[6]

Authenticity is a pivotal life parameter, one of the three key components of the Kaleidoscope Career model. It can take on different forms and be enacted by people in different ways. For some individuals, this may involve a major shift in life focus as they realign their career and life priorities. For others it manifests itself at work as a need to say "This is my decision. Do with it what you will." For some, it may mean standing up to authority and saying "That's wrong. I'll have no part of it," or blowing the whistle, saying "I'm willing to be ostracized by the group. I'm willing to pay the price for doing the right thing." Authenticity is borne from the seasoning of experience over one's life. Terry Ali, a successful information technology entrepreneur and one of the women who was interviewed for this book, said,

> *In my twenties, I was afraid to say "That's wrong." I would go ahead and do what people wanted of me. In my thirties, I would say "Hey, that's wrong." In my forties I would say "That's really wrong," and I would speak up about it. In my fifties, I am willing to say "That's wrong. And I won't do it."*

For both men and women, authenticity is often a drive that increases in intensity throughout life. For most men, the desire to be authentic, to be "one's own person" begins early in life. For most women, authenticity is a drive that is deferred while they take care of the needs of others.[7] Usually when women are in their late forties or fifties they step forward and ask, "What about me? What about what I want to achieve? What about what I want to be?"

Sometimes authenticity becomes a priority when life events bring about other changes. These life events—a serious personal health crisis, the lost of a loved one, or an impending corporate merger—cause many individuals, both men and women, to take stock of their priorities.[8] In the next section, we will examine one of the most common life-changing events, the midlife crisis, and its relation to authenticity.

AUTHENTICITY AT MIDLIFE

The need for authenticity, the desire to be genuine and live according to your values, may intensify during one well-known life event, the midlife crisis. Daniel Levinson wrote about the male midlife crisis in his book *The Seasons of a Man's Life*. The midlife crisis is a crucial turning point when a man in his forties discovers that the life he has created doesn't match the dream of success he had formed in his early twenties.[9] A man going through a midlife crisis may reevaluate his assumptions about himself, his abilities, and his life. This may require a restructuring of his life, including divorce, career change, or reinvention of himself. A midlife crisis may especially hit a man who feels he has failed in his career, as in the case when he loses his job, doesn't climb the corporate ladder as he expected, or has to let go of long-held beliefs about his career (e.g., if you work hard, you'll be rewarded and promoted). At midlife, men may feel more open to express emotions, seek to strengthen their personal relationships, and worry about their legacy.[10]

In Levinson's follow-up book, *The Seasons of a Woman's Life*, he notes that women in midlife often experience a conflict between the traditional woman, or homemaker/mother, and the antitraditional woman, who wanted a career but didn't have full support at home to do so. Other studies of women at midlife have also found that some women do experience a period of reevaluation about the balance of their lives in relation to their careers. Research on midlife in women has centered on a concept of "rebalancing" priorities and roles. This may involve changing roles within the family, building new work strategies, reinstating personal interests, or devoting more time to social relationships.

Midlife women, similar to the midlife men Levinson studied, may develop a new perspective on the use of time and the pace of life. Women at midlife demonstrate a more positive self-image, relinquish their needs for control, and redefine what success means for them.[11] Many of these women expressed a greater need for control over their destinies and for more time for personal reflection about the balance between work and family.[12] They were striving for a more authentic tone to their lives, a "this is me" approach, rather than allowing others to dictate what they should do. A 2005 *Time* magazine cover story reported on women at midlife who were going inward, asking cosmic questions, or reconnecting with a former hobby or passion. They were also confronting the obstacles of middle age and figuring out how to turn those obstacles into opportunities. Several women profiled in the article were writing novels, pursuing further education, starting new businesses, or traveling in search of new adventures.[13]

Midlife may be a time of reckoning, causing some to walk away from the rat race saying "Who needs it" to a corporate career. It may cause individuals to seek out new challenges that are more in line with their values and priorities elsewhere. And while experts disagree on the actual number of Americans who experience a full-blown midlife crisis, with estimates ranging from 10 percent to 26 percent, midlife is an important milestone in life causing most individuals to take inventory of where they've been and where they're headed.[14] A midlife crisis is just one of many events that may trigger the quest for authenticity.[15]

Finding Purpose by Helping Others: Jerri Leinen

Some people develop the need to be genuine, to answer their inner calling, earlier in life. Jerri Leinen is a different kind of CEO. Her motivation is not in the money, the power, or the prestige but is in the challenge of making life better for those around her. Jerri said she recognized this calling to help others when she was just a child.

> *It started when I was a little kid, growing up in a community in which older people never really seem to get their due. People were just too busy for them. I remember a lady who was so gregarious and kind to others. She developed MS [multiple sclerosis], was confined to a wheelchair, then later confined to bed, and no one ever visited her. It was a trigger for me and became my purpose in life, the welfare of older people.*

While attending college, Jerri learned about the field of social work and was hooked. After earning a master's degree in gerontology and then an honorary doctorate in public service, as part of her practicum in social services, she spearheaded a grant proposal to United Way. Although the grant award was fifteen thousand dollars short of what was promised, Jerri said she was optimistic about what could be accomplished and relished the chance to help others.

> *The grant helped us develop a grand reputation of service, of putting people first. It's been very exciting for me to see how people have been helped and lives changed. For example, a catalyst for one of our organizational meetings was a gentleman who walked out of his apartment to pay rent. While counting out his rent money, three fellows came by and pulled the money out of his hands. The older gentleman fought to retrieve his money but literally dropped dead of a heart attack during the fight. People in his building knew his first name but didn't know if he had family or whom to contact and actually didn't know much about him at all. Other people in the building realized it could have been them and that they just didn't know each other. Twenty-five individuals from that area came to our first meeting, thinking about this man's death and thinking, there but for the grace of God go I. From there we made a lot of changes. We started in the family*

arena and just became friends to the neighborhood gaining their trust. We kept branching out to include outreach services and volunteer programs. Today we have five new laws on record at city hall based on our efforts. We filed petitions to make things change. We marched on city hall. We've been on the front pages many times over the years and have gained a lot of visibility, which converts to strength. That gentleman who was [mugged] outside his apartment didn't die in vain.

In addition to the inspiration she draws from the older individuals who benefit from her efforts, Jerri has always surrounded herself with people who have inspired her. Her late husband, Jerry, shared her strong belief in people and public service. Jerri described their unique relationship as a partnership that seamlessly integrated their personal and professional lives.

Jerry was just the most positive human being you would ever want to be around. He was such a believer. As we worked together there was such a synergy that when he died in 1994 it felt like I lost two people. What fun it was to do whatever it took to make some great things happen. Jer had been a Catholic priest, and I had been a nun. It was such an unbelievable joy when we met. I remember the day that made all the difference in the world to me. I was helping prepare an apartment for an elderly woman before she moved into it. It was nasty, and there were cockroaches to deal with. Jer stopped by the office on his way through town, and they told him where I was. He came by totally unprepared for such a situation, and dressed in nice clothes. He asked if I needed help and rolled up his sleeves, and the rest is history. Together we just enjoyed being a part of things and helping others accomplish their goals. We were so focused on what needed to be done and just loved doing it together. When my husband knew he was going to die, he said over and over that the worst thing for him was that he was leaving me to see it all through. Ten years later, people still speak of him, and, as someone said, he taught us how to live and how to die. He was a giant and left big footprints!

Jerri is now president and CEO of the Center for Active Seniors Incorporated (CASI), an accredited, premier nonprofit organization dedicated to providing assistance and programs to those over the age of sixty. CASI provides services to more than five thousand people each year through its educational programs (e.g., senior health information, money management, computer classes), social advocacy (e.g., case management, casework, and outreach services), volunteer programs (e.g., Listen to Me Read, which teams seniors with students in local schools), exercise classes, and meal programs.

Working for a nonprofit organization has its own unique challenges, including the continuous task of fund-raising. Jerri reflected on what keeps her going even when times are tough.

It's the people, the older people, and empowering them to experience a greater quality of life for themselves, that makes it all worthwhile. Sometimes I wonder to myself if something is possible, but then I see someone walk in the door and realize what a sacrifice it was for him or her to come, and I get back to work. It's what it is all about! The other day, I was thinking about how to ask a donor for five hundred thousand dollars. The evening before I met with her I was reading Bruce Wilkinson's The Dream Giver, *and the book just seemed to own me. The main thesis was that you must follow through with your purpose in life. I kept trying to think what it was saying, because I've always known my life is about older people's concerns. Then it dawned on me that what it was helping me understand was that asking for a donation is not about me. I need to get out of the way and realize that I'm asking for money to build a center for the people. I'm just carrying the message to one person after another so they can be a part of something great for the seniors of our area.*

Jerri spoke with excitement about CASI's new projects. She discussed how amazing it is that when things need to be done, people step forward to help. She is proud of her organization's accomplishments, including being accredited as one of the top senior centers in the United States and having a certified adult day care program. She is enthusiastic about the future and how CASI will continue to enhance the lives of seniors. With a laugh, Jerri remarked, "We have come a long way, and we have a long way to go! If my job were easy, I'd probably be blazing new trails [elsewhere]." And that's what keeps Jerri motivated—serving her higher purpose of helping others.

THE MANY FORMS OF AUTHENTICITY

Authenticity serves as a life-career pivot for the Kaleidoscope Careers model because it represents the voice of conscience that remains after trade-offs regarding career challenge and life balance have been made over the course of a life and career. Authenticity is the third nexus, and perhaps the constant, in the life-career equation. Tired of having to serve a corporate master and constantly negotiate a fragile balance between the work and nonwork aspects of life, men and women say "That's it. Now let's talk about what I want, what I need, for a change."

People who are authentic have a good grasp of their values, priorities, and preferences. They take stock of their life experiences to sharpen their values and beliefs, bringing those values and beliefs into focus with the ways in which they spent their time and the masters they served. As such, authenticity represents different things to different people. For Mim Schreck, finding authenticity meant taking stock of her priorities and leaving her hard-earned position at the top of her company to pursue sports and leisure activities from the comfort of her home. For others, like Jerri Leinen, the drive for authenticity manifested itself as an increased need for spirituality, for growth and learning, that occurred throughout life. For others, authenticity became the issue the moment they stepped up to the boss and told the truth about a highly political project that was going down the drain. Authenticity is difficult to describe, but we know it when we feel it. According to Marian Ruderman and Patricia Ohlott of the Center for Creative Leadership, authenticity is a state or condition rather than a personality characteristic. Authenticity involves feeling that daily actions are in concert with deeply held values and beliefs.[16]

Psychologist and best-selling author Dr. Phil McGraw defines the *authentic* self as

> *the you that can be found at your absolute core. It is the part of you that is not defined by your job, or your function, or your role. It is the composite of your unique gifts, skills, abilities, interests, talents, insights, and wisdom. It is all of your strengths and values that are uniquely yours and need expression, versus what you have been programmed to believe that you are "supposed" to be and do. It is the you that flourished, unself-consciously, in those times in your life when you felt happiest and most fulfilled. It is the you that existed before and remains when life's pain, experiences, and expectancies are stripped away. . . . It is the you that wants to require you to be more than you are, that doesn't even know what it is to settle or sell out.*[17]

Authenticity is usually not one solid color but a hue of many different nuances and shades. Many of these shades or forms of authenticity are interrelated and overlap. People searching for life's purpose, for example, often also seek out spiritual guidance. For the individuals in our research, authenticity took on five major forms.

1. A longing for purpose

2. A hunger for spiritual growth

3. A need to follow one's own path

4. A desire for an unrealized dream

5. A force for overcoming a crisis

Authenticity as a Longing for Purpose

For many people, the importance of authenticity becomes clear when they reach a point in their lives where they grow weary of the rat race and instead crave something more. Maryann, one of our early study participants, said, "Life is too short and I am starting to realize that. I want to work to live and not live to work. There are far more important things in life. People are so busy that the little pleasures of life get overlooked."

Having made a series of trade-offs concerning career challenges and life balance, individuals begin to ask the bigger questions about the purpose of it all. Yvonne, another of our study participants, said, "At this point in my life, I have a different life view. I want to be more effective with myself, with those I touch, and in the community and the world."

As individuals grow and age, they come to realize what's most important to them. They've learned that life is fleeting, that every moment should be respected and cherished. They need to make every minute count. Individuals longing for purpose don't want to live what seems to be a false life. They don't want to waste their time working at a job that brings them no joy or contentment. They want to take off their masks and be their true selves.[18]

In recent years, there has been a growing consciousness about people's longing for purpose. Consider the popularity of books on spirituality and purpose, including Marianne Williamson's *The Gift of Change: Spiritual Guidance for a Radically New Life* (San Francisco: Harper, 2004), Richard Carlson's *Easier Than You Think . . . Because Life Doesn't Have to Be So Hard* (San Francisco: Harper, 2005), and Rick Warren's *The Purpose-Driven Life* (New York: Zondervan, 2005). These books, and others like them, have climbed the best-seller lists as people have sought a better understanding of what the purpose of their lives is and how they can fulfill it. Some of these individuals have been successful in their quest for purpose—their quest for authenticity.

For example, consider the case of R. Keith Martin, profiled in Chapter 4. Keith moved from a teaching position as a professor of information systems to a prestigious administrative position as dean of the School of Business at Fairfield University. After serving for many years as dean, Keith decided he wanted to return to teaching.

Later, when he realized how much pleasure he received from using his rich baritone voice, he wanted to devote more time to singing in choral concerts and musicals. He said, "I am retiring early so that I can pursue what I want to do, not what others require me to do. Life is too short to be chained to that desk."

Keith and others like him long for purpose. They've come to realize that life goes by all too fast. They want to do work or engage in other activities that result in satisfaction and pleasure. They want to leave the daily grind behind and live with purpose.

Authenticity as a Hunger for Spiritual Growth

Once relegated to Sunday church services and discussed in hushed, reverent tones, spirituality is more and more in the forefront of discourse and debate. For example, religion figures prominently in the runaway best seller *The Da Vinci Code,* causing some to question basic beliefs and others to denounce the book as nonsense. Popular TV shows have brought questions of spirituality into American living rooms. These shows include the cult classic The *X-Files* as well as newer hits such as *Joan of Arcadia,* about a teen who literally talks with God; *Medium,* based on the experiences of real-life psychic Alison DuBois, who solves crimes by communicating with the dead; and the miniseries *Revelations,* based on the Biblical account of humankind's final days on earth. Major stories on spirituality in the national media include "The Power of Prayer," *U.S.News & World Report*; "Is God in Our Genes?" *Time*; and "Outsourced God Squads: A Thriving Industry," MSNBC.com.[19]

Perhaps the most influential woman in the United States, Oprah Winfrey, has encouraged Americans across religious, social, and economic boundaries to reexamine their beliefs and to use their lives for some higher power. Oprah personifies and models authenticity for the masses. On her show she teaches daily the power of the self and the need to listen to one's own inner voice, and she validates the search for something more. Through her syndicated television show, book club, magazine, production company, and other endeavors, Oprah has provided a forum in which many individuals have begun a spiritual journey to find their authentic selves.

This quest for spirituality has found its way into the workplace, with some organizations expressing their spiritual and religious beliefs through company policies. The firms that have included spirituality as part of their normal at-work routine are varied, and so are the ways in which they express it. For example, Tyson Foods employs over one hundred chaplains to counsel employees, mediate worker disputes, and help bridge cultural differences in its diverse workforce. In each in-flight meal served on Alaska Air, customers receive a card with readings from the book of Psalms. And before each race, NASCAR drivers attend a brief church service and a chaplain blesses them at the starting line. Even when there are no formal company policies about spirituality, workers still bring their beliefs to the job.[20] A March 2005 poll conducted by Hart Research for MSNBC found that, of those surveyed,

- 58 percent reported that their religious beliefs influenced their decision making at work

- 65 percent said that their religious beliefs affected their interactions with coworkers

- 15 percent participated in prayer circles with coworkers.[21]

This hunger for spirituality was expressed in many ways by the individuals in our study. Some connected spirituality to a specific faith and the power of God. Sarah, a respondent to our first survey, said, "I realize now that everything comes in God's time, not mine. And that if I do the groundwork God will help me complete the task if it is meant to be."

Others discussed spirituality separate from an established religion or faith. Instead they described spirituality more broadly, as how one interacts with others and respects differences. Kate, a telecommunications consultant in the wireless communications industry, told about the intersection of her work and spirituality.

I have become much more "spiritually" involved from a universal concept but not any specific religion. This epiphany of self, environment, and world has allowed me to achieve a position where I have become a telecommunications consultant working for a Japanese company, ensuring that our mutual Japanese clients and the American vendor achieve positive communications for a successful product. I can say that my performance has been a success, based on the fact that I was nominated and won as one of the top consultants of 1999, in an almost 95 percent male-dominated industry. Spirituality had to play a huge part in all of this—in maintaining a level of understanding and decorum between the various individuals and cultures.

Many people described their search for authenticity as a visionary or transformational approach to life. One of these was Mary, a fifty-one-year-old corporate entrepreneur.

I left the corporate world at age forty-eight to start my own businesses, fulfilling a long desire to be my own boss and be aligned with my spiritual beliefs and the need to help others reach their full potential. My life is about creating a vision, bringing it to life, engaging others in fulfillment of that vision, having a purpose, making a meaningful contribution to the betterment of people's lives, being able to be my own boss and keep my own schedule, working with other creative, intelligent, caring individuals, and having fun!

Spirituality helps people remain genuine in their decision making. As one survey respondent, Diana, said,

My toughest career decision I finally had to [make] on a spiritual level. I reach that place in making tough business decisions in the course of my day. If I wasn't reaching beyond myself, my ego, for guidance, I would never have come as far as I have in my career.

In an era of corporate scandals and questionable ethics, spirituality serves as a moral compass, pointing people in the right direction. Rather than waiting for others to make a decision that would be ethically or morally uncomfortable, authenticity shows itself in a need to speak up and say what's in one's soul. Spirituality helps individuals to do the right thing—even if everyone else is being rewarded for doing what's wrong. It helps individuals grow and become their real selves. As one survey respondent, Brianne, explained,

My spirituality has helped me maintain the highest level of integrity at all times, even when those around me are displaying little or no integrity. It's also provided a source of comfort by helping me realize that adversity can be a good thing—it makes you strong, it builds character, and helps you grow as an individual. It has also made me a more empathic person.

Brianne, Diana, Mary, and many others have come to see spirituality as an important influence not only in their home lives but also in their work lives. Regardless of whether they define it in terms of an established religion or faith or whether they view it in more universal terms, spirituality helps individuals to be their true selves and provides guidance when difficult ethical decisions need to be made.[22]

Authenticity as a Need to Follow One's Own Path

People who are authentic find their own paths. They makes decisions and take actions that are true to who they are, proudly proclaiming: "I'll do it my way." One such individual is Terry Ali, one of the interviewees for this book. Terry works with her husband in their own information technology start-up business and explained authenticity in the following way.

You know, career decisions over the long haul are not unlike how you deal with each other in a good marriage. In my twenties, I would tell my husband, "If you do that, I am going to throw your clothes out that window." In my thirties I would threaten him seriously and get all mad and huffy about it. In my forties I actually did throw his clothes out the window—in winter, no less, into the pool, and they ended up frozen. He had to fish them out, de-ice them, and wash them. Together we laughed about it later. I've matured, and there are certain things I am not going to take anymore. It's the maturing process. At a certain point, you look up, listen to that voice inside, and decide the phoniness is all baloney. You've got to call it as you see it and mean what you say. The people I work with know I am going to give them the straight story.

There is no more compelling time in a person's career than when the realization hits that a choice must be made between one's values and ambition to speak out against an issue or become a silent accomplice in crime. Making this decision requires going against corporate norms and risking career suicide for standing up for what's right. George, an accountant in a highly recognized consulting/accounting firm, told about one such authentic moment.

> *I had gone along with all the crap over the years and whatever they wanted of me. "Fine," I said. "Tell me how high to jump," and I did. You know, my family was counting on me, and I wanted the money. So I did some things I am not exactly proud of in retrospect—nothing that would get me into jail, but just some of those grey shading things that could be interpreted differently by different people. In my forties, I started to realize how crappy the whole thing was. I had a moment when I decided I was going to call it as I saw it. So the next time my boss asked me to do one of those grey shadings, I found the courage to say, "No, I won't do it." It changed everything—I suddenly was no longer the "go to" man. I was closed out of the loop, and I had to switch firms—but at least now I can sleep in my bed at night and know I am doing the right thing.*

Authenticity can manifest itself in the realization that one must make decisions that are right and true. Research on ethical judgment shows that those in later career stages display higher ethical judgment than those in early career.[23] Rejecting corporate politics can be a situation in which authenticity shines through. Lisette, a banker, said,

> *The challenge for me was to learn and adopt a management style that would feel right for me in my skin, while getting the job done right for the bank. I made a lot of mistakes in the beginning. Once I figured out people want and need to know what is expected of them and that it can be delivered in a positive win-win way, things got much easier. I was able to be the good guy, and I got comfortable delivering bad news when-*

ever necessary. The key to all of it is that I was able to be myself and be consistent, honest, and fair. People can see that, and it helps to build trust and respect. My advice to someone starting their career would be, To thine own self be true.

People who traverse the road less traveled often pay a heavy price for their quest for authenticity. The media has reported on well-known corporate whistle-blowers, like Karen Silkwood, whose stories did not have happy endings. Still others, like Lisette, have found that being true to herself brought her positive career outcomes, including the trust and respect of coworkers. Some, like George, decided to live more authentically and were finally able to get a good night's rest. Still others, like Terry Ali, enhanced their understanding of who they truly are as they matured, permitting them to develop more meaningful relationships.

Authenticity as a Desire for an Unrealized Dream

Authenticity can also take the form of pressure to accomplish something by pursuing a hobby, starting a business, or striving for a yet unrealized dream. As one survey respondent, Debra, said,

You know, you gotta ask, "What's the point of work?" Honestly, I don't know. Other than to put food on the table. But now I am at the point in my life where I am looking around, noticing the mortal time clock, realizing that I may not have much time left. My mother died at fifty-seven, and I'm fifty-three. Why wouldn't I retire right now and pursue my dreams?

Like Debra, several of our respondents discovered their passion overruled their needs for career advancement. Paul Robert, profiled in Chapter 3, is one such case. His passion for cooking led to his entrepreneurial success as an owner of two kitchen product retail stores and a cooking school on the side. Other men and women, like Mim Schreck and R. Keith Martin, discovered the quest for authenticity as they came closer to their retirement years. For example, Charles spoke with joy of his emancipation.

I can't tell you how freeing it is to be on the perch for retire-
ment. After all those years of work, work, work, I am finally
able to do what I want to do. My family has been provided for,
and three of my children have gone to college. One to go. Now
it is about my wife, and my golfing, my fishing, my reading the
newspaper every day, my doing what I feel like [doing], not
what others make me do for them.

For others, pursuing that unlived dream became paramount
when they realized that they were just plain fed up with the
demands of a corporate environment. Several of the women who
had become entrepreneurs expressed an interest in controlling
their own destinies and playing by their own rules. But first they
had to find the courage to venture out on their own. Some, sick of
corporate life, found the strength to break away from the safety of a
regular paycheck and realize their dream of starting their own
businesses. Others found ways of realizing their true passions in
retirement. Although the dream may have been deferred, these
individuals found that it could no longer be denied.

Authenticity as a Force for Overcoming a Crisis

The need for authenticity also arises in response to a crisis. When a
crisis occurs, the chips are down, and one's true character—good or
bad—shines through. The power of authenticity is often revealed as
a force to overcome a difficult challenge or as a way to navigate a
formidable transition period. As Chris, one of our Internet respondents, wrote,

I find it hard to write this, but my son recently died from a
drug overdose. I can't tell you what a change his death, now
several months ago, has wrought in me. It was a cataclysmic
event for my life, my whole family, and for my career. Now I
don't care much about "career," as I used to. I go to the office
and make the motions, but my heart isn't in it anymore. This
event has taught me what is really important. Life is about
people, not about work.

Several survey respondents indicated that various health crises prompted them to live more authentically. Said Jim, a plastics engineer,

Having had a heart attack, I really don't give a —— about the politics of the place. I'm much more interested in saying what I mean and meaning something to the people with whom I come into contact than futzing about dealing with who said what to whom.

For some, it might have been relationship problems, even a looming divorce, that caused them to take stock of their priorities. Some, like Jake, encounter a rough patch in a marriage that causes a rethinking of career ambitions.

I started working right out of college, and I got raises four out of five years and two promotions to date. I make a great salary. But my near divorce caused me to reconsider everything. I thought about changing my career to a lower paying career, one that would make me happier. I realized it is better to work hard here, make good money, and then retire early to pursue my other interests fully.

Others, like Rolan, decided to get out of the corporate world, strengthening their relationships in the process.

Sometimes I am happy that I traveled so much that it caused a temporary separation in my marriage. It sounds strange, but if it wasn't for that, I never would have gone to counseling, where I learned how unhappy I was at work. Two years later, I have started my own business, and my marriage has never been stronger.

For still others, it was a corporate reorganization that spurred them to reconsider their career choices and family needs. Although many fear the loss of a job when companies restructure, others view it as an opportunity for a graceful exit. Toni described why she felt that way.

I have been very fortunate and have achieved significant success monetarily and with personal challenges, as a result of investing time and effort in my career. My early career was a series of developmental management positions, which prepared me for the higher level. Over the years I have made steady progress, culminating in an appointment several years ago to a vice presidency in my firm. However, I have recently experienced family difficulties. These difficulties require more of my time. . . . I have a daughter who will be ready for college soon, and I have aging parents who need more attention. With all these new reorganizations, I am hoping that I will be laid off.

The literature on crisis management shows that taking stock of one's priorities is a normal response to a crisis. Monday morning quarterbacking is a common response to a perceived or real failure.[24] Whether it is the death of a family member, a corporate reorganization that goes awry, or a marriage on the rocks, men and women use these life events as a means of reflection and to propel personal change.

THE QUEST FOR AUTHENTICITY OVER THE LIFE CYCLE

In our interviews and online conversations we found differences between women and men concerning authenticity. For men, authenticity became apparent as they confronted their career dreams, usually in their late thirties and early forties. Men reflected on their careers and lives, taking the time to evaluate their career progression and determine whether their careers were meeting their expectations. If the careers did not, they decided it was time for a course correction; men changed firms or industries, became entrepreneurs, or found other ways to do things their way. The quest for authenticity, defined as "becoming one's own person," appeared earlier in the life cycle for men (late thirties, early forties) than for women (late forties, fifties).

Ronald, a banker, discussed the mergers and acquisitions that forced him to reevaluate his career.

Initially, my job was a place to earn money and feel satisfied about my accomplishments. I never thought of it as a career until I was knee-deep in responsibility on the job and at home. I enjoyed my progression within the company because my work was challenging and the results were recognized and appreciated. My boss gave me enough freedom to learn, and he respected my opinion and judgment. When the mergers took place, the politics began. The direction the company was moving in made less sense, and I had less power to make a difference. The vision of the organization was not clear, and there was a severe lack of communication. Everyone was looking to cover himself as things went wrong. No one looked for solutions—just blame and excuses. So I said, "Is this what I really want?" I decided that it was high time that I take my skills elsewhere. So when the time came to discuss relocation, I respectfully declined and transitioned all my areas. I decided to take a position with a small local firm where my contributions have a greater impact, and I can make my own decisions.

Ace, a forty-three-year-old former student and Wall Street stockbroker, discussed his career path and drive for authenticity along the way.

My zeal to become a stockbroker at age twenty-one was certainly contrary to my Greenpeace T-shirt and my Vote Mondale button, but success seemed to be measured by a scorecard. In school it was grades, best car, best clothes, coolest friends, so in life I assumed I needed major coin to get more of the same. So by age twenty-two I owned a condo and a Mercedes Benz—OK, it was one of the Baby Benzes. By thirty-four I had had it with that lifestyle. I learned very early that slow and steady wins the race, and I never lost the passion to win the race. No, I am not a blood-sucking capitalist.

Over the years I have learned to do everything to the best of my ability and do so with deep moral standards. My drive to succeed is strong but will never be at the cost of my ethics or the sacrifice of my family. I have remained on the investment side of the industry, not for the score, but to help others. This is my turnaround. If I can help people find peace of mind by eliminating financial stress, I feel good. I learned over the years that if you do the right thing, the rewards (or the commissions) will follow; if you simply focus on the carrot, you'll crash into the wall.

Both Ronald and Ace underwent midcourse corrections prompted by reflection associated with their career progress. For Ronald, it was an external change to a new, smaller firm that allowed him to make his own decisions and be more authentic. For Ace, it was the realization that the drive for the "coin" should not replace his ethics or his family—an internal philosophical change— that made him more genuinely aligned with his values and his work.

Men want to be authentic, especially when they hit the wall in their careers. Tired of the politics, some men decide there is more to life than work, work, work. But many men who serve in the provider role find that they cannot be as authentic as they would like to be. For men, the timing of events in their lives can be obstacles to achieving authenticity. Tony, a forty-five-year-old auditor, said,

On the one hand, I am proud of what I have achieved during the last twenty years, both professionally and personally. On the other hand, I feel I have lost some authenticity along the way. Once you get trapped in financial security, it is extremely hard to change, particularly if a family is involved. My needs obviously have to come last.

Although some men experience stumbling blocks in their quest for authenticity, most men tend to consider authenticity around midlife, whereas women tend to focus on authenticity later in life.[25] Why the difference? Women exercise a more simultaneous set of parameters in the kaleidoscopes of their careers than do men. In the midst of multitasking their lives away, women still hear the whisper of that small voice inside them that asks, "What about me? What do I want?" but they are often too consumed with caring for others to heed it. Caught in a nurturing, relational bind, or even compelled by the compulsion to please others before themselves, women subjugate their desires to the needs of others.

This does not mean that women don't value authenticity. In fact, many women told us that they were striving for a life and work situation in which their values and careers could be better aligned. But for many women, authenticity could not be practiced actively until later in life. The timing of other commitments constantly got in the way. Said one of our survey participants, Martha,

> There was this question that I kept dodging—OK, what about me, me, me? In the midst of all the cooking, cleaning, washing clothes, running to the store, filing reports, doing presentations, and serving as carpool master, . . . [it was a question] that I never answered until now, at age fifty. Now I can ask that question and actually get an answer.

As women gain life experience, they strive to identify their priorities and values—and live by them. Many women discover that the hours they are spending on the job are simply not how they want to live their lives. For women, caught in the constant time bind between work and family, the quest for authenticity typically appears later in life, when they are in their late forties or fifties.

The timing must be right. Women must have the time for reflection, and many women simply do not have that time. Between handling children, chauffeuring teenagers to sports games and music lessons, meeting the demands of the boss, caring for elderly parents, and keeping up with household tasks, women don't have the time to engage in pursuits that are more personally self-fulfilling. Forty-five-year-old Kara was in that situation.

> Looking at my situation right now, it appears that all of my choices and decisions I've made lined up to get me to this exact point in my career. It would have been nice to avoid

*some of the significant struggles that I've had that were com-
plicated by my own reactions. That would have entailed
knowing myself better and having more self-confidence,
which I've worked hard on in the last five years. I'm not sure
I would have been ready for this type of personal growth any
sooner.*

Although women might have given a passing thought to the
"What about me?" dilemma in their hectic thirties, the luxury of
true authenticity does not become available to them until they
reached their late forties or fifties. Then for many life became a
pleasure. Monica, a forty-seven-year-old woman who worked in
the high-tech industry felt that way.

*I had a high-powered career in high-tech but am now per-
fectly happy staying home, writing, doing volunteer work, and
taking care of our two dogs. Why the change? Managing
worldwide businesses and making million-dollar decisions
provided a high for a long time and was immensely satisfying,
but then I started to miss the simpler things in life, . . . going
for walks, spending time with friends, connecting with
extended family, and having a home that felt like a home
instead of just a rest stop between work assignments. I can do
what I'm doing now because I had the success I did early on. I
don't have to prove anything to anybody, including myself. As
we live longer, I suspect that more of us are going to find ways
to broaden our life experiences. What I did in my twenties
and thirties didn't make sense in my forties, and since I had
the financial resources to choose a new life path, I did. There's
nothing sacred about working all your life for money.*

Like Monica, fifty-five-year-old Ina worked hard and decided
to make a change later in life.

*The early years were hectic, and I worked for a firm that
actually supported women. At Reader's Digest, for example,
when there was a snow day, it was understood that we did not
have to come in to the office, that we would be home with our*

*children—in fact, the whole building closed down! I worked
and brought up my children, and they have turned out pretty
well. So now I have the time to consider, what about me? I
spend my time painting now. I have always had a passion for
painting. I could not devote myself to my painting while I
worked at* Reader's Digest. *There just weren't enough hours
in the day. But now I have the time, and I have even returned
to my old firm as a part-time consultant, so I have the best of
both worlds.*

Because of the different kaleidoscope patterns of men's and
women's careers, the quest for authenticity usually occurs later in
women's lives than it does in men's. Despite the differences in timing, the quest for authenticity affects the ways in which both men
and women define success.[26]

THE CHANGING DEFINITION OF SUCCESS

Individuals measure success in different ways. Research has found
that some individuals define career success objectively, by the outward trappings. The right car, the big house, and the exotic vacation trip become the standards of success. Individuals focused on
objective success strive for money, position in the organizational
hierarchy, and the corner office. Others use less tangible definitions, gauging success subjectively. These individuals are concerned with having pride in their work and striving for satisfying
and meaningful work and work relationships. So who's better off?
Ironically, there are happy losers (those who have high subjective
success but few of the material outcomes) and unhappy winners
(those who have all the trappings of success yet are unfulfilled by
their work). Thus, while management may believe that their workers are satisfied and content with their jobs because of the material
rewards given, management that does not also provide for intangible rewards may discover that their employees are leaving for more
meaningful, satisfying, and personally rewarding opportunities.
The prevalence of happy losers and unhappy winners supports the
importance of authenticity as a pivot in the Kaleidoscope Career

model. The unhappy winners look at how they are measuring success and decide to change from a focus on external to internal measures, often stunning others when they walk away from their high-powered jobs in search of greater meaning.[27]

Not only does the definition of success differ from person to person but the definition changes as individuals age. We found that the quest for authenticity increases in importance as a life-career parameter as people mature. In early career, success is often defined objectively by such things as earning a bigger salary, getting that expense account, and being assigned an upscale company car. But as the life and career paths change over time, new, less tangible definitions of success become more apparent. Studies examining definitions of success over the life cycle found that material criteria for career success generally decrease in importance with age. Material criteria of success were often replaced by an emphasis on influence and autonomy. Research has found that people may appear for all the world to be hugely successful—living glamorous lifestyles, rubbing elbows with celebrities, and shopping in the most exclusive stores—but still feel like failures. It may be that the behaviors that earned them the material success—devoting so much of their time and energy to their jobs—drained them, and they have nothing left to give their families. Or it may be that successfully completing job assignments has not resulted in any personal growth. Or people may have acquired new knowledge and skills—as is often the case with expatriate assignments and extended off-site training and education—but this new learning couldn't be applied on the job or wasn't valued by their employers. As many people age, they get increasingly frustrated by the disconnect between their external success and their internal feelings that something just isn't right. They become less concerned about what other people think and what their salaries can buy and become more concerned about being true to themselves and discovering meaning in the work they do.[28]

In addition to age, gender has a profound influence on workers' definitions of success. Women tend to define success based on internal criteria as well as relational criteria. Men tend to define success based on material wealth, salary, and the external trappings of success.[29] Our interviewees and survey respondents echoed this gender difference. Susan, a mother of three, said, "I am a success, even though I dropped out of the workforce. My greatest achievements are my children, not my work."

Likewise, Donna, a sales manager, commented,

At this point in my life, I don't care about the car I drive or the clothes I wear or the latest multimillion-dollar deal that's going to make the company rich. I care about what I think, what I can do, what I can accomplish. The kind of work I do is more important than what the salary for the work can buy for me.

But most men defined success largely in financial or hierarchical terms. One respondent, Ryan, said, "In the quest for the meaning of life, I guess it has been the almighty dollar that has influenced me most." Richard also focused on external signs of success: "I have measured success by the number of promotions I have received along the way, and the increase in salary that I have gained for myself and for my family." Throughout our surveys, we found the same theme echoed again and again for men. Pay and position were seen as indispensable markers of career success for most men.

Gen X and Gen Y men, however, defined success more broadly. Kevin, a thirty-year-old computer programmer, stated simply,

Am I going to fight the corporate wars all day in an elusive search to get to the top? Not me. My wife and I eschew the name-brand labels, the fancy new kitchen, and the trappings of success so that we can live a more balanced life with quality time for each other. Of course, we live in an older home that needs more repairs, but you know what? As a computer programmer, I get to work at home and see my kids. It's a simpler life and a better life.

There was a trend for younger women and younger men both to define success in more intangible, less material terms. But this shift in emphasis from external to internal measures of success was not without conflict. Some women, for instance, found that they needed to make peace with their feelings about leaving the work-force and perhaps abandoning the cause of feminism.

Will the shift in the way in which success is defined by younger men and women continue? Will individuals start seeking authenticity earlier in their lives than ever before? For now, the search for authenticity reflects individuals' growing maturity and seasoning over the years. It becomes possible once the parameters of challenge and balance create a space for people to reflect on themselves and the totality of their lives. With the growing number of American baby boomers in midlife and planning for retirement, increasing attention may focus on living with authenticity.[30]

CORPORATE AUTHENTICITY AND THE KALEIDOSCOPE CAREER

Unfortunately, as it stands now, most major corporations don't care in the least about individuals' need for authenticity. But employees do. In a survey of fifteen thousand managers asked to select the seven most admired leadership characteristics from a list of twenty, 87 percent selected honesty. Studies completed by Lou Harris and other opinion research firms, found a gap between the importance workers place on credibility and the belief that it is happening in their own workplaces.[31] This is hardly surprising given the well-publicized ethical scandals that have recently rocked not only corporate America (e.g., Enron, WorldCom) but religious organizations as well.

Employees want leaders who are credible, those who are honest, competent, and inspiring. Credible leaders make workers feel valued. Workers feel proud to be members of the firm. They are willing to put forth the time and effort toward the accomplishment of shared goals. They feel more optimistic about their workplaces and more motivated to help accomplish their firms' missions.[32]

So if being credible, if being honest, if being authentic produces positive outcomes for organizations, why aren't companies doing more to increase organizational and employee authenticity? Even though most companies unfortunately aren't focused on authenticity, some companies are. The efforts by these organizations take on many different forms. For example, a number of companies offer sabbaticals for their employees as a vehicle for personal growth and learning, increasing self-awareness, and being of service to others. One such company that sponsors sabbaticals is Intel. Intel's engineers and technical employees who have seven years of organizational tenure have the chance to take an eight-week paid sabbatical. This leave is in addition to regular vacation time and has been used by employees to teach in public schools and universities, to enhance their own educations, or to do volunteer work.[33]

Other organizations—including American Express, 3M, FedEx, DuPont, and Microsoft—have established support groups to provide a nurturing climate for employees. These resource groups cover a range of needs for groups of working parents, single parents, dads, ethnic groups, those with health problems and disabilities, and many more.[34] Still other companies provide opportunities to combine business necessity with the needs of their employees to express their true, whole selves. For instance, the e-business firm TIS Consulting maintains a low turnover rate of 3 percent by hiring individuals who live well-balanced lives. TIS doesn't want to hire people who will work over the weekend and have no outside interests. Instead, they hire well-rounded individuals and encourage these individuals to bring their passions to work. For example, TIS's Andrew Peterson, a senior software engineer and tightrope walking juggler, often practices—in his circus gear—at the company's Manhattan office.[35]

Other firms focus on helping employees discover their true selves by learning of the potentially life-altering impact of the work they do. For instance, Novo Nordisk, the Danish pharmaceuticals firm that focuses on the treatment of diabetes, expects each of its employees to meet with a diabetes patient and learn about the illness and how it affects that person's day-to-day life. In 2002, 80 percent of Novo Nordisk workers had talked with a diabetes sufferer. Nirmal Kumar Jain, a regulatory affairs executive at the firm's branch in India, said about his experience: "[The talk] made me feel that I should start contributing by whatever means possible."[36] Although some companies are introducing programs to help employees define and reinforce their authentic selves and find meaning in their work, these firms are still few in number.

Despite many organizations' reluctance to foster their employees' authenticity, there is no question that authenticity represents an inner drive that is inherent in the human condition. It is difficult to define, because it means different things to different people. In our research, we saw authenticity displayed as a search for purpose, a hunger for spiritual growth, a need to define one's own path or management style, a quest for an unlived dream, and a catalyst to help overcome a crisis. Above all, it represents the inner voice that suggests *To thine own self be true.*

People want to be genuine, but becoming authentic requires time in self-reflection, of trying new things and experiencing life. As individuals are changed by the lessons learned, they come to know their strengths and limitations as well as the boundaries that have shaped their lives. The authenticity parameter of the Kaleidoscope Career falls into place naturally through trial and error over the life cycle. People start to connect the dots and use the three ABC parameters—authenticity, balance, and challenge—to fit the best equation overall for their lives, their careers, and themselves. The next chapter examines these issues more fully and articulates the parameter of balance as a life-career pivot.

CHAPTER 6

THE SEARCH
FOR BALANCE

Brenda Barnes has been profiled in the media as a role model for other women who have chosen to take a breather from corporate life to spend time with their families. Her early career was a whirlwind as she learned the ropes of management in the competitive, hard-driving culture of PepsiCo. The epitome of the assertive modern-day working woman, she would rise at 3:30 a.m., wake her children at 7 a.m., put them on the bus, and then rush to the office, where she'd spend her time taking meetings, juggling budgets, answering urgent overseas e-mails, and developing strategy for her division. She'd manage to make it home for dinner, put the children to bed, and then finish answering her e-mail. And that was her hectic schedule when she was in town. Her job required constant travel. She relocated seven times, and sometimes she and her husband lived in separate cities, trying to juggle both the demands of work and family.[1]

For many years, her dedication to her work and her long work hours paid handsome dividends. Brenda Barnes was widely considered a real contender for the top job at PepsiCo when CEO Roger Enrico retired. But in September 1997, at age forty-three, she suddenly stepped down, when the demands of work began to take their toll. When she resigned her post as president and chief executive of PepsiCo's North American division, she was widely quoted in the media as saying "I'm not leaving because my children need more of me; I'm leaving because I need more of them."[2]

Many women who make the decision to opt out of the workforce drop out of sight entirely, allowing their lives to become a churn of laundry, play dates, community service, and soccer practices. But there is an epilogue to this story. Brenda Barnes remained active after she stepped off the career track and continued to serve on the boards of six major companies. She also taught at the Kellogg School of Management, and she stepped in as interim president of Starwood Hotels in early 2000. She did not give up her career for her family. Instead, she adjusted her illustrious career to provide more balance in her life.

Like Brenda Barnes, many women face tough decisions regarding work and family. Women ask themselves, should I walk away from work altogether—and the pay, challenge, and prestige that go with it—or make adjustments and try to do it all, and face the potential of doing neither well?[3] Is one decision better than the other? Although each strategy has its own risks and rewards, the question isn't which is better. The question that should be asked is: Is real balance even possible?

BALANCE AS THE HOLY GRAIL
OF THE TWENTY-FIRST CENTURY

Probably the most frequent comment from the women—and even some men—in our study was about balancing work and family. Some swore it couldn't be done and opted out of the workforce to dedicate themselves to their families. Others developed an uneasy set of compromises between work and family. Still others gave up before even trying and found a nanny or professional caregiver, thus delegating the necessary responsibilities of child rearing to others.

For many working people, "balance" is a goal that can never really be attained. Each day represents a struggle to meet the demands of one's boss and the responsibilities of home. When children are sick, when travel commitments extend beyond the time allocated, or when snow days complicate logistics, lives fall apart. "Having it all" may not mean "doing it all." A well-known "secret" is that several of the top Fortune 500 working mothers have husbands who are either writers, teachers, or IT professionals with flexible work hours or the ability to work at home, or who don't work at all.[4] Others have nannies or relatives who serve as caregivers.[5]

Although we can admire famous women who have managed to "do it all," most American women don't have that option. Most two-income households can't afford to become a one-income household. Many workers can't work from home or don't have the option to work flexible hours. Many families no longer live by relatives who can help care for children or can't afford private nannies or other household help.

When the average working woman reads that a celebrity mom has balanced her acting career with her charity work and her clothing design company and her Pilates lessons, all while taking her three adorable children to Mommy and Me classes and planning romantic getaways with her movie-star husband, the average working woman doesn't find the story inspirational. Instead, she wonders why she can't do it all, whether she is failing somehow. Such media stories that readily bombard working women may create unrealistic expectations for those who don't have the support systems and incomes that these famous women have.[6]

In contrast to the celebrity mom stories, Lisa Belkin, writer of the *New York Times* column "Life's Work" and author of the book *Life's Work: Confessions of an Unbalanced Mother,* uses humor to examine the everyday struggles of American workers.[7] She writes about the hectic life of the typical working woman, who is out of town on business yet schedules play dates from a street corner in Denver, brings three laptops on vacation, and sings the Barney song to her son by cell phone while the other moms in the airport waiting room begin to cry. The demands of deadlines, travel, and work commitments in a fast-paced environment lead to unavoidable conflicts between life and work. Belkin publicly raises the question that many of her readers have often silently asked themselves: has searching for balance become the holy grail of the twenty-first century?

IS BALANCE POSSIBLE?

Is balance really attainable, or is it a relic of the old manufacturing economy, a condition that no longer applies in a globalized, Internet-connected world? Literally hundreds of academic articles have been written on various aspects of work-family balance. These articles are filled with stories of women and men trying to juggle work and nonwork demands. And the findings of these studies aren't always so encouraging for the average working man and woman trying to have a successful career and a fulfilling life.

Briefly, the research has found that people experiencing high levels of work-family conflict are more likely than others to

- Have low levels of job satisfaction, career success, and organizational loyalty

- Experience turnover and burnout

- Be unsatisfied with their family lives and their lives in general

- Have high levels of stress and alcohol abuse

- Have problems with their physical health and psychological well-being[8]

We were surprised that the literature on work/nonwork conflict emphasizes married workers or people with children. This emphasis is especially surprising given that 42 percent of the American workforce is unmarried.[9]

Like their married coworkers, single women and men are searching for balance, often in a corporate world that is designed for married workers. Take salary and benefits as an example; single individuals make 25 percent less than married individuals because they cannot take advantage of the health care, retirement, and other benefits that are offered married people.[10] A Conference Board survey of single workers without children found that 25 percent thought they were doing more work yet getting a smaller share of benefits, and 42 percent said they were subsidizing the health care and other benefits of married workers with children.[11]

Many singles, especially those without children, believe that employers are more likely to ask them to work holidays, take last-minute assignments that require travel, work longer hours, accept transfers that require moving to another location, accept international assignments, and pick up the slack of employees who leave work early because of child care responsibilities. And while family-friendly company programs tend to focus on reducing the stress of working parents, singles without children have higher burnout levels than both married individuals and those with children.[12]

Despite single workers' beliefs that they are contributing more and getting less from their employers, singles without children are often viewed as less reliable, less mature, and less responsible than parents.[13] These negative stereotypes invade nonwork as well as the work domains of the lives of singles. Off work, singles find another time bind as their families expect them to be the ones to step up to the plate and take care of aging parents because they are perceived as having "nothing else to do." Most singles would disagree, feeling that their time is equally precious.

Regardless of people's situations—single or married, children or no children, male or female—achieving balance is a constant refrain because the lives of American workers are so biased in favor of work. Both economists and organizational scientists have called attention to the increasing number of hours white-collar professionals work each year.[14] Workweeks of fifty or more hours are now the norm for managerial and professional employees. The number of work hours keeps growing as technology permits workers to be on call 24/7 and as the work schedules of colleagues in different time zones across the globe must be accommodated.[15] With laptops, PDAs, cell phones, and portable conference calling, will employees ever get away from work demands—even in their own homes?

What are the outcomes of devoting so much time and energy to work?

- Individuals who worked the longest hours reported feeling alienated from their families, with men who worked the longest hours experiencing more stress.

- Individuals who worked long hours and didn't feel equitably rewarded experienced lower levels of job satisfaction than others did.

- There are 3.4 million workers, the so-called supercommuters, who travel at least ninety minutes daily to and from work. Commuting has been linked to many health concerns, including musculoskeletal disorders and the increase of negative behaviors such as hostility, absence from work, and tardiness.

- Between 1970 and 1997, the number of hours dual-career couples worked increased by ten hours a week. Couples where one partner was a professional were more likely to be overworked than couples where neither partner had a professional position.

- Single working mothers spent slightly more time with their children than married fathers, but these women had less free time for themselves.[16]

Once considered the workaholics of the world, the Japanese even have a term, karoshi, to describe the phenomenon of death from overwork. Today, Americans are working an average of 2.5 more hours a week than the Japanese. Will Americans soon need a new term to define death by overwork?[17]

CONTEMPORARY STRATEGIES FOR BALANCE

The men and women in our study used different, and sometimes highly creative, strategies for managing the daily work and life struggles and time binds that characterize today's complex environment. The ways in which the men and women in our study described their strategies for balance could be likened to the plate spinners who perform in circuses. Sometimes the spinners have five, ten, or fifteen plates in motion, all in balance. Other times, it seems impossible for them to keep just a few plates spinning. And sometimes the plates crash to the floor, and they have to start from scratch. Like the plate spinners, the men and women in our study had some strategies that worked well, some strategies that worked well most of the time, and some strategies that didn't work so well and needed to be adjusted along the way before everything came crashing down around them.

The Kaleidoscope Career model suggests that the need for balance is a strong pivot that shapes career decisions, especially the career decisions of women. The average working woman is still the primary caregiver for both children and elderly relatives. She is constantly negotiating her career responsibilities and her family's needs. Relationships influence her decisions at every turn. She invariably asks herself:

- Can I continue to work and still fulfill the ever-growing needs of my family?

- To what extent will I allow work to get in the way of my family life?

- Is forgoing my needs and my personal goals the only way to meet the needs of my family?

We found that women—and some men—developed distinctly different strategies for dealing with work and family struggles. The strategies they chose helped to determine the priority they were able to place on their careers at each point in their lives.

Let's look at the major approaches that they used as they rotated the wheel of their career kaleidoscopes to negotiate issues of balance. The five major approaches are

1. Adjusting

2. Consecutive

3. Concurrent

4. Alternating

5. Synergistic

The Adjusting Approach

The issue of balance moves to the forefront of the kaleidoscope as family demands increase. For some women, the tension between work demands on the one hand and family or nonwork demands on the other is too great for these women to continue to pursue their careers at all costs.

Rather than drop out of the workforce entirely, most women rotated the kaleidoscope of their careers to adjust their work to the demands of their more relational selves. They thought of their children, husbands, parents, or friends first; their careers, their own needs came later. Many women reconfigured their work to better balance the demands of home and family. Kaleigh, now an entrepreneur who works from home, explained her approach.

> *Yes, I have turned down work that would be too many hours and go on for too long a period of time. I also do not network as widely as I should, because I know there are only a few clients who will support my being a mother, meaning I have to leave early to get to my child's school event or I have to stay home with a sick child. So last year I started my own editing business, because I wanted to have control of my hours and my clients. After only two years in the business, I doubled my income, even taking the summer off to be with my kids and travel around to see my family. I only take on clients who I will call "family friendly" because my kids and my husband need me.*

Like Kaleigh, many women reported times in their lives when they made adjustments in their careers or sacrificed their own personal needs for the sake of their families. (See the following comments for how some of the women in our study made adjustments to balance work and nonwork demands.) The adjusting pattern is a bargain that is struck when a woman looks at her kaleidoscope of career choices and realizes "something's gotta give." Very often, she puts her career ambitions on the back burner for the sake of family.

The adjusting pattern is often adopted for economic reasons. Many women find they must work to add to the household income. Yet these women take jobs that often pay below their talents and don't meet their need for challenge, because their husbands' jobs usually pay more. If their husbands get transferred, these women give up their jobs and follow rather than tear their families apart.[18]

What Women Said about Meeting the Needs of Family

- While I haven't taken breaks from my work, the reasons for my career change have been (1) for challenge, and (2) to be focused on my son and spending time with him with my current flexible schedule.

- Until the boys started school, [relocating] was not an issue. Now that they are in school, I have turned down several interviews for positions which would involve a move to a different state.

- When I had three older kids, I stayed in a job I strongly disliked because it was very close to home, and I was concerned that commuting a distance would tire me out, and I would not be able to give my other children proper attention. I happen to be an extremely skilled and diligent employee who really enjoys working, but many employers can't understand or respect family needs.

- I have often taken positions which would allow me the flexibility I need to tend to my family. So I look for companies that are comfortable with flextime, telecommuting, etc., so that I can balance work and family.

- I had to take a lower-graded position two years ago to keep my family together to meet both my husband's and my children's needs.

And contrary to what some critics claim, these women aren't working to buy designer clothing, spa treatments, and fancy vacations. They are working to put food on the table, to pay the dentist's bills, and to save for their children's college educations.[19]

But women don't make adjustments in their careers just for their husbands and children. Many women, especially those of the baby boomer generation, are sandwiched between the needs of their children and the needs of their parents. One of our respondents, Karen, told of relocating to help a parent: "I accepted a lesser paying job in a city closer to my mother during her severe illness."

Karen isn't alone. Almost 25 percent of American households are caring for someone age fifty or over, and that number is increasing and will continue to increase as the baby boomers age and need assistance.[20] Many single women face this work-family dilemma, often in organizations that don't realize—or don't care to—that unmarried workers have family and nonwork interests just as married workers have other obligations. Lal's story is typical.

People were shocked when I left my job for a smaller, less prestigious organization. My parents were getting older, and they needed my help, so I packed everything up and moved across country. The new place had recruited me promising great challenges and great autonomy within a family-friendly, slower paced environment. I wanted to be a team player, so when the boss asked me to step in and help someone finish a project or work late so someone could pick up their kids from day care, attend a soccer game, or go home and have dinner with wives and kiddies, I did. But as time passed, it was always me who was expected to work the extra hours, to help one of the men finish up a project—which the boss inevitably would give them full credit for—or serve on a committee that was boring drudge work.

Likewise, many organizations forget that single workers want advancement opportunities and rewards for their performance just as their married coworkers do. Lal's new employer was one of those, as she explained.

When I talked to the boss about a promised promotion, carefully outlining my contributions to the units—no whining or complaining—he told me that the men needed to be paid more money to support their wives and kids, that it was important for the men to get the assignments that could make their careers, and the men needed schedules that gave them the best chance to make the connections needed to move up. He talked about what a great place to work it is and how we are all a team, a family. Yes, it was a great place to work—if you were a married good old boy, with a stay-at-home wife, with 2.4 children. . . . The boss wouldn't share numbers with us, but a friend obtained a copy of the productivity records—the unit statistics showed my productivity was literally carrying the whole department. My friend had the ear of the higher-ups, and there were public statements that more women were needed in the upper ranks. She talked to them about my situation. While they agreed with her that I was the top performer, they needed to promote the men so the men didn't quit and go to work somewhere else. One of them said they wanted to keep me, but if I felt unhappy they understood if I tried to find another job. They even said if I got another offer, maybe they would match it. It's a tight market, I need the job and need to be by my parents. But now I do only my work, document everything, and do only enough work to keep my job. There've been times in meetings when I have the answer, or the information or ideas, but I keep my mouth closed and let the men spin their wheels trying to figure it out. I just got tired of doing all the work so the boys could get the credit. I keep my hand in professional associations building a reputation for excellence and honesty, networking, am constantly developing new abilities, go to any training I can—and when the time is right, I'm outta there!

The Consecutive Approach

Another approach women used in an effort to balance work and nonwork demands was to drop out of the workforce for a period and then reenter when their family demands allowed for greater work accomplishments.[21] Nancy Killie is someone who exemplifies this consecutive approach. Nancy worked at the Social Security Administration as a claims representative. Her husband, Peter, five years her senior, had worked as a criminal investigator with the U.S. Customs Service for a number of years. But Nancy and Peter wanted children. When their twin girls arrived, Nancy dropped out of the workforce to be a stay-at-home mom. Peter worked steadily for twenty years, until it was time for his retirement. When their girls turned ten, right at the time of Peter's retirement, Nancy returned to the workforce—back to the Social Security Administration. When we asked what motivated her return to the workforce, Nancy admitted,

Well, it was simple. My husband was at the point that he simply was tired of the commute. He wanted to work on small security jobs on the side for a while, but he really wanted to retire. The time was right for him to step out of the workforce and for me to return. We needed a steady income, not only to pay the bills but also to save for the girls' upcoming college tuition. So it became a natural decision that when the girls turned ten, it was time for me to return to work full-time.

Nancy is very satisfied with her decision to return to the work-force.

At first, I wasn't sure about going back to work full-time after being away from work for such a long time. I had done some part-time work, but now I am back full-time. I left my grade level fourteen years ago, and they reinstated all my benefits, except my pension, which I took with me when I left. The first day was hard, though. One of my daughters left me a note that said "Have a nice day at work." Now I've been back for three years, and I have grown to really appreciate the work I do. I enjoy listening to people's stories. What I have is a very people-oriented job, and I feel good about the work I do.

Ronnie DiNucci is another woman who used a consecutive approach. Having worked for IBM as a staff manager, she took the company's severance package when her oldest son was born. She then stayed home for sixteen years. But when her husband's business didn't get off the ground, she said she had to make some tough choices.

I had planned on going back much earlier. When my youngest son was finally in elementary school, I called them up and asked if they wanted to have me back. My husband had decided to open his own business, so it was time for me to return for the benefits and everything. They have a policy of allowing people to come back if a position is available. So I returned to a building I had previously worked in, in a com-pletely new organizational area for me. And you know what? It's been great—other than the commute, of course.

The consecutive pattern exists for those women and men who are able to take a career interruption for a period of time and then return later. Sometimes it boils down to an either/or decision. Do I work now or care for family now? Vanessa, from one of our online surveys, sees it this way:

> *My family-inspired break was because I found it too difficult to handle two children under three and a spouse who traveled overseas about 40 percent of the time. I enjoyed my work, but economics made following his career a more logical choice.*

Sometimes the consecutive approach involves a decision on not only when to work but also where to work. Many times spouses can't find jobs in the same cities, or the couple doesn't want to pull children out of schools they love. Jeanne, another survey respondent, explained,

> *We have made many hard decisions over the years to live apart and/or travel extensively. Sometimes the career comes first, sometimes the family comes first—it depends on the situation at the time.*

The Concurrent Approach

Most couples that try to work and rear a family simultaneously find they are living life one day at a time, hoping the other shoe does not drop. Balancing acts between work and family demands are a constant. These couples assume that they can have it all—with a few compromises. So one spouse may fill in while the other takes a trip, but then there is payback when the traveling spouse needs to work late. Couples who use the concurrent approach find that they are always switching between work and family, often making use of technology that allows them to work remotely while attending a child's soccer or baseball game.

For dual career couples, the concurrent approach means that every day is spent juggling work and family. For example, what if seven-year-old Jimmy needs to be at the pediatrician's office at 3:30 p.m.? One of the parents, probably the wife, will need to leave work early and take Jimmy to the appointment. What if the next day the wife needs to work late? Then the husband will need to change his schedule, pick up Ariel from soccer practice, drop

Rennie off for dance class, and take the dog to the vet for her annual check-up. What if there is a snow day, but both husband and wife have important meetings? Frantic phone calls will need to be made to neighbors and friends. Or what if either of them gets sick? Well, forget it. Their allotted sick days were used up when the kids had the flu.

Working concurrently and trying to do it all with technology leads to tight work versus home situations that are ready made for TV sitcom fodder. The following are real stories of how work and family collided—sometimes with a bang.

- Waiting for an important conference call from his new boss, one dad had to rush to school to pick up his son, who was asked to leave because of a sore throat. He took his son home to call the doctor, but he had to take the conference call first. Trying to amuse his son while he was on the phone, he said to his son, who was playing with building blocks, "Put the blue blocks there." Suddenly someone on the call said, "What? Who said something about blue blocks? What blue blocks? Who is talking about blue blocks?" The dad kept mum, as he had a new boss and wasn't supposed to be working from home that day. He thought he was safe when the conversation moved on to other topics, but later there was the resounding sound of a crash—his son's blocks scattering all over the hardwood floor. At that point, the truth was revealed, and the dad had to confess that he was working from home.

- A corporate mom was working at home and was on the phone with Australia. Her children were playing happily outside the door of her home office, and all was going well. Then suddenly her two-and-a-half-year-old daughter barged through the door. She immediately began to retch all over the floor and started crying. Amid the screaming and vomiting, the embarrassed working mom asked for a few moments to control the situation with her daughter. The people on the other end of the phone were glad to call her back.

- A dad received a call from his wife, who was running unavoidably late at work. She reminded him that their son was to attend his team's practice that afternoon. At first he thought he would have no problem—he could go home, pick up his son, run him over to practice, and continue his workday with his Blackberry and his cell phone from the field. But when he got to the field, there was no phone service. So he dropped his son off and rode around in his car to make a connection to call his office. After an hour or so, he returned to the field to pick up his son, feeling happy that he had managed to make work and home life intersect seamlessly that day. He discovered that his son had been taken by ambulance to a hospital because he had been knocked out cold during the practice.

- A working mom, a professor, who brought her four-year-old son to work one day, had a student babysitter lined up to care for the child while she was teaching. Then an important meeting came up, and she had to give a presentation. The student babysitter was willing to extend her hours on the condition that she get to her next class on time, as she had a test. Unfortunately for the mom, while her fellow professors pontificated, the meeting ran late. The babysitter dropped the four-year-old off outside the room where the working mom was giving her presentation. In the middle of her presentation, she furtively kept peeking a look at her son through the window. Fellow professors thought her behavior, turning to the window a lot, was odd, but they understood later when, in the middle of a sentence, she made a mad dash out of the room to reach her young son.

Such is the life of busy parents with professional jobs. They attempt to make compromises between work and home; some days these compromises give balance, and some days the whole thing comes crashing down like a tower of unsteady building blocks.

The concurrent approach works well if both spouses have the option of working at home, at least part-time.[22] This is the approach where the benefits of technology are at a premium. Driven by the need for an equal share of parenting and provider responsibilities, however, couples using this approach can make themselves crazy. Robin Ostrosky, whose husband is a frequent traveler, said,

> *My husband is a big sports person, and he wants our kids signed up for every sport possible. Since he travels, he really doesn't know what it means to go to all the practices during the school week. He goes to the games with his Blackberry and always has that thing in his ear—his cell phone—and he is text messaging back to people on the West Coast all the time. Honestly, sometimes I get so exasperated I want to rip that Blackberry right out of his hand, and I bet there are a lot of wives who agree with me! He has seen games, sure, but ironically he has missed some of the action on the field because he is on the phone or clicking his PDA. One day he came home from India, and he missed time with the kids. So, my husband, being a big sports person, decided to take our two sons to a game—in Philadelphia, of all places, four hours away. I was out shopping with our daughter, and I found out when he left me a note on the kitchen counter. We passed each other on the road. He didn't pack anything for the overnight trip—the boys didn't even have a change of underwear—but they all had a good time.*

Can working parents really have it all and do it all? Can they capture the holy grail known as balance? Author Keith Hammonds bluntly argues that "balance is bunk," saying, "It's the central myth of the modern workplace: With a few compromises, you can have it all. But it's all wrong, and it's making us crazy."[23] Despite the jam-packed schedules, frantic mornings, and organizations that want their workers to work more and more, some are still trying to balance it all.

The Alternating Approach

Sometimes, couples believe the best approach to balancing work and family is to take turns. One spouse works, the other stays at home. Then, when the time is right, they switch, or alternate.

Rob Spillman, a writer-editor married to writer-editor Elissa Schappel, takes turns playing the role of the 1950s housewife with his spouse.[24] After years of frustration, bickering, and seething resentment, he and his wife gave up on their attempt to have an egalitarian, postfeminist marriage. Like many couples, they couldn't figure out how to share everything—work, kids, household chores—without driving each other crazy. Originally in their marriage, they attempted to be as equitable as possible in the distribution of family responsibilities, sharing everything from financial duties to domestic chores. Rob writes, "We operated on the assumption that our time was equally valuable and we should share all the parenting burdens."

Rob met his wife when they were both twenty-one, and they married at age twenty-three. When they met, they were in complete agreement about rejecting any kind of gender stereotypes and splitting everything down the middle. However, when children came into the mix, Rob writes that their utopian vision of being able to work and somehow spend time with the kids fell apart.

> Early on we discovered there was a fundamental problem with our flexible, sustenance level approach to life: children are inflexible. They need to eat regularly and sleep regularly. They like routine and certainty. And while it used to be charming and artsy for us to be financially crunched—eating canned soup or peanut butter and jelly while we waited for an overdue paycheck—our children weren't as amused or sustained by the creative dishes one can create with 29 cents worth of dry noodles. Reality set in one late night when our overdraft was tapped out and our credit card was denied when we tried to buy diapers. At this low moment, we wondered aloud if this wasn't the time for one of us to get a Real Job.

Rather than succumb to the notion that the husband should get the "real job," they decided to redouble their creative efforts and take on as much freelance work as each of them could handle. Because they couldn't afford to hire out all domestic and childcare needs, somebody had to pick up the slack. Rob writes about how they tried dividing up tasks on an as-needed basis, but accusations quickly flew and they had to modify their approach.

> *There was a constant weighing of tasks. Does one easily pre-pared dinner really equal a load of laundry? Didn't I shop the last time? Can't you for once change the damn light bulb? On a weekly basis, one parent was "on"—meaning, fully dedi-cated to their work—while the other parent was "off"—fully dedicated to childcare and household tasks. I proposed that we become Ward and June Cleaver. We'd alternate, on a weekly basis, who is Ward and who is June. Each week, who-ever is June gets fully burdened with the domestic duties from Monday through Friday, and whoever is Ward disappears to his "office" all day. There is no negotiating and no trading chores. It's just the way it is.*

This system has worked well for Rob Spillman, his wife, and their two children. Weekends, though, are a "murky swamp." Resentment creeps in now and then. But their alternating weeks have given them back their sanity—and their paychecks. Says Rob, "We do manage to have it all. Just not at the same time."

The Synergistic Approach

Is it possible to have it all? Is there a way to combine work and fam-ily so that each enriches the other? Are there some jobs that natu-rally lend themselves to this approach? One job that does is a position in academia, and one of our respondents, Amanda, has made it work.

Amanda earned her PhD from a prestigious university and embarked on a full-time teaching and research career. During the day, she devoted herself to teaching, and late into the night she worked writing articles to meet the tenure and promotion require-ments of her university. She obtained tenure and promotion, and with that goal achieved, she was lucky enough to get pregnant—right before her sabbatical year. She recalled that she had the entire year on sabbatical to nurse her newborn son.

I worked during his naps, so it was easy. My research and writing is the kind of work you do in front of the computer, so I could work easily with a baby. The following year when I returned to teaching, my schedule only required me to be on campus for a few hours on Tuesdays and Thursday mornings. I had a mature caregiver for my son for those times I was teaching, but my son slept much of the time, so he didn't even know I was gone.

But things changed when child number two came along. Amanda's life became more complicated.

At that point my son was in kindergarten and my daughter needed me. So I took a year's leave to be with her. When I returned to teaching full-time, I didn't have adequate time to pursue research and consultation work. My job has three prongs—teaching, research, and consultation. When my children were young, I focused on the teaching more and the research second. But when they entered my world, I dropped the consultation entirely.

For several years, Amanda divided her time, spending half on teaching and the other half on research and writing. Now that her children are older, she is producing more research, teaching steadily, and thinking of returning to consulting.

I have been able to have it all, . . . do my research and writing at home so my children have me fully accessible to them. I also have the summers off, and my vacation weeks coincide with my children's school calendars. I am home so much that people in my town think I am a stay-at-home mom! I go into my office for face time with students and for actual teaching hours. Sometimes I have requested night classes so that my husband could be with our children while I was out working. If I need help with cleaning the house, I'm happy to go out and hire someone. I volunteer at my children's schools, but I'm not ashamed to bring store-bought cookies to school functions. On top of that, I've taken three sabbaticals, which has allowed me time to devote to my children and my research. With each sabbatical, I have produced a book, a child, or moved. Finally I am at a point where all the pieces of my life are coming together. I am so grateful for a job structure that has truly allowed me to do it all, without sacrificing a single important moment with either of my children. I'm a better parent because my children see that I enjoy the challenging and fulfilling work I do—and that it's possible to be both a good mother and a good worker. I'm a better teacher and researcher because I know that most workers don't have the kind of job that permits this synergy—so I encourage my students to think about these issues and what companies can do better.

Wouldn't it be wonderful if more jobs were structured this way?[25] Amanda's job is synergistic because she was able to downplay certain aspects of her work—teaching, research, or consultation—at different points in her career and life. She made adjustments to her workload without giving up her career. She was also allowed year-long career interruptions that facilitated getting work done while taking time for family issues and transitions. The trade-offs and adjustments Amanda made as she negotiated her work and nonwork roles were not always easy—she works extremely hard, and her life is not without stress. In the end, though, Amanda believes that such negotiations between work and family permitted her to have the best of both worlds.[26]

Unfortunately, not many workplaces, or even other academic institutions, allow time for career interruptions and adjustments to workload as needed. But why not? Will permitting balance result in the company's demise? Best-selling author Bill George, who wrote *Authentic Leadership: Rediscovering the Secrets to Creating Lasting Value* (2003), argues that the opposite is true. He suggests that leaders who permit their employees to enjoy more balanced lives will have more successful firms.[27] He argues that the careers of leaders themselves are rarely straight journeys to success but instead the leaders' experiences—such as the sensitivity gained through community service work—make the person a better leader and contribute to overall success. Thus, overall success, not just financial or professional success, is the result of leading a balanced, rich life—a life that realizes the importance of family, friends, service, and faith as well as work. George contends that by living a balanced life themselves and enabling all employees to do so also, leaders have ensured that employees will demonstrate higher levels of organizational commitment, which will have a positive impact on the firm's bottom line.

Women desiring a more synergetic lifestyle have often turned to entrepreneurial careers as a means of creating synergy between work and family demands for themselves—and often for others. Madolyn Johnson, who was profiled in Chapter 2, is a case in point.[28] Madolyn explained how she integrated work and family.

> *Family was my first priority. I managed to integrate it all, work and family. Some people don't know their child's favorite color, but I did because I balanced work and family. I resigned from teaching to start the business because when I had my daughter, I realized while it was great to have her, it was not great to be broke. I left teaching not because I lost my passion for teaching but [because] my passion for my daughter was stronger. When I was five years into the business, my second daughter was diagnosed with a life-threatening lung disease, but I was able to maintain my business by relying on my employees and asking for help. I was able to be at my daughter's side in the hospital whenever she needed me, and, with help, I was able to keep the business growing while I dealt with her health crisis. That crisis made me realize that there are lots of women who would love to have the opportunity that I had to focus on priorities and still have financial security. With help, I was able to keep the business growing while I dealt with her health crisis.*

Madolyn is so happy with her ability to integrate job, career, and family life that she now tells other women, "You've got to start your own business!"

Although relatively few women in our research chose the synergistic approach, and few jobs today are structured for its implementation, synergism is more than a utopian ideal. With flexible workplaces—brought about by changes in corporate cultures that encourage employees to lead full, whole lives and careers that can ebb and flow with the tides—synergism can become a reality.[29]

THE DEFINITION OF SUCCESS

Most women are engaged in a creative dance; they are seeking challenge and meaning in their work while at the same time balancing their work and nonwork demands. Because of this need for balance, some in the media have questioned whether women lack ambition. They don't believe in advancement at all costs. If ambition is measured solely by movement up a male-dominated hierarchy and advancement at any cost, then, yes, it does appear that women are less ambitious than men.[30]

However, we think the answers are more complex than they appear on the surface. Evidence suggests that the aspirations of women, and some men, have changed from the dog-eat-dog 1980s, when it was common to step over others on your way to the top. Men and women define success differently today. Advancement may be just one factor among many that motivate women and men today.

What do we know about the way people define success and aspiration in the twenty-first century? We do know that men and women perceive success much differently.[31] For men, success is often defined as salary and rank. For women, success is seen as a process of personal development that combines challenging work with balance between work and nonwork issues. For women, pay is not central to their definition of success; rank wasn't valued for itself but as a means of obtaining more interesting work, greater influence, or recognition of contributions.

If an organization is led by men and has a male culture, then success (or ambition) is likely to be defined in male terms, as salary and rank. Male behaviors are more likely to be rewarded. Female behaviors, such as helping others, are less likely to be valued.[32]

A nationwide telephone poll on women's attitudes about success found that an overwhelming majority of the 1,200 women interviewed felt successful, though not in the traditional sense. "Happiness," "peace of mind," "fulfillment," "freedom," and "balance" were the words that best captured contemporary women's view of success. Most women—82 percent—felt that they were more successful than their mothers, and 52 percent agreed that combining children and career is the best strategy for success. Finally, 84 percent felt that the meaning of success is up to every individual woman to decide on her own.[33]

If organizations continue to look at only one aspect of success—career advancement—they will fail to recognize that working women are motivated by complex factors and have a broader definition of success than do most men. Likewise, if organizations don't look beyond narrow definitions of success or ambition, they may also fail to keep talented men who may shift priorities as they age, and Gen X and Gen Y men who may measure career success much differently from their fathers and grandfathers.

MEN AND BALANCE

Although some men in our study agreed to more equitable work and family household sharing arrangements with their spouses, most did not.[34] The majority of men viewed themselves in the role of family provider, and issues of balance, in the sense of adjusting work priorities to favor family needs, were often not even considered. Balance for most men meant something much different than it did for most women. Men talked about balance as an issue in the background, an issue affecting them only peripherally in their careers. As their careers progressed, some men began to think more about the value of balance. One of these, Peter, said,

> *I have had to learn about the importance of "balance" in my life over the years. My wife and I had our children early in our marriage. My wife chose to stay home, and I was the provider. That was the deal. Even though my boss would say, "Go ahead, take time off," I rarely did so. The problem was me, not the company. I believed that it was my job to provide*

for my family. So I worked overtime and did not ask for much extra time. Yes, I missed baseball games and birthday parties. And, yes, I do regret it, looking back. As time passed, it started to occur to me that there was more to life than work. My children were growing up. I found that balance was something I had to work at. I had to remind myself that my children were not going to be children forever, so my only time was now to be a Little League coach so that I could be visible to my kids. Eventually, with some prodding from my wife, I started to bend a little, loosen up with the work hours. Now I am glad I did.

When asked whether family balance was an issue in their careers, the majority of men in our study left the question entirely blank, or answered "No, it was not an issue" or "Did not apply" or "Marriage and family did not alter my career plans."[35] Most men never questioned their role as the breadwinner and became the providers for their families as a matter of course. Rich, an MBA student, said,

Early in my career, I worked long hours, not because I had to but because I wanted to. This continued after I got married, as both my wife and I were at work more than at home. Then we had our first child, and we decided she would put her career on hold to stay home with the baby. I really respect her for that decision, as it worked out for all of us.

Sexist? Perhaps. But it was the reality for most of the couples with whom we spoke on the subject of balance. For men, balance was not an issue until later in life, when responsibilities for providing were over and they could enjoy a bit of free time associated with retirement. Sixty-seven-year-old Patrick captured this idea when he said,

I'm retired, and I want nothing to do with work. My joy each day is reflecting upon my family—how each of my sons has grown and become his own man, with children of his own. I am grateful I have been a small part of that legacy by provid-

ing what they needed while they were young. Now I can enjoy my grandchildren and spend time with my grown sons in ways I was never able to do before. One of my sons and I just took a trip to the Grand Canyon. My other son and I are building a fence at his house. This is the best time of my life, when I can finally sit back and appreciate my family.

Most men, especially those of the baby boomer generation, grew up watching their fathers go off to work every morning while their housewife mothers nurtured the children. This image was reinforced by the social structure of the day. After World War II the hardworking Rosie the Riveters were told they were no longer needed now that the men were home, that they should go back to cooking and cleaning and leave the real jobs for the boys returning from the front. And the media of the day supported this system well into the 1950s, when TV shows like *Father Knows Best* and *Ozzie and Harriet* reigned.

But times were changing, at least on TV. Soon TV fans had new models of the American family and working women. Audiences met characters such as glamorous "That Girl," Ann Marie, who wanted a career before marriage; beloved Mary Richards, who created the TV ideal of the single working woman that many modern TV heroines still emulate; working moms like Claire Huxtable, who juggled being a lawyer with caring for her ever perplexing husband and growing children; and Murphy Brown, who gained national attention when the wrath of Vice President Dan Quayle fell on her for choosing to be a single mom while remaining in a high-powered career. Thus, television reflected some of the changes that were happening in American society, including redefinitions of the roles of people in the workplace and in families, redefinitions that are continuing as a younger generation deals with these issues.

YOUNGER MEN RETHINKING BALANCE

With the growing number of married women sharing the provider role with their husbands, and the greater societal acceptance of

men who want to nurture their children, more men are facing conflict between their roles as workers and their roles as fathers.
Following are some indicators of the trend.

- Younger men (Gen X and Gen Y men) are more likely to
  decrease their work hours upon having a child, whereas
  older men (baby boomers) were more likely to increase
  their work hours upon the birth of a child.

- Men are now sharing more of the household chores and
  child-rearing tasks; men spend 2.3 hours each workday on
  household tasks compared to 1.8 hours two decades ago.

- A *Time*/Spike TV poll found that 72 percent of men agreed
  with the statement "I would sacrifice exciting opportunities
  and higher pay at my job for more time with my family,"
  while only 27 percent agreed with the opposite: "I would
  sacrifice family time for exciting opportunities and higher
  pay at my job."

- The *New York Times* reported that 68 percent of men would
  take advantage of flextime if possible.

- A *Management Today* survey of five hundred British men
  found that 30 percent of them agreed that their job seriously interfered with their family lives, 24 percent admitted
  that they had recently neglected their children, and 62 percent felt more guilty about neglecting domestic duties than
  their fathers did.[36]

For the new generation of men, work-family balance is not just
a women's issue—it's a men's issue as well.[37] Men, however, are still
less likely than women to ask about family-friendly benefits. The
majority of working fathers do not expect family-friendly practices
to be made available to them and are less likely to take advantage of
existing ones.[38] For instance, although the Family Medical Leave
Act (FMLA) of 1993 allows employees to take up to twelve weeks
of unpaid leave for the birth or adoption of a child, many men take
vacation days instead. Some men may fear that it will hurt their
promotion opportunities if they take paternity leave. Others may

work in companies that have organizational cultures that discourage men's use of family-friendly programs.

But why does anyone care if men have balance anyway if their wives devote most of their time to child care and household tasks? As long as mom is watching out for the kids, why bother dad? Stewart Friedman and Jeffrey Greenhaus, authors of *Work and Family—Allies or Enemies? What Happens When Business Professionals Confront Life Choices,* believe that we should all care, because of the powerful influence fathers have upon their children. Their research found that although high career involvement of mom often benefits the children, high career involvement of dad doesn't. Mothers who are highly involved in their careers have higher self-esteem and can serve as positive role models for their children. Fathers who are highly involved in their careers, however, are less psychologically available for their children. When fathers are not there for their children, the children are more likely to have behavioral problems. And what may surprise many of these fathers is that children rate lowest the parental performance of the parents who earn the most money. Many children would rather have dad home than have the latest, most expensive toy or designer clothes.[39]

But some firms are beginning to take men's roles as fathers more seriously and are offering new benefits. The accounting firm KPMG, for instance, is one of those. In 2002, KPMG introduced two weeks of paid paternity leave. The firm's management expected that 10 percent of eligible men would take advantage of the new policy. They were surprised when almost 30 percent of fathers took the leave in 2002—and nearly 70 percent did so in 2003.[40]

Likewise, management at Apple Computer was surprised when they instituted family-friendly policies in the hopes of attracting more top female employees and discovered that the company's then predominately male workforce was just as interested in such programs. Companies such as Marriott International, Merrill Lynch, and Texas Instruments have found that fatherhood seminars are a big draw for their male employees.[41] Microsoft, J. P. Morgan Chase, and other firms are joining the ranks. Johnson & Johnson has developed its own lunch-and-learn seminar for fathers.[42] Seminars such as Daddy Stress/Daddy Success and Effective Fathering, which help men identify the techniques that help workers succeed both at work and with their children, are growing in popularity.[43] Although such father-friendly policies, workshops, and seminars are few in number, they are a beginning. Such programs have permitted men to address the unique pressures faced by working fathers and have let them know that there are other men experiencing the same conflicts.

And as firms offer more family-friendly programs and change their cultures to truly encourage both men and women to make use of these policies, a time may come when *not* taking a paternity leave or *not* using a family policy is frowned upon at the office.[44] Until now, men have been the "silent majority" at work, refusing to vocalize their needs for work-family balance. Part of the male straitjacket has been the "put up and shut up" mentality. A vicious cycle sets in: men hide their desire for work-family programs, employers continue to define work-family issues as women's issues, and men's reluctance to express their needs is thereby reinforced, thus bringing the cycle full circle with men continuing to hide their desire for family-friendly policies.

But, more important, what will happen next? Will more men buck tradition and have the courage to take advantage of family leave policies and fatherhood seminars? Will the men taking part in these programs be promoted and rewarded? Once promoted, will these men champion the expansion of family-friendly policies and work cultures? Once men join women in demanding more work/nonwork balance, will a tipping point occur so these issues are seen as needed worker policies rather than as women's concerns? Only time will tell.[45]

The tide may have turned already in providing more balance in the lives of working women and men. But balance is not enough. Both women and men desire challenging work, work that permits them to test themselves, to use their knowledge and skills, and to contribute to society. In the next chapter, we will look at how the drive for challenge changes for women and for men over time, and explain why challenge is an important parameter of a Kaleidoscope Career. In the next chapter we will look at issues of challenge and see how they develop for women and for men over the course of their life cycles.

CHAPTER 7

THE DRIVE
FOR CHALLENGE

Patti Hutton is a woman who loves turning the challenges of her job into opportunities for success. As executive vice president and chief financial officer for NBC Universal, she works in a highly competitive, creative, and goal-directed environment. But it took years of dedicated work and a talent for identifying challenges before she was nominated for numerous leadership awards at General Electric and eventually attained her current executive position.

Patti graduated from Fairfield University in 1985 with a BS degree in finance and received an offer from General Electric to work in their credit training program. Soon she was off to Atlanta where she spent two years learning the business. Then she entered GE's prestigious Financial Management Program, which is known as an incubator within GE for upper management. Patti earned her stripes by working as a credit analyst for the eastern region and then landed a demanding job on the corporate audit staff as an auditor for GE's business units. Patti reflected on her early career days.

The time I spent in the Financial Management Program was terrific, a real challenge, where you are competing with the best of the best. But I really enjoyed my time as an auditor,

*too. As an auditor, I became comfortable going into a business
and learning how to ask the right questions. I learned about
risk assessment and how to add value in a short time. You
really have to know a business to audit it.*

Patti's long hours and dedication to service caught the attention
of higher management, who within a five-year period promoted
her from an associate auditor to an executive audit manager position, where she had responsibility for auditing three to four businesses and implementing company-wide initiatives. Then she
switched to GE's Plastics-Americas Division. For several years, she
traveled around the world, working with people from Mexico and
Canada as well as other countries as the manager of both Manufacturing Finance and Commercial Finance.

*Jeff Immelt was running Plastics at the time, and there was a
large restructuring of the business. I worked with him on the
restructuring, and he drove the business to be more product-
line oriented. When my work there was completed, I had a
choice to work on the product-line side of the business or to go
to a commercial finance job in Pittsfield, Mass., which is what
I chose to do.*

After her tour of duty in a series of solid financial positions,
Patti started looking for something more. She had a few
exploratory discussions with people within GE about New York
possibilities, and then a challenging opportunity landed in her lap
to become senior vice president of finance for NBC, West Coast,
which includes NBC Entertainment, NBC Studios, and NBC Enterprises. She took the job and found working in the entertainment
business required the best of her management talents.

*When I first went out to the West Coast, they viewed me as
the NBC/GE "bean counter" finance person. Walking into
those meetings, I could have focused solely on the bottom line.
But I decided to approach the problem in a different way. I*

asked them, "What are your challenges? How can I help?" rather than, "OK, I'm the suit here, tell me all about your financials." I had my guys set up meetings where we assessed the risks and challenges along with them, and we took the attitude "How can we help? We're partners here. My responsibility is to help you get the best results." So rather than looking at me as a bean counter, we set the bar so that we were partners solving challenges and looking for creative opportunities to improve the business. It worked.

Her dedication to GE's bottom line was noticed, and she was summoned back to corporate headquarters to work as an analyst for Gary Rogers, GE's vice chairman. In her corporate headquarters assignment, she learned about the issues for GE companywide from a corporate strategy perspective. She then returned to NBC, first as the chief financial officer of NBC and Telemundo's twenty-eight owned and operated TV stations based in New York. Following the merger with Universal Studios in May 2004, she was named as executive vice president and chief financial officer of Universal Studios, including NBC's Universal Motion Picture Group as well as the Universal theme parks. On the twists and turns of her GE career, Patti said,

My career has been a whirlwind, and I have worked hard every minute of it. But there are rewards, too. I was on the golf course with a friend who has come up through the business with me, and we were saying, "How did we get here?" Did you ever think that the two of us back in our GE Plastics days would end up with jobs in the movie business, going to the Cannes Film Festival? The two of us shook our heads—not in a million years would I have predicted my financial career would have ended up on the West Coast in the entertainment business. It's great—I love what I do, and I am always looking forward to see what the new day will bring. Every day is a new series of challenges, and that's the fun of the job. I am having fun in this job.

At this point in her career, Patti has developed a style of management based on challenge.

You know, I have learned it's not about outshining others, it's about energizing others to do what they do best. It's about possibilities, not alternatives. It's not about punching tickets, but it's about growth, your growth as a manager and as a person. I tell people "Go for the big challenges." If you are challenged, then you will naturally work hard to show results. Each of my jobs has challenged me, and I took the attitude, from a very early point in my career, that it's not about the business problems that need to be solved, it's about the process of finding the challenges and surmounting them.

THE MANY ASPECTS OF CHALLENGE

For Patti, turning "problems" into "challenges" sustains her motivation. Doing business requires identifying and solving problems. But for Patti, finding solutions to insurmountable problems challenges her to develop her skills and improve her capabilities as a manager.

Challenge. Confidence. Identity. These are the words that kept surfacing again and again as we talked to men and women about *why* they worked. For some, accepting challenges was a type of self-validation, a mentality of "If I can do this, I can do anything." For others, the challenges they sought were about having an impact on the larger organization or on other people; about growth, learning, and exercising creativity; or about becoming experts in their fields. We found five major ways in which men and women searched for challenge in their careers, especially early in their careers.[1]

1. Challenge as a way of gaining motivation

2. Challenge as a way of obtaining validation

3. Challenge as a way of developing and growing

4. Challenge as a way of having an impact

5. Challenge as a way of establishing expertise

Challenge as a Way of Gaining Motivation

The drive to be challenged is a potent motivating force in early career. "Challenge," defined as "a summons to take part in a contest or a trial of strength," was the reason—other than money—that most people gave when asked why they worked.[2] Men and women who accepted high challenge described their work as a frenzy of exhilaration, exhaustion, tension, ambition, intensity—even addiction—as they did something they had to do, not only to make money but for themselves.[3]

People for whom challenge is a powerful motivator can easily—and enthusiastically—answer questions such as "What was the biggest challenge you ever faced professionally?" "If you had to name a project, innovation, or event that you are really proud of in your career, what would it be?" "Why do you work? And what's next?"

For some people, challenge is viewed as a natural motivator. One of our respondents, Mark, explained the excitement of being challenged.

> *Our CEO likes to practice the ready-fire-aim method of planning. Everything is changing around here, and I am in the thick of it. We are rolling three businesses into one, buying two divisions from a troubled sister firm, and starting a new office in a new market, all to be completed within the next thirty to sixty days! Our completely revised organizational chart was rolled out at 7:30 a.m. today. Now that the org chart has been broadcast to the troops, it becomes my responsibility to provide answers to who, what, when, where, and why. This is a challenge that I accept, but I won't have any time for my life!*

Workaholism and the desire for challenge are partners in crime. Responding to e-mails at midnight, being on call all day, and running on empty can actually be fun. Research shows that work hours have increased over the past decade, with workers spending many more than the standard forty hours on the job. Some even suggest that 25 percent of Americans are workaholics, making workaholism our country's most widespread addiction. Chapters of Workaholics Anonymous have popped up throughout the United States, and companies like Strategic Coach are holding seminars, with workaholics paying fees ranging from four thousand to ten thousand dollars for help with their "addiction."[4] Leaving the office at 3 p.m. to meet a child's bus while remaining connected via cell phone or the Internet is common. Logging on to the Internet to check for e-mail messages from a Blackberry at a child's soccer game is a technological marvel. One person who admits he is a workaholic, Denzel, is happy about it.

> *OK, so I'm a workaholic. But working eleven to fourteen hours a day makes me happy. I love to go in to the office and mix it up. Every day I have no idea what will be thrown across my desk, and I just continue to respond to e-mails when I leave the office. The chaos and confusion of the workday can be a turn-on. It fuels my fire.*

Many people, like Denzel, enjoy working long hours and feel the rewards justify the time devoted to work. Research has found that there are differences between workaholics (those who work too much but believe that the rewards from work are equitably distributed) and overworkers (those who work too much but believe the distribution of rewards is inequitable, favoring their employers). Workaholics have significantly higher levels of career satisfaction than the overworkers. But for both groups working long hours was negatively related to life satisfaction.[5]

Technology allows workers to remain challenged by their work, even if they are not physically present at the work site. For those in early career, cutting deals remotely, being available 24/7 in order to get the best assignments, and traveling to adventurous locations—living to work, rather than working to live—is a powerful motivator and a natural high.

Challenge as a Way of Obtaining Validation

The successful resolution of a challenge or a problem is a marker event in a person's career that helps the individual become a seasoned manager. In their book *The Lessons of Experience,* authors

Morgan McCall, Michael Lombardo, and Ann Morrison describe the lessons learned by managers as they ascend the corporate ladder.[6] Often these lessons include building new skills, such as strategic thinking, handling politics, and working with people in other areas of the business. What they describe is a confidence-building process that becomes the cornerstone of one's work identity.

Tatiana, who worked for a former defense supplier to the Pentagon, told about how in her early career a briefing with the Joint Chiefs of Staff at the Pentagon helped her to build her identity.

> *I was a nervous wreck. It was my first time to do a briefing. I called my contact from the front and said, "I'm here, you can come pick me up." Except there were over twenty entrances! My purposefully early arrival turned into a "Where's Tatiana?" When I finally found the right entrance, we had to sprint to make the presentation, as these are not guys you want to leave waiting. Here I am, in pantyhose and heels, sprinting down the hall to my first major briefing, on an extremely polished slick floor. As I walked—or ran—into the room, I dropped my folder and presentation notes all over an air force general! The upside was I was so worried about nearly being late that I didn't get nervous about the presentation. I gave the best presentation of my life. It was that day I realized we're all just people (even the president himself), and titles don't matter. It's about how confident you are with yourself and whatever it is you do in a situation that matters.*

Some, like Tatiana, told stories about challenges that allowed for personal reflection and marked the building of self-confidence. Many told stories about challenging projects that shaped their work identities. For example, Daniel discussed a challenge in which he had the responsibility to turn around a failing bank. This project served as a marker event in his career, allowing him to gain greater visibility and respect.

> *My greatest challenge at work was when we purchased a troubled bank in Indiana that was given the choice from the FDIC [Federal Deposit Insurance Corporation] to either sell*

or close. I was primarily responsible for turning things around in less than three years. The turnaround led the bank into a new building and doubled the size of the assets under management during the next three years. The success of the project really put a feather in my cap and made me very marketable. I can honestly say I received fifteen years' experience during those six years. Of course, I also probably worked enough hours to equate to fifteen years in that time frame, too.

As was the case with Tatiana and Daniel, the successful resolution of a challenge or problem is a marker event in a person's career that helps the individual become a seasoned manager. Research has shown that as managers climb the corporate ladder, they learn important lessons—such as strategic thinking, handling politics, and working with people in other areas of the business—along the way. As individuals learn these lessons and experience success, they also gain confidence, which helps them become leaders. These experiences help the managers discover who they are.[7]

For one of the participants in our online career conversations, John, the opportunity to manage a large division within his firm was one of his greatest challenges. He had been given the opportunity to manage several units of his business, the first time he had been given a more strategic management role.

My biggest challenge occurred in January of 2000 when I was given the opportunity to manage the operations, sales management, and investment groups. While I had been in the organization for a while, my roles in the firm put me in positions where I worked alone or managed small to midsize groups. The challenge was in understanding or learning about my new position, which made me responsible for 350 people. [It required] change, motivation, conveying a mission and vision that was understood and then knowing that change would have to take time. [It was] moving the Titanic rather than working independently about who needed to come along for the ride.

Being involved in such a change effort challenged John as a manager and as a person. He described how using his skills and abilities had an impact on his team, his organization, and, most important, on himself. He discovered what he was capable of and what type of manager he really was.

> *I am not a salesperson by trade, yet I used the skills I had—planning, logistics management, communication skills—to create a clear and understandable message to the troops. I lined up each group's accountabilities and implemented reward systems that they could understand and self-track. I went to the project planning mode to create success. I thought the first step was to ensure that the team understood its mission. We have had a great two years—tons of promotions, exceeding expectations, breaking through milestones. My proudest accomplishment was working through my skill set to accomplish a task and not trying to become someone I was not.*

For people like John, challenge helps them gain insights into who they are and who they are not. Challenge can also serve as an important means of fulfilling personal dreams. One of our survey participants, Rich, said, "My desire for challenge is born from my desire to have freedom and unlimited opportunity and to give myself a chance to pursue my dreams and utilize my talents."

For many people, challenge builds self-identity because it helps them understand what kind of work they prefer, what roles they play in comparison to others, and what part they play in their firm's operations. Missy described things she learned about herself.

> *I thrive on variety and change. I like to have stimulating challenges and have some control over how I get my job done. I am a results-oriented individual, and I don't like to be told how to do what I am supposed to do. I also like to know what's going on in the company from a big-picture standpoint. It keeps me focused on my role within the company.*

Research has found that individuals who have a strong sense of identity, those who are self-aware and understand themselves, are more likely to report greater career success.[8] And there's a growing trend among young workers to delay adulthood in an effort to discover who they really are early in their lives. Unlike the baby boomers, Gen Xers and Gen Yers are extending their college educations from the traditional four years to five years, delaying marriage and children, and are, in some cases, even moving back in with their parents in order to find themselves. Many of these "kidults" work a series of full-time or part-time jobs, trying them on for size. They move frequently, with 47 percent of those between the ages of eighteen and twenty-nine having had at least three addresses in the past five years. They use cell phones, e-mail, and text messaging to stay in almost constant contact with friends. And they stay in touch with their parents; almost half of those between the ages of eighteen and twenty-nine talk to their parents daily. With so many choices—from the eight hundred thousand job ads posted on monster.com to the 15 million personal ads on match.com to the 205 channels on DirecTV—many Gen Xers and Gen Yers are just overwhelmed by the opportunities available to them. Some want to try them all (or as many as they can), while others are paralyzed by indecision, afraid to make the wrong decision. So many Gen Xers and Gen Yers have decided to take the time early in their careers to figure out which life path is right for them. But they aren't just looking for a job, they are searching for a calling, a way to express their identity.[9]

Challenge as a Way of Developing and Growing

Sometimes challenges take the form of stretch assignments in which important lessons are learned. Such stretch assignments present individuals with the opportunity to learn new skills and go beyond their current capabilities. Doing work that is beyond one's comfortable skill set makes for stimulating workdays, to put it mildly.

Jeanine, a former student of one of the authors, told of such a stretch assignment that came early in her career and shaped her management style. While working for General Electric Credit Corporation, she was assigned to a project in Chile. She was to travel to factories in Chile and determine their needs. This assignment required a six-month stint in Chile, living at the plant, reviewing financials, watching how truckers handled distribution, and observing a host of other logistics. Jeanine described how this assignment turned out to be a terrific growth opportunity.

I felt like I was thrown into the assignment feet first. But because of that I had to think on my feet. I had to pretend like I knew what I was doing. Fortunately, I had a few good mentors along the way, and I modeled my style after them. When the assignment was over, I returned to headquarters and reported on what I found. They told me I had done a marvelous job. It was a Six Sigma–level accomplishment. I had accepted the challenge without really knowing what I was getting into, but I had arrived.

Jeanine's project was a tremendous success. She gained the respect of the Chilean team members and became their advocate with GE headquarters. She not only learned about the Chilean operations but developed a management style that worked for her.

Many individuals, like Jeanine, who are in the early part of their careers, are thrown into sink-or-swim situations.[10] Whether it is a stretch assignment, a sink-or-swim assignment, or a combination of the two, these challenges can be frightening, causing the person to wonder: "Am I really ready for this?" Another respondent, Frederick, discussed a big promotion that made him wonder at first what he had gotten himself into.

At the beginning of this year I was promoted to the president of the region. This is something I have been preparing for and now that I have reached my goal, I am not sure if I am happy or sad. In my first two weeks in my role, I wondered if I hadn't made a serious mistake in accepting my new position. Change is something that I adjust to slowly, so I guess I should have expected some reluctance on my part. After two weeks in the new position I started to leave my comfort zone and began to accept my new role as leader for the region. Now

after two months in the job, I have accepted my new assign-
ment and am beginning to have fun. The biggest challenge
that I see for myself is going forward and becoming a better
manager inside and outside this organization.

But sometimes individuals aren't given stretch assignments or promotions but are forced instead to create their own challenges. They may redesign their jobs to invent opportunities for learning and growth. One of the bankers in our online career conversations, Martin, told about how developing an innovative project in his area of customer collections resulted in his chance to learn and grow. Often customer collections is considered to be the dead-end area of the banking business. Martin had worked in collections for many years when he conceived of an unconventional idea: collections should support the bank's relationship with the customer and, what's more, should even enhance that relationship. After all, Martin reasoned, if a bank supports a customer through the hard times, in turn that customer will feel a sense of gratitude, increased loyalty, and goodwill toward the bank. For example, although collections may have been called in because a customer started a business and the business failed, that doesn't mean that the customer will never need a bank again. By creating a positive experience, the bank can build the foundation for a continuing relationship with the customer that may be fruitful for both parties for many years to come.

From his position in a supposedly dead-end area of the business, Martin started with a problem, developed a pilot program to deliver a "relationship-based" marketing program linked to the collections system, and changed the mind-set of how collections should and could be handled. He explained the program.

The innovation I am most proud of is a pilot we are currently
running. It has taken me twenty years and two different
banks to convince our risk management group that we needed
to take a holistic view of our customers and provide debt col-
lection and counseling based on that entire relationship. The
focus is rehabilitation, not pressure, attempting to preserve
the customer's dignity and deepening their loyalty and finan-

cial relationships with our organization. The initial results, from both a customer and bank perspective, have been extremely positive.

Martin needed to be challenged, but his job and his bosses weren't giving him challenging assignments. So Martin created the challenge for himself. He took what could have been a boring, dead-end job and made it exciting work that he looks forward to doing.

The literature on job redesign is clear in its message: the more challenging the work, the more likely that employees will be motivated to achieve. Studies show that workers on a factory shop floor who were given tedious, boring assembly work to perform improved their performance when their jobs were redesigned to allow for a greater variety of tasks and skills or for the completion of a whole and identifiable task that had meaning and significance. Workers also improved performance when they were given greater autonomy and discretion in decision making.[11]

Organizations that want to retain highly talented professionals need to provide them work assignments that continue to challenge them as they grow and achieve mastery. For instance, scholar Tim Hall recalls the career journey of Jane, who requested a new position from her team leader after quickly becoming bored with her first assignment. From that experience, Jane gained the confidence that the organization would support the future changes and the related challenges she needed to avoid becoming stale. Over her sixteen years with the firm, Jane changed positions five or six times, working in many different units within the firm and eventually becoming a team leader. Jane's career comprised a series of two- to three-year learning cycles. As she gained mastery during one cycle, she craved the next challenge, the next opportunity to learn and grow, and began a new cycle of learning.[12]

Challenge as a Way of Having an Impact

People also define challenge as having influence over decisions and making things happen. Many people find it satisfying to be in a place where they can have an impact on others. If their careers lead them to this goal, they flourish. Marcia, for example, enjoys achieving goals and seeing others learn. She said, "I love to watch plans and objectives come together, seeing the light go on when someone understands a new concept."

Some, such as Sam, define challenge as being a mentor or coach who helps others achieve their personal best.

> *My proudest moment in my career was when I started up a commercial loan department that accumulated assets in excess of $500 million. [Another was] developing and promoting a staff that was second to none. My proudest moments have been seeing others reach their personal and professional goals.*

Many people need a workplace where they feel that they can affect others' lives. Such is the case with Kelsey, who said, "I need challenging work with people I respect who in turn respect me. I need to work somewhere where I feel I can make a difference."

Challenge, in the sense of having an impact, was a profound theme and is an important parameter for the Kaleidoscope Career model. Making things happen, connecting with people to bring them into a work situation to solve a problem, developing a new business, creating new ideas as part of a team, or seeing how one's work positively affects people's lives can be deeply satisfying. Deanna, a human resources professional, talked about her work as an outplacement consultant.

> *I am motivated by the work we do, which is helping people. We are a human resources consulting firm, and I head our career transition division. I work with individuals who have lost their jobs through downsizings and plant closings and help them get back on their feet and secure new positions. This is very rewarding work, and I am grateful to have such an impact.*

Many men and women talked about the sheer exhilaration of having an impact on others as the reason why they remained with their firms. Betty was excited by *the sense of accomplishment when a job has been well done and you see the effect of your efforts. I like to make things happen. I am motivated by connecting with people to bring them into a work situation to solve a problem, develop the business, or create new ideas. I love to motivate, orchestrate, and congregate.*

For people like Kelsey, Deanna, and Betty, there is nothing sweeter than the challenge of helping people change their lives for the better.

Occupations like teaching, social work, or medicine readily lend themselves to influencing and helping others, but many people seek out ways to have an impact on others regardless of the environment in which they work.[13] Moreover, while some people's drive for challenge has tangible outcomes, sometimes the outcomes of this drive are less visible or take a longer time to materialize. Wilma, an engineer for a utility firm, described her drive for challenge.

I am a trained and educated engineer working in a field dominated by individuals without balance or perspective. I work because I enjoy it. Work, love, and home are all part of life and are inseparable. I work for my future well-being. I work because as I do I can change the work environment and make positive contributions to the projects I work on based on my abilities and influenced by my gender.

Wilma may see right away how her contributions affect certain short-term work projects, but it may be years before she sees an impact from her actions to change the work environment or to introduce a new sense of balance among her colleagues.

Challenge as a Way of Establishing Expertise

An oft-quoted axiom of career development is "Build your expertise early." Tommy, a data professional, took this career advice to heart. In the early days of his career, Tommy was faced with the challenge of ensuring that there was minimal disruption to customers when his firm decided to bring its data processing capabilities in-house. This major computer conversion was a career-building experience for Tommy.

There are always so many time-sensitive and other issues to deal with along with ensuring minimal customer impact. Mapping data from one system to another is no treat, particularly when you are so tired you can't stay awake! But the challenge of doing it within a restricted (three-month) time frame was very exciting, and I became the go-to person for the whole company. It really established my expertise in the area, and I have built my career around that project. I became more confident in my abilities and was able to demonstrate it to my peers. I made changes to my career because I needed to expand my areas of knowledge and to increase my skills.

People like Tommy enjoy being the expert, the go-to person. They thrive when they can expand their expertise and then use that expertise to solve problems or bring about change. They also realize that the more a person's expertise is in demand, the more valuable that person becomes. When a firm downsizes, those with needed expertise will keep their jobs. When people become dissatisfied with their work situations, those with high levels of transferable expertise can find new jobs.[14] Data professionals, engineers, and other technically trained professionals often make or break their careers based on their areas of expertise. If those who thrive on establishing their expertise are thwarted in their attempts to do that, they may leave their firms.

In addition to the career benefits, some people enjoy establishing a base of expertise from which to operate. George, for example, was a premier scientist who worked at a well-known chemical firm that produces agricultural chemicals. He built his career early as a scientist, developing patents that the firm could use to manufacture chemical innovations, publishing scientific papers, and working on cutting-edge manufacturing processes. One of his innovations allowed for a fine-tuning of the manufacturing process that saved the production facilities at his firm hundreds of thousands of dollars. George explained his satisfaction with this work.

I love getting in there and fixing problems. It was never about the money. It wasn't even about getting published or getting the patent approved. It was about the satisfaction of solving the problem and becoming an expert that charged me up about my career. I was willing to work long hours to solve thorny problems.

Anne, a professional author, speaker, and media consultant, described this drive for developing and sharing one's expertise.

I am motivated by the opportunity to provide good information within my areas of expertise. I have an MBA and a PhD in law and policy, and I am president of a nonprofit organization. So you can tell I like challenges.

People with this drive for expertise thrive when they can use that expertise to solve problems or bring about change. They find themselves in what athletes call "the zone," when they are lost in the joy of their work, often not even noticing the passage of time.

There may be a downside, however, in this thirst for challenge through expertise. Given the increasing rate of technological change, many types of expertise can quickly become obsolete, requiring individuals to invest considerable time and money in constantly updating their knowledge and skills to remain employable.[15] And the situation is even worse for those experts over the age of fifty. Many businesses assume that older individuals have less up-to-date knowledge and skills as well as less energy to devote to their work than younger workers. For example, a survey conducted by the Society for Human Resource Management reported that 53 percent of HR managers agreed that older workers don't keep up with technology and 28 percent think older workers are less flexible than younger workers. Organizations often prefer to hire younger workers or outsource jobs rather than pay higher salaries to older experts. So while the challenge of becoming and remaining the expert fuels many careers, many individuals experience the downside of an involuntary early retirement or involuntary freelance employment when they are laid off and are unable to find equivalent work.[16]

CHALLENGE AND THE KALEIDOSCOPE
CAREER PORTFOLIO FOR WOMEN

Our research showed that both men and women begin their careers with a desire for challenge, to grow, to learn. But the Kaleidoscope Career portfolios of men and women take a sharp turn away from each other in midcareer. While men forge ahead and continue to pursue challenges in their corporate careers, women often back out of corporate careers to embrace concerns of balance. Does this mean that women suddenly lack ambition? Must we conclude that we live in a sexist world where the man remains the breadwinner and the wife returns to an Ozzie and Harriet existence at the mere mention of children in the offing?

Not necessarily, as the reasons for this shift in the kaleidoscopes of men and women in midcareer are more complex than they appear on the surface. While women have more choices than they once did in the kinds of lives they want to lead, they do not have control over basic biology. Consider the common life pattern for an educated woman. Upon graduating from college, during her most fertile years, when she actually has the most energy for child rearing, she gets a job. Sometime in her late twenties or early thirties she marries—just at the point when she has acquired the training in her job to be considered for a management position. Then, when she is ready for advancement and has acquired the maturity to make intelligent career choices, she takes time off from work to rear her children. Several years later, she seeks to reenter the labor force. She discovers that she has lost pace with her colleagues, needs to update her skills, or may even need to find an alternate career. So she finds a job, works for a while, and then exits the workforce.

A woman's drive for challenge is not diminished while she is taking time off to rear her children or caring for her elderly parents. Instead, it becomes sublimated into her care-giving role or surfaces as the desire to open her own entrepreneurial business that provides challenge while permitting her to still fulfill her caregiver responsibilities.

Books like Judith Warner's *Perfect Madness: Motherhood in the Age of Anxiety* detail how life on the soccer field is rapacious, the world of play dates can be inhuman, and the selection of volunteers for the school play can be an exercise in cruelty.[17] Some highly competitive, stay-at-home moms find challenges not by returning to work but through their parenting accomplishments. This may be why some PTA moms are so fond of discussing the many activities their children have become involved in, rather than their children's growth and development. The drive for challenge remains, but it is being channeled through their children's accomplishments. A voluminous literature echoes the point that women are looking for opportunities for growth, creativity, task enjoyment, self-fulfillment, education, variety, and feedback in their jobs.[18] However, because of discrimination, stereotypes, societal gender expectations, the "maternal wall," and a host of other problems, women are often prevented from finding challenge within the confines of corporate America. A recent study showed that women at the middle levels of management had less challenging experiences in their job tasks than did men.[19] Some women remain trapped within companies that prevent them from using all of their abilities or from taking on greater responsibilities. Others break free to find challenging work, sometimes finding it in nontraditional organizations or in unexpected ways. Still others find ways to do it all—have challenge as well as balance and authenticity.

A Challenging Career as an Astronomer: Heidi Hammel

Heidi Hammel is one of the new vanguard of women who can work at home while maintaining a high-challenge job—as an astronomer and researcher. Heidi earned her BS from the Massachusetts Institute of Technology and her PhD from the University of Hawaii. After a postdoctoral position at the Jet Propulsion Laboratory, she worked at MIT as principal research scientist studying planetary systems. Working with a scientific team, she used the Hubble Space Telescope to make observations of Neptune and was a prime researcher on the team that discovered that the Great Dark Spot on Neptune had disappeared. A great advocate of science, especially the need to get more women interested in science careers from an early age, Heidi is now employed by the Space

Science Institute, located in Boulder, Colorado, and serves as its codirector of research. This position gives her the ability to work on cutting-edge space science research as part of a loosely connected group of professionals, scientists, and administrators—from her home base in Connecticut. She shared her thoughts about the challenges of her work.

> *There are so many wonderful challenges in the work I do. For many of us studying the universe, it is a pleasure to be able to look up at the sky and investigate interesting questions and add to the sum of celestial knowledge. The work I do is truly fundamental to science and contributes to the sum total of human knowledge. I do my primary research from my home office. This includes writing research papers associated with the projects I am currently involved in, analyzing the data I am collecting with some of the largest telescopes in the world, and working with the teams of researchers I am involved with. I also do public outreach regarding science, such as contributing to the museum exhibit on Mars, and currently I am working on an exhibition concerning the giant planets. I also travel all over the world giving talks to the general public about my research; attending scientific conferences to exchange information and ideas with my colleagues; serving on national boards, advisory committees, and review teams; and participating in planning meetings for future space and astronomy projects.*

One would think that many astronomers must work at night, staring into space—but not anymore. Much of the data that serves as the foundation of space science research is collected by computers and through cutting-edge technology, while astronomers work at home or from remote locations, analyzing the data. Furthermore, actual work time is very limited for these big telescopes, often just a few half-nights out of a whole year. Even so, as Heidi admits, working from home to pursue her passion for her science has not been an easy transition. Now that she is a mother of three young children, she has had to face many dilemmas balancing her challenging work with the needs of her family.

I love the work that I do, and the challenge of the work drives me forward, but working from home required a huge transition for me. I had to train myself and my husband that my work from home is work and not time to do household chores. It took me a full year to realize that I didn't have to do laundry, clean the kitchen, or work in the garden when I am home. I have had to find ways to really focus on the work while my children are in school or in day care. The science has to come first. My husband would come home from his office and would say, "Hey, why aren't these toys picked up? You've been home all day," to which I would respond, "Because I was at work today, my dear."

Heidi loves the challenge of her work and the flexibility of working at home. She finds true meaning in contributing to science and rearing her children. But maintaining the delicate interplay among authenticity, balance, and challenge isn't always easy. Says Heidi,

I work 9 to 5:30 p.m. each day, when I am lucky. I don't work at night when my children are home, and I don't work weekends. Weekends are family time. And I just am too tired to work each evening, so that's where I draw the line. Instead, I live a life of constant desperation—I have several papers waiting to be worked on, and many more that I could be working on. I just don't have enough hours in the day to get it all done. My greatest challenge is to work my way through the piles of data, reports, research, proposals, administrative tasks, meetings, travel—there just aren't enough hours to get through it all!

Finding Authenticity, Challenge, and Balance through Entrepreneurship

Many women would like to find a challenging and important job situation like Heidi Hammel's that allows them to work at home. But given the way that most corporations are structured and with face time in the office still king, most women find they cannot negotiate job situations that permit truly integrated authenticity, balance, and challenge. These women may be locked in to low-paying and monotonous jobs, or their workplaces may discriminate against them, or their boss won't permit flexibility so home and work can be balanced—so they opt out of corporate America.

Becoming an entrepreneur is one way to have a more flexible work schedule, take on a significant challenge, and at the same time do meaningful work. In 2004, 48 percent of all privately held U.S. firms, 10.6 million companies, were owned at least 50 percent by women. Since 1997, women-owned firms have grown at about twice the rate of all other firms. One in seven of U.S. workers is employed by a woman-owned business, and these businesses spend an estimated $546 billion annually on salaries and benefits. And those with their own businesses had an average net worth six times that of women heads of households without a business.[20]

What may surprise many is that balancing work-family demands may not be the major driving force behind women entrepreneurs' decisions to leave corporate America. In an early study of women entrepreneurs, small-business experts Dorothy Moore and E. Holly Buttner found that the 129 women they studied had complex reasons for leaving firms to start their own businesses.[21] The top-ranking reasons women reported for becoming business owners were the desire for challenge and the need for self-determination. These reasons were followed by concerns about managing work and family, and obstacles to advancement including discrimination, and organizational dynamics (e.g., low quality standards, little motivation to produce).

Following up on her original study, Moore, in her book *Careerpreneurs: Lessons from Leading Women Entrepreneurs on Building a Career without Boundaries,* found that women are still starting their own businesses in search of greater challenge.[22] Most of the one hundred women she studied acquired important skills while working in corporate America and decided that the rewards of calling their own shots outweighed the risks of striking out on their own. So instead of remaining in an environment that lacked challenge, these savvy women packed up their skills, abilities, and knowledge and left corporations to blaze new career paths. They created their own opportunities so they could make the rules and chart their own courses.

Research on careers in the entertainment industry also found that women broke away from major organizations to start their own companies.[23] Of the fifteen women executives studied, 80 percent opted out of the major firms to start their own entrepreneurial endeavors. These women left to start their own firms for two major reasons: (1) to gain access to more challenging work or to get their "big break"; and (2) to gain more flexibility in managing work/nonwork demands. Some also said that forming their own firms permitted them to be authentic, allowing them to express their visions and match their work to their values. As one production company owner explained,

I wanted to work in a place that was respectful, family-oriented, and allowed people to grow. People who work for me seem to feel the same way. I started the company with three people three years ago. Now we have seventy people who work for us, and we are producing six cable TV shows.[24]

Even though, like Maureen Smith (profiled in Chapter 2), most of the women returned to the corporate environment, these entrepreneurial time-outs served as important training experiences for these women. The challenge of running their own businesses helped them to develop important skills, to see what type of work environment they preferred, and provided a showcase to demonstrate what they could really accomplish. Some of the women were lured back into the corporations when the decision makers saw what these women achieved and wanted that kind of talent working for them.

The bottom line is clear: women who can't find the challenge they desire within the bounds of corporate America are going to leave. Corporations troubled by the "brain drain" of talented women need to ensure that they are providing stimulating, uplifting, meaty assignments to their women employees. Researchers at the Center for Creative Leadership found that men and women receive different types of developmental opportunities in their jobs, and this complicates women's ability to qualify for the executive level.[25] Tasks with high levels of visibility and clear deadlines, jobs with large scope and responsibilities for managing multiple functions, and jobs with external pressure characterized most jobs held by men. Women reported receiving less personal support from peers and greater demands for influencing people over whom they did not have direct authority. This suggests a more subtle form of discrimination that prevents women from qualifying for positions that would track them to the upper levels.

Despite greater awareness and laws to promote fair treatment, discrimination against women is alive and well in corporate America. For example, Catalyst, an organization that tracks the progress of women in corporations, conducted a survey of women in the financial services industries, long a bastion of male exclusivity. Following is a summary of what they found.[26]

- 65 percent reported that they have to work harder than men to get the same rewards

- 51 percent reported that women are paid less than men for doing similar work

- 42 percent believed that projects and clients are assigned fairly within their firms

Discrimination. Boring and repetitive work. Subtle yet exclusionary good-old-boy practices. These reasons give women the impetus to display their need for challenge in other ways—outside of the bounds of corporations—through mothering duties or through entrepreneurial activities or a combination of both. For this reason the Kaleidoscope Career portfolio takes an abrupt and dramatic turn for women. The parameter of challenge does not drop out of the kaleidoscope equation because women suddenly lack ambition when they give birth. Rather, a complex convergence of events leads many women to find alternate career approaches, approaches that sublimate the need for challenge while the parameter of balance takes center stage. For this reason we see women's career kaleidoscopes as more simultaneous than men's. Women follow alternate, more circuitous, more simultaneous routes to achieve their goals, while men's careers remain linear. It is not a lack of ambition on the part of women that drives the drop-out rate. Instead, the challenges women continue to seek in their simultaneous, relational career kaleidoscopes take place in alternative ways.

THE STRUCTURE FOR CHALLENGE IN CORPORATIONS

For women's need for challenge to be sustained in corporations, companies must change how work is designed, developed, and distributed across the ranks. Companies have an opportunity to do so: they are already changing their structures in the light of globalization and the outsourcing of accounting, human resources analysis, and information systems work to countries like India. There is a hope that American companies will finally wake up and recognize that the jobs that remain in the United States can (and must) be reconfigured to provide more intrinsic challenge and motivation, thus decreasing the opt-out rate of talented workers and encouraging women to seek challenge inside of corporate boundaries.

Management that discounts women's need for challenge in corporations creates a loss both for the woman and the firm. Treating a significant portion of employees as dead weight because they have nurturing responsibilities is not productive for the corporation or the economy. Quality of performance drops, and, intentionally or otherwise, that system puts a lid on the contributions individual women can make. There are high-potential women out there who want to remain challenged in their jobs but who also want to take a more important role in responding to family caregiving needs.

The Kaleidoscope Career model could help corporations capitalize on a tremendous opportunity. Knowing that women's needs for challenge do not diminish even though they need to meet their relational needs, corporations could create systems to allow women (and men) to pursue challenges outside the confines of corporate offices. With portable technology in place—such as PDAs, wireless data systems, and Wi-Fi Internet-access mobile offices—project-based work could be assigned to allow for linkages back to the office that nonetheless keep the employee in the loop and provide a sense of personal challenge.

The study of job design has long suggested that work that provides a sense of meaning, responsibility, and discretion in decision making is inherently motivating. Although money provides extrinsic motivation, research has repeatedly shown that work can be designed to provide intrinsic motivation as well. Jobs should be redesigned so that people are permitted to develop and grow. Work should allow people not only to excel but also to contribute to something bigger than themselves. People want to be appreciated and rewarded for outstanding performance, for meeting challenges head on.[27]

When corporations change their structures to allow project work to take place untethered, outside the boundaries of the corporate walls, the climate for productivity will change. When employees—women and men—realize that caregiving is valued and that the kaleidoscope of life requires treating work and family as part of the same gestalt, women's work will also be recognized as a central resource. When individuals realize that organizations value integrity and making work and career decisions based on being true to oneself, employees will realize that opting out isn't the only answer, or the best answer.

The Kaleidoscope Career model suggests that corporations need to value women as a central resource, not discourage their participation, especially in midcareer. When the sense of challenge in a corporation diminishes and there are few opportunities for advancement available, women shift their kaleidoscopes to a new life parameter—that of balance. The structure of corporate life, not a lack of women's ambition, causes women to make a midlife course correction. Put simply, something's gotta give. In the next chapter, we will explore how corporations need to change their work policies and cultures so that employees can have successful Kaleidoscope Careers.

CHAPTER 8

NO MORE BUSINESS AS USUAL

For more than a decade, Motek, a quiet little software company in Beverly Hills, California, has been making waves. According to *Fortune Small Business* magazine, it may very well be the best place in the world to work.[1] Ann Price, the company's founder, has blended new age business ideas, personal beliefs, and nonconformist practices into a successful start-up company in the highly competitive software industry. The company's mission, according to Price, is not to make money for shareholders. Its employees and its founder *are* its shareholders. So the company defines its mission this way: to improve the life of its employees as well as its customers.

Motek's culture is employee focused. For example, Motek's employees are required to take a mandatory lunch hour, in which shoptalk is forbidden. Price believes everyone should be able to walk to work so she subsidizes employees' glitzy Beverly Hills neighborhood addresses. She provides employees up to five hundred dollars a month for a car lease to ease travel to customers or for long commutes. No one is supposed to take on more assignments than he or she can accomplish by the end of the week, so most tasks discussed in the weekly meeting will have to wait until the next week. Employees are rewarded for issuing "Thursday-alerts," which communicate that a task will not be completed so that others can work on the task or, if needed, the customer can be told that more time is needed. Said Price, "We know we'll get there. But instead of doing it in five years, we'll do it in ten and have a life along the way."[2]

Motek's employees are truly empowered. Motek's twenty-one employees vote on everything from the size of their bonuses to project assignments to the office furnishings they need. This democratic process extends to the company's pay system. Everyone except the CIO and sales manager makes one of three salaries at Motek. All three pay levels are under seventy thousand dollars, and the highest is only thirty thousand dollars more than the lowest. Often when there have been opportunities to improve compensation, the employees have decided they'd rather pay down debt than award themselves a bonus. Price has promised each founding employee 1 percent of Motek's value when the company is sold, and employees feel they have a piece of the company. In addition, despite Price's urging, the employees concluded that they couldn't afford to give everyone an additional week of vacation. Motek's annual vacation benefit stayed at five weeks, with each employee receiving a vacation voucher for up to five thousand dollars a year based on the belief that vacations reduce worker stress.

What inspired Ann Price to develop such a revolutionary management style? Her previous work experience at General Electric Consulting allowed her to be promoted quickly; she was managing a major project for Southern California Edison within six months. But she didn't feel she fit into GE's hard-driving, winner-take-all culture. Before working at GE, she had lived on a kibbutz in Naan, Israel, that had invented a drip-irrigation system—and she became smitten with the fairness and prosperity of communal life. She decided to merge the two—business and communal life—to create a "capitalist kibbutz," dedicated to making the lives of her workers and her customers better while making money at the same time. Motek is already profitable and continues its rapid growth. It has successfully installed its reliable, revolutionary software in more than forty warehouses for more than thirty major customers. Said Price, "I'm not willing to build an organization that's a modern software sweatshop. No matter what happens to these people later, . . . while they were here they had quality of life."[3]

For women and men negotiating the issue of balance, Price's management strategy of promoting trust, autonomy, and a well-balanced life is a breath of fresh air. So many women, and in recent years men, have left corporations due to the inflexibility of their jobs. While working from nine to five used to be difficult enough, the added burden of travel, long corporate hours that extend past a child's bedtime, early morning staff meeting requirements, and weekend take-home work leave no time for family life or personal pursuits. As the Kaleidoscope Career model makes clear, careers are no longer static entities. Gen X and Gen Y men and women as well as baby boom knowledge workers have new requirements. A career must fit into their lives, and allow for balance, rather than overwhelming all other life parameters.

Companies like Motek may sound like utopia, but they are not without problems. Issues of surviving a corporate growth cycle (Motek was reaching the point where it would need to hire more employees soon), increasing salaries (Motek's salaries paled in comparison to the more typical one hundred thousand dollars and up for good software programmers), and meeting increasing demands for customers (Motek's success was causing customers to start to line up) create bureaucratic pressures.[4] But while companies like Motek may face growing pains in maintaining their employee-focused strategies, other corporations cannot remain so inflexible. These companies are tearing apart the basic fabric of our society. They are breaking the bond between parent and child by their relentless demands for long hours and time spent in travel. These companies are causing people—men and women—to lose sight of what is authentically important for them as individuals.

What these companies may not realize is that these practices may be viable in the short term, but in the long term they are not. These practices cost companies in obvious ways like employee burnout, higher health care costs due to stress-related illnesses, and reduced employee creativity, efficiency, and effectiveness. These practices also eat away at the firm in less obvious ways, like a cancer as employees do their jobs and nothing more. Employees keep money-saving suggestions to themselves, they don't take the initiative to solve problems or help fellow workers, and they don't truly care about the company and its long-term survival—it's just a job, a way to pay the bills.

WHAT IS CONSIDERED
"FAMILY-FRIENDLY" IS OFTEN NOT

Everyone has heard of "family-friendly" firms. These firms—such as those profiled in *Working Mother* magazine, *Fortune, Working Woman, NAFE Magazine* (from the National Association for Female Executives), and Catalyst publications—often include benefits in their HR policies that are deemed family friendly.[5] For example, *Working Mother*'s top ten firms offered the following types of coveted family-friendly benefits: child care options, subsidized day care, flexible scheduling, on-site child care, maternity leave and adoption benefits, job-guaranteed leaves, and retirement benefits. But according to Catalyst, an organization that tracks such policies, many of these benefits, while coveted, are the exception and not the rule in most companies.[6]

The problem is that what is often touted by the media as "family friendly" simply is not. Even for those firms that are moving toward more of a family-friendly environment, creating a family-friendly firm involves more than offering employees an annual family picnic. Many firms wrongly believe that providing "family-friendly" policies such as child care vouchers or employee discounts is sufficient to make their firms attractive to potential recruits and retain current high-performing employees. But what firms traditionally think is "family-friendly" simply isn't anymore. Such policies, while welcome, do not address the fundamental issue raised in this book: how to create a workplace where authenticity, balance, and challenge—the ABCs of the Kaleidoscope Career model—are recognized and enhanced.

With the new Gen X and Gen Y mentality, firms will need to do more than simply offer cosmetic benefits. Firms will need to undergo normative change. They will need to restructure policies concerning careers, benefits, and pay. They will need to reexamine central assumptions about how work gets done and recognize work/nonwork balance as a strategic concern. They must embrace the Kaleidoscope Career model and all that it implies.

Based on the research that forms the foundation of this book, we think that there are two important caveats for those who want to implement successful work-life programs. First, organizations must be truly committed to work-life programs and not use them solely for publicity.[7] If organizations have work-life policies but foster a hostile culture that makes use of these programs unacceptable, the policies become worthless and will fail to produce the positive outcomes intended.[8] Men who believe, for example, that they will be ridiculed for taking advantage of an extended paternity leave policy, or that taking such a break will truncate their career advancement options, will not make use of family-friendly policies. Men (and women) must feel that the corporate culture validates their choices about having a life beyond work. The belief must be woven into the organization's strategic mission and culture that employees who have full and rich lives outside the office bring all their experiences to the office and produce better work because of them.

Second, establishing work-life programs is not enough. Our research shows that women make career decisions based on a complex and interrelated set of factors that include opportunities to be challenged on the job and opportunities for advancement. It is still common practice for promotion decisions, especially in law and consulting firms, to be based on long hours or travel as surrogate measures for commitment and ambition rather than on actual performance.[9] Although work-life programs are a beginning, they must be coupled with challenging jobs and advancement opportunities for women at different points of the life cycle. Gender-based inequities in wages, job placements, and training opportunities across the board must be eliminated. Treating issues of work-life balance in isolation from organizational strategy and culture cannot continue. Providing child care or gym memberships while denying working women fair treatment and equal opportunities for pay and advancement is not family friendly.

Standards of what makes a company a great place to work must be raised. Companies must be held to a higher level of responsibility than ever before. If workers cannot be their true selves at the office and must deny their connections to family, friends, and community, then the firm becomes nothing more than a place to go to earn the rent; for the firm, any chance to gain from the positive influence of the nonwork aspects of life on work performance is lost.[10] The old model of business as usual isn't good enough anymore. A whole new way of doing business is needed.

THE FIVE MYTHS OF
THE FAMILY-FRIENDLY FIRM

Today's employees want flexible scheduling options. We asked women and men what they wanted from a more flexible work environment. The results were hardly surprising. More than fifteen hundred workers were surveyed online and asked to rank their top five most wanted company benefits. The three choices ranked number one most often were "a firm that maintains health care benefits for part-time positions," "a firm that allows part-time scheduling," and "a firm that builds flextime into jobs at all levels." Other top choices included "a firm that encourages telecommuting as an alternative to travel," "a firm that has pay systems designed to pay for outcomes rather than face time," and "a firm that values diversity and promotes from within."

Although the technology is in place for such possibilities, what firms actually offer pales in comparison to what employees want and need. Most firms offer few of these benefits, and the ones they do offer are often hampered by restrictions on their use.[11] By failing to offer benefits, or by discouraging their use, organizations are creating hostile corporate cultures that constantly demand "more, more" from already overstressed, overburdened workers. Unfortunately, many organizations don't seem to realize the damage they are doing—both to their own long-term viability and to society as a whole. Firms are adhering to five major myths, assuming what they are doing is sufficient to be considered family-friendly. We disagree. Instead, firms should be putting policies and programs into place that support the Kaleidoscope Career model. The five myths of family-friendly firms are the following.

1. "We offer flexible schedules for those jobs where it is appropriate."

2. "We offer child care options, such as sponsored day care."

3. "We say that we support the advancement of women."

4. "We have a traditional rewards system, based on seniority, performance, and bonuses."

5. "We offer the same benefits that other family-friendly firms are offering, so there's no need to do anything more."

Myth 1: "We offer flexible schedules for those jobs where it is appropriate."

Many firms—especially those commonly noted in publications such as *Working Mother* magazine, *Fortune* magazine, *NAFE Magazine,* and Catalyst publications—offer flexible schedules. Flexible scheduling allows employees to choose their work hours within the limits established by their employer. But while some flextime programs allow workers a great deal of leeway and truly help employees gain better work/life balance, others provide very little flexibility, or the flexibility comes at the price of stalled career advancement or challenge.

Although most employers using flexible scheduling require their employees to report for work during predetermined core work hours, flexible programs can be implemented in a variety of ways. Flexible scheduling may include the following limitations.

- Some employers enforce bands of time during which employees may start and finish work. The bands may range in length from as little as fifteen minutes to two hours or more.

- Some employers require their workers to stay on the schedule they select for six months or longer, while others let employees vary their hours from day to day or week to week.

- Some employers require staffers to work the same number of hours every day, while other firms let their workers balance shorter days with longer days.[12]

There is no consistency in how firms define flexible schedules, so firms that say they permit flexibility may have policies that are so restrictive that they are basically worthless in helping employees achieve balance. Moreover, while many firms may say they offer flexible schedules, the flexibility only extends to special circumstances or for certain types of work.

So who is most likely to actually have flexible work hours? A 2001 Society for Human Resource Management (SHRM) study conducted by the Bureau of Labor Statistics reports the following percentages of workers in each occupation who have the option of flexible schedules.

- 45.5 percent of executives, administrators, and managers

- 40.7 percent of sales workers

- 18.3 percent of precision production, craft, and repair workers

- 13.7 percent of operators, fabricators, and laborers[13]

The SHRM survey indicates that flexible schedules were most prevalent among managerial and administrative employees. Although these employees fared much better than many lower-income workers—who are probably less able to afford child care, elder care, and other services—still more than half of these managerial and administrative workers didn't have the option of flexibility. So how helpful are these programs for the typical worker? Take, for example, the stressed-out mom of three who lives in Columbus, Ohio, and who must drop baby Seth at the child care center that opens at 9 a.m. and yet be home from work in time to meet Kate's bus at 3:30 p.m., take Johnny to karate class, and engage in a 9 p.m. conference call with project team members working in Sydney and Hong Kong. For her the programs would probably not help much. For flexible scheduling to have an impact, a norm of flexible scheduling must be created throughout the workforce. For true flexibility to work as part of the Kaleidoscope Career mind-set, leaders at the highest level must value flexible schedules.

Technology is now available that makes it possible for an employee to work from home, work different (and perhaps longer) hours than the standard 9 a.m. to 5 p.m., attend a daughter's baseball practice in the afternoon, and complete unfinished work in the evening before she goes to bed. Smart cell phones, PalmPilots with e-mail, and networks open up new avenues to women and men for effectively balancing work and family issues. However, these technologies alone are not the answer. Corporations must reinvent their career paths to accommodate flexibility so that those working outside the traditional 9 to 5 hours are not subject to career penalties.

True flexibility must be the goal. If professionals can accomplish weekly goals, what difference does it make if they work forty hours or thirty-five hours? What difference does it make if they work in their offices or at home? As long as high-quality work is produced, does it make much of a difference if employees communicate with coworkers via telephone and e-mail rather than travel to their locations? Those organizations that focus on performance outcomes rather than time clocks and effectively use technology to help resolve work-life conflict will be able to recruit the most gifted and talented individuals—and, more important, will be able to retain them.

Myth 2: "We offer child care options, such as sponsored day care."

Consider Eve, who works a half hour away from home. Her child attends public school, which gets out at 3 p.m. Eve must attend a meeting that no doubt will extend beyond 5:30 p.m. So what is she to do? Drive home, pick up little Billy and bring him to the company-sponsored child care center, taking an hour out of her day? Stay late and frantically call a neighbor to meet Billy's school bus? Start calling the names on her emergency babysitter list? Angrily demand that her husband drive to school in the middle of his day to pick up the stranded child? Send Billy to a town-sponsored after-school day care program? Which option works? Actually, few of them work well. Most companies don't sponsor child care centers on-site. Likewise, odds are there are few individuals available to call in times of emergency. That's why many working women end up taking a sick day to stay home and care for an ill child. Most fathers work at firms that assume their male employees' wives will handle child care emergencies and that frown upon those men who do take time off from work to care for their children. Most cities don't sponsor after-school day care programs, so chances are this isn't an option either. And most neighbors won't be home to meet the school bus, because they're probably at work too.

Most working mothers find their lives are a patchwork of child care plans and backup plans if emergencies arise. As the baby boom generation ages, elder care responsibilities for many will further complicate the situation. And, yes, there are times when individuals can pay others to take care of household duties, especially items such as maintaining the lawn, cleaning the house, and doing the laundry, freeing them to more readily meet company demands. There are other occasions, however, when individuals themselves cannot be reasonably replaced by paid labor. For example, who wants someone else to take her place at her child's parent-teacher conference, fifth grade play, or birthday party? Who wants someone else to go with her best friend to her chemo treatments or be with her husband at his uncle's funeral? Who wants someone else to help her sister pick out her wedding dress, take notes during her father's medical appointments, or attend her family reunion?

Most organizations need to update traditional work-life initiatives. Take child care for example. Most U.S. firms' child care centers are open only from 9 to 5; such hours are of little help to individuals who must work past 5 p.m. or on weekends, or who regularly work the night shift. But it doesn't have to be that way. The Toyota plant in Georgetown, Kentucky, took the traditional child care center and turned it into a twenty-four-hour operation. Toyota's twenty-four-hour center permits parents to work the night shift on the assembly line while their children slumber.[14] Now, that's true commitment to family values. Firms need to be inspired by stories like the Georgetown Toyota's twenty-four-hour day care center and recognize that many traditional work-life initiatives must be updated and that others are just the tip of the iceberg. Human resources professionals need to question if employees are being treated as the valuable assets they are, or as disposable workers. Corporate leaders should examine how their culture and mission can be reinvented to better meet the needs of their employees—while still remaining profitable.

Myth 3: "We say that we support the advancement of women."

Women have made great strides in gaining entrance to firms and cracking the glass ceiling. Despite these advances, women still largely advance to middle management and no further. Researchers at the Center for Creative Leadership found that there were significant differences in the criticality, visibility, and breadth of responsibility in management positions held by men and women.[15] Women were more likely to be placed in positions where they lacked authority to influence others, lacked network support, and experienced greater stress.

Although some corporations are now making a concerted effort to place more women in the pipeline to executive positions in their firms, Catalyst reports that women in the largest U.S. firms still hold less than 10 percent of the profit-and-loss line jobs that eventually lead to the top positions.[16] In an effort to promote and retain women, firms must provide real advancement opportunities that allow for executive development. Companies can benchmark the practices of other firms to improve their own policies. For example, the National Association of Female Executives' "Top 30 Companies" list focuses not only on how many women hold senior profit-and-loss positions but also on how many women in middle management have experience to be viable pipeline candidates. Many of these firms follow the motto "What gets measured gets done" by setting specific numerical goals for the number of women in profit-loss and executive positions and by regularly reviewing compensation and succession plans for gender equity.[17] Moreover, the top-rated companies have cultures that support and reinforce the advancement of women and hold senior managers accountable for those numbers.

Organizations need to do more than just say they support women. They need to actively level the playing field and enforce antidiscrimination policies. And career management and mentoring programs based on male models are inadequate. Simply expecting women to work longer hours and accept transfers to other cities and countries without taking into account their caregiving responsibilities fails to recognize that women are whole beings with lives outside the office. Organizations must realize that a woman does not make career decisions without considering the impact of her choices on her family and friends. The standard linear career model must be replaced with one that recognizes fully the reality of the ABCs of the Kaleidoscope Career model. Advancing women is not only the right thing to do; it is the smart business decision to make.

Myth 4: "We have a traditional rewards system, based on seniority, performance, and bonuses."

Many women know that after all the juggling of home and work demands, after the realization that no matter how hard they work a top position in the firm will never be theirs, there is the paycheck to consider. Women who take advantage of flextime benefits discover that their pay suffers, making it less attractive to remain employed. For example, 90 percent of law firms in the United States offer part-time career options to employees, but only about 4 percent of employees choose this option because many of them (33 percent) believe that doing so will hurt their careers and their pay.[18] Gender discrimination in pay across the board is also tied to part-time pay and benefit discrimination. Most pay studies include only information on full-time workers, so the real wage gap between men and women is often obscured. But women have babies and are usually the caregivers of both children and the elderly, so they are more likely to work part-time or take leaves. Between 1983 and 1998, women worked 67.5 percent as many hours as men and subsequently earned $449,101 less. Without paid family leave and subsidized quality child care, this gender wage gap, as Table 5 on the following page shows, will continue.[19]

Even for men, pay-for-performance systems have not kept pace with the changing workplace. Consider the case of one of our respondents, Bob, who initially had been paid through a system of commissions and bonuses based on the number of sales clients he activated. Yet once his job was changed to a more flexible project

TABLE 5
Wage Gap between Highly Educated Men and Women

Occupation	Women's Salary	Men's Salary
Human Resource Specialists*	$39,260	$49,504
Accountants and Auditors*	$43,784	$52,832
Registered Nurse*	$46,540	$53,612
Mathematical Computer Scientist	$58,000	$65,900
Pharmacists*	$74,464	$87,568
Public Relations Professionals	$75,498	$107,960
Senior Mechanical Engineer	$81,100	$87,000
College/University Full Professors	$82,874	$94,235
Lawyers*	$65,260	$88,920
Anesthesiologists	$265,72	$336,747

Source: Riss, S. 2005. "2005 Salary Survey: How Can We Close the Gender Wage Gap?" *NAFE Magazine* 28, no. 4: 18–21.
*Indicates median; other salaries are based on average income.

management role, permitting him to work from home, Bob's commission pay remained, despite the fact that he no longer had clients and there was no basis upon which commissions could be drawn. Examples like these proliferate in organizational life. Pay systems need to catch up to the nature of work rather than forcing work to fit into an outdated compensation plan.

Flexible project-based work and salary systems that pay for outcomes rather than hours worked may be the answer, because such systems fit the Kaleidoscope Career model. People we surveyed were demanding that corporations get away from the concept that the only work of value is work done on-site, in one's office. Organizations must trust that their professional employees will do their work without being monitored and punching the invisible time clock that pervades firms that focus on face time rather than actual output. Our survey found that for both men and women, pay systems based on outcomes rather than attendance were a popular choice.[20]

Additionally, organizations need to completely overhaul their benefit systems to recognize families beyond the traditional definition of husband as breadwinner with a wife at home with the children. Firms should move away from policies that focus on marriage, making changes such as the following.

- Extending family benefits such as health care coverage to include a domestic partner, parents, and adult children

- Giving employees an allowance to be spent on benefits of their choice rather than imposing one-size-fits-all programs that may be of little use to some workers (e.g., child care programs for single employees without children)

- Eliminating biases in pay systems that give married employees, especially men, higher salaries regardless of performance

- Permitting singles to designate someone to inherit their pensions if they should die before receiving benefits

- Providing ample personal days, rather than sick days, that can be used for whatever the employee chooses—illness of self or family members, child care or elder care emergencies, family events—with supervisor notification still required but without the requirement to explain why the personal day is being taken[21]

Traditional rewards systems were designed for the traditional family: the male breadwinner, the stay-at-home wife, and the 2.4

"perfect" children who don't have problems and place no demands on their parents' time. Those traditional families are rare. Families today are more likely to include divorced or single parents, blended stepfamilies, single workers caring for elderly or disabled relatives, and dual career couples. Rewards systems must be designed for today's family—in all its permutations.

Myth 5: "We offer the same benefits that other family-friendly firms are offering, so there's no need to do anything more."

Many of the women in our study talked about forgoing career opportunities to care for ailing family members, to be near aging parents, and to nurture small children. Likewise, many of the men regretted not spending more time with family. But while the list of corporate firms that offer favorable parental leave or work-life management programs is increasing, stellar examples are still rare. *Working Mother*'s 2004 list of the best companies highlighted firms such as Bristol-Myers Squibb, which provides a full range of child care options, and Eli Lilly and Company, which offers job-guaranteed leaves for new moms. Such programs should be benchmarked and serve as blueprints for change.[22]

But even this is not enough. Corporations must adopt kaleidoscope-oriented job policies, such as time banks of paid parental leave, reduced-hours careers, job-sharing opportunities, and options for career interruptions to retain workers caught in a parental work bind. Similar programs should be developed to help working women manage elder care issues (e.g., paid leave, subsidized day care for the elderly), including expanding the definition of elder care to include not only one's parents but also other elderly relatives. Firms must recognize employees' needs for authenticity, balance, and challenge, and the journey to fulfill these needs must permeate the very fabric of the workplace to make it truly family friendly. Organizations that assume that providing minimum benefits or the same outdated benefits as other firms is enough to be truly family friendly are shortsighted. Today's workforce is changing, and pay and benefit systems must also evolve if organizations are to remain competitive. It's no longer enough to just follow the pack. To attract, recruit, and retain the best workers, organizations must take the lead and proactively introduce change. They must remake themselves based on the principles of the Kaleidoscope Career model. Table 6 presents changes that forward-looking companies can adopt.

Do some companies balk at such ideas? Say that business is no place for personal needs? Say it is just impossible to do? Yes, there are nay-sayers. But they are wrong. It is possible, and it is already being done.

IT IS POSSIBLE: LESSONS FROM ABROAD

The countries of Europe, which decades ago gave up working long hours in favor of a more balanced lifestyle, provide some good examples of how to do it right. Some countries have initiated policies that provide considerable support for working parents and are truly based on the idea of family values. Following are five international examples of note:

- In the Netherlands, maternity benefits include four to six weeks of prenatal leave and sixteen weeks of postnatal leave with 100 percent salary. The leave laws allow parents, after twelve months on the job, to take up to thirteen weeks full-time or six months part-time unpaid leave to care for children up to four years old. Surprisingly, these laws even cover those working less than twenty hours a week.[23]

- In France, mothers receive a year-long paid maternity leave and can place their three-year-olds in public nursery schools free of charge. In addition to free health care, mothers receive a cash allowance for each child, to be used as the mother chooses; the allowable choices include paying a nanny or other household help.

- In Italy, where the *pranzo* (an extended midday lunch period) is still part of the daily routine, employees work in the morning, take time off for a long lunch with family or for errands and a nap, and then return to work, clocking hours from 9 a.m. to 1 p.m. and again from 3 to 7 p.m., often bringing children with them if needed.

TABLE 6

Changes to Help Firms Retain and Advance Women and Gen X Men

What Corporations Think Is Sufficient to Be "Family Friendly"	New Approaches for Firms Committed to the Advancement and Retention of Women
Offering flexible schedules where they are appropriate.	Redesign work so it can be made flexible. Provide "tech for flex" (technology for flexibility) so that workers can work remotely from their homes or other locations at all hours of the day. Allow videoconferencing to eliminate unnecessary travel. Reward and promote individuals who effectively use flexible schedules and are role models for others.
Offering linear career paths.	Embrace kaleidoscope thinking and alternative career paths. Build on-ramps as well as off-ramps so that professionals and workers of all types can take career interruptions and return later. Reward women who return with advancement possibilities. Maintain employee alumni networks to make possible ongoing communication.
Stating that the company supports the advancement of women.	Make top-level managers accountable for turnover and advancement rates of women. Provide career succession plans that include time off for career interruptions, with rewards for reentry. Monitor the number of men and women in the pipeline for general management and upper-management positions. Consider early field experiences for women who have not yet taken a career interruption, and profit-and-loss experience for women who return once they have reacclimated.

continued

TABLE 6

Changes to Help Firms Retain and Advance Women and Gen X Men cont'd

What Corporations Think Is Sufficient to Be "Family Friendly"	New Approaches for Firms Committed to the Advancement and Retention of Women
Offering a traditional rewards system based on face time, long hours, and travel commitments.	Create rewards systems based on outcomes and actual performance, not face time. Eliminate gender discrimination in wages and benefits, and gender inequities in training and promotion systems. Include feedback from family and friends on work/nonwork balance as part of the evaluation process. Reward managers for developing unique compensation packages.
Offering family-friendly programs.	In addition to programs, foster an organizational culture that encourages and rewards the use of family-friendly programs. Redefine "family" beyond children and provide programs that support caregiving. Consider radical new benefits, such as tuition reimbursement programs for employees' children offered based on length of service, or on-site summer camp programs for employees' children. Make sabbaticals available for long-term employees to encourage fresh new thinking.
Paying lip-service to efforts by government and community groups to create programs that value families.	Support lobbying efforts for government initiatives to help working parents, initiatives such as government-funded day care and paid family leaves, as well as securing the rights of parents and caregivers to a shorter workweek without fear of penalty.

- In Sweden, new mothers receive a year's paid leave, the right to work a six-hour day with full benefits until the child enters primary school, and a governmental stipend to help pay child care expenses. Married couples are taxed independently; women earning less than their husbands are taxed at a lower rate, making it economically worthwhile for women to work.[24]

- In Canada, firms considered family friendly offer the following options: on-site day care, maternity leave, and flexible work options (including telecommuting and job-sharing, extended vacation allowances, extra personal days off, and unpaid leaves of absence as necessity dictates).[25]

- In Norway, there is a "minister of children and equality" position in the governmental cabinet. Norway has recently created legislation to require over the next several years that 40 percent of the board members of that nation's large, publically traded companies be women.[26]

- A 2004 Harvard research report found that 166 of the 168 countries studied provide paid family leave. Only the United States and Australia did not. Australia does give workers a full year of unpaid family leave. In the United States, workers get only twelve weeks of unpaid leave.[27]

In Europe and Canada, citizens think there are solutions—such as shorter workweeks, more flexibility, and longer vacations—to help employees balance work-life issues. People in these countries demand change from their governments and reinforce work-life balance by the way they live their own lives. The Scandinavian countries are seen as the leaders in this arena and are also leading the pack in education reform and social equality as well as the strength of their economies.[28] It should come as no surprise that in Sweden more than 50 percent of the members of the Swedish parliament and 50 percent of cabinet members are women. The more women in high government positions, the greater the likelihood that the country will have positive work-life initiatives.[29]

In Europe, there have been a number of economic, social, cultural, governmental, and legal factors that have contributed to the establishment of family-friendly policies. Several European governments have actively worked to increase women's equality in all areas of life, including employment. These governments have focused on initiatives such as changing societal attitudes toward cohabitation and childbirth outside of marriage; governmental provisions for maternity and child care leave for parents; direct monetary or tax credit support of child care facilities; taxation systems that favor, or at least don't penalize, married women who work; and legislated changes that promote equal opportunities. As an example of the latter, Norway requires that 40 percent of all board seats are filled by women.[30] Governmental initiatives are just some of the factors that have helped individuals in Europe to reconcile family and work responsibilities.

However, the Europeans still have their struggles, with women in particular still finding themselves constrained by their children's school schedules. In France, students have Wednesday afternoons off. In Germany, classes start especially early. In the Netherlands, children are still sent home for lunch. In the United Kingdom, where people still struggle with long work hours, many are rebelling against the idea of spending so much time in their offices and are questioning the concept of "presenteeism" as a means of getting work accomplished. Despite the struggles, these countries have introduced ideas that offer numerous possibilities for U.S. governmental initiatives and organizational actions to help Americans gain better work-life balance.

Perhaps one of the most important lessons that Americans can learn from Europeans relates to their attitude toward work. The philosophy of working to live, rather than living to work, has been widely adopted among many European communities, resulting in a less chaotic and stressful work-family lifestyle. Americans need to reexamine basic attitudes about work and scrutinize whether current governmental policies and typical organizational practices are having a positive effect on working men and women, families, and especially children.

Plus, the United States hides a dirty secret about the real possibility of transforming American organizations and culture to become more family friendly. It's already been done. In 1945 the

United States had child care centers to help the 6 million women who went to work during World War II. Rosie the Riveter would drop off her children, as well as any mending that needed to be done, at the center. While she worked, her children got any immunizations they needed and were taken care of in the center's infirmary if they became ill. When she picked her children up at the end of her shift, she also retrieved the bags of groceries and ready-made dinners she had preordered that morning from the center. However, when the war ended, so did these marvelous centers.[31]

The United States still subsidizes child care for more than two hundred thousand children whose parents are in the military. More than 75 percent of these centers have been independently accredited, compared to 7 percent nationwide. Military caregivers must pass a thirteen-unit course covering subjects such as child development, health and safety, and psychology. These caregivers receive guidance from a monthly newsletter that outlines ideas on scheduling and daily activities as well as from a supervisor who visits daily.[32] So it is possible for U.S. corporations to provide great child care support to working parents; other countries as well as the U.S. government have already shown how it can be done.

FROM MOMMY TRACK TO FAMILY TRACK TO LIFE TRACK

Several years ago, Felice Schwartz published a seminal article in *Harvard Business Review* on the need for flexibility in career pathing so corporations could retain stellar female talent. She believed that, on the one hand, women who are "career-primary" view their careers as the single most important aspect of their lives.[33] These women should receive full training, benefits, and field experiences necessary to ascend to the general management level. On the other hand, some women prefer to prioritize issues of family balance ahead of other concerns. These women should be allowed greater flexibility, but at the price of relinquishing prospects for future advancement. Schwartz's ideas were later dubbed by the media as "the mommy track."

The article created a firestorm of controversy at the time because it suggested a dual ladder for women that would keep some women—those who were "career and family driven," or those who were just "family driven"—set apart from opportunities for advancement. Schwartz argued that the losses for corporations by not providing a flexible workplace for women were considerable. If women aren't granted flexible work arrangements, then of course they will leave. And that's what did happen. Women who didn't have flexible options (plus not having advancement opportunities or challenging work but having plenty of negatives to deal with such as discrimination), opted out.

Although the so-called mommy track isn't the complete answer, today's corporate executives need to expand beyond policies driven by the linear career to consider both women and men who lead lives with a broad spectrum of interests. Parenthood is finally becoming valued. Corporations are starting to realize that employees *do* have a life outside of the office. So it's not just a mommy track or a parent track but a family track. The needs of workers caring for elderly relatives or involved in helping others are also being recognized.

But even the family track is not enough. A quantum cultural leap has taken place in the minds and hearts of employees. With Gen X and Gen Y employees in the workplace, a seismic shift in work values and cultural norms has ripped apart traditional reverence for the corporate pyramid. Employees have moved from mommy-track thinking to daddy-track thinking to parent-track thinking to family-track thinking to *Life-Track* thinking.[34] People are realizing that it is better to work to live, rather than to live to work.

Corporations that recognize the value of their human capital and use the Life-Track approach will encourage men and women to take advantage of family-friendly policies without fear of career or social reprisals. In the past, programs that had the potential to help individuals lead more balanced lives have been implemented by some firms but have been unsuccessful because employees haven't taken advantage of them. For example, parental leave has been available in many firms for quite a while. Yet for years many men refused to take advantage of such policies, fearing that their coworkers would make fun of them for doing so or that they would be taken off the fast track in their careers. In the legal case of *Knussamn v. Maryland,* for instance, a Maryland state trooper brought suit because he was denied parental leave "unless [his] wife [was] dead or in a coma."[35] Unfortunately, many men fail to make use of parental leave because of such negative attitudes, and despite evidence that that the presence of the father at the time of birth and through the early months of an infant's life is necessary for the infant's effective orientation to the world.[36] Likewise, many women who work for hard-driving, competitive firms feel forced to take the shortest maternity leave possible, fearing that they will be seen as less serious about their careers. These women and men end up managing work-life balance in spite of organizations, not with the help of effective policies.[37]

Some companies, however, are implementing polices that recognize that employees have lives outside of work. In their book *Leveraging the New Human Capital,* Sandra Burud and Marie Tumolo examined companies that have transformed themselves into firms that value the idea that individuals want a whole life— one that includes both work and nonwork interests.[38] The four firms are the following.

- DuPont found that employees who were using work-family initiatives were the company's most productive workers, causing leadership to realize that supporting their employees' interest in both work and nonwork pursuits was not only socially responsible but also good business.

- Baxter International was led by CFO Harry Kraemer, who served as a living example of the company's new emphasis on investing in human capital. Kraemer sometimes left meetings to care for a sick child, engaged in community activities such as teaching Sunday school, and regularly posted updates on his daughter Suzie's fourth grade softball team on the home page of the company's Web site.

- First Tennessee Bank found that human capital outcomes, just like financial ones, can be measured and evaluated.

- SAS, a start-up company designed according to the needs of the employees' work and nonwork interests, offers a standard thirty-five-hour workweek, unlimited employee sick days, cutting-edge benefits such as an on-site health center for employees and their families, and learning centers with teaching staff rather than the typical day care centers.

According to Burud and Tumolo, "dual-focus" employees, who emphasize both work and nonwork life aspects, outnumber those who are primarily work focused by three to one.[39] Thus, organizational decision makers, executives, and HR professionals must question entrenched assumptions about their firm's mission and culture that are based on the false idea that the majority of workers are focused primarily on work. They must ask themselves, Does our firm have a culture that permits our employees to be authentic? To be challenged? To have balance? If leaders recognize their employees as the foundation of their company's success—the true source of competitive advantage—they will build a culture that not only values them but that fosters an environment where employees can be their best selves and make their best contributions to the firm.

The Kaleidoscope Career model argues for such a total life perspective. But, unfortunately, most organizations have been loath to recognize these changes. Researcher Jeffery Pfeffer found that only about half of organizations and managers truly believe that people really are their most important asset.[40] And only about half of those organizations actually put the belief into action by adopting human resources initiatives. And only half of these true believers stick with these initiatives over time. While Pfeffer found that some firms like Southwest Airlines and Microsoft do give more than lip service to human resources development, most corporate policies have not kept pace with reality. Requiring employees to remain inside office doors while there is ample wireless technology available for remote work is nothing short of misguided in the current free-agent climate. And there will be a future penalty to pay for such Neanderthal corporate policies. Workers are increasingly becoming disenchanted with vampirelike organizations that fail to provide opportunities for authenticity, balance, and challenge. The exodus of talented women from corporate America has already begun. Which workers are next headed toward the door? But, more important, can organizations do anything to keep qualified workers—women and men—from leaving?

KALEIDOSCOPE CAREERS
AND STRATEGIC THINKING

In Chapter 1, we discussed the concept first articulated by management strategist Rosabeth Moss Kanter, who encourages CEOs and business leaders to think more flexibly. According to Dr. Kanter, kaleidoscope thinking is a blend of concepts, competencies, and connections. It encourages new and innovative ways of branching across systems, strategies, and philosophies to rethink how business can and should be accomplished. Time and space are no longer barriers to working anywhere in the world; the Internet permits continuous transactions, and work can be produced on a worldwide clock. Winning the war for talent will require aspects of mastery, membership, and meaning—the three dimensions of commitment.[41] The best companies, according to Dr. Kanter, realize that "brainpower is to the global information economy as oil was to the industrial economy. Business strategy thus means multi-dimensional and multi-local thinking."[42]

We agree wholeheartedly with Dr. Kanter's approach. Firms that wish to follow the Kaleidoscope Career model must foster a culture that encourages creative ways to blend work, family, and personal needs. This will require a redesign of that work to include more opportunities for challenge, balance, and even authenticity. To do so will require more innovative and inspirational kaleidoscope thinking to break down well-entrenched corporate norms that bifurcate "work" and "family," to discover a new *kaleidoscope* pattern, a pattern that goes beyond the typical *Alpha* and *Beta* patterns that we found in our research.

As an example, an executive at U.S. Robotics shared with *Fortune* magazine an epiphany she had about work-family issues.[43] Shortly after one of her babies was born, she was scheduled to attend a big company event in Salt Lake City. Still breast-feeding, this employee asked her boss if she could bring the baby, as well as her assistant to watch the baby, with her while she attended the meetings. Her boss wondered why someone responsible for a budget worth millions was asking permission for an expenditure of less than one thousand dollars. The woman responded that it was not the money but the precedent. The boss asked what was best for the business: for her to come to Salt Lake City, any way she could, or for her to stay home with the baby? Obviously, it was better for the business for the nursing mother to attend the meetings in Salt Lake City—so she did.

Corporations need to take seriously the moral to the story: that the intersection of work and family often affects business decisions and that there are options—win-win solutions—that are best for both the business and family. This would be the foundation of the future kaleidoscope pattern—a career and life pattern that integrates both work and family lives. It is possible to re-create a company culture that truly supports personal lives as well as business goals. Organizational leaders will then begin to recognize that what is good for employees is also good for business and give more than lip service to the idea that people are the most important asset.

How then can organizations put the Kaleidoscope Career model into motion? It boils down to these five basic steps.

1. Create a vision based on the fundamental principle that workers want authenticity, balance, and challenge in their lives.

2. Build commitment to the vision at all levels, especially with the help of change champions who not only talk about integrating the ABCs of the Kaleidoscope Career model throughout all organizational systems but also walk the talk in their own lives.

3. Take action to turn the vision into reality, because vision without action, without successful implementation, kills employees' hope.

4. Continuously support the vision and its implementation by committing adequate resources to training, development, incentives, equipment, and the like. Ensure not only that performance is equitably rewarded but that benefits are equitable and employees who need the most assistance but may be the least able to afford it receive more benefits.[44]

5. Measure attitudes, behaviors, and other outcomes and, based on the data obtained, make changes—big and small—

to keep pace with, and even anticipate, organizational and environmental changes.

CREATING INNOVATIVE KALEIDOSCOPE CAREER HR PRACTICES

Firms that accept the necessity of the Kaleidoscope Career approach can start to experiment with new ways to structure themselves to permit employees to experience authenticity, balance, and challenge. But changes in structure must occur within the context of a culture that recognizes that all employees are on the life track and that great synergies can exist between work and life roles.

The leaders of the company JetBlue Airways know this well.[45] In the global, wired economy, companies often set up reservation offices or telephone help desks in many different cities—or even countries. But JetBlue, based at New York's Kennedy Airport, is unusual in that its entire workforce of 550 reservation agents work from the comfort of their own homes, most of them near Salt Lake City. Mothers serve JetBlue as reservation agents while watching their kids play outside a living room window. The new phrase for this concept is "homeshoring," as opposed to "outsourcing." Rather than send jobs around the globe, com-panies can utilize the talents of a cadre of stay-at-home moms and dads who work when then their children are at school or playing in the backyard.[46]

JetBlue found a win-win solution to a common work/life dilemma. And, an added bonus, JetBlue saves 20 percent for each flight booked by agents working from home instead of from a call center. The turnover rate for these JetBlue employees is a mere 10 percent. JetBlue doesn't care what its reservation agents wear while taking calls—robes and slippers are fine—but the company does insist that customers don't hear sounds of the home, such as crying children or blaring cartoons in the background. Employees attend monthly meetings to check in, and supervisors monitor calls from time to time to ensure that all a customer hears is a friendly voice and a keyboard. JetBlue has made technology work for them; and what was best for the employees has had a measurable impact on the firm's bottom line. JetBlue has happy employees and happy customers. JetBlue has won numerous awards; in 2004, these included Best U.S. Airline by the University of Nebraska Airline Quality Survey; Best Domestic Airline by *Conde Nast Traveler* Readers' Choice Awards; Best Domestic Airline by *Conde Nast Traveler* Business Travel Awards; Airline Customer Loyalty Award from *Brandweek* magazine; and Airline Excellence, Best Low Cost Airline, and Best North America Cabin Staff from Skytrax Airline of the Year Survey.[47]

Traditional brick-and-mortar companies built on the hierarchical manufacturing age structure are no longer necessary. For example, firms can be conceived not as pyramids but as "jungle gyms," where opportunities for lateral, diagonal, downward, upward, and opting-out career moves are legitimate.[48] Within the jungle gym there are many avenues to the top, and there is more room at the top because power and rewards are shared among many rather than the few. On the jungle gym, there is freedom to move laterally without being seen as plateaued. Some move diagonally into new areas of cross learning. Others even move out and then back in, returning with knowledge and skills gained in other organizations or entrepreneurial endeavors, or during leaves taken for personal development, to nurture children, to care for elderly relatives, or to provide service to the community. The jungle gym concept permits the horizontal entry and exit of people into the core from the bottom, side, and even the top. Individuals are free to move about and decide where their motivation and talent will carry them. Individuals are also free to choose the pace at which they move; they can climb quickly or take a slower, more flexible approach.

Such changes in structure don't occur in isolation. Compensation and benefit systems must be adjusted so that salary and raises are tied not to level or organizational tenure but to performance. Likewise, training processes must be adjusted to meet the needs of many different types of workers with different needs beyond the traditional orientation training and educational programs linked to life stage (e.g., retirement planning). Old assumptions that focused training on new employees and fast trackers need to be replaced with the idea that individuals—regardless of age or organizational level—desire training opportunities and the chance for challenging on-the-job growth assignments. Leaders, subordinates, and co-workers take on developmental roles, sometimes providing information and feedback, other times serving as mentors, coaches, or guides. Learning is not confined to the classroom or special conferences but occurs every day.

Applying a kaleidoscope approach to formulate career development requires creativity in thinking—and in planning. Beverly Kaye, in her book *Up Is Not the Only Way*, identified seven career options: upward, downward, lateral, exploratory, enrichment, realignment, and diagonal.[49] This set of options closely aligns with the Kaleidoscope Career approach. The truth is that not everyone gets to the top of his or her firm—nor does everyone have that goal. A multitude of options—such as learning in place (enrichment); moving downward to forge a new career path, say from engineering to marketing (realignment); and pursuing an educational alternative or taking two years off to rear a family (exploratory)—are all part of the mix for the new employee. At different points in the kaleidoscope life cycle, workers may wish to move up, down, or allow themselves to become realigned. Corporations need to legitimize these Kaleidoscope Career options so that employees are aware that development can take place in a multitude of ways depending on their interests and the company's creativity in making a variety of options and benefits available.

The Kaleidoscope Career model requires that corporate human resources planning be turned inside out so that focus is placed on the total experience of people's lives. Because our research shows that people have needs for authenticity, balance, and challenge, and that sometimes these needs interact differently at unique points of the life cycle, especially for women, corporations must be redesigned to accommodate this natural human search for need fulfillment. The Kaleidoscope Career pattern is possible. Corporations can be ethically authentic, responsible toward balance, yet provide challenges for productivity. In fact, these ideas can and should be used to recruit and attract the best talent as well as to retain those workers for the future. In the following sections we give some specific ideas that corporations can use as the basis for rethinking their structures to better attract and retain qualified, competent people.

Ways to Support the Quest for Authenticity

Our research found that individuals are searching for meaning in their work and in their lives. They want to discover (or rediscover) who they are. They want to come to know and to express their true selves. They are tired of putting on a false mask and hiding their real wants and needs when they enter the office door. Organizations can help employees fulfill this parameter of the Kaleidoscope Career model. We offer three major ways in which organizations can assist employees in their quest for authenticity.

First, to aid the quest for authenticity, firms should focus on corporate social responsibility. In this age of Enron and the Arthur Andersen implosion, stock market scandals, and CEO debacles, there is a growing interest in corporate ethics and social responsibility. Gen X and Gen Y workers are more likely to be attracted to firms that have a strong sense of corporate social responsibility than ever before. For example, the ice cream company Ben and Jerry's is well known for behaving as a good corporate citizen. The company not only supports its local community through its employee-led community action teams but also funds grassroots organizations for social change though the Ben and Jerry's Foundation. The company Web site provides "50 Ways to Promote Peace" as well as information on its initiative to "Lick Global Warming." Ben and Jerry's goes out of its way to help others; for example, the company secures its vanilla beans from disadvantaged countries and its brownies from a New York bakery that employs those who have a hard time becoming employed. Additionally, the firm honors its own roots by providing advice to small business owners, especially those led by minorities.

Timberland, the maker of boots and shoes located in New Hampshire, also has strong social objectives. The firm has developed several community programs targeted to improving youth leadership in Boston and has actively worked with Habitat for Humanity. Repeatedly recognized by *Fortune* magazine as one of the best companies to work for in America, Timberland is known for nurturing the whole employee through programs that provide paid time off for volunteer work, monetary aid for adoptions, and paid time off for elder care. On the firm's twenty-fifth anniversary, the company closed operations so employees could contribute to community activities.

And one of the best-known corporations that models authenticity is Harpo Productions. Lead by CEO Oprah Winfrey, who has not received the recognition she deserves as an excellent business leader, Harpo Productions has not only raised awareness of world problems but is involved in building rural schools in ten countries (e.g., China, Mexico, Haiti, Ghana), supporting women's shelters, and building youth centers and homes. The Oprah Winfrey Scholars Program gives scholarships to students dedicated to using their education to give back to their communities. The Use Your Life Awards helps individuals who have made a difference in the lives of others expand their programs and help even more people. The Angel Network has raised more than $27 million for charity, with all administrative costs covered personally by Oprah. Through her daily TV show, magazine, telefilms, motion pictures, and Web site, Oprah and Harpo Productions spread the message that individuals should create their own best lives and do something meaningful with those lives. Oprah says, "I want you to open your hearts and see the world in a different way. I promise this will change your life for the better."[50] The types of socially responsible programs exemplified by Ben and Jerry's, Timberland, Harpo Productions, and other companies attract younger workers while providing older workers who are searching for greater authenticity in their lives a way to find meaning through their work.

Second, firms should renew company efforts to promote total wellness—in mind, body, and spirit. Some companies have realized the importance of focusing on employee health beyond the corporate health care copay. Companies have provided their employees with on-site gyms, sponsored stress management and relaxation classes including yoga and tai chi, provided mental health and family counseling, funded treatments for addictions, and provided on-site ministers and spiritual guides. Nationwide Financial Services, the insurance and financial services company, for example, used an approach that combined many different wellness programs. Motivated by creating a competitive company environment in an effort to compete in a possible war for talent, the company upgraded its employee work-life benefits programs to include a full fitness center at its headquarters in Columbus, Ohio, and clubs geared to employee interests, whether in astronomy, bird watching, or chess.[51]

Other companies have gone beyond programs to infuse their employees with the sense that the company truly cares about their well-being. For instance, Townsend Engineering, a company that designs and manufactures meat-processing equipment, provides each employee with a free five-hour medical exam. One of those physicals allowed physicians to discover that an employee's long-standing liver disease had reached the critical point and a transplant was needed. When he heard of the employee's plight, the CEO of Townsend put his three company pilots on standby for when a donor liver became available.[52]

Companies also promote total wellness by leaders inspiring and empowering their workers. Madolyn Johnson, CEO of Signature Homestyles (formerly The Homemaker's Idea Company), left the teaching profession to become an entrepreneur for a combination of reasons, including her desire to empower women as other women had empowered her. Madolyn told the story of how one of her employees was battling breast cancer. The woman said that she was able to beat the disease because the company had given her the opportunity to learn who she was and what she could accomplish. Madolyn said,

Nothing can compare to reaching out to another person and watching them blossom and grow as an individual. As women, we wear so many hats. We're often not recognized for our own accomplishments. The greatest excitement for me is to recognize and help women as they personally grow and achieve their dreams. At Signature Homestyles, they learn that they can dream and follow their dreams.

There are many types of programs that companies can initiate to enhance the total person—mind, body, and soul. Some companies, such as Xerox and the Container Store, offer sabbaticals. At PricewaterhouseCoopers, for instance, trainees are offered leaves that can be used to care for dependents, to increase maternity leave, for paternity leave, to do volunteer work, or for travel.[53]

Every seven years, partners at the accounting and consulting firm Plante and Moran are given a paid four-week sabbatical; they are encouraged to do no work whatsoever, including no e-mail or voice mail.[54] The J. M. Smucker Company gives their workers unlimited paid time off to volunteer in their community.[55] Still other companies, such as NerveWire and Netscape, have pet-friendly office policies.[56] The Container Store offers yoga, stretching classes, monthly chair massages, and online exercise and nutrition diaries that are personalized to each individual employee. TDIndustries, a facilities management and construction company, pays 100 percent of an employee's tuition, fees, and books at any state-supported university, provides twelve weeks of paid personal time off after three years of employment, and indexes health insurance premiums to income so entry-level employees can more easily afford to cover their whole families.[57]

Third, firms should help individuals find meaning in their work so employees can make a difference, have an impact on others, and come to know themselves better. Giving employees freedom and trust can help them fulfill their potential. The Container Store (TCS) is a firm that treats its employees with respect and creates a culture of support. In addition to being a leader in extrinsic rewards, paying above the industry averages in salary and benefits, TCS has created a work environment that provides high levels intrinsic rewards. In a survey of TCS employees 94 percent said their work for the company "made a difference." The survey showed that there is a climate of mutual respect that pervades the firm; 98 percent thought it was a friendly place to work, and 97 percent believed that people at TCS care about one another. The company's books are open, so everyone knows the firm's financial status. Employees have the freedom to address customer concerns and are even able to spend money to fix problems without first seeking permission from management to do so. TCS encourages employees to expand their minds, with first-year employees receiving 235 hours of formal training and all employees receiving 162 hours of training a year. Employees with ten years of tenure are encouraged to take a sabbatical. People think TCS is such a great place to work that over 40 percent of the firm's new hires come from referrals from current employees.[58]

Likewise, many companies go to great lengths to foster the pride employees feel in working for the firm. In her book *HR from the Heart: Inspiring Stories and Strategies for Building the People Side of Great Businesses,* former Southwest Airlines employee Libby Sartain describes the enduring pride workers at Southwest have for the firm as demonstrated at the funeral of a longtime employee.[59] Sartain writes, "I approached her open casket to say farewell and was thunderstruck to see what she was wearing. Of all the beautiful clothes in her closet, her family had chosen the garment that meant the most to her in her adult life: her People Department denim shirt."

While some firms focus on creating mutual trust or pride in the firm, other companies focus on instilling freedom in their employees. For instance, consider how the software company Great Plains (now a division of Microsoft) demonstrated the respect they had for their employees by not only showing trust in them and giving them freedom but also by respecting the needs of the whole person. One of the firm's valued employees was offered a promotion but didn't want to leave her home in California to transfer to Fargo, North Dakota. The company was able to come up with a win-win solution to this problem that companies often face. The firm still promoted her to the senior position in marketing, and she still stayed in California; because the firm wanted to retain this talented individual and wanted her to be happy, they permitted her to telecommute to Fargo. The same employee also worked part-time for three months so she could finish her MBA. Doug Burgum, Great Plains chairman and CEO at the time, explained why the company's system worked so well: "We put people through a vigorous hiring process and through a lot of interviews. Once they're part of the team, we say, 'We trust you. From day one, you get a key to the building. You get a laptop. You become an equal member of our community, and we trust that you're going to pull your weight.'"[60]

Following is a summary of ways organizations can support authenticity in Kaleidoscope Careers.

- Give paid corporate sabbaticals of three to six months to pursue education or community service activities

- Provide corporate wellness programs, focusing on health and the whole person

- Offer workshops on spirituality and finding a higher purpose in life and work

- Establish corporate social responsibility programs that allow employees to participate in programs such as Habitat for Humanity or in walk-a-thons for charity

- Provide centralized corporate gyms and recreation centers so employees can maintain their health while on-site

- Offer workshops that address hot-button issues such as assertiveness or negotiating skills

- Establish a time bank of free hours that employees can use for leisure interests

- Establish employee clubs for interests such as golf, tennis, chess, crafts, and dancing

Ways to Achieve Improved, More Realistic Balance

Until recently flexibility has been treated with a passing nod and little real change. With the advantages of technology, firms can help reshape career paths to recognize the increasing complexities of Kaleidoscope Careers, especially in the area of improving balance. Workers are tired of having to "hide" their children, their elderly relatives, and their personal concerns. Although there are some companies that provide ample leave for medical appointments, snow days when children are home from school, and the last-minute necessity of picking up poster paper for a child's forgotten project assignment, the culture of work causes people to feel that such activities are devalued. The fact is that people have lives to lead, and if their work for the day is accomplished and no urgent meetings or e-mails are pending, why must they sit in their offices? Work can and should be made flexible, not just in daytime hours, but over the arc of a career.

Flexibility can exist beyond the boundaries of standard corporate rules. Job-sharing, reduced work hours, and other flextime

arrangements become possible when the work is designed cre-
atively. When systems are in place so that employees can make rec-
ommendations for improved work schedules—and see their
suggestions actually implemented—then the very fabric of work
will be redesigned so that it is truly family friendly.[61] One example
of such work redesign was suggested by Sally, a female security
guard. Sally requested flextime, the ability to determine her own
hours, and a laptop so she could work at home. Her request was
initially met with a resounding no. Yet as Sally explained her
rationale, it became apparent that the security guards—men and
women alike—had already developed a workable solution: a flexible time schedule in which all hours were covered but were different from the standard eight-hour corporate shift. In addition, the
security guards were responsible for some paperwork that could be
accomplished from home if they were provided with laptops. The
answer to Sally's and the other guards' time needs seems simple in
retrospect. It illustrates that employees themselves often hold the
key to maintaining workplace effectiveness while permitting work-
life balance.[62]

Reduced load options and job sharing may be a real alternative
for overly stressed workers. In their large-scale study on reduced-
load work for professionals and managers, professors Ellen Ernst
Kossek and Mary Dean Lee found that 77 percent of their sample
of fifty-four employers stated that "compared to five years ago,
there are more professionals and managers working reduced loads
in their firms."[63] Even top jobs can be job shared, as shown by Gary
Newman and Dana Walden, presidents of 20th Century Fox Television. Both are company presidents responsible jointly for the performance of the entire company. As a consequence of sharing the
top job, both Newman and Walden have greater freedom to participate in their families' lives.[64]

How pervasive are flexible work schedules? The U.S. Department of Labor reports that about 29 million full-time, salaried
workers have schedules that permit them to vary the start and end
time of work, a number that represents a 50 percent increase from
just ten years ago. Approximately 33 percent of these individuals
worked flexible hours as part of a formal employee-sponsored pro-

gram. Surprisingly, men (30 percent), perhaps because of higher positions in their firms, were slightly more likely to have flexible schedules than women (27 percent).[65] Although about 29 percent of the labor force has some degree of schedule flexibility, it's puzzling that the percentage is not greater, especially because firms typically rated as the best to work for often emphasize this aspect. For example, *Working Mother* magazine's recent list of "Best Companies for Working Mothers" reported the following major trends among their winners: no rollbacks of work-life benefits despite the recent economic downturn; increased emphasis on flexible scheduling; and augmented use of family leave.[66] Stellar examples include companies such as

- Bristol-Myers Squibb, which provides a full range of child care options and gives managers training on flexible scheduling

- Eli Lilly and Company, which offers comprehensive flexible scheduling and job-guaranteed leave for new moms

- Fannie Mae (Federal National Mortgage Association) and General Mills, both of which offer programs for the advancement of women and promote flexible scheduling options

Fortune magazine's recent list of the "100 Best Companies to Work For" also emphasized companies that have adopted flexible schedules. *Fortune*'s list includes such winners as Sun Microsystems, where an overwhelming 95 percent of its workforce enjoys flexible schedules, and PricewaterhouseCoopers, where once unheard of flexibility has penetrated the management ranks of this traditional accounting firm and 10 percent of the partners have adopted flexible schedules.[67]

Work-family benefit cultures have been positively related to commitment and negatively related to intentions to leave the firm.[68] Maureen Smith, who was profiled in Chapter 2, related a story about bringing her baby, her firstborn son, to her office at Fox Broadcasting.

My husband and I were both working at Fox in 1990. I was
the first female there in the executive ranks who was married
and had a baby. My boss said, "Let's try something new."
I was able to bring in my baby—crib and all—to the office for
the first six months, three days each week. My son went with
me to meetings and everywhere I went. People in the building
would take "baby breaks" to come play with him and get reju-
venated. In fact, after the first three months, my husband's
boss felt she wasn't seeing enough of the baby, so she arranged
that he could bring in our son to my husband's office on
Fridays. I remember a story she told me about my husband
giving a presentation via conference call and at the same time
changing a diaper on the conference room table. I'm proud to
say he never missed a beat and the people on the other end of
the call never even knew he was multitasking.

Firms that develop a culture that honors work and family are
likely to create true flexibility in the workplace. When bosses
encourage workers to blend the line between work and family as
part of the work culture, parents can be more productive. Recently,
Maureen left TLC Entertainment and headed to the television network Animal Planet as executive vice president and general manager, in a quest to create even more creative, family-oriented
programming—this time about animals. When asked why she
returned to a programming position despite loving the lifestyle of
running her own production company and coming and going as she
pleased, she responded:

I love the opportunity to work at Animal Planet, because this
allowed me to pursue my childhood dream of working with
animals while also being a perfect outlet for my career skills.
Most importantly, I am working for a company [Discovery
Communications] that celebrates and nurtures work-life bal-
ance. That was a critical factor in my decision to return to the
corporate world. Judith McHale, our president and CEO, is
an amazing woman, and Discovery is always ranked as one of
the top companies for working parents. Here there is a recog-

nition that we are people with a full life, and that makes us better employees.[69]

Moreover, firms that redesign work by eliminating unnecessary tasks and by encouraging flexible and alternative work arrangements reduce the need for many traditional work-family programs. For example, the JetBlue reservations agents—and other telecommuters—don't need child care centers because they work from home. Although no company can be perfect in its management systems, flexible practices from top-rated firms can serve as starting points for other firms considering how to slow the climbing attrition rates of women in their firms. Moreover, although face time in the office is lower in family-friendly firms, job performance is just as high, and organizational commitment is higher than in firms with less family-friendly environments, suggesting that work-life programs are good for both employees and the bottom line.[70]

But flexibility in work arrangements is only part of the solution. Developing programs that allow for natural "stop-outs" (long-term, five years or more, absences) and "opt-outs" (short-term, one to two years' absences from the firm) over the course of a career is vital if the Kaleidoscope Career model is to be actualized in high-performing firms. A recent study of long-term career interruptions suggests that the negative career stigma may be decreasing for those who take a career interruption, or "stop out."[71] Realizing that the Kaleidoscope Career model suggests that women may need to take time off to handle aspects of their lives, firms can create career pathways that allow women to do so without penalty of losing their jobs. Corporations need to create better on-ramps as well as off-ramps—positions that allow for career interruptions or part-time downscaling of the work at hand.

Paid and unpaid corporate sabbaticals are slowly catching on, with General Mills and other firms offering a carrot of a one-year leave to women on global assignments so that they can obtain international experience needed for corporate advancement.[72] Deloitte Touche Tohmatsu has created an unpaid leave policy of up to five years as a means of facilitating career interruptions for employees who wish to take time off to settle family or personal concerns.[73] IBM has long been a leader in developing "alumni relations networks," policies that allow former employees in good standing to be readmitted to the firm. These so-called boomerangs often do not return to jobs equivalent to their previous level, but they usually are placed within the former area of responsibility.[74] For instance, one of our interviewees, Ronnie DiNucci, is an IBM boomerang. She left IBM for sixteen years and returned to a job in her old department. Ronnie maintained the tenure she had from her previous years of working for the firm, so her vacation time and all the perks she had at the time she departed were reinstated. Said Ronnie, "I chose not to return to a management job because I wanted time to catch up on new systems and procedures. After all, I had been gone sixteen years! There are people who have returned to their former jobs, others to new jobs in other departments, and still others who return at a lower level." IBM matches returning employees to positions on an individual-by-individual basis, balancing job availability with the wishes of the returning employee.

HR professionals must identify innovative policies to create such stop-out and opt-out options. One case example from our research concerned Mallory, a woman who left her job at the Social Security Administration to rear twins and care for an elderly relative. Ten years later, feeling the pressure of college tuition on her, Mallory elected to return to her old job in the same area of responsibility. She was denied a management position so instead took basic pay as an assistant claims officer. Two years later, the HR office recommended that Mallory receive a promotion to manager of the unit. Five years later she earned the position of administrative head. The HR department monitored Mallory's progress, rewarding her based on performance and not on uninterrupted company tenure.

Human resources managers must carefully examine the lives of their women employees and redesign career planning and development so as to adopt more of a total life cycle perspective. They need to develop corporate-sanctioned options on how careers can be enacted over the life cycle. HR planning should be flexible enough so that employees have choices. Some employees may prefer to use alternate work arrangements and rear children simultaneously.

Others may prefer to focus first on their careers and then take time out later to rear children or work part-time.

Researchers, like those at the Center for Work-Life Policy (CWLP), have begun to study how companies can develop better on-ramps as well as off-ramps for women.[75] The CWLP team reported that among women who do take off-ramps, the overwhelming majority fully intend to return to the workforce someday. Many of the women studied cite financial reasons for wanting to get back to work: 46 percent wanted their own source of income, 35 percent reported that their household income was no longer sufficient for family needs, and 24 percent said that their partner's income was no longer sufficient for family needs. But other women, most notably teachers and physicians, said "the enjoyment and satisfaction" they derive from their careers was an important reason to return to the workforce. Unfortunately, the CWLP found that only 74 percent of women who want to rejoin the ranks of the employed manage to do so, and only 40 percent return to full-time professional jobs.

Likewise, researchers at the MIT Workplace Center, a think tank that examines work-life issues, suggest that basic assumptions about how work is designed must be challenged to support women.[76] They recommend that firms examine how to streamline work processes. For instance, an important distinction to be made is the difference between "quiet time," time in which work is accomplished without unnecessary interruptions, and "interactive time," time in which high-quality communication among workers is required. Managers and coworkers learn to respect these differences so that time is used effectively, reducing the need for working late nights and weekends.

Some firms are beginning to apply the principles suggested by these research studies. For instance, companies, like the consulting firm Booz Allen, have attempted to find ways to allow their consultants to balance work and life and still serve clients.[77] The key to the program is Booz Allen's effort to unbundle the standard series of tasks that run on and on in consulting engagements and identify chunks that can be done by telecommuting or short stints in the office. For Booz Allen, this is a way to maintain ties to consultants who have already proved their worth with a client while allowing them time to ramp up or ramp down as needed. Many of these part-timers will return to full-time employment, and it is most likely that they will return to Booz Allen when the time is right. The experiences of Booz Allen and other firms demonstrate that off-ramps don't have to be one-way tickets out of the corporation. While those choosing to use off- and on-ramps are more likely to have slower progress in career advancement, such options give employees choices and permit them to remain connected to the workforce and on track with the firm.

Another company that is using a more integrative approach is Covenant Healthcare of Milwaukee. The company offers workers a choice of shift lengths, ranging from four to twelve hours, as well as solid benefits, ample maternity and time off policies, and laptops so work can be done at home. And the firm realizes that some working mothers prefer part-time work; 80 percent of Covenant's nurses work part-time.[78]

Corporations need to create better on-ramps as well as off-ramps—positions that allow for career interruptions or part-time downscaling of the work at hand. They can also create "slow lanes" and "fast lanes," which are no different than the current systems used by HR professionals to identify individuals who may be high-potential versus average performers, except that in this case employees rather than the HR office choose which lane to take. Now is the time for HR professionals and their organizations to be proactive, creative, and innovative, rather than reactive. By constructing a corporate culture that allows for and respects all pathways—allowing employees to opt out, stop out, take interruptions, be boomerangs, maintain alumni relations, and work part-time— the Kaleidoscope Career model will reduce barriers and provide a smoother natural process of career development.

Such on-ramps and off-ramps may also be useful in helping older workers phase into retirement, or "unretire" and return to work for the firm on a part-time or project-to-project basis. Although retirement used to be described as the time when workers declined and older workers were seen as contributing less and less to their organizations as they disengaged to play golf and spoil their grandchildren, that is no longer the case. Our research found that retirement does not have to be a black hole for productivity. As older individuals yearn for greater authenticity in their lives, they wish to pursue leisure pursuits and volunteer activities. Some people, like the late Johnny Carson of NBC's *Tonight Show*, may retire and never look back. Others may wish to continue to stay connected part-time but have more freedom to travel and pursue leisure activities. Some may take a time-out for a few years, test the retirement waters, and then return as a consultant, mentor, or outsourced or part-time employee.

As more Gen X and Gen Y men, who typically have more similar values and career patterns to women than the baby boomer and Greatest Generation men, continue to move into the workforce and start families or care for their elderly parents, these issues that have long been highly relevant for working women may also become more and more relevant for men. For example, a poll by Radcliff Harris reported that 70 percent of men in their twenties said that they would trade money for time with their children.[79] In the same way that not all women should be treated as part of the same mold, Gen X and Gen Y men are not like previous generations of men. In our survey, for example, younger men said their number one choice for corporate benefits was "a firm that built flextime into all levels."[80] HR managers should begin to plan for how this total life cycle approach can be more fully applied to men's, as well as women's, Kaleidoscope Career patterns.

In addition to organizational programs, there needs to be better integration of governmental policy with work-life balance. For example, in an effort to ensure better work-life balance and attract corporations to the city, the businesses and the public school district of Des Moines, Iowa, joined forces to create the Downtown School.[81] This revolutionary project began in 1990 when nineteen local firms donated office space, used furniture, carpets, and office supplies to create a school located in the city's business district. Skywalks connect the elementary school's two locations with nearby office buildings, making it easy for working parents to drop off and pick up their children and even stop by during the day for school-sponsored activities. Des Moines' innovative school program, coupled with its low cost of living, is attracting workers and companies alike. Des Moines provides a model for other cities of how work-life balance can be an integrated seamless balance.

Cities should follow Des Moines' example and examine ways to create such innovative work-life programs. The federal government should also take steps to improve work-life balance of U.S. workers. Such actions might include reducing the length of the paid workweek; increasing paid vacation time; classifying child care and elder care as allowable business expenses for tax purposes; fostering the creation of more quality part-time jobs, with prorated benefits and pension plans; giving tax breaks to individuals who are reentering the workforce; and providing tuition reimbursement programs for loyal employees. Executive women and men should argue for policies within their own firms as well as vote with their checkbooks and political ballots for policies that enhance the quality of life at work. Following is a summary of the ways organizations can support balance in Kaleidoscope Careers.

- Give each employee a time bank of paid parenting leave

- Restructure retirement plans

- Allow opt-out career interruptions of one or two years

- Allow stop-out career interruptions of two to ten years

- Offer reduced-hours careers to allow employees to return home for children's after-school activities

- Allow job-sharing

- Maintain active part-time job listings

- Offer alumni status with rehiring programs, creating "boomerangs"

- Provide "tech for flex" programs so workers can work remotely from home or other locations

- Provide health care benefits for part-time workers of long standing

- Offer on-site day care or make it readily available

- Provide benefits for long tenure, benefits such as partial college tuition reimbursement for employees' children

- Reward and promote individuals who effectively use flexible schedules and are role models for others in their use

- Redefine family to include relatives besides children and provide programs that support caregiving

- Offer vacation and summer camp programs so children can be on-site when school is not in session

Ways to Achieve Greater Challenge and Less Discrimination

Challenge is a potent motivator, and when workers no longer have a sense of challenge in their work, they move on to other firms (men) or move out of the workforce (women). The Kaleidoscope Career model suggests that challenge remains a visible and powerful drive for many men, but also for women who choose to challenge themselves through other venues inside and outside of the office. Firms wishing to retain talented workers need to examine the level of challenge and support they are providing.

In an effort to promote and retain qualified workers, firms must provide advancement opportunities that allow for executive development, especially for women, who are leaving corporate America in record numbers. Rather than the standard progression from entry-level analyst to associate to manager, and in midcareer assignments that include international and field experience, why not invest in field and international experience early—when people usually have fewer family obligations and are more willing to travel? For example, by investing in women's talents from the beginning, firms will be able to allow women to opt out and opt back in more easily so that career paths aren't truncated later. When the kaleidoscope turns, and women choose to return to the firm, because they already have the necessary field experiences, a vital profit-and-loss assignment might be considered within a few years of rejoining the workforce.

Likewise, men who opt out to become Mr. Moms for a period of time should not be dismissed out of hand during the recruitment and selection process. As Ann Crittenden details in her book *If*

You've Raised Kids, You Can Manage Anything, parenting skills are transferable to the workplace.[82] Demeaning stereotypes of the empty-headed stay-at-home mom or the out-of-touch, unassertive Mr. Mom need to be revealed for the falsehoods they are. Parenting needs to be seen as a valuable training ground for business.

Moreover, the top-rated companies for the advancement of women have cultures that support and reinforce the advancement of women and hold senior managers accountable for these numbers. Managers must be held accountable for the attainment of goals regarding the promotion and advancement of women and be granted rewards for doing so. Research has found that structured hiring and promotion procedures that hold managers accountable reduce decision-making biases.[83] Structured procedures and specific measures should be used to determine whether managers are providing women with key learning and work experiences that will cultivate the skills necessary for advancement. For example, NAFE's "2004 Top 30 Companies" list focuses not only on how many women hold senior profit-and-loss positions but also on how many women in middle management have experience to be viable pipeline candidates.[84] NAFE's "2005 Top 30 Companies" had the practice of setting goals regarding women's advancement and measuring whether these goals had been met. Some made use of traditional human resources policies but with a twist. For instance, Colgate-Palmolive spends four of its yearly succession-planning meetings examining high-potential women and minorities. Procter and Gamble has a policy that top managers must identify three possible successors, one being a woman or minority to be groomed for the position. Compuware supports female employees' participation in Menttium, a one-year mentor program that pairs protégés with mentors external to the firm.[85]

Likewise, firms should collect and analyze data to eliminate gender inequalities. Companies can benchmark their practices against those of other companies to improve their own policies. For instance, IBM conducts annual audits of the base pay of women and minorities. When an inequity is found, a recommendation is made to the manager, who either implements the raise or provides a written explanation of why the raise should not be given. The manager's manager must also explain in writing why the raise was not implemented. If the department lacks funding for the raise, headquarters provides it. IBM's system is unique in that it looks for one standard deviation of difference while other companies that use this process typically look for two standard deviations.[86]

Top companies for women engage in activities such as monitoring the number of women and men rotating into operating roles; developing formal job rotation policies that identify and train high-potential women; developing women's networks; developing skill-based mentoring programs for women that focus on solving specific operating and management problems; fostering a culture that is favorable to the development of informal mentoring relationships; making available on-the-job learning assignments designed to prepare women for leadership positions; and offering leadership forums, conferences, and training programs for women that sharpen the type of bottom-line skills that lead to career advancement. NAFE provides the following examples of female-friendly programs:

- Formal job rotations, similar to the health insurer Well-Point's program, which trains and identifies high-potential women for profit-and-loss responsibilities

- Skill-based mentoring programs, such as IBM's "subnets" of ten to twenty women who meet monthly to brainstorm about specific operational and management programs

- Flexible fast tracks, such as Federated Department Stores' part-time executive program that supports women's decisions to work part-time by permitting them to retain their management positions[87]

Firms wishing to retain talented women need to examine the level of challenge and support they are providing and ensure that professional women gain critical field experience early in their careers—perhaps ahead of their child-rearing years—and that training continues throughout their careers. A renewed focus on the early development of women, knowing that some might take time off to rear their children or care for elderly relatives, may be the key. Some practices that might support a Kaleidoscope Career approach include the following.

- Long-term succession planning that allows for career interruptions

- The requirement of early field experience, especially for women

- International assignments early in the career

- Training programs that ease reacclimation of boomerangs on their return to the workforce

- Alumni networks that keep former employees "in the know"

- Training on new processes, equipment, and services for potential boomerangs and those on sabbaticals and leaves

- Recognition of skills and knowledge gained during personal leaves, career interruptions, and nonwork activities, including parenting and community service, in job placement decisions

- Job banks that give potential boomerangs first priority of consideration over external candidates

- Corporate expectations that former employees will be welcomed back with open arms as full-time, part-time, or contract workers

But challenge involves more than removing structural sources of discrimination that insidiously or openly affect career planning. The Kaleidoscope Career model suggests that real challenges, in the form of meaty, interesting, stimulating work assignments, are the key. With the advent of worldwide outsourcing of heretofore menial tasks, the remaining jobs may need to be redesigned so that they have a more full, complete, strategic challenge component. Noted *New York Times* columnist Thomas Friedman relates a story of a visit he made to the front lines in Afghanistan, permitting him a glimpse of how the U.S. Armed Forces conduct their business and provide challenge to "employees."[88] He noted that on one computer screen pictures were being uploaded from one of the "drone" aircraft that patrol the skies. Although in the past army generals would be right on the scene issuing orders, the new army merely sends the drone images to a location in the United States, where a lower-level officer takes the input, makes strategic decisions for the drone aircraft, and plots a new course. With the advent of technology, lower-level workers may have more opportunities to make strategic decisions than in the past when such decisions were made by only the few of the highest ranks. These types of technology-driven jobs challenge workers' intellects and infuse pride for their work, while permitting them to work with teammates and gather information from distant locations.

HR managers need to examine jobs and determine how to instill them with challenge and meaning so that workers stay motivated and prideful. One key is making technology work for the workers rather than having workers become slaves to technology. For instance, consider how one manager used technology to change how business was usually done at Ford Motor Company. Traditionally, e-commerce teams (based in Dearborn, Michigan) moved to a pilot retail site full-time, having weekly in-person meetings with architects and other agencies. This required a major relocation for the team that would sometimes last for weeks or even months. For the company's planned pilot retail store in San Diego, the manager and her team decided to stay in Dearborn, replacing face-to-face meetings with conference calls and videoconferencing. Travel expenses were greatly reduced, and team members could spend more time with their families.[89]

Global business perspectives present new challenges, and employees' talents must be upgraded to serve the new purposes and missions of firms as they evolve. Firms may need to make regular efforts through education and company seminars to upgrade the qualifications, skills, and talents of their workforces so that they can remain competitive on the worldwide stage. Companies may need to foster learning, teaching, and growing at all levels, perhaps through training employees on new management philosophies articulated in the latest business best sellers, or by upgrading skills and equipment usage. Companies will need intrapreneurship and flexible thinking so they can remain competitive. As Rosabeth Moss Kanter has suggested in her book *Evolve! Succeeding in the Digital Culture of Tomorrow,* "brainpower, flexibility, and alliances across nations will be the key."[90] Kaleidoscope thinking is a way of constructing new patterns from the fragments of data available— patterns not yet imagined because they challenge conventional assumptions about how pieces of the organization, the marketplace, and the community fit together. A rethinking, a reordering of the data can create change. Companies need to challenge their people to question the prevailing wisdom around conventional business assumptions and status quo procedures in order to invent new ways of looking toward the future. Following is a summary of the ways organizations can support challenge in Kaleidoscope Careers.

- Redesign work so that workers at the lower levels are empowered to do more tasks

- Outsource menial work

- Find ways to "chunk" work so that meaningful work can be chosen

- Create opportunities for early field experiences for women and men

- Encourage early international experiences for women and men

- Give women as well as men profit-and-loss experience

- Redesign bureaucratic work methods and organizational relationships to increase learning opportunities and reduce boundaries between functions and levels

- Offer job rotation to increase early skill development across departments

- Redesign bureaucratic work methods and organizational relationships to increase learning opportunities and reduce boundaries between functions and levels

- Make top-level managers accountable for turnover and advancements rates for women

- Provide career succession plans that include time off for career interruptions without penalty

- Create rewards systems based on outcomes and actual performance, not face time

KALEIDOSCOPE CAREERS
AND THE BOTTOM LINE

A new concept in HR is starting to take hold. Smart HR departments are moving HR planning from a focus on processes and policies to an analysis of tangible results and outcomes.[91] By the application of techniques such as human resources accounting, HR managers are putting dollar amounts to the costs and benefits of HR activities, documenting how human capital affects the bottom line. HR managers are clearly demonstrating to other organizational decision makers how human capital—not physical capital—is today's competitive advantage. But how can HR activities, which often have "feel-good" outcomes, be measured? Following are some examples.

- College Summit, a program to help low-income children prepare for college, focuses not on satisfaction with the process but on actual outcomes by comparing the college enrollment rates of their students (75 percent) to the national enrollment rates of students at the same income level (about 37 percent).[92]

- At DPR Construction, anyone on a job site can submit an "opportunity for improvement" or OFI form, to suggest how a task can be done better. Every OFI is logged in to a database that any employee can search. A committee reviews these suggestions, implements the ones that make sense, and calculates the impact of the change. A recent suggestion, that fax machines be installed where the tradespeople were actually working rather than having workers walk to the site office to handle faxes, was estimated to save $42,000 a year.[93]

- Pat Brown, First Tennessee Bank's vice president and manager of family matters, calculated that 85 percent of the employees who changed from full-time work schedules to the new reduced-time work with full benefits would have left the bank had that option not been available. The bank estimated that it saved $5,000 to $10,000 for each nonmanagerial employee and $30,000 to $50,000 for each executive in replacement costs.[94]

By measuring results of programs to enhance authenticity, balance, and challenge, including time saved, employee retention, increased productivity, reduced absenteeism, and reduced health care costs, HR managers can demonstrate the real value and impact initiatives have on the bottom line. And HR managers must be the ones leading the way in showing how the human heart, mind, and soul make the difference in this global, technology-driven environment. Following are ten important questions an HR director must answer.

1. Will professionals who shift into slow-lane jobs be allowed to pick up velocity in their careers when their children have grown or their circumstances change?

2. How can long-standing performance systems based on face time be changed to systems based on outcomes regardless of whether the employee works at home or uses alternative work arrangements?

3. Should workers who indicate a willingness to travel and work long hours at any cost be placed on high-potential career paths over those who do not, or should they be encouraged to develop a fuller life balance?

4. Should benefits be retained and reinstated for employees who take career interruptions but return later? What kinds of benefits will attract employees so they will remain loyal to the firm over the long haul?

5. Should opt-outs be differentiated from stop-outs? Will there be a difference in career advancement based on the amount of time away from the office?

6. How can work be reorganized and "chunked" so that part-time professionals can stay in the loop and contribute to organizational projects?

7. Will sufficient part-time work be available through job-sharing programs and the like so that employees who wish to adopt flexible options can do so for lengthy periods of time?

8. How can corporate cultures be shaped so it is perfectly acceptable for employees, both men and women, to move in and out, stop out and return as alumni later?

9. How should senior management model and show their support for flexible options?

10. How can executives be convinced of the urgency of changes to HR planning, compensation, and strategic initiatives that should be in place in preparation for the labor shortage projected for 2012?

And what kind of financial impact do these life track, employee-focused programs really have? Wegmans Food Markets, which was named *Fortune* magazine's "2005 Best Company to Work for in America," has demonstrated that it pays to be a good employer. In a market known for cheap wages, Wegmans bucks the industry trend by paying its employees well. Wegmans' labor costs are between 15 and 17 percent, compared to the 12 percent standard in the industry. In the past twenty years, Wegmans has contributed $54 million for college scholarships to more than 17,500 employees, including both full- and part-time workers. Workers are empowered to fix customers' problems—even if it means cooking a Thanksgiving turkey in the store because the customer's oven was too small—get credit for making suggestions for improvement, and receive excellent training and development opportunities. Although Wegmans does spend money to promote a positive employee culture, their returns on their investments have been great. Wegmans' annual turnover rate for full-time employees is 6 percent, compared to similar grocery chains' rate of 19 percent. In an industry in which annual turnover costs can exceed profits by more than 40 percent, Wegmans' employees are happy to stay with the firm, with 20 percent of employees having ten or more years of tenure.[95] And Wegmans is not alone in coming out a winner by treating its employees well. According to *Fortune* magazine, the stock prices of 55 of their "1999 Best 100 Companies to Work For in America" had an annual growth rate of 25 percent, compared to 19 percent for comparable firms.[96]

Are there other payoffs to organizations that embrace the kaleidoscope career model? Yes, in terms of employee goodwill and the avoidance of costly lawsuits. Many talented women who are discriminated against walk away from those firms, taking their creativity and knowledge with them. Others remain but silently contribute less to balance the scales of their unfair treatment. Still others fight back, sue, and win large monetary awards. Employers who discriminate against women are being held accountable by our legal system. Consider the following legal cases: in 1996, Mitsubishi settled for $34 million; in 1997, Home Depot settled for $104.5 million; in 1998, Merrill Lynch settled for an undisclosed amount; in 2002, American Express settled for $42 million; in 2004, Boeing settled for $72.5 million; and in 2004, Morgan Stanley settled for $54 million. And technology makes it easier for employees to join and win these lawsuits. Plaintiffs' lawyers can more readily collect and analyze data from diverse geographic locations. Potential members of class action lawsuits are just a mouse click away.[97]

It is critical that firms take note, and quickly. Because of the proliferation of the outsourcing of information systems jobs, accounting jobs, and other back-office positions to India and China, as well as the climbing value of the Euro against the U.S. dollar, there is a growing concern that the best workers from other countries will no longer flock to U.S. shores in search of the American dream as in the past.[98] The Internet permits would-be immigrants to stay in their home countries and prosper as entrepreneurs. No passport, no travel, and no becoming a U.S. citizen are required. And the United States loses the direct economic contributions of these lost immigrants.

In the past, the founding fathers' American ideal of welcoming immigrants to U.S. shores to contribute to society led to a great entrepreneurial culture. Now, with technology allowing work to take place remotely, products are shipped from distant locations all over the globe, and outsourced work, even personal U.S. tax returns, is completed in India and other countries. There is less motivation for the best and brightest to immigrate to the United States, to prosper on these shores, and to enrich the diversity that has made the United States great.

The United States is facing a unique juncture—a collision of economic, worldwide, and demographic forces. Such trends are creating major human resources challenges and opportunities for the next decade. Beginning in 2012, the annual growth rate of the U.S. labor force will decline. There will not be enough younger workers to replace workers who retire as part of the baby boomer bubble. As the boomers exit the workforce, rapid changes in technology will require that every worker receive adequate training to keep up with change. More than 10 million jobs will open up in highly skilled service occupations over the next ten years. There will be a very significant gap in professional, skilled, and leadership talent across multiple industry sectors.[99]

Within the next decade, smart corporations will realize that they need to develop new career pathing opportunities to attract and retain qualified workers. Executives perplexed by the brain drain of female employees must realize that advancement prospects, as well as relationship issues and family, have a great influence on women's—and a growing number of male Gen X and Gen Y workers'—career decisions. The Kaleidoscope Career model shows that women and men have distinctly different needs that ache to be filled at unique points in the life cycle. Therefore, the key to retaining workplace talent and human capital is to offer flexibility alongside advancement opportunities, as appropriate, and in the total arc of a career, not just within the workday.

Applying the Kaleidoscope Career model allows for all kinds of far-reaching HR career development possibilities. With the new technologies that are available, work can and should be redesigned around the concept of performance outcomes rather than hours logged sitting in an office. Technology permits individuals to telecommute, hold meetings virtually, and stay in contact by e-mail and telephone. More and more managers should question policies that require unnecessary face time and travel. Instead of assuming that employees should demonstrate their commitment and ambition through nonperformance factors, firms must focus on actual productivity. Organizations must recognize that employees have both work and personal obligations—and individuals should not be made to sacrifice their personal lives for career success.

Solutions to these issues are complex and may require organizations to rethink and completely revise the fundamental ways in which they conduct business. But the solutions are not impossible to implement. They simply require a creative mind-set on the part of courageous organizational leaders, human resources professionals, and other champions of change to adopt new, far-ranging approaches. With the advent of new technology that permits employees to work untethered, away from their offices, a whole new mind-set of how work gets done that was heretofore unimaginable is now possible. And given how rapidly technology continues to advance, the future realities of how technology will enhance worker opportunities for authenticity, challenge, and balance would read like science fiction today.

The Kaleidoscope Career model is a new way of blending careers, work-family needs, and personal identities in a way that is meaningful for individuals as well as organizations (see fig. 3). Time and time again it has been illustrated that companies can put people first and still be profitable. Our research shows that Kaleidoscope Career ideas require that a new culture of change be embraced in corporations, one that values the intersection of work with family.

The times in which we live present an exciting blend of global chaos and technological opportunities in the world of work. With the advantages of technology, firms can help reshape career paths to recognize the increasing complexities of Kaleidoscope Careers. Until now, corporations have given lip service to programs such as flextime and reduced-hours schedules. While firms have adopted one or more "solutions" to the work-family balance issue, there has not been any urgency to provide integrated benefits and support. Specifically, there has not been a model of career development to articulate which programs and benefits are needed to retain talent. The Kaleidoscope Career model provides such a foundation. It offers corporations a smorgasbord of possibilities in the areas of

FIGURE 3
The ABCs of the Kaleidoscope Career Model in Action

recognizing employee needs for authenticity, balance, and challenge. Corporations must tailor their benefits and work-life programs over the life cycle and help employees satisfy these three
parameters to retain talent. The kaleidoscope approach to career
development recognizes that sometimes life can get in the way of
work. By integrating these three parameters into a meaningful
career plan that recognizes this reality, corporations can find ways
to make work fulfilling while retaining talent for the years to come.

The Kaleidoscope Career model involves reinventing the wheel
of the corporation so that all the colors of the kaleidoscope of life
and work can shift into new and innovative patterns. By accepting
nontraditional career paths within the firm; by broadening compensation and benefits policies to encompass alternative forms of

work; by recognizing that everyone is on the Life Track and abolishing obsolete norms such as using long hours or travel as a surrogate measure for commitment and promotability; by establishing ethics programs that address wholeness issues, spirituality, and leisure interests; and by encouraging a variety of measures for work-life balance, corporations will have an easier time recruiting, retaining, and shaping talent. The time is right for organizations to create such options. In fact, it is necessary that it be done—and quickly—to alleviate the predicted labor shortage of 2012.[100] Once policies are in place that both support the advancement of women as well as men and simultaneously allow for men and women to participate in flexible work arrangements over the total arc of their careers without penalty, we will be able to say that true equality has been achieved, and the workplace will be a better place to actually live a life.

RESEARCH METHODS AND STUDY INFORMATION

This book is the product of a five-year-long effort to better understand the complex issues surrounding individuals' choices regarding career, family, and nonwork aspects of life, as well as the ways in which other factors, such as gender and societal roles, influence these decisions. This approach is different from many past studies in that we used four major online surveys plus additional in-depth interviews. The quantitative sections of the project drew from a large and diverse sample, which permitted us to empirically examine many questions regarding career decisions, including the "opt-out revolution." The extensive qualitative sections of the project provided for a richer understanding of the choices made by men and women, told in the words of the individuals affected by the changing work environment. We used the real names of interviewees where appropriate and when granted permission to do so by the interviewee. For quotes from our anonymous surveys, executive students, and for all other individuals, we adopted pseudonyms, as appropriate given research convention, to protect the identities of those who participated during this five-year research undertaking.

Advances in technology permitted us to use Internet-based surveys for Studies 2 and 4. There are strong arguments in favor of Internet-based surveys as a valid method to collect large-sample data. First, the online panel we used is one of the largest established marketing research panels in the United States. To ensure a representative panel, the firm uses a variety of methods so that a diverse composition and sufficient response rate can be obtained.[1] Research suggests that Internet-based samples compare favorably to traditional survey methods used in psychology, and Internet samples are comparable to large-scale telephone samples of the general population.[2] Gosling found that Internet samples are generally more diverse than samples published in highly selective psychology journals where student populations are frequently used, and Internet samples are more representative with respect to gender, socioeconomic status, geographic location, and age than traditional samples, and are about as representative as traditional samples with regard to race.[3]

The following table summarizes the research methods we used and numbers of participants in each of our surveys and interviews.

Research Methods and Sample Sizes

Method	Sample Size
Study 1: Web-Based Survey	109
Study 2: GOI Internet Survey 1*	1,647
Study 3: Online Interviews	27
Study 4: GOI Internet Survey 2	1,525
Study 5: Interviews	52

*"GOI" is Greenfield Online, Inc.

Study 1

This study was an online survey of women members of a national organization of female professionals that had more than 100,000 members in 2001. One hundred and nine women answered the 20-question survey by e-mail. Participants were asked to describe their careers and detail the reasons behind their career transitions. Questions included the following: "Please rank-order what motivates you in your career," "Please list the transitions you have made over the course of your career," "Please describe what motivated you for each transition you have made," and "How have issues regarding balancing work and nonwork demands influenced your career decisions?" In return for completing the survey, a donation to each respondent's choice between three charities was made. The respondents ranged in age from 20 to 68, with an average age of 41.5. Eighty percent were white, 71% had a spouse or significant other, and 42% had children living at home. Forty percent of the women had a college degree, and 36% had an advanced degree (e.g., MBA, PhD). The respondents worked in a variety of industries, including banking, biomedical research, manufacturing, education, health care, and law. Sixty-seven percent had children living at home. Participants' work experience averaged 14.5 years.

Three coders examined the comments women made to the open-ended questions asked in the survey. The coders sorted the commentaries into three categories, which were labeled "authenticity," "balance," and "challenge." Fifty-seven "authenticity" comments were coded overall, with 6 from women ages 20 to 35; 22 from women ages 35 to 50; and a large proportion (29 comments) from women over age 50. Eighty-one "balance" comments were coded, with 18 from women ages 20 to 35, 52 from women ages 35 to 50, and 11 from women over age 50. Finally, 73 "challenge" comments were coded, with 23 from women ages 20 to 35; 35 from women ages 35 to 50, and only 15 from women ages 50 plus. This led us to understand that these three factors—authenticity, balance, and challenge—were important for women at different points over the life cycle. The total number of comments exceeded 211, allowing for commentaries outside these main categories. This study also provided many female case histories that are included in this book. We are very thankful to each of the women who participated in this study and took the time needed to complete this detailed survey.

Study 2

This online survey of 1,647 individuals—837 men and 810 women—was conducted in partnership with an Internet market research firm, Greenfield Online, Incorporated (GOI), in 2002. GOI periodically surveys subjects of all ages, races, backgrounds, corporate industries, and titles on various subjects for purposes of market research. GOI holds lists of thousands of respondents who have agreed to participate for a fee. Respondents are guaranteed confidentiality and are required to participate in two surveys per month to maintain their status with the firm. They are not required to purchase products for market research purposes, but they are told their logins will be entered into a drawing for a chance to win a $100 cash prize. Our survey was self-contained and was not merged with any other surveys that GOI was conducting at that time. Survey results were checked, coded, and compiled by GOI from the period March 15, 2002, through May 30, 2002.

Respondents reflected the overall population of the GOI Web site. The respondents by race were 87.7% Caucasian (men 87%, women 88.8%), 3.6% African American (3.7% men, 3.6% women); 3% Asian (3.1% men, 3% women), 1.9% Latin American or Hispanic (1.7% men, 2.1% women), 4% other or preferred not to say. Seventy-six percent worked full-time (84.9% men, 66.7% women); 13.9% worked part-time (6.3% men, 21.7 % women), and 10.1% were self-employed (8.7% men, 11.6% women). The following industries were represented: education (12.2%), health care (9.5%), government (10.1%), manufacturing (7.6%), retailing (8.9%), telecommunications (2.5%), Internet/computer/hardware (5.6%), financial services/banking (4.4%), media/publishing (1.3%), market research (0.3%), public relations (0.2%), real estate (2.1%), and other occupations (40.1%). Only 6.7% of the sample ranged in age from 18 to 24, 23.1% were 25 to 34, 30.4% were 35 to 44, 28.6% were 45 to 54, 10.2% were 55 to 64, and 0.9% were age 65 or older. Income categories broke down as follows: under $20,000, 5.8% (men 4.2%, women 7.5%); $20,000 to $29,999, 10.3% (men 9.4%, women 11.2%); $30,000 to $49,999, 27.3% (men 24.3%, women 30.3%); $50,000 to $74,999, 29.9% (men 32.8%, women 16.8%); $75,000 to $99,999, 13.1% (men 13.6%, women 12.7%); $100,000 to $199,999, 10.9% (men 12.5%, women 9.3%); and $200,000 or more, 1.3% (men 1.4%, women 1.7%). Income levels were tested for bias and found significant at the $p < 0.05$ level for a difference in income. Education categories broke down as follows: less than four-year college degree, 58.5% (men 57%, women 59.6%); four-year college degree or more, 41.5% (men 42.9%, women 40%). Forty-six percent of the respondents had children (men 41%, women 51%).

Forty questions were asked of respondents, of which ten were demographic profile questions, including questions on race, income, education level, industry affiliation, and age. Responses to the primary items we used in the study were prompted by the question "Select the statement that best describes your career now." Response categories were 1 (does not describe my career) to 3 (partially describes my career) to 5 (directly describes my career). Respondents were also asked to respond on a 1 to 5 scale (1 = do not agree to 5 = agree strongly) to the following prompt: "Using a scale, please tell us which of these transitions and changes have happened in your career." Participants were told that this survey was for research purposes only, not for market research purposes. Participants made the choice to answer the questions in the survey; if they preferred not to answer, they could click on an alternate GOI survey to fulfill their monthly obligation for market research. GOI does not track how many individuals click to an alternate survey; therefore, the exact response rate for any of their surveys cannot be determined. However, because GOI's response rates normally range from 20% to 30%, the response rate for our survey was considered "good," as more than 33% of individuals available chose this survey for participation.

From this study, we examined the strategies men and women used in their careers, their transitions over time, and the factors that motivated them. Selected highlights of this study are reported in Appendix B.

Study 3

This study consisted of a series of online conversations conducted with 5 women and 22 men enrolled in an executive MBA program in March 2003. Participants ranged in age from 25 to 55, had achieved income levels that ranged from approximately $60,000 to $200,000, and worked in various locations all across the United States. This study employed an online interactive format for discussion on each topic and was undertaken to learn more about men, as considerable data had been collected regarding women in Study 1. Participation was voluntary, and respondents were assured of confidentiality. Sixteen percent of the individuals were under the age of 30, 44% were ages 30 to 45, and 40% were 45 or older. Questions asked included "Tell me about your career to date," "What changes and transitions have you experienced in your career?" "How have you handled issues of corporate politics at your firm?" "Can you describe some of your experiences in early career?" "Are you satisfied with the way in which your career has progressed?" "How do you handle issues of life, career, and family balance?" "Have gender issues affected your career in any way?" and "Tell me about your future plans." Online conversations occurred in response to question prompts offered each week and in response to comments made by other participants. Responses were in a conversational tone; they were checked for variable status and coded by an independent coder as being in the categories "authenticity," "balance," and "challenge" as well as being chosen for descriptions of career histories and paths for purposes of illustration in this book.

From this study, we not only derived case histories of men and women but learned more about men's career decisions. This study was an attempt to balance the focus of the overall qualitative aspects of the project, as the subjects of Study 1 were all women. We gathered qualitative commentary on family balance issues, on motivation at different points in the career cycle (authenticity, balance, challenge for men), on gender issues, and on career regrets. These case histories and commentaries appear throughout the book.

Study 4

This study, an online survey of 1,525 individuals (675 men and 850 women), was conducted to refine and capture some of the reasons why women and men leave the workforce and the reasons behind their career transitions. This study was conducted in 2004 in partnership with GOI, the Internet market research firm described in Study 2. Survey results were checked, coded, and compiled by GOI from the period July 2004 through August 2004. Respondents reflected the overall population of the GOI Web site and had similar sample characteristics as reported in Study 2. Thirty-seven questions were asked of respondents, of which eight were demographic profile questions, including questions on gender, race, income, education level, industry affiliation, and age. The primary items in the study were questions such as the following: "How would you describe the timeline of your career to date?" "Please describe the transitions you have made in your career, from the point you left high school or college until the present time." "Have you been unemployed? If so, what was the reason?" "When you attempted to return to work after a period of unemployment, how difficult was it for you to find another job that suited your circumstances?" "When you were first starting your career, what was your central motivation at work?" "As you progressed in your career, has your motivation changed in midcareer?" "At the end of your career, what do you expect will be your central motivation?" "What parts of your life claim the biggest energy now, for whatever reasons?" "At this point in your life, what do you find challenging?" "If you could live your life over again, what choices would you make?" Respondents checked a variety of responses or were also asked to respond on a 1 to 5 scale (1 = strongly do not agree to 5 = agree strongly). Participants were told that this survey was for research purposes only, not for market research purposes. Participants made the choice to answer the questions in the survey; if they preferred not to answer, they could click on an alternate GOI survey to fulfill their monthly obligation for market research. GOI does not track how many individuals click to an alternate survey; therefore, the exact response rate for any of their surveys cannot be determined. However, because GOI's response rates normally range from 20% to 30%, the response rate for our survey was considered "good," as more than 33% of individuals available chose this survey for participation.

From this study, we examined the strategies men and women used in their careers, their transitions over time, and the factors that motivated them. Selected highlights from this study are reported in Appendix B.

Study 5

From April 2004 to May 2005, we conducted 52 additional interviews to gather case histories for this book. The interviews were conducted by one of the coauthors and took the form of a telephone interview, a face-to-face discussion, or an online conversation about each individual's career. Quotations from approximately 35 of the interviewees appear in the chapters. Subjects came from all walks of life and were chosen based on the authors' knowledge that these individuals had "interesting" careers. In conducting the interviews, questions were first asked to gather information on the individual's career history. Then questions concerning authenticity, balance, and challenge were asked. Also, interviewees were asked if there were any other issues they would like to discuss or any comments they would care to add. Notes were taken on each interview, and responses were incorporated into the chapters of this book for illustrative purposes. Most of the interviews required an additional follow-up for clarification; the follow-ups were conducted by e-mail or by telephone. The authors are grateful to all the individuals who participated in this sometimes lengthy process, and especially to the members of the Ridgefield Women's Network for their participation.

STATISTICAL SUPPORT FOR THE RESEARCH

Appendix B contains selected statistics that provide additional details on some of the issues examined in this book. Please also visit our Web site at www.theoptoutrevolt.com for additional information.

TABLE B-1

Career Experiences of Men and Women

To what extent does the following statement describe your career?		
Linear Career Experiences:	**% Men**	**% Women**
I have pursued my career goals at several different firms, all within the same industry.	25.5*	17.6
I was promoted several times after working hard to achieve my goals.	31.8*	25.1
I have developed a certain level of expertise in my field.	42.9*	28.6
I enjoy using my skills and talents in a variety of different ways.	17.9*	11.7
Work-Family Experiences:		
Nothing is more important to me than my family.	4.7	18.8*
Family needs necessitated that I change jobs or careers so that I could achieve a better balance for my work and family.	14.2	29.4*
I took a break from work/career to care for family, children, or elders.	5.6	27.7*

Note: From Study 2.
* Statistically significant at p <0.05 level. Total N =1,647 (837 men, 810 women).

Reasons for Career Transitions for Men and Women

Check the statement describing why you made a career transition.		
	% Men	**% Women**
I made changes due to family demands.	24.4	41.1*
My spouse moved to another geographic location, and I followed.	15.0	42.7*
I wanted to simplify my life and reduce stress.	19.3	30.1*
I was bored and wanted greater challenge.	17.3	23.5*
An opportunity presented itself for more money, greater security.	30.7*	24.4
A risky opportunity presented itself that had a greater long-term payoff.	18.1*	11.8
My firm made the decision for me.	13.8*	9.8
Corporate politics got in the way.	12.2	14.6

Note: From Study 2.
* Statistically significant at p <0.05 level. Total N =1,647 (837 men, 810 women).
Percentages for men and women, respectively, total more than 100%, because respondents were permitted to check more than one reason for making a career change.

TABLE B-3

Reasons for Opting Out of the Workforce by Gender

If you left the workforce, what was the reason?		
	% Men	**% Women**
Housework and child care too complicated.	14.0	86.0*
I left because it was important to be home with my kids.	1.6	98.4*
Too many work hours interfered with family life.	18.8	81.2*
I left to travel and seek adventure.	66.7*	33.3
My firm no longer required my services.	67.3*	32.7
I left due to corporate downsizing.	54.3*	45.7
I needed to find challenges elsewhere.	63.3*	36.7
It was time to retire.	65.3*	34.7
I never left the workforce.	58.1*	41.9

Note: From Study 4.
* Statistically significant at p <0.05 level. Total N =1,525 (675 men, 850 women).

TABLE B-4

Mean Scores on Agreement or Disagreement with Questions Affecting Self-Identity

To what extent do you agree/disagree with the statements below?		
	% Men	**% Women**
My work describes who I am.	3.26*	3.01
The number of promotions I have received is my greatest accomplishment.	2.43*	2.10
One's salary defines one's worth.	2.35*	2.03
My family is more important to me than my work.	4.13	4.34*
Work is meaningless if there is no time for family.	3.95	4.14*
My children are my legacy, and I want to rear them well.	3.63	3.93*
My spiritual growth is important to me.	3.58	3.95*
There must be more to life than work.	4.25	4.41*
It is important to stop and smell the roses.	4.18	4.37*

Note: From Study 4.
* Statistically significant at p <0.05 level. Total N = 1,525 (675 men, 850 women).

TABLE B-5

Mean Scores on Top Ten Number 1 Rankings for Flexible Options in the Workplace

Please read the list of flexible options. Please rank-order, from 1 to 5, which options you would be most interested in at your workplace.		
Rank	**Flexible Option Choice**	**Mean**
1	A firm that maintains health care benefits for part-time workers	2.52
2	A firm that allows part-time scheduling	2.57
3	A firm that builds flextime into jobs at all levels	2.63
4	A firm that takes advantage of telecommuting as an alternative to travel	2.81
5	A firm that values diversity and promotes from within	2.82
6	A firm that has pay systems designed to pay for outcomes rather than face time	2.88
7	A firm that allows ample personal days for employees to take time off for personal reasons	2.93
8	A firm that is encouraging women to advance to the upper levels	3.01
9	A firm that allows parents flexible schedules to attend after-school programs	3.04
10	A firm that offers on-site day care	3.09

Note: From Study 4, Q 11. Total *N* =1,525 (675 men, 850 women). Respondents were asked to rank-order their top five options out of a total of 25 possible choices, including a write-in option. These results depict the options receiving the highest numbers of number 1 rankings as indicated by the means. Analysis by gender shows that the option that was most often ranked number 1 by men was "A firm that has pay systems designed to pay for outcomes rather than face time" and by women, "A firm that allows part-time scheduling."

Notes

Chapter 1

1. Bureau of Labor Statistics, May 2005.
2. Bureau of Labor Statistics, June 9, 2005. In 2004 there were 35.4 million families with children under the age of eighteen. In 1997 the percentage of families in which only the husband worked was 28.2 percent, which increased slightly to 31.2 percent in 2004.
3. Bureau of Labor Statistics, May 2005. Women with college degrees who worked full-time earned a median weekly wage that was 75 percent of their male counterparts ($860 for women, $1,143 for men). However, despite media headlines questioning the value of a college degree for women because college-educated women still earn less than college-educated men, it should be noted that in 2004, women college graduates earned 76 percent more than women with only a high school degree.
4. Bureau of Labor Statistics, May 2005. In 2004, about 26 percent of employed women and 11 percent of employed men worked part-time. Bureau of Labor Statistics, May 24, 2001; Dunham 2003. See also www.slowlane.com (accessed August 31, 2005) for more information on stay-at-home dads.
5. Arthur and Rousseau 1996; Sullivan and Arthur 2006.
6. Sullivan 1999; Arthur and Rousseau 1996; Sullivan and Arthur 2006. Mike Arthur and Denise Rousseau coined the term "boundaryless career" and changed the way many scholars think about how careers are enacted.
7. Kaye 2002. Beverly Kaye, a consultant who has written about career options, has developed a model that includes six options: upward movement, downward movement, realignment to a different division or career path, lateral movement, enrichment options (redesigning job challenges and skills), and exploration options (finding out about new career paths or pursuing educational opportunities). This model first appeared in the 1980s but has recently caught people's attention as it represents a more flexible way to view career movement.
8. Hall 1996. Douglas T. Hall is a scholar in the area of careers, whom many consider the father of modern career theory. He has contributed

countless new ideas to the study of careers, including introducing the idea of the protean career. Scholars are indebted to Tim for his many contributions to the field, which have helped us better understand the true nature of careers.

9. There is considerable career literature that describes how women do not fit traditional masculine-defined models of linear careers. See, for example, Powell and Mainiero 1992 and 1993; Gallos 1989; and Woodd 2004 for a discussion of the issues.

10. Morris 2002. *Fortune* magazine reported that 30 percent of the women who attended their Most Powerful Women in Business Summit in spring of 2001 had househusbands, and about 33 percent of the women on *Fortune*'s 2002 list of powerful women had a husband at home full- or part-time. Some of these men have careers that permit them to work at home. Others work part-time or are retired. *Fortune* found that many of the women executives and some of the househusbands didn't want to discuss their arrangements.

11. See Appendix A for complete survey information. Please note that to protect the identities of those involved in our research, the names of survey respondents, online participants, and some other individuals have been changed in the career stories that appear in this book.

12. Friedman 2005. Thomas Friedman's book *The World Is Flat* is a must-read for understanding the rise of outsourcing and the impact it has had on the U.S. economy.

13. Rosabeth Moss Kanter has used the kaleidoscope metaphor, specifically "kaleidoscope thinking," to spur executives to free their thinking regarding strategic problems. See Kanter 2000, 2001, and 2004 for her work on kaleidoscope thinking.

14. Kanter 2000. Kanter is the Ernest L. Arbuckle Professor of Business Administration at the Harvard Business School. She has authored or coauthored sixteen books and advises major organizations and CEOs on strategy and change. She has been named one of the "50 Most Powerful Women in the World," one of the "50 Most Influential Business Thinkers in the World," and one of "18 Business Gurus to Watch." The *Academy of Management Executive* (vol. 18, no. 2, 2004) printed a special series of articles highlighting Dr. Kanter's career. See articles by Sheila M. Puffer, Warren Bennis, and Herminia Ibarra in that issue.

15. Kanter 2001; Kanter 2004, n. 282.

16. Cappelli 2000.

17. Pink 2001.

18. Ibid. See page 106.

19. DeFillipi and Jones 1996; Jones 1996.

20. Drucker 1993.

Chapter 2

1. Pearson 2002. This book is a delightful tale of the work-life balance issues working women face.

2. *Executive Female,* Spring 2003. Maureen Smith's decision to step down is recounted in "Get a Life!" from this issue, p. 11.

3. In July 2004, Maureen Smith took a position as general manager of the television network Animal Planet and has been developing programming for that channel. We are grateful to her for her interview and her permission to also use quotations.

4. Belkin 2003. See also Tischler 2004; Mero and Sellers 2003; Wallis 2004; and Story 2005 for further media articles related to the opt-out revolt

5. Hewlett 2002; Schor 1991; Hochschild 1997.

6. There have been a number of authors focusing on "the time squeeze," or the number of hours worked by employees and the impact on their lives. See also Townsend 2002; Clarkberg and Moen 1998; Jacobs and Gerson 2000; and Moen, with Harris-Abbott, Shinok, and Roehling 1999.

7. Williams 2000. See note page 2.

8. Crittenden 2001. Crittenden's excellent detailing of cost of motherhood is a must-read, especially for working mothers.

9. Spence 2004; Riss 2005.

10. Winkler 2002. Interestingly, Winkler found that when examining the perceived gender gap within married couple households, wives report they spend 19.5 hours per week more on household activities than their respective husbands do, whereas their husbands think the gap is smaller, at 16.9 hours. The difference in the husbands' self-reports and the wives' reports of their spouses' hours is statistically significant, suggesting that men may still overestimate their contributions to household chores and child care.

11. Hewlett 2002.

12. Crittenden 2001.

13. Arlie Hochschild has written eloquently on this theme. See her book *The Second Shift: Working Parents and the Revolution at Home* (New York: Viking Penguin, 1989), 23.

14. Hochschild 1989, 23.

15. Enrensaft 1994; Williams 2000; Bureau of Labor Statistics, September 20, 2005.

16. Quoted from Williams 2000, 146; Darnton 1990, 64–65.

17. Spence 2004; Riss 2005; Bureau of Labor Statistics, May 2005.

18. Rosie's story also illustrates how working moms will place a lower priority on their own well-being, such as skimping on sleep, in order to spend time with their children. Rosie explained why she made the trade-off between much needed sleep and her daughter's project: "My daughter asked me why I stayed up and helped her even though I was so tired. She

tells me that no one else's mom would have done it. I told her, 'Honey I want to help you to succeed and help you get through school. Education is so important to your future. And as you go through life, this is one thing you'll always remember. This is a moment we had together as mother and daughter.' She tells people to this day about that night. But that's what I've done all her life. For Rachael and my son, Jason, I'm their mother, and I'm there to help them succeed in life. "

19. Hewlett 2002; Hewlett and Luce 2005.
20. Story 2005; Riss 2005.
21. Merrill-Sands, Kickul, and Ingols 2005.
22. Eby, Casper, Lockwood, Bordeaux, and Brinley 2005; Friedman and Greenhaus 2000; Greenhaus and Beutell 1985; Allen, Herst, Bruck, and Sutton 2000; Frone, Russell, and Cooper 1995.
23. You can learn more about Barbara Pasternack at her Web site: barbara pasternack.com and on realitynewsonline.com.
24. Hewlett and Luce 2005.
25. Yankelovich survey in Morris 1995; Deutch 2005.
26. Deutch 2005.
27. Gersick and Kram 2002.
28. See Catalyst 2003. Also see CGO Insights, Simmons College of Management, *Women Pursuing Leadership and Power,* Briefing 20, Boston, MA, 2005.
29. Center for Women's Business Research 2002; Morris 2004.
30. Association of American University Professors 2004.
31. Wooton 1997.
32. See Lyness and Judiesch 1999; Kirchmeyer 2002; Ornstein and Isabella 1993; Ragins, Townsend, and Mattis 1998; Schneer and Reitman 1995; Tharenou, Latimer, and Conroy 1994; and Vinnicombe and Singh 2003 for additional information on discrimination as a barrier to women's career advancement. Many in the field remain concerned about the media's push to describe the opt-out revolt as merely family-driven; for years these scholars have tracked the progress of women in organizations and found that discrimination clearly affects women's decisions to opt out.
33. Catalyst survey in Ragins, Townsend, and Mattis 1998. Also see Gibbs 2005.
34. Catalyst 2003.
35. Hewlett and Luce 2005.
36. Stroh, Brett, and Reilly 1996.
37. Lyness and Judiesch 2001. Also see Stroh, Brett, and Reilly 1996.
38. Lombardo and McCauley 1988; Lombardo, Ruderman, and McCauley 1987; McCall, Lombardo, and Morrison 1988.
39. Fels 2004; Metz 2005.
40. *Women Pursuing Leadership and Power,* 2005.

41. Korabik and Rosin 1995. Also see Kirchmeyer 1998.

42. Maccoby 1998; Maccoby and Jacklin 1974.

43. Singh and Vinnicombe 2004. See also Kluger, Cray, Ferkenhoff, Isackson, and Whitaker 2005.

44. Center for Women's Business Research 2002 and 2004.

45. Moore 2002.

46. Our thanks to Robin Diamond for putting us in contact with Madolyn Johnson.

47. Formerly known as the Homemakers Idea Company. You can see the firm's new Web site at www.signaturehomestyles.com.

48. Ensher, Murphy, and Sullivan 2002a and 2002b.

49. Haas 2005.

50. Tu and Sullivan 2001.

51. Schneer and Reitman 1997; Sullivan 1999; Gallos 1989; Mavin 2001; Sullivan and Crocitto forthcoming; Sullivan forthcoming.

52. Levinson 1996.

53. Quote from Levinson 1996, 415.

54. Bardwick 1980; see also Roberts and Newton 1987.

55. A number of authors have described the link of biology to a woman's career decisions. For example, in 1977 Gail Sheehy discussed two patterns: the woman who nurtures first and defers achievement, and the woman who achieves first and then nurtures a family. Age 35 is seen as the important decision point for women. McKaughan's *The Biological Clock* (1987) also examines in detail how women's biological clocks frame their decisions. See also Rossi 1972.

56. Gilligan 1982.

57. Gallos 1989; Gilligan 1978 and 1982.

58. Kram 1996. Also see Fletcher 1996.

59. Hales 1999, notes for Chapters 11 and 12; Gur and Gur 1994.

60. Shaywitz and Shaywitz 1995; Hoptman and Davidson 1994; Beaton 1997.

61. George et al. 1995.

62. Taylor, Klein, Lewis, Gruenewald, Gurung, and Updegraff 2000.

63. See also Latak, Kinicki, and Prussia 1995; Greenglass 2002.

64. Fletcher 1999. It should be noted that any discussion of differences in the behavior and personal characteristics of men and women are generalizations and won't apply to all men or all women. For example, although women tend to be better communicators than men, there are many men (e.g., John F. Kennedy and Martin Luther King Jr.) who are excellent communicators, just as there are many women who are poor communicators.

65. Eagly, Karau, and Makhijani 1995.

66. Rosener 1990 and 1995.

67. Belasco and Stayer 1993; Byhams and Cox 1994; Case 1998.

68. Powell and Mainiero 1992. A number of researchers have studied the experiences of women at work and have contributed to our better understanding of women's leadership styles. Although we cannot list all of these researchers, we are indebted to the outstanding research of Dr. Gary Powell. He has authored or coauthored 8 books, including the *Handbook of Gender* (1999) and *Women and Men in Management* (1993). He has also published 20 book chapters and more than 80 articles.

69. Ibid.

70. Eby, Casper, Lockwood, Bordeaux, and Brinley 2005; Friedman and Greenhaus 2000.

71. Bielby and Bielby 1989.

Chapter 3

1. Gwyther 2003; Rogers and Brocklehurst 2002.

2. Super 1957; Super, Thompson, and Lindeman 1988; Levinson 1978, 1986, and 1996. Researchers Donald Super and Daniel Levinson made major contributions to our understandings of career patterns, especially the careers of men. Their theories were the jumping-off point for many of the newer models of careers, such as Driver's (1979 and 1982) career types and Sullivan, Carden, and Martin's (1998) Career Grid. Their ideas are still the subject of a great deal of research on career processes. Researchers in the field of careers are indebted to the foundation laid by Super and Levinson.

3. Arthur and Rousseau 1996.

4. For further perspectives on how careers have changed, see Bird 1996; Hall 1976 and 1996; Mohrman and Cohen 1995; Osterman 1996; Peiperl and Baruch 1997; Rousseau and Wade-Benzoni 1995; Sullivan and Crocitto forthcoming; Weick 1996; Baruch and Hall 2004; Baruch and Peiperl 2005.

5. Despite the fact that our workplace has greatly changed, theories such as Super's continue to exert a strong influence in the study of careers. For instance, in a 1999 review of the empirical careers literature, Sullivan (1999) found only 16 studies that examined careers in nontraditional contexts. More recently, Arthur, Khapova, and Wilderom's (2005) 11-year review of 80 articles found very little that contributed to an understanding of nonlinear careers.

6. The way in which the research was completed—cross-sectional research rather than a longitudinal design that tracks individuals as they progress through their careers—means we are at a loss to say whether or not these issues and stages exist for individuals over the life cycle. While Super thought his theory applied to both men and women, women's careers follow a drastically different set of assumptions. Linear career stage models like Super's also are suspicious from the point of view that age or organi-

zational tenure has been used as a proxy for psychological career stage, which may not reflect reality. For more on the measurement of career stage, critiques of the career stage literature, and reviews of stage models, see Chao 1986; Cooke 1994; Cytrynbaum and Crites 1989; Dalton 1989; Feldman 1989 and 1990; Greenhaus and Parasuraman 1986; Hackett, Lent, and Greenhaus 1991; Ornstein, Cron, and Slocum 1989; Ornstein and Isabella 1990 and 1993; Powell and Mainiero 1992 and 1993; Power and Rothausen 2003; Smart and Peterson 1994 and 1997; Stoltz-Loike 1996; Sullivan 1999; Swanson 1992; and Watkins and Subich 1995.

7. From Study 2.
8. From Study 2.
9. Results here quoted from Study 4.
10. Martins, Eddleston, and Veiga 2002.
11. Moen, with Harris-Abbott, Shinok, and Roehling 1999.
12. Maier 1999.
13. Bielby and Bielby 1989.
14. Maier 1999. Mark Maier's chapter in Powell's *The Handbook of Gender and Work* (1999) is a tremendous source that examines and distills complicated gender-based life-world perspectives in a concise manner that has applicability to men's and women's lives in the workplace.
15. Pleck 1977 and 1985.
16. Levinson 1978.
17. Friedman 2005.
18. See Helyar 2005.
19. Bureau of Labor Statistics 2001.
20. These examples were drawn from Mahler 2003 and Helyar 2005.
21. There have been some contradictory findings on how men and women adapt to layoff decisions. In our own research, we found marked differences between men and women; women were more comfortable with being laid off as it meant they could "opt out" and take time with their families. Men were more agitated, angry, and upset, and felt unfairly treated. Others have found no differences in responses based on gender; see Leana and Feldman 1991. Still other research points to differences; see Armstrong-Stassen 1998.
22. From Study 2.
23. From Study 4.
24. In Study 2, regression analysis was completed on these data specifically examining reasons for career transitions for women and men. For the model for transition 1, "pursued career goals at different firms," men were more likely than women to show an "active" career path, r-square for the full model = 0.10; for transition 4, "took break to care for family," women were more likely than men to change jobs due to family demands, r-square for the full model = 0.24. Factor analysis on these data showed

distinct clusters for early and midcareer: an organizational/challenge factor (0.66), a self/creative/authenticity factor (0.57), and a single-loading
family factor, which dropped out in late career.

25. HR Briefing 2000; Bailyn, Rayman, Bengsten, Carré, and Tierney 2001.
Also see Wilkie 1993 and Marsiglio 1993.

26. "Generation and Gender in the Workplace," produced by the Families and
Work Institute in collaboration with the American Business Collaboration, 2004.

27. Karp, Fuller, and Sirias 2002.

28. Kupperschmidt 2000.

29. Smola and Sutton 2002; Jurkeiwicz and Brown 1998. Also see Kupperschmidt 2000.

30. See Smola and Sutton 2002; also Karp, Fuller, and Sirias 2002. There is
disagreement about the exact age ranges of the Gen Xers and Gen Yers
and baby boomers, so we used the most common ranges.

31. See Catalyst's (2001) report titled *The Next Generation: Today's Professionals, Tomorrow's Leaders.* Also see the press release of December 11,
2001, titled "Catalyst 2001 Study Dispels Myths about Generation X Professionals and Sheds Light on What This New Generation of Leaders
Seeks at Work." See www.Catalystwomen.org (accessed January 20,
2005).

32. Bureau of Labor Statistics 2004.

33. National Sleep Foundation 2001; Breus 2003.

34. Bureau of Labor Statistics 2001 and 2004; Lawlor 2004.

35. Gwyther 2003.

36. Lawlor 2004.

37. McNamee 2004.

38. "Generation and Gender in the Workplace," 2004.

39. As more Gen Xers (and Yers) move into the workforce, we may see an
increase in the number of men who are intentionally seeking nonlinear
career paths and more balance in their lives. See also "Generation and
Gender in the Workplace," 2004.

Chapter 4

1. From Study 3. "Leah Bateson" and "Greg Varscroft" related their career
stories in our online survey. We gave them fictitious last names to corre-
spond with other chapter introductions. All other survey respondents are
characterized by a fictitious first name only throughout this book. Where
first and last names are listed for our interviewees, permission for use of
their names was granted.

2. A recent study found women could be classified into three categories:
achievers, representing the traditional model of career advancement; nav-
igators, those who operate outside of corporate boundaries; and accom-
modators, who had emergent careers that were developed in accordance

with family needs and demands. Only one-third of women were "achievers"; instead, the majority of women had boundaryless, protean, or family-driven careers. O'Neil, Bilimoria, and Saatcioglu 2003. Also see O'Neil and Bilimoria 2005 for a further conceptualization.

3. We are indebted to earlier work with our noted colleague Gary Powell, who was coauthor on "Cross-Currents in the River of Time" (Powell and Mainiero 1992; 1993). We both view this work as instrumental for the foundation of our later thoughts and ideas about women's careers.

4. The term "Kaleidoscope Career model" has evolved through research analysis and has been presented in paper/symposium format numerous times. It was first cited by Sullivan in 1996: "Kaleidoscope Careers: A New Direction in Career Theory," Southern Management Association *Proceedings,* New Orleans, 177–179. Later it was used as the focus of annual symposium presentations by both authors jointly at the Annual Academy of Management and regional meetings during 2000 (Toronto, National Academy of Management), 2001 (New York City, Eastern Academy of Management), 2002 (Denver, National Academy of Management), and 2003 (Clearwater, Florida, Southern Management Association) as the theory was being developed. We thank those who attended those sessions and provided us with feedback. We are also grateful to Rosabeth Moss Kanter, who also simultaneously pioneered the term "kaleidoscope thinking" in her book *Evolve!* (Harvard Business School Press, 2001), and in "A Note on Leadership" in Sumir Chowdhury's *Management 21C,* in the context of looking at how organization leaders and business in general need to develop more flexible, simultaneous, and less rules-bound strategic approaches to adapt their businesses to a global, technology-driven economy.

5. Ironically, past research has discussed how women have sequential careers, either focusing first on family and later on career or first on career and then on family. So it is a unique discovery that we found men to have sequential patterns and women to have simultaneous patterns.

6. The development of the ABC parameters for the Kaleidoscope Career model not only provides a richness to the model but also helps us better understand why much of past research found that women's careers simply could not be classified by the linear pattern—women's careers are complex and cannot be easily explained. Likewise, with changing values and social norms, as exhibited by the Gen X men in our study, we suspect that the career patterns of men will become increasingly complex over time. The *Alpha* and *Beta* patterns help to explain and identify some of the differences between women's and men's careers. We hope that other scholars find our research useful in their continuing study of careers and that our ideas are tested as Gen X and Gen Y workers enact their careers.

7. See also Ruderman and Ohlott 2002 for their definition of authenticity as it appeared as a theme in the lives of high-achieving women.

8. The Web site for Deborah Ann's Chocolates is www.deborahanns.com.
9. These statistics reflect results from questions 12, 13, and 14 from Study 4. Authenticity was not significant for late career, but increased steadily across the age ranges and was nearly significant for late career.
10. While our Kaleidoscope Career model is unique, we appreciated seeing similar themes between the 61 high-achieving women Ruderman and Ohlott (2002) studied and the vast numbers of women in our samples. For example, they discovered a theme of "agency" in early career similar to our theme of "challenge." Balance predominated in the middle years, while in late career both "agency" and "authenticity" were apparent.
11. These themes are derived from Study 1, which had frequencies of coded comments in each category as follows: for challenge, 58 coded comments in early career; for balance, 52 coded comments in midcareer; and for authenticity, 51 coded comments from age 35 to beyond age 50 (considered late career). These data suggested three lines of issues—challenge, balance, and authenticity—that peaked at different points in the life/career cycle (early, mid, late). Subsequent data were collected to further examine these ideas.
12. A few other researchers have also begun to examine women's career development issues at midlife. See O'Neil and Bilimoria 2005; Gersick and Kram 2002; Gordon and Whelan 1998; as well as Terjesen's (2005) article on women managers' transitions to entrepreneurship and embedded career capital. As the research evolves, we are developing a clearer picture of women's career processes and issues within the context of changing work environments. Our work on the Kaleidoscope Career model used a triangulation approach employing multiple methods (surveys, qualitative data, personal accounts, interviews) in an effort to better understand the working lives and careers of women (and men). Although such a process required more than five years to complete, we believe that the extensive research provided us with a strong foundation for this book. We also realized that studying women's careers in isolation, without a counterpoint of understanding men's careers, seemed incomplete, as men's careers were undergoing radical changes as well. No research is done in isolation from past works, and we recognize our debt of gratitude to those scholars whose work has preceded ours. Many of the earlier models of careers, such as Super's Career Stage model (1957), the River of Time model as developed by Powell and Mainiero (1992 and 1993), and Sullivan, Carden, and Martin's (1998) Career Grid influenced our thinking. We are indebted to the many colleagues who provided us with feedback, encouragement, and suggestions throughout this lengthy endeavor.
13. Ruderman and Ohlott 2002.
14. Gordon and Whelan 1998.
15. There is a voluminous literature in work-family conflict that supports the notion that men are more focused on their careers while women resolve

work-family conflict by bifurcating the decision between work and family. See Martins, Eddleston, and Veiga 2002; Tenbrunsel, Brett, Maoz, Stroh, and Reilly 1995; Veiga 1983; and Stroh, Brett, and Reilly 1996. Chapter 6 of this book provides additional information on work-family research.

16. Kaufman and Uhlenberg 2000; Gordon and Whelan 1998.
17. Bielby and Bielby 1989 and 1992.
18. Ternbrusel, Brett, Maoz, Stroh, and Reilly 1995.
19. Martins, Eddleston, and Veiga 2002.
20. Veiga 1983.
21. Mainiero (1994) recognized this trend in her study of executive women. See also Morris 2002. When examining couples in which the wife has a high-level career and the husband is the stay-at-home caregiver, Morris notes that decisions regarding who will be the breadwinner and who will be the stay-at-home parent are influenced by partner interests as well as who earns the most money. Many of these relationships began as dual-career marriages. The husbands have or had jobs as navy pilots, physicists, engineers, lawyers, and marketing executives. Some of these role reversals haven't been easy, as some men said being a stay-at-home dad was a "jolt" to the ego, while others came to learn that caring for children is often a difficult, thankless job. Some of the women likewise felt the burden of being the sole breadwinner and experienced guilt over being "a bad mother."
22. Mainiero 1994.
23. *Fortune* magazine runs an annual list of the top fifty women in corporations.
24. Morris 2002.
25. Hewlett 2002.
26. Hamilton, Gordon, and Whelan-Berry 2005.
27. DeLong and Vijayaraghavan 2003.
28. De Janasz, Forret, and Haack 2003.
29. Young 1996.
30. Gibbs 2005. Also see Hochschild 1997.

Chapter 5

1. Brady and Grow 2004. After her self-imposed two-year midlife break as CEO for Young and Rubicam, Ann Fudge has recently returned to the workforce.
2. Conference Board 2005.
3. Mahler (2003) paints a particularly poignant picture of how men who lose their jobs feel and react.
4. Ann Crittenden, in her book *If You've Raised Kids, You Can Manage Anything* (New York: Gotham Books, 2004), writes about how women executives are still outsiders in much of corporate America. Crittenden argues

that many of these women grow tired of maintaining this "inauthentic persona" and quit their jobs. They realize it is just too much to maintain a pretense while working long hours on a demanding job.

5. Douglas and Michaels 2004.

6. Other scholars have also examined the needs of individuals to be true to oneself. For example, Abraham Maslow (1943) wrote about self-actualization, the need to be all that one can be. Similarly, Marian Ruderman and Patricia Ohlott (2002) of the Center for Creative Leadership define "authenticity" as a vital developmental goal that is a state or condition rather than a personality characteristic. Kernis (2003) believes that individuals must be authentic to experience optimal self-esteem.

7. Researchers Ruderman and Ohlott (2002), who study the midlife issues of women, found that women must "accept egocentrism" in themselves to fulfill their dreams. Likewise, Miller (1976) states that a key developmental task for a woman is learning how to claim her own needs. See also Levinson 1978 and 1996. Note that Newton (1994) reports that Levinson's 1996 book was completed after his death and the interviews were conducted during the 1980s.

8. Sullivan, Martin, Carden, and Mainiero 2004.

9. In Levinson's book *The Seasons of a Man's Life* (1978), he developed a punctuated equilibrium model of life development. He suggested that men develop through alternating periods of relative continuity or stability, in which they build life structures, with periods of transition, or changes. See Power and Rothausen (2003) for a model of midcareer development, Crocitto (2006) for a review of midcareer issues, and Sulllivan and Crocitto (forthcoming) for a review of the developmental theories.

10. Mahler 2003.

11. Gordon, Beatty, and Whelan-Berry 2002.

12. For more on midlife and the midlife crisis, see Levinson 1978 and 1996; Gordon and Whelan 1998; Gersick and Kram 2002; Ruderman and Ohlott 2002; and Roberts and Newton 1987. Additionally, Gayle Sheehy is often credited with popularizing the idea of career stages and bringing this idea to the attention of nonacademic audiences. She found that men tend to take the "this is me" approach at midlife. In her books *Passages* (1974) and *New Passages* (New York: Ballantine, 1996), Sheehy also focuses on the impact of the midlife crisis for men and for women. Later, as her work evolved to encompass 500 interviews, she sought to explain various life issues that affect people as they move through adulthood—from the "try-out twenties" to the "turbulent thirties," "flourishing forties," "flaming fifties," and "serene sixties."

13. See Gibbs 2005 as well as Shellenbarger 2004.

14. Of all the transitions described by Levinson (1978), his ideas on the midlife crisis have garnered the greatest interest, especially in the popular press. Unfortunately, the midlife crisis has become negatively stereotyped as a time in which men behave erratically and try to recapture their youth, as depicted in such popular movies as *10* and *The First Wives Club*. The midlife crisis, as well as other parts of Levinson's theory, have been widely criticized and challenged (Cytrynbaum and Crites 1989). For example, Lawrence (1980) found that relatively few individuals actually experience a midlife crisis, suggesting that such a crisis is a myth. On the other hand, Lawrence Steinberg, a psychology professor at Temple University and coauthor of a recent book about midlife crisis called *Crossing Paths* (with Wendy Steinberg), estimates that about 50% of all women and at least 40% of all men will go through a reassessment period in their thirties or forties (Steinberg and Steinberg 1995). He argues that in addition to this reassessment period, 15% of both groups may be headed for a full-blown crisis. Also, Wethington (2000) used semistructured telephone interviews of 724 individuals to study the midlife crisis. She found that 90% of the subjects could describe the midlife crisis with definitions similar to those being used in psychological and psychoanalytic theories, with these definitions being especially consistent with Levinson's theory of adult development. Although the subjects on average reported that the midlife crisis occurs at age 40, the age at which they reported experiencing their own midlife crisis did not match the ages suggested by developmental theories. Overall, 26% reported they had a midlife crisis, with women just as likely as men to have experienced one. Most individuals thought their midlife crisis was caused by a major life event rather than aging. Wethington suggests that differences in study findings regarding the number of people who report experiencing a midlife crisis could be due to the fact that she used self-report measures of midlife crisis rather than investigator judgments. It could also be argued that individuals in this sample (ages 28 to 78) who were younger than age 40 and reported already experiencing a midlife crisis were actually describing other transitions. In sum, Wethington found that 14.4% of those age 39 and over reported experiencing a midlife crisis.

15. Ibarra (2003) examined how 39 professionals engaged in the identity transition process. See also Arthur and Rousseau 1996; Hall 1996; and Peiperl, Arthur, and Anand 2002.

16. Ruderman and Ohlott 2002.

17. P. C. McGraw, *Self Matters: Creating Your Life from the Inside Out* (New York: Simon and Schuster, 2001), 30.

18. Smith (2000) discusses how individuals describe the false lives they are living. Some people talk about living behind masks, while others describe

their lack of authenticity as the disease to constantly please others, as not being the main character in the story of their lives, or as the inability to express a full range of emotions, especially "forbidden feelings" such as anger. In his article, he provides practical advice for removing the mask and becoming one's true self. We have also witnessed a rise in the number of entrepreneurial firms that have been developed in response to an individual's longing for purpose. For example, Room to Read was launched by a former Microsoft executive to help villages in southeast Asia build schools, libraries, and computer language labs based on the assumption that education ends poverty. Room to Read is just one of the many organizations that have won a Fast Company/Monitor Group Social Capital Award for their efforts to solve social problems using entrepreneurial know-how (Dahle 2006). See also www.fastcompany.com for a description of other winners.

19. Sheler 2004; Szegedy-Maszak and Hsu 2004; Kluger, Chu, Liston, Sieger, and Willams 2004.

20. Johnson 2005; Rhee 2005; MSNBC 2005.

21. MCNBC poll (2005). The poll on religion and American life was conducted by Peter D. Hart Research. Eight hundred adults were interviewed by telephone between March 8 and 10, 2005. The poll has a margin of error of plus/minus 3%.

22. For more information on spirituality in the workplace, see the *Journal of Management, Spirituality and Religion,* online at www.jmsr.com (accessed November 1, 2005), and Cash and Gray 2000.

23. Weeks, Moore, McKinney, and Longenecker 1999.

24. See Mitroff and Alpaslan 2003, and Watkins and Bazerman 2003, for more information on crisis management.

25. Minter and Samuels's (1998) study supports Levinson's theory of women's development. Minter and Samuels surveyed 300 women between the ages of 40 and 50. They found that 70% of the women had formulated a dream in early adulthood, the most popular of which was marriage and family (61%), followed by occupation (36%), personal growth and fulfillment (27%), and travel (13%). As women entered middle adulthood, the content changed. For the 69% with a current dream, "personal" (43%) was the most popular, followed by occupation (27%), marriage and family (26%), and travel (10%).

26. A 2005 special issue of *Journal of Organizational Behavior* examined the concept of career success. In the special issue, Gunz and Heslin (2005) examine the multifaceted nature of career success and call for its reconceptualization given changing social contexts. Similarly, Arthur, Khapova, and Wilderom's (2005) 11-year review of the career success research reported that few of the 80 articles examined conceptualized success in ways meaningful to understanding nontraditional careers. For instance,

only a third of the articles recognized any two-way interdependence between objective and subjective career success, and few acknowledged the influence of either career mobility or extra-organizational support on career success. Heslin (2005) examines how success is measured and evaluated by researchers. He suggests that because an increasing number of individuals are choosing careers outside the borders of traditional organizations (i.e., boundaryless careers), objective measures of success such as titles and promotions may be less meaningful to them. Likewise, he argues that some people may inherently focus on subjective measures of success, desiring less tangible outcomes, such as a sense of well-being or purpose. He suggests that scholars be more aware of the context in which research is conducted and recommends examining how individuals themselves conceptualize and evaluate career success. See also Ng, Eby, Sorenson, and Feldman 2005.

27. Nicholson and De Waal-Andrews 2005.

28. Hall and Chandler (2005) discuss careers as a calling, in the sense that people feel this is the work they were meant to do. Although "calling" is often thought of in the religious sense, individuals can have a career calling that is not associated with any religion.

29. Konrad, Ritchie, Lieb, and Corrigall (2000) found that men are more likely to value objective success (e.g., money, advancement), whereas women tend to value subjective outcomes (e.g., feelings of accomplishment, growth, challenge, interpersonal relationships). See also Sturges 1999.

30. Are you wondering if your values are aligned with your work? Have you been concerned lately that who you are does not match what you do? Have you taken time in your life to "smell the roses"? Are you finding that lately you are asking "meaning of life" questions? If so, you may be on the threshold of using authenticity as a life and career pivot to shape your kaleidoscope as you make a life and career transition. Here are some guidelines for you to consider as you negotiate this transition.

    First, do a "values life sort" on what is important to you. Lay out, on a piece of paper, all the aspects of life that you value or have valued in the past. Key career values (types based on Driver 1979 and 1982) might include variety, autonomy, creativity, influence, expertise, status, and (financial) security. Key life values might include humor, duty, adventure, collaboration, community, courage, diversity, enjoyment, friendship, health, inner harmony, integrity, justice, love, order, personal development, physical fitness, self-respect, leisure, spirituality, and wisdom. Identify the top 10 values that describe you from your early career. Then re-sort and see if you can prioritize the top 5 values of your life right now. If your values sorts are similar, then you might as well stay the course, as your values match your career for the moment. But if more of your current values fall in the life values category, you might be ready to consider your options concerning how you can move out of your current job and into a more fulfilling career that more adequately suits your dreams.

Second, keep a journal of your life and work experiences. Jot down pearls of wisdom at the end of each day. What was interesting that happened today? What bothered you about your day? At which points in the day did you feel unfulfilled? Sad? Lonely? Happy? Don't worry about writing too much or too little; you will find the writing gets easier each day. After a month's worth of entries, look back at your journal and see what you can discover about yourself. What themes repeat? Themes about how you use your time, about your wishes and dreams, or about what makes you content versus frustrated may begin a process of self-discovery that will lead you to a more authentic path.

Third, discover the point where your passion meets your destiny. Many of us have spent years in unfulfilling careers that we started simply because back in college it seemed like the right thing to do. But times—and you—have changed. Do you still serve the world best in an accountant role? Could you have a life as a teacher? A book author? Is it time to finally open your own business? What obstacles might be in the way? A good adage is that if we love what we do, the money will follow. If you don't love what you are doing, why do it?

Fourth, prepare a life plan for your future. If you won the lottery and had all the time in the world, what would you do? Would you play golf? Hike up a mountain? Garden? Travel? Sleep? Watch TV? Cook? And once you had your fill of leisure activities, what would be next? Think about how you would spend your time if you had time to spare. Would you volunteer in your community? Doing what, exactly? Would you work for the environment? Work with children? Help the local government make policy decisions? Run a charity fund-raiser? Assist in the care of the elderly? Defining your leisure time highlights what is most important to you and can help you find your road to authenticity.

31. Cited in Kouzes and Posner 1993.
32. Ibid.
33. Gomez-Mejia, Balkin, and Milkovich 1990.
34. Society for Human Resource Management 2002.
35. Conlin, Coy, Plamer, and Saveri 1999.
36. Lachnit 2003.

Chapter 6

1. Tischler 2004. In February 2005, Brenda Barnes took over as CEO at Sara Lee Corporation. On her new position, see Monica Roman's "Brenda Barnes: No Piece of Cake" (*Business Week,* May 17, 2004), as well as Kevin

Helliker's article "Sara Lee Hires Brenda Barnes as President, Operating Chief" (*Wall Street Journal,* May 3, 2004, B2).

2. Tischler 2004; Roman 2004; Helliker 2004. See also the September 22, 1997, issue of *Time,* where Barnes is quoted (online at www.time.com/verbatim). In their *Business Week* article called "Act II," Brady and Grow (2004) also profile other executive women who have made these tough decisions. They discuss Ann Fudge, for example, who quit a high-level position at Kraft Foods. Fudge's leaving was especially unexpected, because one year prior to her departure, she had been promoted to run a $5 billion division. After two years of charity work, travel, and watching movies, she was recruited to head up Young and Rubicam. Although these profiles provide illustrations of how some high-powered women have been able to move in and out of the workforce, it is unclear how the average managerial-level woman can successfully navigate such transitions. Past research has shown that career interruptions have a negative impact on salary and promotion rates of women. An issue for future study is the impact of such time-outs on the career of the average professional woman. How do these hiatuses influence the ability to maintain employment in a similar job, and what are the effects on retirement benefits? Does the length of the time-out matter? Does the reason (e.g., children, health, stress) for the time-out matter?

3. For this book, we focused on the changing nature of work and its impact on men and women living in the United States. Although many of our findings may be generalizable to other Western countries, additional research in other countries is needed. For more information on the changing workforce composition outside of the United States, see Martin and Kats (2003), who analyze data for 12 countries.

4. Morris 2005.

5. Orenstein, in her book *Flux* (2000), suggests that women give up what she calls the "Perfect Mother" syndrome; in other words, women shouldn't feel they are a failure if they don't do all the work around the home. Women have to ask their partners to help. Further, she argues that because women normally see themselves as the primary caregivers of children and home, they often self-select into careers that they believe will allow them more flexibility. These careers, however, tend to be lower paying and usually don't lead to executive positions. Also, it may be that higher-level positions would actually allow these women more control over their time and workloads and in fact provide them more flexibility. Women who do assume executive positions could also influence company policies for the better and help themselves and other women create work environments that encourage authenticity, balance, and challenge for all workers. Other authors, such as Crittenden (2004), Douglas and Michaels (2004), and Tomlinson (2004), have raised similar issues.

6. Crittenden 2004; Douglas and Michaels 2004.
7. Belkin 2002.
8. There is a large literature that has examined how individuals manage their work/nonwork lives and the potential conflict between the two. The research of Jeff Greenhaus and Saroj Parasuraman is especially noteworthy, not only for the large number of articles they have written on the topic and their long time in the field, but also for the remarkable quality of their work. Both have provided outstanding insights into how individuals can cope with the demands of work and family life. Both have also contributed substantially to the field by training doctoral students who also conduct important research on work-family conflict and carry on their legacy. In addition there are a number of other individuals who are doing research in this area and a number of university centers, such as at Cornell University, that focus on the work-family interface. The numbers are too great to mention all these fine researchers and centers by name.

   A number of review studies and books are also noteworthy. These include Stewart Friedman and Jeff Greenhaus's *Work and Family: Allies or Enemies?* (2000) and Saroj Parasuraman and Jeff Greenhaus's *Integrating Work and Family: Challenges and Choices for a Changing World* (1997). For reviews and meta-analyses of the literature on the topic, see Allen, Herst, Bruck, and Sutton 2000; Eby, Casper, Lockwood, Bordeaux, and Brinley 2005; Greenhaus and Parasuraman 1999; and Kossek and Ozeki 1998. Eby and associates, for example, reviewed 190 studies on work and family research. They recognize the complexities of studying these issues and suggest that we not only look at the negative aspects of the work-family interface but also the potential positive outcomes, such as work to family depletion and work to family enrichment.
9. Conlin 2003.
10. Ibid.
11. Burn 1998.
12. De Janasz, Forret, and Haack 2003; Young 1996.
13. Eby and Allen forthcoming.
14. Filer, Hammermesh, and Rees 1996; Bell and Hart 1999; Babbar and Aspelin 1998.
15. Hochschild 1997. Feldman (2002) uses a four-level framework (individual level, job level, organizational level, and economic level) to conduct an in-depth analysis of the many factors that can contribute to managers working increased hours. His article suggests many avenues for future research and asks some provocative questions about why Americans work so much.
16. Schabracq and Cooper (2000) examine how changes in our environment, including rapid technological growth and globalization, have affected the everyday lives of workers. They detail some of the potential costs of the

changing nature of careers, including increased stress and nonstop workdays. Likewise, Brett and Stroh's (2003) article is of interest, because it empirically tests the much-hyped explanation that people who work longer hours do so to avoid the pressures at home. Their findings did not support the idea that employees who work the most hours are the most dissatisfied with, and stressed about, their family lives. Instead, they reported that both men and women who work long hours have the least family stress. Those people, however, did feel significantly more alienated from their families. Moreover, regardless of the hours worked, men spent approximately 20 hours per week on child care and 11 hours per week on household chores. Similarly, regardless of hours worked, parents spent approximately the same number of hours with their children. See also Peiperl and Jones 2001; Conlin, Gard, Doyle, and Arndt 2005; and Townsend 2002.

17. Maidment (2003) reports that of industrialized nations, Americans spend more time on the job than anyone except for the South Koreans, who have a six-day workweek, and the Czechs, who work 113 hours more than the Americans each year. Research has found that men who work more than 60 hours per week and are missing sleep are twice as likely to have a heart attack than men working 40 hours a week. In his article, Maidment asks, Are Americans working too hard? We believe the answer is *yes!* And maybe we should be asking, Are Americans working themselves to death—physically, mentally, and spiritually? See also Berg, Apelbaum, Bailey, and Kalleberg 2004.

18. Eby (2001) found that workers who follow their transferred spouses usually don't lose ground with interfirm mobility in terms of intrinsic job characteristics such as challenge, quality of work life, and potential for learning. However, they do experience downward moves in terms of pay and opportunities for promotions. Eighty-two percent of the accompanying spouses were women, with women being more likely than men to be involved in multiple moves accompanying their husbands.

19. Crittenden 2004.

20. See Bureau of Labor Statistics 2004.

21. Sullivan 1992.

22. Moen and Sweet (2002) did an interesting study of interlocking couples. They compared couples who were also coworkers (250 individuals) and couples who were not coworkers (627 individuals). In their sample, 4 of every 10 couples were coworking couples. Half of the coworking couples met on the job and then developed relationships. Half of the men in coworking couples and 40% of the women in coworking couples said that neither of the partner's career took priority. In contrast, 20% of the men and 20% of the women who were not coworkers said that neither partner's career was more important than the other's career. The study found

that men, especially younger men without children who were part of a coworker couple, had higher job prestige, tenure, and work commitment. Likewise, women, especially younger women without children, who were part of a coworker couple had increased income and increased spillover from their work to their family lives.

23. Hammonds 2001.

24. Spillman 2004. Parker and Arthur (2004) detail a counseling method, based on the intelligent career framework, that permits partners in dual-career relationships to make sense of their own career within the context of their relationship.

25. Unfortunately, not all academics work in a university that permits the type of work/life balance of Amanda. Women academics have also shared stories of child care nightmares, such as missing "hand-offs," so that children who were supposed to be with their fathers while their mothers attended meetings or taught classes ended up staying with their mothers, as well as the dilemma of sick children and out-of-town conferences.

26. Ruderman, Ohlott, Panzer, and King's (2002) study of managerial women supports the positive benefits of an approach like the one exhibited by Amanda. In their qualitative analysis, they found that women's personal roles enhance their managerial effectiveness. In their quantitative analysis, they reported that women with multiple roles had higher life satisfaction, self-esteem, and self-acceptance, as well as improved managerial skills. When considering the different approaches available to manage work/nonwork balance, it is interesting to note the findings of a study conducted by Greenhaus, Collins, and Shaw (2002). They found that for those who invest time in both career and family roles, those who focus more on family than work have a higher quality of life than those who try to equally balance the two. Those who try to balance the two, however, have a higher quality of life than those who spend more time on work.

27. George 2003. See his book *Authentic Leadership: Rediscovering the Secrets to Creating Lasting Value* (San Francisco: Jossey-Bass, 2003) for a full discussion of these concepts.

28. Madolyn Johnson has served as a role model for many women because of the way she has managed her own work/family demands while founding and operating her own successful business. In May 2005, Madolyn was named one of the women who is "changing the game of business" by *Fast Company* magazine. She was number 9 on the list. On December 13, 2004, Crain's *Chicago Business* newspaper (online at www.chicagobusiness.com) named the Homemaker's Idea Company the 13th largest woman-owned firm, up from the number 16 spot in 2003. Crain's list included such companies as Turtle Wax and Oprah Winfrey's Harpo Productions. In 2004, Madolyn earned the Stevie Award for Women Entrepreneurs in the Women Helping Women category. In 2004, Madolyn also earned the

National Association of Female Executives' (NAFE's) highest honor, its Women of Achievement Award. She has also been recognized as the Illinois Entrepreneur of the Year in the retail category (2002), has received the Influential Women in Business award from the Business Ledger (2002), has made *Working Woman* magazine's list of the top 500 women-owned businesses in the United States, and was a 1999 inductee to the Entrepreneurial Hall of Fame. Madolyn's firm is also involved in charitable activities and a number of other endeavors. For more information on Madolyn Johnson and her company, see www.signaturehomestyles.com.

29. Hacker and Doolen (2003) suggest that the metaphor of balance itself is causing problems. The idea of balance sets up a win-lose situation; this competition of priorities doesn't recognize the potential blending of various aspects of life. Instead, Hacker and Doolen offer the metaphor of "soaring in life." Using parasailing to explain their ideas, they suggest that although this sport can be scary at first and requires a "leap of faith," once airborne, the individual is keep aloft by the updrafts (of life's purpose). As one's purpose is better understood, the power of the updraft increases, lifting the individual higher.

30. There has been some debate about whether women aren't reaching the top because they lack ambition. A number of parties have weighed in on the topic, each using a different perspective to examine the issue. Korabik and Rosin (1995) look at the issue of ambition by studying young children. Research shows there are few, if any, gender differences regarding aspirations, from childhood to adulthood. Fels (2004), a psychiatrist who has also examined women's ambition, says a lack of recognition affects women in the workplace. According to Fels, if women do not feel recognized for a job well done, they are less likely to pursue their goals. For women's ambition to thrive in corporations, both the development of expertise and the recognition of accomplishments are required. In contrast to Fels, Singh and Vinnicombe (2004) argue that it is not women's ambition that is lacking but the fact that women are persistently socially excluded from the decision-making networks. Likewise, Van Vianen and Fischer (2002) did find women to be less ambitious than men but suggest it is because women face two barriers in breaking the glass ceiling. First, women are less likely to move into middle management positions because they don't take to the masculine culture that pervades management. Second, women are less likely to move into top management positions in an effort to maintain work-home balance; this may be especially important to women given that they are usually more responsible for the home and children than are men. Thus, the different sides of the debate illustrate that women's career choices are not simple. Rather, their decision-making process is complex, and a number of different factors influence choices women make. See also Brim 1992 and Kirchmeyer 1998.

31. Sturges 1999; Powell and Mainiero 1992 and 1993.
32. Hall 1996.
33. Welch 2004.
34. Qualitative results from Study 3.
35. From Study 3.
36. A recent study conducted by Gayle Kaufman and Peter Uhlenberg (2000) showed that while for older men the association between fatherhood and work effort tends to be reversed, younger fathers are following a different track. Younger men, usually Gen X men, had different profiles than men of the baby boom generation. What some are calling the "modern men"— those age 30 and under, usually white, college-educated professionals— expect their work hours to decrease upon having a child. Traditional men, in contrast, were more likely to increase their work hours after the birth of a child. Further, as the number of children increases, modern men expect to continue to reduce their workloads, while traditional men expect an increase or no change in work hours. Men are starting to take on more responsibilities at home despite the fact that, according to a new *Time*/Spike TV poll of 1,302 men, 68% work more than 40 hours per week, 62% work weekends, and 60% of men with children work 41 to 59 hours per week (Orecklin 2004). These results suggest that while most men still see themselves as working to provide, they are starting to pitch in around the home when they can. And there are tasks men accomplish at home that often do not fit the category of "housework," for example, fixing a flat tire, taking out the garbage, doing plumbing work, or shoveling snow. Says Leah Fisher, codirector of the Center for Work and the Family in Berkeley, California: "I call it cultural lag time. Society hasn't caught up yet. Men are expected to do more at home without that being recognized at work." Poe 1999. See also Gwyther 2003.
37. Wilkie (1993), using longitudinal data from the National Research Center, General Social Surveys from 1972 to 1989, studied men's changing attitudes to the breadwinner role. In general, American men have become more egalitarian. However, although men have a greater acceptance of women earning money, they are hesitant to lose their status as family provider. Likewise, Botkin, Weeks, and Morris (2000) examined longitudinal data from 1961 to 1996 and found significant changes in expectations regarding egalitarian marriages. See also Gwyther 2003.
38. Personnel Today 2003.
39. Friedman and Greenhaus 2000.
40. McNamee 2004.
41. Carbonara 1998.
42. McNamee 2004.
43. Poe 1999; Orecklin 2004.
44. Hammonds (2001) says that balance is just plain bunk. It is an unattainable pipe dream and that mostly rhetoric is offered as a solution to prob-

lems of logistics and economics. He suggests that trying to obtain balance between work and life is a losing, hurtful, destructive proposition. See also Hammonds, Aneiro, Clayton, Korn, and Yankus 2004.

45. We believe that as male baby boomers move into retirement and out of the labor force, and as Gen X and Gen Y workers take their place, the issues of balance may change dramatically. It may be that if this study were to be replicated years from now, that population of mostly Gen X and Gen Y men would be seeking balance and would show patterns similar to the majority of the women in our sample. See Bond, Galinsky, Kim, and Brownfield 2005.

Chapter 7

1. As can be seen by the examples presented, the five major ways of experiencing challenge are not mutually exclusive. People often experience challenge as, say, a motivator, as a validation of identity, or in various other combinations.

2. *Oxford Desk Dictionary and Thesaurus,* ed. Frank Abate, American edition, 1997.

3. Peiperl and Jones 2001.

4. Ibid.; Schwartz 2001; Jervey 2003.

5. Peiperl and Jones (2001) studied 174 individuals who worked long hours to see if these people experienced different job outcomes. On average, both the workaholics and overworkers did work long hours. The workaholics worked an average of 58.08 hours per week and the overworkers worked an average of 59.54 hours per week.

6. McCall, Lombardo, and Morrison 1988.

7. DeFillippi and Arthur (1994) created the model of the Intelligent Career, which details three ways of knowing. One of these ways, knowing why, examines self-identity. Their model has been used to examine self-identity in a number of ways; see de Janasz and Sullivan 2004, as well as de Janasz, Sullivan, and Whiting 2004 for more details. Parker and Arthur (2000) have taken the Intelligent Career model to develop a counseling method to help individuals explore self-identity as well as the other two ways of knowing: knowing how and knowing whom. See also Parker and Arthur 2004. Others, ranging from Donald Super (1957) to Hall and Mirvis (1996) have also discussed the self-concept and self-identity. For a review of the developmental career theories and the development of self-identity, see Sullivan and Crocitto forthcoming.

8. Eby, Butts, and Lockwood 2003.

9. Grossman 2005. This is an excellent article that contrasts with previous views of Gen Xers as slackers.

10. John P. Wanous is a renowned scholar in the area of organizational entry. He developed the idea of Realistic Job Previews (RJPs), which suggest that recruiters provide job applicants with both the positives as well as

the negative aspects of the job, work unit, and organization. RJPs permit individuals to better match their needs and values with what the organization can offer in terms of meeting those needs and also what the organizational values are (i.e., organizational culture). Those job seekers who don't believe there is a good fit between themselves and the organization can self-select out of the recruitment process, saving the firm time and money by reducing turnover. See Wanous 1992 for a complete discussion of the organizational entry process.

11. Hackman and Oldham 1976.

12. Hall 2004.

13. Holland 1973.

14. Sullivan, Carden, and Martin 1998.

15. Schein 1978 and 1996.

16. Helyar 2005.

17. Warner 2005.

18. Konrad, Ritchie, Lieb, and Corrigall 2000. Alison Konrad is an award-winning scholar who has written extensively on gender issues.

19. DePater 2005.

20. Fairlie 2004; U.S. Small Business Administration 2001.

21. Buttner and Moore 1997. To examine the many myths about women entrepreneurs, see Menzies, Diochon, and Gasse 2004. For more information on women entrepreneurs and entrepreneurship, see the United States Association for Small Business and Entrepreneurship Web site (www.usa be.org) as well as the Web site for the Small Business Administration (www.sba.gov).

22. The fields of entrepreneurship and careers are indebted to Dorothy Moore for her pioneering research on the careers of women entrepreneurs. Her 2002 book *Careerpreneurs,* together with her 1997 book, *Women Entrepreneurs: Moving beyond the Glass Ceiling,* coauthored with E. Holly Buttner, brought increasing attention to the growth of small businesses owned by women while encouraging other scholars to study this underresearched topic. Additionally, Moore, a former entrepreneur herself and a fellow of the United States Association for Small Business and Entrepreneurship, has written numerous articles for practitioners on how to be a successful entrepreneur and is currently writing a book to provide additional guidance.

23. Ensher, Murphy, and Sullivan 2002a and 2000b.

24. Ensher, Murphy, and Sullivan 2002a, 239.

25. Ohlott, Ruderman, and McCauley 1994.

26. Catalyst 2001, *Women in Financial Services.*

27. This theme—the importance of challenge—has been echoed repeatedly in recent best-selling business books, including *Peak Performance: Aligning the Hearts and Minds of Your Employees* (Katzenback 2000) and Jim

Collins's *Good to Great* (2001). Unfortunately, not all organizations and managers have embraced these ideas and many workers are still seeking challenging work.

Chapter 8

1. Motek is becoming well known for its innovative business practices and has been the subject of a great deal of positive press. We based our discussion on several sources, including Spragins and Keeney 2002; Schneider 1998–1999; Winning Workplaces 2002; and the company's Web site, www.motek.com. *Fortune*'s best company to work for in 2006, pharmeceutical company Genentech, shares many of the same characteristics as Motek. In addition to the good stock options, on-site day care, concierge service, and a host of other perks, Genentech fosters a culture that promotes authenticity (e.g., doing work that really matters; the science is not driven by market data or return on investment); balance (e.g., offering sabbaticals to prevent burnout); and challenge (e.g., scientists and engineers are encouraged to spend 20 percent of each workweek on pet projects). Like Motek, Genentech is doing well financially. In December 2005 it was named the twentieth most valuable company, ahead of well-known competitors Merck and Eli Lilly. Genentech's stock price doubled in 2005 to $95 a share, with expected revenues of $6.6 billion. Morris 2006.

2. Ann Price is quoted in Spragins and Keeney 2002.

3. Spragins and Keeney 2002; Schneider 1998–1999; Winning Workplaces 2002; as quoted in Schneider 1998–1999, Web exclusive.

4. Ibid.

5. The firms profiled on these lists of best companies to work for can serve as valuable examples of what is possible. It should be realized that these companies are not 100% perfect and may be on a list one year and then lose their positive status the next year if they fail to keep up with the current needs of their employees.

6. Catalyst 2003. Tomlinson (2004) found that women who worked full-time and held a higher level position were better able to negotiate for a part-time management position or flexible arrangements after maternity than were women with fewer skills and in lower levels of the organization. For women with less senior positions and skills that were less in demand, the flexibility of part-time work may come at the cost of job quality and future advancement opportunities. See also Barnett, Gordon, Gareis, and Morgan 2004.

7. Powell 1999.

8. Fursman and Jacobsen 2003.

9. Landers, Rebitzer, and Taylor 1996.

10. Crittenden's (2004) book provides a highly detailed description of why she thinks parenting skills are transferable to the workplace and should

be recognized as such. See also Hall 1996 for further discussion of how experiences in the nonwork areas of life can enrich the work skills. Also see Forret and Sullivan 2002.

11. Catalyst 2003.

12. Pritchard 2002.

13. Ibid.

14. See the *Fortune* (1995) article "There Are No Bedtime Stories Here."

15. Ohlott, Ruderman, and McCauley 1994.

16. Ragins, Townsend, and Mattis 1998.

17. Cleaver and Spence 2004; Spence 2005; Larson 2005. While researching companies for NAFE's 2005 "Top 30 Companies for Executive Women," Larson found that many companies don't track profit-and-loss jobs by gender. NAFE's report shows that in the top 5 companies, women hold 74% of profit-and-loss positions that report directly to the CEO and 42% of total profit-and-loss positions. These firms also use a variety of tools to help prepare women for profit-and-loss positions. For instance, Liz Claiborne holds a two-day business simulation retreat in which teams create mock companies and make strategic decisions. Using a combination of computer programs and role-playing situations, the participants learn important skills, including reading profit-and-loss documentation. Liz Claiborne also sends employees to women-only programs at the Center for Creative Leadership and Women Unlimited. Likewise, in addition to providing simulations, 360-degree evaluations, and mentoring programs, Hewlett-Packard sends high potential women to UCLA's Women's Leadership Institute to learn more about breaking through the glass ceiling. It is clear, by reviewing NAFE's criteria for their top companies for executive women, that NAFE is looking for firms that use a combination of approaches that actively focus on developing a culture that supports the advancement of women. These firms can be used as benchmarks for other firms wanting to increase the number of women ascending the ranks of their own organizations. As NAFE's president, Dr. Betty C. Spence, writes, "We hope the NAFE Top 30 list will put the gender P&L issue on the radar screen of corporate America" (Spence 2005, 3).

18. A good source that examines these aspects of reduced-load work is Bailyn and Fletcher 2002.

19. Larson 2004.

20. From Study 3, the result was 20%. Larson 2004; Riss 2005.

21. For more examples of company programs to benchmark, see *Fortune* magazine's yearly lists of the best companies to work for in America; Branch 1999, Wheat 2002, Boyle 2005, and Riss 2005..

22. Working Mother 2003.

23. United Nations 2000.

24. Crittenden 2001.

25. Vermond 2004; Larson 2004. Also see Berg, Applebaum, Bailey, and Kalleberg 2004.
26. Bernstein 2006.
27. Larson 2004.
28. Ibid.
29. Crittenden 2001.
30. Lee 2004.
31. Douglas and Michaels 2004.
32. Crittenden 2001.
33. Schwartz 1989. This article, much maligned originally, really represents the first such recognition that the structure of business was not in accord with the needs of women. We recognize the real intent of Schwartz's article, taking it a step further by discussing the Life Track and the use of our Kaleidoscope Career model. Also see Schwartz 1992 for additional valuable insights.
34. Others have also examined how individuals are often torn between their work and nonwork lives. One excellent example is the work of Sandra Burud and Marie Tumolo, who use the term *dual focus* to describe today's new ideal worker. In their book *Leveraging the New Human Capital* (2004), Burud and Tumolo present a compelling argument for why organizations should permit individuals to have a focus beyond work. They suggest that in the past, when firms hired an employee, they really were getting two for the price of one—the employee himself and the second invisible partner, his wife, who made it possible for her husband to focus on work by managing his personal life. Today the work-primary employee has been replaced by the new ideal worker. This ideal worker has a dual focus, work and family, and is capable of effectively managing both simultaneously. Also, Rhona Rapoport, Lotte Bailyn, Joyce Fletcher, and Bettye Pruitt (2002), in their book *Beyond Work-Family Balance: Advancing Gender Equity and Workplace Performance* suggest that work can and should be redesigned around a "dual agenda" so that individuals can contribute to their organizations while having meaningful personal relationships. Galinsky, Salmond, and Bond (2003) discuss the "dual-centric" worker who places the same priority on work and life. While 61 percent of the executives they surveyed were "work-centric," 32 percent had the dual-centric focus. They found that the dual-centric people worked five fewer hours per week, but felt more successful and were less stressed. See also Friedman and Greenhaus 2000 for an extensive study of the relationship between work and family.
35. Williams 2004.
36. Pruett 2000.
37. Ward and Wolf-Wendel 2004.
38. Burud and Tumolo 2004.

39. Ibid.
40. Pfeffer 1998.
41. Kanter 2004, 204.
42. Ibid.
43. Fisher 2003.
44. Unfortunately, many recent business practices have enacted the exact opposite of equity. Take Enron, for example, where top executives walked away with millions while workers lost their jobs. Questions about the fairness of CEO pay and retirement payments versus the pay and pension of the typical worker have been the subject of debate for some time. Organizations need to consider such issues when redesigning their cultures and structures to meet the needs of today's workers, especially when the firm is facing financial hardships.
45. Begun 2002; Anderson 2004; Salter 2004. For more information on Jet-Blue, see the Web site, www.jetblue.com.
46. Conlin 2006.
47. Begun 2002; Anderson 2004; Salter 2004.
48. Schwartz 1992. We modified Schwartz's jungle gym metaphor slightly.
49. Kaye 2002.
50. From www.oprah.com, in the section "About Oprah's Angel Network." We encourage readers to visit Oprah's Web site, as well as the Web sites of Ben and Jerry's (www.benjerry.com) and Timberland (www.timber land.com) to learn more about these companies. Fast Company also recognizes social capitalists, describing numerous company examples; see www.Fastcompany.com. See also Branch 1999 and Dahle 2006a, b.
51. Koeppel 2004.
52. Fishman 1999.
53. Luthans and Youssef 2002.
54. McGregor 2004.
55. Luthans and Youssef 2002.
56. Layne 2000; Schneider 1998–1999. Layne 2000; Schneider 1998 and 1999. Although perks such as on-site dry cleaning services are nice, what is most important is that a firm develop a culture that demonstrates on a daily basis the value placed on work and life balance. The use of such programs, such as pet-friendly work environments, is one example of how a balanced culture can begin to be built. Netscape, for example, is well known for its pet-friendly culture. The company offers many programs that encourage work-life balance, including flexible schedules, a casual dress code, tuition reimbursement, and sabbaticals. In addition, the firm fosters an "open book" environment, in which information is readily shared with employees. The company has minimal bureaucracy, provides exciting work to employees, and permits employees to take risks and make mistakes without fear of punishment. In these ways, Netscape has

created a culture that makes it a place where people want to work; it provides employees with the ABCs of the Kaleidoscope Career model.
57. Gavin and Mason 2004.
58. Ibid.
59. Sartain 2003.
60. Reich 1998.
61. See Rapoport, Bailyn, Fletcher, and Pruitt 2002.
62. See also Belkin 2004.
63. Kossek and Lee 2005.
64. Miller and Miller 2005.
65. Bureau of Labor Statistics 2002.
66. Working Mother 2003.
67. Levering and Moskowitz 2003.
68. Thompson, Beauvais, and Lyness 1999.
69. Personal communication by telephone with Maureen Smith, May 25, 2005.
70. Friedman and Greenhaus 2000.
71. Reitman and Schneer 2005. This study, which examines the long-term impact of managerial career interruptions, illustrates that over a twenty-year-plus period, the career stigma associated with employment gaps may be decreasing. However, significant pay discrepancies remain between those who stay in the workforce and those who do not on a long-term basis.
72. Cited in Cleaver and Spence 2004.
73. Catalyst 2003.
74. Working Mother 2003.
75. Hewlett and Luce 2005.
76. Bailyn and Fletcher 2002; Kochan 2002. These are well-respected researchers in the area of work-life balance, whose research has identified multiple barriers and possibilities for increasing the quality of work-life issues. Bailyn and Fletcher have also been recognized for their study of the advancement of women.
77. Hewlett and Luce 2005.
78. Usigan 2005.
79. Tischler 2004. See also Brady 2004.
80. The percentage was 29%.
81. Overholt 2003.
82. Crittenden 2004.
83. Powell 1999.
84. Cleaver and Spence 2004.
85. Larson 2005.
86. Spence 2004; Larson 2005. Some people believe that women need to develop their negotiation skills as well as learn to document their

accomplishments and ask for salary increases, promotions, P&L experiences, training, and needed benefits. For instance, one woman executive explained how she provided her boss with a written "business plan" proposing that she freelance. She detailed the initial costs of setting up a home office and the short- and long-term benefits to the company of her doing so, including retaining a top employee and saving money when she transferred to her husband's health care plan. See Spence 2005, 40.

87. These examples, as well as others, can be found in Cleaver and Spence 2004 and Larson 2005.
88. Friedman 2005.
89. Hammonds, Aneiro, Clayton, Korn, and Yankus 2004.
90. Kanter 2001. We are indebted to Dr. Kanter for her fresh approach and thinking regarding strategic change and "kaleidoscope thinking," as discussed in her book *Evolve!* and in "A Note on Leadership" (Chowdhury 2000).
91. Ulrich 1997.
92. Dahle 2005.
93. Randsdell 1998.
94. Martinez 1998.
95. Boyle 2005.
96. Branch 1999. The companies on the 1998 list also had higher than average annual returns.
97. Morris 2004.
98. Friedman 2005.
99. Bureau of Labor Statistics 2004. There has been some debate about the impact of the predicted labor shortages (Cappelli 2005), with some instead focusing not on projected overall labor supply and demand but on the possible shortage of skilled, qualified workers. The potential skill gap may be a concern especially in the expanding health-care and computer fields (Grossman 2005). See also Fisher 2005.
100. Ibid.

Appendix A
1. See www.greenfieldonline.com (accessed November 1, 2005).
2. Berrens et al. 2003 and 2004.
3. Gosling et al. 2004, 99.

References

Abate, F., ed. *Oxford Desk Dictionary and Thesaurus.* New York: Oxford University Press, 1997.

Allen, T., D. E. Herst, C. S. Bruck, and M. Sutton. 2000. "Consequences Associated with Work-to-Family Conflict: A Review and Agenda for Future Research." *Journal of Occupational Health Psychology* 5, no. 2: 278–308.

Anderson, T. 2004. "First-Class Treatment: JetBlue Rises above Industry in Employee Relations." *Employee Benefit News,* online at www.benefitsnews.com (accessed September 1, 2004).

Armstrong-Stassen, M. 1998. "The Effect of Gender and Organizational Level on How Survivors Appraise and Cope with Organizational Downsizing." *Journal of Applied Behavioral Science* 34, no. 2 (June): 125–142.

Arndt, M., and M. Roman. 2004. "No Piece of Cake." *Business Week,* no. 3883 (May 17): 48.

Arthur, M. B., D. T. Hall, and B. S. Lawrence, eds. 1989. *Handbook of Career Theory.* New York: Cambridge University Press.

Arthur, M. B., S. N. Khapova, and C. P. M. Wilderom. 2005. "Career Success in a Boundaryless Career World." *Journal of Organizational Behavior* 26, no. 2: 177–202.

Arthur, M. B., and D. M. Rousseau. 1996. "The Boundaryless Career as a New Employment Principle." In *The Boundaryless Career,* ed. Arthur and Rousseau, 3–20.

Arthur, M. B., and D. M. Rousseau, eds. 1996. *The Boundaryless Career.* New York: Oxford University Press.

Arvey, R. D., I. Harpaz, and H. Liao. 2004. "Work Centrality and Post-Award Work Behavior of Lottery Winners." *Journal of Psychology* 138, no. 5: 404–420.

Association of American University Professors. 2004. "Research Director Reports on Gender Gap." *Academe* 90, no. 3 (May–June): 26–27.

Babbar, S., and J. Aspelin. 1998. "The Overtime Rebellion: Symptom of a Bigger Problem?" *Academy of Management Executive* 12, no. 1: 68–76.

Bailyn, L., and J. K. Fletcher. 2002. "Work Redesign: Theory, Practice, and Possibility." Cambridge, MA: MIT Workplace Center.

Bailyn, L. P. Rayman, D. Bengsten, F. Carré, and M. Tierney. 2001. "Fleet Financial and Radcliffe Explore Paths of Work/Life Integration." *Journal of Organizational Excellence* 20, no. 3 (Summer): 49–64.

Bardwick, J. M. 1980. "The Seasons of a Woman's Life." In *Women's Lives: New Theory, Research and Policy*, ed. D. McGuigan, 35–37. Ann Arbor: The University of Michigan.

Barnes, B. 1997. Quoted in "Verbatim." *Time*, September 22, online at www.time.com/verbatim (accessed January 25, 2005).

Barnett, R. C., J. R. Gordon, K. C. Gareis, and C. Morgan. 2004. "Unintended Consequences of Job Redesign: Physiological Contract Violations and Turnover Intentions among Full-Time and Reduced-Hours MDs and LPNs." *Community, Work & Family* 7, no. 20: 227–246.

Baruch, Y. 2003. "An Empirical Assessment of Sonnenfeld's Career System Typology." *International Journal of Human Resource Management* 14, no. 7: 1267–1283.

———. 2004. "The Desert Generation: Lessons and Implications for the New Era of People Management." *Personnel Review* 33, no. 2: 241–256.

Baruch, Y., and D. T. Hall. 2004. "The Academic Career: A Model for Future Careers in Other Sectors?" *Journal of Vocational Behavior* 64, no. 2: 241–262.

Baruch, Y., and M. A. Peiperl. 2003. "An Empirical Assessment of Sonnenfeld's Career Systems Typology." *International Journal of Human Resource Management* 14, no. 7: 1266–1282.

Beaton, A. 1997. "The Relationship of Planum Temporale Asymmetry and Morphology of the Corporus Callosum to Handedness, Gender, and Dyslexia: A Review of the Evidence." *Brain and Language* 60, no. 2: 255.

Begun, B. 2002. "Special Report, Business and Technology: Moving into the Future." *Newsweek* 139, no. 17 (April 29): 40–42.

Belasco, J. A., and R. C. Stayer. 1993. *Flight of the Buffalo*. New York: Warner Books.

Belkin, L. 2002. *Life's Work: Confessions of an Unbalanced Mother.* New York: Simon and Schuster.

———. 2003. "The Opt-Out Revolution." *New York Times Sunday Magazine*, Oct. 26, Sec. 6, 42.

———. 2004. Presentation at the Society for Human Resource Management (SHRM), Fairfield, CT, April 11.

Bell, D. N., and R. A. Hart. 1999. "Unpaid Work." *Economica* 66: 271–290.

Bennis, W. 2004. "Owed to Rosabeth Moss Kanter: Impact on Management Practice." *Academy of Management Executive* 18, no. 2: 106–107.

Berg, P., E. Appelbaum, T. Bailey, and A. R. Kalleberg. 2004. "Contesting Time: International Comparisons of Employee Control of Working Time." *Industrial and Labor Relations Review* 57, no. 3: 331–349.

Bernstein, R. 2006. "Men Chafe as Norway Ushers Women into Boardroom." *New York Times*, January 12, A3

Berrens, R. P., A. K. Bohara, H. C. Jenkins-Smith, C. L. Silva, and D. L. Weimer. 2003. "The Advent of Internet Surveys for Political Research: A Comparison of Telephone and Internet Samples." *Political Analysis* 11: 1–22.

———. 2004. "Telephone versus Internet Samples for a National Advisory Referendum: Are the Underlying Stated Preferences the Same?" *Applied Economics Letters* 11: 173–176.

Bielby, W. T., and D. D. Bielby. 1989. "Family Ties: Balancing Commitments to Work and Family in Dual Earner Households." *American Sociological Review* 54: 776–789.

———. 1992. "I Will Follow Him: Family Ties, Gender Role Beliefs, and Reluctance to Relocate for a Better Job." *American Journal of Sociology* 97, no. 5 (March): 1241–1267.

Bird, A. 1996. "Careers as Repositories of Knowledge: Considerations for Boundaryless Careers." In *The Boundaryless Career*, ed. M. B. Arthur and D. M. Rousseau, 150–168.

Bond, J. T., E. Galinsky, S. S. Kim, and E. Brownfield. 2005. "2005 National Study of Employers." New York: Families and Work Institute.

Botkin, D. R., M. O'Neal Weeks, and J. E. Morris. 2000. "Changing Marriage Role Expectations: 1961–1996." *Sex Roles* 42, no. 9/10: 933–942.

Bowes-Sperry, L., and J. Tata. 1999. "A Multiperspective Framework of Sexual Harassment: Reviewing Two Decades of Research." In *Handbook of Gender and Work*, ed. G. Powell, 263–280.

Boyle, M. 2005. "The Wegmans Way." *Fortune,* online at www.Fortune.com, Jan. 10 (accessed June 1, 2005).

Brady, D. 2004. "Hopping Aboard the Daddy Track." *BusinessWeek,* November 8 (no. 3907), 100–101.

———. 2005. "Employment Characteristics of Families in 2004." Washington, DC: United States Department of Labor News, USDL 05-876, June 9.

———. 2005a. "Women in the Labor Force: A Datebook." Washington, DC: United States Department of Labor Report 985, May.

Brady, D., and B. Grow. 2004. "Act II." *Business Week,* March 29, 72–79.

Branch, S. 1999. "The 100 Best Companies to Work for in America." *Fortune,* online at www.fortune.com, Jan. 11 (accessed June 1, 2005).

Brett, J. M., and L. K. Stroh. 2003. "Working 61 Plus Hours a Week: Why Do Managers Do It?" *Journal of Applied Psychology* 88, no. 1: 67–78.

Breus, M. 2003. "Chronic Sleep Deprivation May Harm Health." *WebMD* feature, online at www.webmd.com, May 6 (accessed May 27, 2005).

Brim, G. 1992. "Ambition." *Psychology Today* 25, no. 5 (Sept.): 48–55.

Bureau of Labor Statistics. 2001. "Contingent and Alternative Employment Arrangements, February 2001." USDL News Release 01-153, online at www.bls.gov, May 24 (accessed January 28, 2005).

———. 2002. "Workers on Flexible and Shift Schedules in 2001." USDL News Release 02-225, online at www.bls.gov, April 18 (accessed January 28, 2005).

———. 2004. "Employment Characteristics of Families in 2003." USDL News Release 04-719, online at www.bls.gov, April 20 (accessed January 28, 2005).

———. 2005a. "Employment Characteristics of Families in 2004." Washington, DC: U.S. Department of Labor News, USDL 05-876 (accessed online June 9, 2005).

———. 2005b. "Women in the Labor Force: A Datebook." Washington, DC: U.S. Department of Labor Report 985 (accessed online May 30, 2005).

Burn, T. 1998. "Single Workers: Do Bosses Assume Your Job Is Your Life?" *Washington Times*, April 20, D13.

Burud, S., and M. Tumolo. 2004. *Leveraging the New Human Capital.* Mountain View, CA: Davies-Black Publishing.

Buttner, E. H., and D. P. Moore. 1997. "Women's Organizational Exodus to Entrepreneurship: Self-Reported Motivations and Correlates with Success." *Journal of Small Business Management* 35, no. 1: 34–47.

Byhams, W. C., and J. Cox. 1994. *Heroz: Empower Yourself, Your Co-Workers, Your Company.* New York: Harmony Books.

Cappelli, P. 2000. *The New Deal at Work.* Boston: Harvard Business School Press.

———. 2005. "Will There Really Be a Labor Shortage?" *Human Resource Management* 44, no. 2: 143–149.

Carbonara, P. 1998. "Most Companies That Help Their Employees Juggle Work and Family Target Working Moms. This One Helps Working Dads." *Fast Company* 15 (June): 62.

Case, J. 1998. *The Open-Book Experience.* Reading, MA: Addison-Wesley.

Cash, K., and G. Gray. 2000. "A Framework for Accommodating Religion and Spirituality in the Workplace." *Academy of Management Executive* 13, no. 3: 124–134.

Catalyst. 2001a. *The Next Generation: Today's Professionals, Tomorrow's Leaders.* New York: Catalyst.

———. 2001b. *Women in Financial Services: The Word on the Street.* New York: Catalyst.

———. 2003. *Women in U.S. Corporate Leadership.* New York: Catalyst.

Center for Women's Business Research. 2002. "Women-Owned Businesses in the United States: A Fact Sheet." Jan. 11. Washington, DC: Center for Women's Business Research.

———. 2004. "Capturing the Impact: Women-Owned Businesses in the United States." Fact Sheets. Washington, DC: Center for Women's Business Research.

Chao, G. 1986. "An Empirical Exploration of Career Stages." Paper presented at Annual Meeting of the Academy of Management, Chicago, August.

Chowdhury, S., ed. 2000. *Management 21C: Someday We'll All Manage This Way.* London: Prentice-Hall.

Clarkberg, M., and P. Moen. 1998. "Understanding the Time Squeeze: Married Couples Preferred and Actual Work-Hour Strategies." *American Behavioral Scientist* 77, no. 7: 1115–1136.

Cleaver, J., and B. Spence. 2004. "All the Right Stuff: NAFE's Top 30 Companies." *National Association of Female Executives Magazine* 1: 16–27.

Collins, J. C. 2001. *Good to Great.* Boston: Harvard Business School Press.

Conference Board, n.a. 2005. "U.S. Job Satisfaction Keeps Falling." *Business Credit* 107, no. 4 (April): 67; also online at www.conference-board.org, Feb. 28 (accessed October 19, 2005).

Conlin, M. 2003. "Unmarried America." *Business Week,* Oct. 20, 106–110, 114.

———. 2006. "Call Centers in the Rec Room." *Business Week,* January 23, 76–77.

Conlin, M., P. Coy, A. T. Plamer, and G. Saveri. 1999. "The Wild New Workforce." *Business Week,* Dec. 6, 39–46.

Conlin, M., L. Gard, R. Doyle, and M. Arndt. 2005. "Extreme Commuting." *Business Week,* Feb. 21, 80–81.

Cooke, D. K. 1994. "Measuring Career Stage." *Human Resource Management Review* 4, no. 4: 383–398.

Crittenden, A. 2001. *The Price of Motherhood.* New York: Henry Holt and Company.

———. 2004. *If You've Raised Kids, You Can Manage Anything.* New York: Gotham Books.

Crocitto, M. 2006. "Middle Career Stages." In *Encyclopedia of Career Development,* ed. Jeff Greenhaus and Gerard Callanan. Thousand Oaks, CA: Sage Publications.

Cytrynbaum, S., and J. O. Crites. 1989. "The Utility of Adult Development Theory in Understanding Career Adjustment Process." In *Handbook of Career Theory,* ed. M. B. Arthur, D. T. Hall, and B. S. Lawrence, 66–88.

Dahle, C. 2005. "Fast Company: Information on Their Criteria and Awards for Social Capitalism." *Fast Company,* online at www.fastcompany.com, January (accessed October 25, 2005).

———. 2006a. "Filling the Void." *Fast Company,* online at www. fast company.com, January (accessed January 24, 2006).

———. 2006b. "The Good Business of Social Change." *FastCompany,* online at www.fastcompany.com, January (accessed January 22, 2006).

Dalton, G. W. 1989. "Developmental Views of Careers in Organizations." In *Handbook of Career Theory,* ed. M. B. Arthur, D. T. Hall, and B. S. Lawrence, 89–109.

Darnton, N. 1990. "Mommy v. Mommy." *Newsweek* 115, no. 23 (June 4): 64–67.

DeFillippi, R. J., and M. B. Arthur. 1994. "The Boundaryless Career: A Competency-Based Model." *Journal of Organizational Behavior* 15, no. 4: 307–324.

DeFillippi, R. A., and C. Jones. 1996. "Back to the Future in Film: Combining Industry and Self-Knowledge to Meet Career Challenges of the 21st Century." *Academy of Management Executive* 10, no. 4: 89–103.

de Janasz, S. C., M. Forret, and D. Haack. 2003. "No Family, No Benefits, No Fair: Are Employees without Families Feeling Left Out?" Presentation at the Southern Management Association, November, Clearwater, Florida.

de Janasz, S. C., and S. E. Sullivan. 2004. "Multiple Mentoring in Academe: Developing the Professorial Network." *Journal of Vocational Behavior* 64, no. 2: 263–283.

de Janasz, S. C., S. E. Sullivan, and V. Whiting. 2004. "Mentor Networks and Career Success: Lessons for Turbulent Times." *Academy of Management Executive* 17, no. 4: 78–82.

DeLong, T. J., and V. Vijayaraghavan. 2003. "Let's Hear It for B Players." *Harvard Business Review,* Reprint R0306F, June, 96–102.

DePater, I. 2005. "Employees' Challenging Experiences as Cues for Promotion Evaluations: A New Perspective on the Glass Ceiling." Presentation at the Academy of Management Meeting, Honolulu, Hawaii.

Deutch, C. H. 2005. "Behind the Exodus of Executive Women: Boredom." *New York Times,* May 1.

Douglas, S. J., and M. W. Michaels. 2004. *The Mommy Myth.* New York: Free Press.

Driver, M. J. 1979. "Career Concepts and Career Management in Organizations." In *Behavioral Problems in Organizations,* ed. C. L. Cooper, 79–139. Englewood Cliffs, NJ: Prentice-Hall.

———. 1982. "Career Concepts: A New Approach to Career Research." In *Career Issues in Human Resource Management,* ed. R. Katz, 23–32. Englewood Cliffs, NJ: Prentice-Hall.

Drucker, P. 1993. As quoted in the *Chicago Sun Times,* Nov. 21. Cited in Moore, T. F. 1994. "Rightsizing: Living with the New Reality." *Healthcare Financial Management* 48, no. 9: 48–54.

Dunham, K. J. 2003. "Stay-at-Home Dads Fight Stigma." *Wall Street Journal,* eastern edition, 242, no. 40 (Aug. 26), B1.

Eagly, A. E., S. J. Karau, and M. G. Makhijani. 1995. "Gender and the Effectiveness of Leaders: A Meta-Analysis." *Psychological Bulletin* 117, no. 1: 125–145.

Eby, L. T. 2001. "The Boundaryless Career Experiences of Mobile Spouses in Dual-Earner Marriages." *Group and Organization Management* 26, no. 3: 343–368.

Eby, L. T., and T. D. Allen. Forthcoming. "Perceptions of Singles and Single Parent: A Laboratory Experiment." *Journal of Applied Social Psychology.*

Eby, L. T., M. Butts, and A. Lockwood. 2003. "Predictors of Success in the Era of the Boundaryless Career." *Journal of Organizational Behavior* 24, no. 6: 689–708.

Eby, L. T., W. J. Casper, A. Lockwood, C. Bordeaux, and A. Brinley. 2005. "Work and Family Research in IO/OB: Content Analysis and Review of the Literature, 1980–2002." *Journal of Vocational Behavior* 66: 124–197.

Enrensaft, D. 1984. "When Women and Men Mother." In *Mothering: Essays in Feminist Theory,* ed. J. Trebilcot, 41–60. Totowa, NJ: Rowman & Allanheld.

REFERENCES **349**

Ensher, E. A., S. E. Murphy, and S. E. Sullivan. 2002a. "Reel Women: Lessons from Female TV Executives on Managing Work and Real Life." *Academy of Management Executive* 16, no. 2: 106–102.

———. 2002b. "Boundaryless Careers in Entertainment: Executive Women's Experiences." In *Career Creativity: Explorations in the Remaking of Work,* ed. M. Peiperl and M. Arthur, 229–254. Oxford: Oxford University Press.

Executive Female, n.a. 2003. "Get a Life!" *Executive Female* (Spring): 11.

Fairlie, R. W. 2004. "Self-Employed Business Ownership Rates in the United States: 1979–2003." SBA Office of Advocacy Contract SBAHQ04M0248, Research Summary 243, online at www.sba.gov, December (accessed October 25, 2005).

Families and Work Institute, n.a. 2004. "Generation and Gender in the Workplace: An Issue Brief." New York: Families and Work Institute. Published jointly with the American Business Collaboration.

Feldman, D. C. 1989. "Careers in Organizations: Recent Trends and Future Directions." *Journal of Management Review* 15, no. 2: 135–156.

———. 1990. "Reconceptualizing the Nature and Consequences of Part-Time Work." *Academy of Management Review* 15, no. 1 (January): 103–112.

———. 2002. "Managers' Propensity to Work Longer Hours: A Multilevel Analysis." *Human Resource Management Review* 12: 339–357.

Fels, A. 2004. "Do Women Lack Ambition?" *Harvard Business Review* (April): 50–60.

Filer, R. K., D. S. Hammermesh, and A. E. Rees. 1996. *The Economics of Work and Pay.* New York: HarperCollins.

Fisher, A. 2003. "The Rebalancing Act." *Fortune* 148, no. 7 (Oct.): 110–114.

———. 2005. "How to Battle the Coming Brain Drain." *Fortune* 151, no. 6 (March 21): 121–128.

———. 2006. "What Do Gen Xers Want?" *Fortune,* online at www. fortune.com, January 20 (accessed January 21, 2006).

Fishman, C. 1999. "The Way to Enough." *Fast Company* 26 (July): 160.

Fletcher, J. K. 1996. "A Relational Approach to the Protean Worker." In *The Career Is Dead, Long Live the Career,* ed. Hall, 105–131. San Francisco: Jossey-Bass.

———. 1999. *Disappearing Acts: Gender, Power, and Relational Practice at Work.* Cambridge, MA: MIT Press.

Forret, M., and S. E. Sullivan. 2002. "A Balanced Scorecard Approach to Networking and Career Development." *Organizational Dynamics* 31, no. 3: 245–258.

Fortune, n.a. 1995. "There Are No Bedtime Stories Here." *Fortune* 132, no. 4: 82–88.

Friedman, S. D., and J. H. Greenhaus. 2000. *Work and Family—Allies or Enemies? What Happens When Business Professionals Confront Life Choices.* New York: Oxford University Press.

Friedman, T. 2005. *The World Is Flat: A Brief History of the 21st Century.* New York: Farrar, Strauss, Giroux.

Frone, M. R, M. Russell, and M. L. Cooper. 1995. "Relationship of Work and Family Stressors to Psychological Distress: The Independent Moderating Influence of Social Support, Mastery, Active Coping, and Self-Focused Attention." In *Occupational Stress: A Handbook,* ed. R. Crandall and P. L. Perrewé, 129–152. Washington, DC: Taylor and Francis.

Fursman, L., and V. Jacobsen. 2003. *Work and Family Balance: An Economic View.* Working paper 03/26, September. Wellington: New Zealand Treasury.

Galinsky, E., K. Salmond, and J. T. Bond. 2003. "Leaders in a Global Economy: A Study of Executive Women and Men." Families and Work Institute, online at www.familesandwork.org (accessed January 21, 2006).

Gallos, J. V. 1989. "Exploring Women's Development: Implications for Career Theory, Practice, and Research." In *Handbook of Career Theory,* ed. M. B. Arthur, D. T. Hall, and B. S. Lawrence, 110–132.

Gavin, J. H., and R. O. Mason. 2004. "The Value of Happiness in the Workplace." *Organizational Dynamics* 33, no. 4: 379–392.

George, B. 2003. *Authentic Leadership: Rediscovering the Secrets to Creating Lasting Value.* San Fransico: Jossey-Bass.

George, M., et al. 1995. "Brain Activity during Transient Sadness and Happiness in Healthy Women." *American Journal of Psychiatry* 152, no. 3 (March): 341.

Gersick, C. G., and K. E. Kram. 2002. "High Achieving Women at Midlife: An Exploratory Study." *Journal of Management Inquiry* 11, no. 2: 104–127.

Gibbs, N. 2005. "Midlife Crisis: Bring It On!" *Time,* May 16, 53–63.

Gilligan, C. 1978. "In a Different Voice: Women's Conception of the Self and of Morality." *Harvard Educational Review* 47, no. 4: 481–517.

———. 1982. *In a Different Voice: Psychological Theory and Women's Development.* Cambridge, MA: Harvard University Press.

Gomez-Mejia, L. R., D. B. Balkin, and G. T. Milkovich. 1990. "Rethinking Your Rewards for Technical Employees." *Organizational Dynamics* 1, no. 1: 62–75.

Gordon, J. R., and K. S. Whelan. 1998. "Successful Professional Women in Midlife: How Organizations Can More Effectively Understand and Respond to the Challenges." *Academy of Management Executive* 12, no. 1: 8–27.

Gosling, S. D., S. Vazire, S. Srivastava, and O. P. John. 2004. "Should We Trust Web-Based Studies? A Comparative Analysis of Six Preconceptions about Internet Questionnaires." *American Psychologist* 59: 93–104.

Greenhaus, J. H., and N. J. Beutell. 1985. "Sources and Conflict between Work and Family Roles." *Academy of Management Review* 10, no. 1: 76–88.

Greenhaus, J. H., K. M. Collins, and J. D. Shaw. 2002. "The Relation between Work-Family Balance and Quality of Life." *Journal of Vocational Behavior* 63: 510–31.

Greenhaus, J. H., and S. Parasuraman. 1986. "Vocational and Organizational Behavior, 1985: A Review." *Journal of Vocational Behavior* 29: 115–176.

———. 1999. "Research on Work, Family, and Gender: Current Status and Future Directions." In *Handbook of Gender and Work,* ed. G. N. Powell, 319–412. Thousand Oaks, CA: Sage Publications.

Greenglass, E. R. 2002. "Work Stress, Coping, and Social Support: Implications for Women's Occupational Well-Being." In *Gender, Work Stress, and Health,* ed. D. L. Nelson and R. J. Burke, 85–96. Washington, DC: American Psychological Association.

Grossman, L. 2005. "Grow Up? Not So Fast." *Time,* January 24, 42–54.

Grossman, R. J. 2005. "The Truth about the Coming Labor Shortage." *HR Magazine* 50, no. 3: 46–53.

Gunz, H. P., and P. A. Heslin. 2005. "Reconceptualizing Career Success." *Journal of Organizational Behavior* 26: 105–111.

Gur, R., and R. C. Gur. 1990. "Gender Differences in Regional Cerebral Blood Flow." *Schizophrenia Bulletin* 16: 247–254.

———. 1994. "Methods for the Study of Brain-Behavior Relationships." In *Biological Bases of Brain Function and Disease,* ed. A. Frazer, P. B. Molinoff, and A. Winoker, 261–279. New York: Raven Press.

Gwyther, M. 2003a. "Men at Work . . . and Men at Home." *Management Today* (April): 8.

———. 2003b. "Working Dads Who Want It All." *Management Today* (April): 44–52.

Haas, N. 2005. "Hollywood's New Old Girl's Network." *New York Times,* April 24, sec. 2.

Hacker, S. K., and T. L. Doolen. 2003. "Strategies for Living: Moving from the Balance Paradigm." *Career Development International* 8, no. 6: 283–290.

Hackett, G., R. W. Lent, and J. H. Greenhaus. 1991. "Advances in Vocational Theory and Research: A Twenty-Year Retrospective." *Journal of Vocational Behavior* 38: 3–38.

Hackman, J., and G. Oldham. 1976. "Motivation through the Design of Work: Test of a Theory." *Organization Behavior and Human Performance* 16: 250–79.

Hales, D. 1999. *Just Like a Woman: How Gender Science Is Redefining What Makes Us Female.* New York: Bantam.

Hall, D. T. 1976. *Careers in Organizations.* Pacific Palisades, CA: Goodyear.

———. 1996. *The Career Is Dead, Long Live the Career.* San Francisco: Jossey-Bass.

———. 2004. "The Protean Career: A Quarter-Century Journey." *Journal of Vocational Behavior* 65: 1–13.

Hall, D. T., and D. E. Chandler. 2005. "Psychological Success: When the Career Is a Calling." *Journal of Organizational Behavior* 26: 155–176.

Hall, D. T., and P. H. Mirvis. 1996. "The New Protean Career: Psychological Success and the Path with a Heart." In *The Career Is Dead, Long Live the Career,* ed. Hall, 15–45.

Hamilton, E. A., J. R. Gordon, and K. S. Whelan-Berry. 2005. "We're Busy Too: Understanding the Work-Life Conflict of Never-Married Women Without Children." Paper presented at the Academy of Management Meeting, Careers Division, Honolulu, Hawaii.

Hammonds, K. H. 2001. "Ford's Drive for Balance." *Fast Company,* online at www.fastcompany.com/article/2001/05/ford-balancingact, May (accessed October 25, 2005).

Hammonds, K. H., M. Aneiro, M. Clayton, M. Korn, and M. Yankus. 2004. "Balance Is Bunk." *Fast Company* 87 (Oct.): 68.

Hayghe, H., and S. Bianchi. 1994. "Married Mothers' Work Patterns: The Job-Family Compromise." *Monthly Labor Review* (June): 24–30.

Helliker, K. 2004. "Sara Lee Hires Brenda Barnes as President, Operating Chief." *Wall Street Journal,* May 3, B2.

Helyar, J. 2005. "Permanent Vacation? 50 and Fired." *Fortune* magazine, online at www.fortune.com, May 2 (accessed June 1, 2005).

Heslin, P. A. 2005. "Conceptualizing and Evaluating Career Success." *Journal of Organizational Behavior* 26, 113–136.

Hewlett, S. A. 2002. *Creating a Life: Professional Women and the Quest for Children.* New York: Talk/Miramax Books.

Hewlett, S. A., and C. B. Luce. 2005. "On Ramps and Off Ramps." *Harvard Business Review* 83, no. 3 (March): 43–54.

Hochschild, A. R. 1989. *The Second Shift: Working Parents and the Revolution at Home.* New York: Viking Penguin.

———. 1997. *The Time Bind: When Work Becomes Home and Home Becomes Work.* New York: Henry Holt.

Holland, J. L. 1973. *Making Vocational Choices: A Theory of Careers.* Englewood Cliffs, NJ: Prentice-Hall.

Hoptman, M., and R. Davidson. 1994. "How and Why Do the Two Cerebral Hemispheres Interact?" *Psychological Bulletin* 116, no. 2: 195.

HR Briefing, n.a. 2000. "Work/Family Policies Aren't Just for Women," *HR Briefing,* October 1, 7.

Ibarra, H. 2003. *Working Identity: Unconventional Strategies for Reinventing Your Career.* Boston: Harvard Business School Press.

———. 2004. "Men and Women of the Corporation and the Change Masters: Practical Theories for Changing Times." *Academy of Management Executive* 18, no. 2: 108–111.

Ismail, M., R. M. Rasdi, and N. W. A. Wahat. 2005. "High-Flyer Women Academicians: Factors Contributing to Success." *Women in Management Review* 20, no. 2: 117–132.

Jacobs, J. A., and K. Gerson. 2000. "Do Americans Feel Overworked? Comparing Actual and Ideal Working Time." In *Work and Family: Research Informing Policy,* ed. Toby L. Parcel and Daniel B. Cornfield, 71–95. Thousand Oaks, CA: Sage Publications.

Jervey, G. 2003. "Workaholics Anonymous: The Sweet Science of Slowing Down." *Fortune* magazine, online at www.fortune.com, February 18 (accessed June 1, 2005).

Johnson, J. 2005a. "Outsourced God Squads—A Thriving Industry: Spiritual Teams." MSNBC, online at www.msnbc.com, March 24 (accessed October 25, 2005).

———. 2005b. "Walking on the Assembly Line with God." MSNBC, online at www.msnbc.com, March 24 (accessed October 25, 2005).

Jones, C. 1996. "Careers in Project Networks: The Case of the Film Industry." In *The Boundaryless Career,* ed. Arthur and Rousseau, 58–75.

Jurkeiwicz, C. E., and R. G. Brown. 1998. "GenXers vs. Boomers vs. Maturers: Generational Comparisons of Public Employee Motivation." *Review of Public Personnel Administration* 18: 55–59.

Kanter, R. M. 2000. "Kaleidoscope Thinking." In *Management 21C: Someday We'll All Manage This Way,* ed. S. Chowdhury, 250–262.

———. 2001. *Evolve! Succeeding in the Digital Culture of Tomorrow.* Boston: Harvard Business School Press.

———. 2004. *Confidence: How Winning Streaks and Losing Streaks Begin and End.* New York: Crown Business.

Karp, H., C. Fuller, and D. Sirias. 2002. *Bridging the Boomer Xer Gap: Creating Authentic Teams for High Performance at Work.* Mountain View, CA: Davies-Black Publishing.

Katzenback, J. R. 2000. *Peak Performance: Aligning the Hearts and Minds of Your Employees.* Boston: Harvard Business School Press.

Kaufman, G., and P. Uhlenberg. 2000. "The Influence of Parenthood on the Work Effort of Married Men and Women." *Social Forces* 78, no. 3 (March): 931–947.

Kaye, B. 2002. *Up Is Not the Only Way.* Mountain View, CA: Davies-Black Publishing.

Kernis, M. H. 2003. "Toward a Conceptualization of Optimal Self-Esteem." *Psychological Inquiry* 14, no. 1: 1–26.

Kirchmeyer, C. 1998. "Determinants of Managerial Career Success: Evidence and Explanation of Male/Female Differences." *Journal of Management* 24, no. 6: 673–692.

———. 2002. "Gender Differences in Managerial Careers: Yesterday, Today, and Tomorrow." *Journal of Business Ethics* 37: 5–24.

Kluger, J., J. Chu, B. Liston, M. Sieger, and D. Willams. 2004. "Is God in Our Genes?" *Time,* online at www.time.com/time/archive, October 25 (accessed October 25, 2005).

Kluger, J., D. Cray, E. Ferkenhoff, N. Isackson, and L. Whitaker. 2005. "Ambition: Why Some People Are Most Likely to Succeed." *Time* 166, no. 20 (November 14): 48–59.

Kochan, T. A. 2002. "An Employment Policy Agenda for Working Families." Working Paper Series. Cambridge, MA: MIT Workplace Center.

Koeppel, D. 2004. "The New Cost of Keeping Workers Happy." *New York Times,* March 7, Executive Life, Business Section, 11.

Konrad, A. M., J. E. Ritchie, P. Lieb, and E. Corrigall. 2000. "Sex Differences and Similarities in Job Attribute Preferences: A Meta Analysis." *Psychological Bulletin* 126, no. 4: 593–641.

Korabik, K., and H. M. Rosin. 1995. "The Impact of Children on Women's Career Behavior and Organizational Commitment." *Human Resource Management* 34, no. 4: 513–528.

Kossek, E. E., and M. D. Lee. 2005. "Benchmarking Survey: A Snapshot of Managers' Perspectives on Implementing Reduced-Load Work for Professionals." East Lansing, MI: Michigan State University.

Kossek, E. E., and C. Ozeki. 1998. "Work-Family Conflict, Policies, and the Job-Life Satisfaction Relationship: A Review and Directions for Organizational Behavior-Human Relations Research." *Journal of Applied Psychology* 83, no. 2: 139–149.

Kouzes, J. M., and B. Z. Posner. 1993. *Credibility.* San Francisco: Jossey-Bass.

Kram, K. E. 1996. "A Relational Approach to Career Development." In *The Career Is Dead, Long Live the Career,* ed. Hall, 132–157. San Francisco: Jossey-Bass.

Kupperschmidt, B. R. 2000. "Multigeneration Employees: Strategies for Effective Management." *The Health Care Manager* 19, no. 1 (Sept.): 65–76.

Lachnit, C. 2003. "A People Strategy That Spans the Globe." *Workforce,* June, 76.

Lamb, M. E., J. H. Pleck, E. L. Charnov, J. A. Levine. 1987. "A Biosocial Perspective on Paternal Behavior and Involvement." In *Parenting across the Lifespan: Biosocial Perspectives,* ed. J. B. Lancaster, J. Altman, A. Rossi, and L. R. Sherrod, 11–42. New York: Academic Press.

Landers, R. M., J. B. Rebitzer, and L. J. Taylor. 1996. "Human Resources Practices and the Demographic Transformation of Professional Labor Markets." In *Broken Ladders,* ed. P. Osterman, 215–245. New York: Oxford University Press.

Larson, C. 2004. "The Penny Pinch." *NAFE Magazine* 28, no. 4: 14–19.

———. 2005. "The Top 30 Companies for Executive Women, 2005." *NAFE Magazine* 28, no. 1: 16–23.

Larwood, L., and B. A. Gutek. 1987. "Working Towards a Theory of Women's Career Development." In *Women's Career Development,* ed. Larwood and Gutek. Thousand Oaks, CA: Sage Publications.

Latack, J. C., A. J. Kinicki, and G. E. Prussia. 1995. "An Integrative Model of Coping with Job Loss." *Academy of Management Review* 20: 311–342.

Lawlor, J. 2004. "When Stay-at-Home Fathers Return to Work (Elsewhere)." *New York Times,* Aug. 1, Sec. 10, Job Market, 1, 3.

Lawrence, B. 1980. "The Myth of the Midlife Crisis." *Sloan Management Review* 4, no. 21: 35–49.

Layne, A. 2000. "Keep Your Balance." *Fast Company,* online at www.fastcompany.com, November (accessed January 28, 2005).

Leana, C. R., and D. C. Feldman. 1991. "Gender Differences in Responses to Unemployment." *Journal of Vocational Behavior* 38: 65–77.

Lee, K. 2004. "Getting on Board." *NAFE Magazine* 25, no. 4: 6.

Levering, R., and M. Moskowitz. 2003. "100 Best Companies to Work For." *Fortune* 24 (Feb.): 127–50.

Levinson, D. 1978. *The Seasons of a Man's Life.* New York: Knopf.

———. 1986. "A Conception of Adult Development." *American Psychologist* 41: 3–13.

———. 1996. *The Seasons of a Woman's Life.* New York: Knopf.

Lombardo, M. M., and C. D. McCauley. 1988. "The Dynamics of Management Derailment." *Tech Report* 34. Greensboro, NC: Center for Creative Leadership.

Lombardo, M. M., M. N. Ruderman, and C. D. McCauley. 1987. "Explanations of Success and Derailment in Upper Level Management Positions." *Journal of Business and Psychology* 2: 199–216.

Luthans, F., and C. M. Youssef. 2002. "Investing in People for Competitive Advantage." *Organizational Dynamics* 33, no. 2: 143–160.

Lyness, K. S., and M. K. Judiesch. 2001. "Are Female Managers Quitters? The Relationships of Gender, Promotions, and Family Leaves of Absence to Voluntary Turnover." *Journal of Applied Psychology* 86, no. 6: 1167–1178.

Lyness, K. S., and D. E. Thompson. 2000. "Climbing the Corporate Ladder: Do Female and Male Executives Follow the Same Route?" *Journal of Applied Psychology* 85, no. 1: 86–101.

Maccoby, E. 1998. *The Two Sexes.* Cambridge, MA: Harvard University Press.

Maccoby, E., and C. Jacklin. 1974. *The Psychology of Sex Differences.* Stanford, CA: Stanford University Press.

Mahler, J. 2003. "Commute to Nowhere." *New York Times Magazine,* April 13, Sec. 6, 44.

Maidment, F. 2003. "Do Americans Work Too Hard?" *Human Resource Executive,* October, 72.

Maier, M. 1999. "On the Gendered Substructure of Organization: Dimensions and Dilemmas of Corporate Masculinity." In *Handbook of Gender and Work,* ed. Powell, 69–93.

Mainiero, L. A. 1994. "Getting Anointed for Advancement: The Case of Executive Women." *Academy of Management Executive* 8, no. 2: 53–64.

Mainiero, L. A., and S. E. Sullivan. 2005. "Kaleidoscope Careers: An Alternative Explanation for the Opt-Out Revolution." *Academy of Management Executive* 19, no. 1: 106–123.

Marsiglio, W. 1993. "Contemporary Scholarship on Fatherhood: Culture, Identity, and Conduct." *Journal of Family Issues* 14, no. 4 (December): 484–509.

Martin, G., and V. Kats. 2003. "Families and Work in Transition in Twelve Countries, 1980–2001." *Monthly Labor Review* 126, no. 9: 3–32.

Martinez, M. N. 1998. "An Inside Look at Making the Grade." *HR Magazine* 43, no. 4 (March), online at www.shrm.org (accessed June 5, 2005).

Martins, L. L., K. A. Eddleston, and J. F. Veiga. 2002. "The Moderators of the Relationship between Work-Family Conflict and Career Satisfaction." *Academy of Management Journal* 45, no. 2 (April): 399–410.

Maslow, A. 1943. "A Theory of Human Motivation." *Psychological Review* 50: 370–396.

Mavin, S. 2001. "Women's Career in Theory and Practice: Time for Change?" *Women in Management Review* 16, no. 4: 183–192.

McCall, M. W., M. M. Lombardo, and A. M. Morrison. 1988. *The Lessons of Experience: How Successful Executives Develop on the Job.* New York: Macmillan.

McGregor, J. 2004. "Balance and Balance Sheets." *Fast Company* 82 (May): 96.

McKaughan, M. 1987. *The Biological Clock.* New York: Doubleday.

McNamee, M. 2004. "Paternity Leave: The New Revolution." *Child Magazine,* July, 81–87.

Menzies, T. V., M. Diochon, and Y. Gasse. 2004. "Examining Venture-Related Myths Concerning Women Entrepreneurs." *Journal of Developmental Entrepreneurship* 9, no. 2: 89–107.

Mero, J., and P. Sellers. 2003. "Power: Do Women Really Want It?" *Fortune* 148, no. 8 (October): 80–88.

Merrill-Sands, D., J. Kickul, and C. Ingols. 2005. "Women Pursuing Leadership and Power: Challenging the Myth of the Opt-Out Revolution." CGO Insights Briefing Note, no. 20 (February): 1–4.

Metz, I. 2005. "Advancing the Careers of Women with Children." *Career Development International* 10, no. 3: 228–245.

Metz, I., and P. Tharenou. 1999. "A Retrospective Analysis of Australian Women's Representation in Management in Large and Small Banks." *International Journal of Human Resource Management* 10: 201–222.

Miller, J. B. 1976. *Toward a New Psychology of Women.* Boston: Beacon Press.

Miller, J., and M. Miller. 2005. "Get a Life!" *Fortune,* November 16, 108–125.

Minter, L. E., and C. A. Samuels. 1998. "The Impact of 'the Dream' on Women's Experience of the Midlife Transition." *Journal of Adult Development* 5, no. 1: 31–43.

Mitroff, I. I., and M. C. Alpaslan. 2003. "Preparing for Evil." *Harvard Business Review* 81, no. 4 (April): 109–116.

Moen, P., with D. Harris-Abbott, L. Shinok, and P. Roehling. 1999. "The Cornell Couples and Careers Study." Ithaca, N.Y.: Cornell Employment and Family Careers Institute, Sloan Center for Working Families.

Moen, P., and S. Sweet. 2002. "Two Careers, One Employer: Couples Working for the Same Corporation." *Journal of Vocational Behavior* 61, no. 3: 466–483.

Mohrman, S. A., and S. G. Cohen. 1995. "When People Get Out of the Box: New Relationships, New Systems." In *Changing Nature of Work,* ed. A. Howard, 365–410. San Francisco: Jossey-Bass.

Moore, D. P. 2002. *Careerpreneurs: Lessons from Leading Women Entrepreneurs on Building a Career without Boundaries.* Mountain View, CA: Davies-Black Publishing.

Moore, D. P., and E. H. Buttner. 1997. *Women Entrepreneurs: Moving beyond the Glass Ceiling.* Thousand Oaks, CA: Sage Publications.

Morris, B. 1995. "Yankelovich Study as Cited in Executive Women Confront Midlife Crisis." *Fortune,* September 18, 61–72.

———. 2002. "Most Powerful Women in Business—Trophy Husbands." *Fortune,* online at www.fortune.com, September 27 (accessed May 27, 2005).

———. 2004. "How Corporate America Is Betraying Women." *Fortune,* online at www.fortune.com, December (accessed May 27, 2005).

———. 2006. "Genentech: The Best Place to Work." *Fortune,* online at www.fortune.com, January 20 (accessed January 21, 2006).

MOW—International Research Team. 1987. *The Meaning of Working.* London: Academic Press.

MSNBC, n.a. 2005a. "Faith in America: Ten Companies with a Mission." Online at www.msnbc.msn.com (accessed October 25, 2005).

MSNBC, n.a. 2005b. Poll on religion. Online at www.msnbc. msn.com/id/7224318 (accessed October 25, 2005).

National Sleep Foundation, n.a. 2001. "Sleep in America" poll. Washington, DC: National Sleep Foundation; online at www.sleepfoundation.org (accessed October 25, 2005).

National Women's Business Council, n.a. 2005. "Women Business Owners and Their Enterprises: Fact Sheet." Online at www.nwbc.gov, March (accessed May 3, 2005).

Newton, P. M. 1994. "Daniel Levinson and His Theory of Adult Development: A Reminiscence and Some Clarifications." *Journal of Adult Development* 1, no. 3: 135–147.

Ng, T. W. H., L. T. Eby, K. L. Sorensen, and D. C. Feldman. 2005. "Predictors of Objective and Subjective Career Success: A Meta-Anaylsis." *Personnel Psychology* 58: 367–408.

Nicholson, N., and W. De Waal-Andrews. 2005. "Playing to Win: Biological Imperatives, Self-Regulation, and Trade-offs in the Game of Career Success." *Journal of Organizational Behavior* 26, no. 2: 137–154.

Ohlott, P. J., M. N. Ruderman, and C. D. McCauley. 1994. "Gender Differences in Managers' Developmental Job Experiences." *Academy of Management Journal* 37, no. 1: 46–56.

O'Neil, D. A., and D. Bilimoria. 2005. "Women's Career Development Phases: Idealism, Endurance, and Reinvention." *Career Development International* 10, no. 3: 168–189.

O'Neil, D., D. Bilimoria, and A. Saatcioglu. 2003. "Women's Ways of Instituting Careers: A Typology of Women's Career Development." Paper presented at the Academy of Management, Best Conference Paper Careers Division, Seattle, WA.

Orecklin, M. 2004. "Stress and the Superdad." *Time,* August 23, 38–39.

Orenstein, P. 2000. *Flux: Women on Sex, Work, Love, Kids, and Life in a Half-Changed World.* New York: Doubleday.

Ornstein, S., W. L. Cron, and J. W. Slocum. 1989. "Life Stages versus Career Stage: A Comparative Test of the Theories of Levinson and Super." *Journal of Organizational Behavior* 10: 117–133.

Ornstein, S., and L. Isabella. 1990. "Age vs. Stage Models of Career Attitudes of Women: A Partial Replication and Extension." *Journal of Vocational Behavior* 36: 1–19.

———. 1993. "Making Sense of Careers: A Review, 1989–1992." *Journal of Management* 19, no. 2: 243–267.

Osterman, R. 1996. *Broken Ladders.* New York: Oxford University Press.

Overholt, A. 2003. "The Hippest City in the USA." *Fast Company* 75 (October): 96.

Parasuraman, S., and J. H. Greenhaus. 1997. *Integrating Work and Family: Challenges and Choices for a Changing World.* Westport, CT: Quorum Books.

Parker, P., and M. B. Arthur. 2000. "Careers, Organizing, and Community." In *Career Frontiers,* ed. M. Peiperl, M. Arthur, R. Goffee, and T. Morris, 99–121. New York: Oxford University Press.

———. 2004. "Giving Voice to the Dual-Career Couple." *British Journal of Guidance and Counseling* 32, no. 1: 3–23.

Pearson, A. 2002. *I Don't Know How She Does It: The Life of Kate Reddy, Working Mother.* New York: Knopf.

Peiperl, M., M. Arthur, and N. Anand. 2002. *Career Creativity.* Oxford: Oxford University Press.

Peiperl, M., and Y. Baruch. 1997. "Back to Square Zero: The Post-Corporate Career." *Organizational Dynamics* 25, no. 4: 6–22.

Peiperl, M., and B. Jones. 2001. "Workaholics and Overworkers. Productivity or Pathology?" *Group and Organizational Management* 26, no. 3: 369–393.

Personnel Today, n.a. 2003. "Working Dads Lose Out with Family-Friendly Policies." *Personnel Today,* online at www.personneltoday.com, May 6 (accessed October 25, 2005).

Pfeffer, J. 1998. *The Human Equation: Build Profits by Putting People First.* Boston: Harvard Business School Press.

Pink, Daniel H. 2001. *Free Agent Nation: The Future of Working for Yourself.* New York: Time-Warner.

Pleck, J. H. 1977. "The Work-Family Role System." *Social Problems* 24, no. 4: 417–427.

———. 1985. *Working Wives, Working Husbands.* Thousand Oaks, CA: Sage Publications.

Poe, A. C. 1999. "The Daddy Track." *HR Magazine* 44, no. 7 (July): 82.

Powell, G. A. 2003. *Women and Men in Management*. Thousand Oaks, CA: Sage Publications.

Powell, G. N. 1999. "Reflections on the Glass Ceiling: Recent Trends and Future Prospects." In *Handbook of Gender and Work*, ed. Powell, 325–346.

Powell, G. N., ed. 1999. *Handbook of Gender and Work*. Thousand Oaks, CA: Sage Publications.

Powell, G. N., and L. A. Mainiero. 1992. "Cross-Currents in the River of Time: Conceptualizing the Complexities of Women's Careers." *Journal of Management* 18: 215–237.

———. 1993. "Getting Ahead—in Career and Life." In *Women and Men in Management*, ed. G. N. Powell, 186–224. Thousand Oaks, CA: Sage Publications.

Power, S. J., and T. J. Rothausen. 2003. "The Work-Oriented Midcareer Development Model: An Extension of Super's Maintenance Stage." *Counseling Psychologist 31*, no. 2: 157–197.

Pritchard, K. H. 2002. "Flextime." Society for Human Resource Management whitepaper, online at www.shrm.org/hrresources/whitepapers-published, July (accessed January 25, 2005).

Pruett, K. 2000. *Fatherneed: Why Fathercare Is as Important as Mothercare for Your Child*. New York: Simon and Schuster.

Puffer, S. M. 2004a. "Changing Organizational Structures: An Interview with Rosabeth Moss Kanter." *Academy of Management Executive* 18, no. 2: 96–105.

———. 2004b. "Introduction: Rosabeth Moss Kanter's Men and Women of the Corporation and the Change Masters." *Academy of Management Executive* 18, no. 2: 92–95.

Ragins, B. R., B. Townsend, and M. Mattis. 1998. "Gender Gap in the Executive Suite: CEOs and Female Executives Report on Breaking the Glass Ceiling." *Academy of Management Executive* 12, no. 1: 28–33.

Randsdell, E. 1998. "Building the New Economy." *Fast Company* 20 (December): 222.

Rapoport, R., L. Bailyn, J. Fletcher, and B. Pruitt. 2002. *Beyond Work-Family Balance: Advancing Gender Equity and Workplace Performance*. San Francisco: Jossey-Bass.

Reich, R. B. 1998. "The Company of the Future." *Fast Company* 19 (November): 124.

Reitman, F., and J. A. Schneer. 2005. "The Long-Term Impacts of Managerial Career Interruptions: A Longitudinal Study of Men and Women MBAs." *Group and Organization Management* 30, no. 3: 243–262.

Rhee, A. 2005. "God in NASCAR." MSNBC, online at www.msnbc.com, March 24 (accessed October 25, 2005).

Roberts, P., and P. Newton. 1987. "Levinsonian Studies of Women's Adult Development." *Psychology and Aging* 2, no. 2: 154–163.

Riss, S. 2005. "2005 Salary Survey: How Can We Close the Gender Wage Gap?" *NAFE Magazine* 28, no. 4: 18–21.

Rogers, B., and M. Brocklehurst. 2002. "What Now for the War for Talent?" *Executive View*, online at www.stork-may.com (accessed January 20, 2005).

Roman, M. 2004. "Brenda Barnes: No Piece of Cake." *Business Week*, May 17, 2004.

Room to Read staff. 2006. "Social Capitalist, Room to Read, Company Profile." *Fast Company*, online at www.fastcompany.com, January (accessed January 24, 2006).

Rosener, J. 1990. "Ways Women Lead." *Harvard Business Review* 68, no. 6 (November-December): 119–126.

———. 1995. *America's Competitive Secret: Women Managers.* New York: Oxford University Press.

Rossi, A. 1972. "Sex Equality: The Beginning of Ideology." In *Toward a Sociology of Women*, ed. C. Safilos-Rothschild, 72–98. Lexington, MA: Xerox Publishing.

Rousseau, D. M., and K. A. Wade-Benzoni. 1995. "Changing Individual-Organization Attachments: A Two-Way Street." In *Changing Nature of Work*, ed. A. Howard, 290–321. San Francisco: Jossey-Bass.

Ruderman, M., and P. Ohlott. 2002. *Standing at the Crossroads: Next Steps for High-Achieving Women.* San Francisco: Jossey-Bass.

Ruderman, M. N., P. J. Ohlott, K. Panzer, and S. King. 2002. "Benefits of Multiple Roles for Managerial Women." *Academy of Management Journal* 45, no. 2: 369–387.

Sacks, D. 2006. "Scenes from the Culture Clash." *Fortune*, no. 102 (January-February): 72–77.

Salter, C. 2004. "Calling JetBlue." *Fast Company* 82 (May), online at www.fastcompany.com/magazine/82/jetblue-agents.html (accessed October 25, 2005).

Sartain, L. 2003. *HR from the Heart: Inspiring Stories and Strategies for Building the People Side of Great Businesses.* New York: AMACOM.

Schabracq, M. J., and C. L. Cooper. 2000. "The Changing Nature of Work and Stress." *Journal of Managerial Psychology* 15, no. 3: 227–242.

Schein, E. H. 1978. *Career Dynamics: Matching Individual and Organizational Needs.* Reading, MA: Addison-Wesley.

———. 1996. "Career Anchors Revisited: Implications for Career Development in the Twenty-First Century." *Academy of Management Executive* 10, no. 4: 80–88.

Schneer, J. A., and F. Reitman. 1995. "The Impact of Gender as Managerial Careers Unfold." *Journal of Vocational Behavior*, no. 47: 290–315.

———. 1997. "The Interrupted Managerial Career Path: A Longitudinal Study of MBAs." *Journal of Vocational Behavior* 51, no. 3: 411–434.

———. 2002. "Managerial Life without a Wife: Family Structure and Managerial Career Success." *Journal of Business Ethics* 37, no. 1: 25–38.

Schneider, P. 1998–1999a. "Debunking the Sweatshop." *CIO Magazine,* December–January, online at www.cio.com (accessed June 10, 2005).

———. 1998–1999b. "The Renaissance Company." *CIO Magazine,* December–January, online at www.cio.com (accessed June 10, 2005).

Schor, J. 1991. *The Overworked American: The Unexpected Decline of Leisure.* New York: Basic Books.

Schwartz, F. N. 1989. "Management Women and the New Facts of Life." *Harvard Business Review* 67, no. 1 (January–February): 65–77.

———. 1992. *Breaking with Tradition: Women and Work, the New Facts of Life.* New York: Warner Books.

Schwartz, T. 2001. "My Name Is Tony, and I'm a Workaholic." *Fast Company,* online at www.fastcompany.com, April (accessed May 10, 2005).

Shaywitz, B. A., and S. E. Shaywitz. 1995. "Sex Differences in the Functional Organization of the Brain for Language." *Nature* 373, no. 6515: 607.

Sheehy, G. 1976. *Passages: Predictable Crises of Adult Life.* New York: E. P. Dutton.

Sheler, J. L. 2004. "The Power of Prayer." *U.S.News & World Report,* online at www.usnews.com/usnews/culture/articles/041220/20prayer.htm, December 24 (accessed October 25, 2005).

Shellenback, K., and P. Moen. 2002. "The Next Human Resource Challenge: Workers Who Are Caregivers." Cornell Employment and Family Careers Institute, Bronfenbrenner Life Course Center, Issue Brief 3, no. 2 (Winter): 1–4.

Shellenbarger, S. 2004. *The Breaking Point: How Female Midlife Crisis Is Transforming Today's Women.* New York: Henry Holt.

Singh, V., and S. Vinnicombe. 2004. "Why So Few Women Directors in Top U.K. Boardrooms? Evidence and Theoretical Explanations." *Corporate Governance* 12, no. 4 (October): 479–488.

Sluis, W. 2005. "Revolving Door in CEO Suites; Fiorina out at HP; Barnes in at Sara Lee." *Chicago Tribune,* final edition, February 13, 3.

Smart, R., and C. Peterson. 1994. "Stability versus Transition in Women's Career Development: A Test of Levinson's Theory." *Journal of Vocational Behavior* 45, no. 3: 241–260.

———. 1997. "Super's Career Stages and the Decision to Change Careers." *Journal of Vocational Behavior* 51, no. 3: 358–374.

Smith, R. 2000. "Living Behind a Mask." *O: The Oprah Magazine,* November, 212–215, 282.

Smola, K. W., and C. D. Sutton. 2002. "Generational Differences: Revisiting Generational Work Values for the New Millennium." *Journal of Organizational Behavior* 23, no. 4: 363–382.

Society for Human Resource Management, n.a. 2002. "What Are Employee Networks and Should They Be Part of Our Diversity Initiative?" February 13. Online at www.shrm.org (accessed October 25, 2005).

Spence, B. C. 2004. "Think It's Just a Penny?" *NAFE Magazine* 27, no. 4: 3.

———. 2005. "Bring on the Best!" *NAFE Magazine* 28, no. 1: 3.

Spillman, R. 2004. "Ward and June R Us." *Real Simple* 5, no. 3 (April): 257–259.

Spragins, E., and J. Keeney. 2002. "Is This the Best Company to Work for Anywhere?" *Fortune Small Business* 12, no. 9 (November): 66–71.

Steinberg, L., and W. Steinberg. 1995. *Crossing Paths*. New York: Simon and Schuster.

Stoltz-Loike, M. 1996. "Annual Review: Practice and Research in Career Development and Counseling, 1995." *Career Development Quarterly* 45: 99–140.

Story, L. 2005. "Many Women at Elite Colleges Set Career Path to Motherhood." *New York Times,* September 20.

Stroh, L., J. Brett, and A. Reilly. 1996. "Family Structure, Glass Ceiling, and Traditional Explanations for the Differential Rate of Turnover of Female and Male Managers." *Journal of Vocational Behavior* 49, no. 1: 99–118.

Sturges, J. 1999. "What It Means to Succeed: Personal Conceptions of Career Success Held by Male and Female Managers at Different Ages." *British Journal of Management* 10, no. 3: 239–252.

Sullivan, S. E. 1992. "Is There a Time for Everything? Attitudes Related to Women's Sequencing of Career and Family." *Career Development Quarterly* 40, no. 3: 234–243.

———. 1999. "The Changing Nature of Careers: A Review and Research Agenda." *Journal of Management* 25, no. 3: 457–484.

———. 2006. "Early Career Stage." In *Encyclopedia of Career Development,* ed. Jeff Greenhaus and Gerard Callanan. Thousand Oaks, CA: Sage Publications.

Sullivan, S. E., and M. B. Arthur. 2006. "The Evolution of the Boundaryless Career Concept: Examining Physical and Psychological Mobility." *Journal of Vocational Behavior.*

Sullivan, S.E., W. A. Carden, and D. F. Martin. 1998. "Careers in the Next Millennium: A Reconceptualization of Traditional Career Theory." *Human Resource Management Review* 8, no. 2: 165–185.

Sullivan, S. E., and M. Crocitto. Forthcoming. "Process Theories of Careers." In *Handbook of Career Studies,* ed. H. Gunz and M. Peiperl. Thousand Oaks, CA: Sage Publications.

Sullivan, S. E., D. F. Martin, W. A. Carden, and L. A. Mainiero. 2004. "The Road Less Traveled: How to Manage the Recycling Career Stage." *Journal of Leadership and Organization Studies* 10, no. 2: 34–42.

Super, D. 1957. *Psychology of Careers.* New York: Harper and Brothers.

Super, D., A. Thompson, and R. Lindeman. 1988. *Adult Career Concerns Inventory: Manual for Research and Exploratory Use in Counseling.* Mountain View, CA: CPP, Inc.

Swanson, J. L. 1992. "Vocational Behavior, 1989–1991: Life Span Career Development and Reciprocal Interaction of Work and Nonwork." *Journal of Vocational Behavior* 41: 101–161.

Szegedy-Maszak, M., and C. Hsu. 2004. "How We Talk to God." *U.S.News & World Report,* December 20, online at www.usnews.com/usnews/culture/articles/041220/20poll.htm (accessed October 25, 2005).

Taylor, S. E., L. C. Klein, B. P. Lewis, T. L. Gruenewald, R. A. R. Gurung, and Updegraff. 2000. "Biobehavioral Responses to Stress in Females: Tend and Befriend, Not Fight or Flight." *Psychological Review* 107, no. 3: 411–429.

Tenbrunsel, A., J. Brett, E. Maoz, L. Stroh, and A. Reilly. 1995. "Dynamic and Static Work-Family Relationships." *Organizational Behavior and Human Decision Processes* 63, no. 3 (September): 233–246.

Terjesen, S. 2005. "Senior Women Managers' Transition to Entrepreneurship: Leveraging Embedded Career Capital." *Career Development International* 10, no. 3: 246–259.

Tharenou, P., S. Latimer, and D. Conroy. 1994. "How Do You Make It to the Top?" *Academy of Management Journal* 37: 899–931.

Tomlinson, J. 2004. "Perceptions and Negotiations of the Business Case for Flexible Careers and the Integration of Part-Time Work." *Women in Management Review* 19, no. 8: 413–420.

Thompson, C. A., L. L. Beauvais, and K. S. Lyness. 1999. "When Work-Family Benefits Are Not Enough: The Influence of Work-Family Culture on Benefit Utilization, Organizational Attachment, and Work-Family Conflict. *Journal of Vocational Behavior* 54, no. 3: 392–415.

Tischler, L. 2004. "Where Are the Women?" *Fast Company* 79 (February): 52–60.

Townsend, B. 2002. "Dissecting the Time Squeeze." Cornell Employment and Family Careers Institute, Bronfenbrenner Life Course Center Issue Briefs, Issue Brief 3, no. 1 (Spring): 1–4.

Tu, H. S., and S. E. Sullivan. 2001. "Striking It Rich in the Gold Rush of the New Millennium: IT Careers." Paper presented at the annual meeting of the Midwest Academy of Management, Toledo, OH.

Ulrich, D. 1997. *Human Resource Champions.* Boston: Harvard Business School Press.

United Nations. 2000. "Families and the World of Work: Four Country Profiles of Family-Sensitive Policies." New York: Department of Economic and Social Affairs, Division for Social Policy and Development, Family Unit. Online at www.un.org/esa/socdev/family/ publications/workandfamily/s.PDF (accessed October 25, 2005).

U.S. Small Business Administration, n.a. 2001. "Women in Business, 2001." Office of Advocacy Report, online at www.sba.gov, September (accessed January 10, 2005).

Usigan, Y. 2005. "Family Friendly Careers." Online at www.summerbridge.org/doc/pressroom/AOL12405.doc, April 20 (accessed October 25, 2005).

Van Vianen, A. E., and A. H. Fischer. 2002. "Illuminating the Glass Ceiling: The Role of Organizational Culture Preferences." *Journal of Occupational and Organizational Psychology* 75, no. 3 (September): 315–337.

Veiga, J. 1983. "Mobility Influences during Managerial Career Stages." *Academy of Management Journal* 26, no. 1 (March): 64–85.

Vermond, K. 2004. "Workplace Winners: The Top Family Friendly Employers in Canada." *Today's Parent* 20, no. 11 (January): 7.

Vinnicombe, S., and V. Singh. 2003. "Locks and Keys to the Boardroom." *Women in Managment Review* 18, no. 6: 325–333.

Wallis, C. 2004. "The Case for Staying Home: Why More Young Moms Are Opting Out of the Rat Race." *Time*, March 22, 52–58.

Wanous, J. P. 1992. *Organizational Entry: Recruitment, Selection, Orientation, and Socialization of Newcomers.* Reading, MA: Addison-Wesley.

Ward, K., and L. Wolf-Wendel. 2004. "Fear Factor: How Safe Is It to Make Time for Family?" *Academe* 90, no. 6: 28–31.

Warner, J. 2005. *Perfect Madness: Mothering in the Age of Anxiety.* New York: Penguin/Riverhead Books.

Watkins, C. E., and L. M. Subich. 1995. "Annual Review, 1992–1994: Career Development, Reciprocal Work/Nonwork Interaction, and Women's Workforce Anticipation." *Journal of Vocational Behavior* 47, no. 2: 109–163.

Watkins, M. D., and M. H. Bazerman. 2003. "Predictable Surprises: The Disasters You Should Have Seen Coming." *Harvard Business Review* 81, no. 3 (March): 72–81.

Wayne, J. H. 2001. *Psychology Today* 34, no. 5 (September-October): 18.

Weeks, W., C. W. Moore, J. A. McKinney, and J. G. Longenecker. 1999. "The Effects of Gender and Career Stage on Ethical Judgment." *Journal of Business Ethics* 20, no. 4: 301–313.

Weick, K. 1996. "Enactment, and the Boundaryless Career: Organizing as We Work." In *The Boundaryless Career,* ed. Arthur and Rousseau, 40–57.

Welch, L. 2004. "Success Stories." *Real Simple* 5, no. 7 (September): 256.

Wellington, S., M. B. Kropf, and P. R. Gerkovich. 2003. "What's Holding Women Back." *Harvard Business Review* 81, no. 6: 18–20.

Wethington, E. 2000. "Expecting Stress: Americans and the 'Midlife Crisis.'" *Motivation and Emotion* 24, no. 2: 85–103.

Wheat, A. 2002. "Best Companies to Work For: The Anatomy of a Great Workplace—a Look at Four of the Top 100." *Fortune,* online at www. Fortune. com, January 24 (accessed June 10, 2005).

White, B. 1995. "The Career Development of Successful Women." *Women in Management Review* 10, no. 3: 4–15.

Wilkie, J. R. 1993. "Changes in U.S. Men's Attitudes toward the Family Provider Role, 1972–1989." *Gender and Society* 7, no. 2: 261–279.

Williams, J. 2000. *Unbending Gender: Why Family and Work Conflict and What to Do About It.* New York: Oxford University Press.

———. 2004. "Hitting the Maternal Wall." *Academe* 90, no. 6: 16–20.

Winkler, A. E. 2002. "Measuring Time Use in Households with More than One Person." *Monthly Labor Review* 125, no. 2 (February): 45–54.

Winning Workplaces, n.a. 2002. "Success Stories: Motek." *Winning Workplaces,* online at www.winningworkplaces.org, December 14 (accessed June 5, 2005).

Winters, J. 2001. "The Daddy Track." *Psychology Today* 34, no. 5 (September-October): 18–21.

Wolfe, A. 1997. "The Moral Meaning of Work." *Journal of Socioeconomics* 26, no. 6: 559–570.

Woodd, M. 1999. "The Move Towards a Different Career Pattern: Are Women Better Prepared than Men for a Modern Career?" *Women in Management Review* 14, no. 1: 21–28.

Wooton, B. H. 1997. "Gender Differences in Occupational Employment." *Monthly Labor Review* 120, no. 4 (April): 15–23.

Working Mother, n.a. 2003. "*Working Mother Magazine* Announces Top Ten Best of the Best." *Working Mother,* online at www.workingmother.com, October (accessed June 6, 2005).

Young, M. B. 1996. "Career Issues for Single Adults without Children." In *The Career Is Dead, Long Live the Career,* ed. Hall, 196–219.

Index

"abandoned careerist," 102
adjusting approach to balance,
    193–197
age, success based on, 182
Ali, Terry, 159, 171–172
Alpha Kaleidoscope Career pattern,
    134–144, 147
alternating approach to balance,
    202–204
ambition, 44–45, 103
Arthur, Mike, 9
authentic self, 166
authenticity
    characteristics of, 115, 165
    in decision making, 172
    definition of, 159
    description of, 12, 154
    desire for, 160
    employee, 184–186
    forms of, 165–176
    life events that affect, 160
    as longing for purpose, 166–168
    manifestation of, 159
    by men, 178–179
    men's need for, 136–137, 140, 143
    at midlife, 160–165
    need for, 115–116, 131, 154
    as need to follow one's own path,
        171–173
    organizational, 184–186
    for overcoming crisis, 174–176
    quest for, 176–181, 270–275

    search for, 158–160
    self-reflection and, 176, 186
    spiritual growth and, 168–171
    throughout life cycle, 176–181
    unrealized dreams and, 173–174
    visionary or transformational
        approach to life and, 170
    by women, 178–179
    for women, 160
    women's need for, 131

baby boomers, 89–90, 211, 295
balance. *See also* work-family balance
    achieving of, 275–285
    adjusting approach to, 193–197
    alternating approach to, 202–204
    attainability of, 188–192
    concurrent approach to, 199–202
    consecutive approach to, 197–199
    contemporary strategies for,
        192–208
    men's approach to, 144–147,
        209–211
    need for, 116–117
    organizational support for,
        284–285
    prioritization as method of
        achieving, 116–117
    by single women and men, 190
    synergistic pattern, 204–208
Bardwick, Judy, 50
Barnes, Brenda, 187–188

Belkin, Lisa, 25, 189
Berman, Gail, 48
Beta Kaleidoscope Career pattern
    by men, 151–152
    by women, 130–134, 147–148
biobehavioral stress response, 54
biological clock, 50–51
boomerangs, 280
boundaryless career
    description of, 8
    development of, 9
Burgum, Doug, 274
Burud, Sandra, 263–264
Buttner, E. Holly, 236

Canada, 259
career. *See also* men's careers;
    women's careers
    adapting to changes in, 86–89
    boundaryless, 8
    derailment of, 42
    holistic approach to, 12
    interruptions in, 59
    men's approach to, 110
    new models of, 10
    reasons for assessing, 113
    sacrifice of, 194
    self-reflection on, 176
    success in, 159
    Super's stages of, 69
    women's approach to, 57–58, 110
career advancement
    company accountability for, 286
    in family-friendly firms,
        251–252
    opportunities for, 285
    for single workers, 196–197
    success and, 208–209
    traditional model of, 69
    for women, 251–252, 257,
        285–286, 295
career boundaries, 9
career challenges, 118–119

career changes
    by choice vs. circumstance,
        85–86
    description of, 11
    gender differences in reasons
        for, 85–86
    by men, 85–86
    reasons for, 84, 195
    by women, 85–86
career development
    corporate strategy effects on, 15
    gender influences on, 154
    kaleidoscope approach to, 269,
        297
career experiences, 308
career interruptions, 279, 282
career models
    early, 69–70
    in 1950s, 48–49, 70
    present-day changes in, 49
    "river of time," 57, 110–111
    traditional, 48–49, 57
career options, 269
career path
    differences in, 4–8
    flexibility in, 261
    linear. *See* linear career
    new opportunities, 295
career patterns
    "abandoned careerist," 102
    differences in, 107–111
    "late-blooming careerist," 62–63
    "linear careerist," 101
    for men, 100–104
    "nonconformist," 63–64
    "opt-out prioritizer," 62
    "resilient careerist," 101–102
    "stay-at-home dad," 103–104
    "supermom heroine," 61–62
    "tech-flex dad," 101
    "traditionalist," 63
    for women, 61–64
career setbacks, 109

career success
  defining of, 181
  male definition of, 182–183
career transitions, 309
careerists
  "abandoned," 102
  "late-blooming," 62–63
  "linear," 101
"career-primary" women, 261
caregiving
  for older parents, 195
  by working women, 193
Carlson, Richard, 167
Center for Work-Life Policy, 281
challenge(s)
  achieving of, 285–291
  career example of, 233–235
  case examples of, 215–218
  changes during lifetime, 119–121
  in corporations, 239–240
  decision-making benefits of,
    227–228
  definition of, 219
  description of, 12, 218
  development and growth from,
    224–227
  of entrepreneurship, 236–237
  expertise established through,
    229–231
  impact on others gained through,
    227–229
  men's approach to, 134
  motivation gained through,
    219–220, 227, 285
  need for, 118–119, 218
  organizational support for, 288,
    290–291
  self-identity building through,
    223–224
  validation obtained from,
    220–224
  women's drive for, 232–233
  work-life programs and, 245

child care
  at family-friendly firms, 249–251
  subsidizing of, 261
  during World War II, 260–261
child rearing
  by men, 29
  by working women, 193
command-and-control leadership
  style, 80
competence, 14
concepts, 14
concurrent approach to balance,
  199–202
connections
  description of, 14
  establishing of, 17
consciousness, 167
consecutive approach to balance,
  197–199
co-preneurs, 45
corporate America, 2
corporate ladder, 18
corporate restructurings, 70
corporate social responsibility,
  270–271
corporate strategy
  career development affected by,
    15
  changes in, 15
corporations
  challenge in, 239–240
  kaleidoscope-oriented job poli-
    cies in, 255
crisis, authenticity as force for overcoming, 174–176
Crittenden, Ann, 285–286

decision making
  authenticity in, 172
  challenge as method of, 227
  development and growth through
    challenges, 224–227
DiNucci, Ronnie, 280

discrimination
    costs of, 294
    description of, 40–44, 238, 252,
       286–287
downsizings
    age groups affected by, 82
    effects of, 82–85, 88
    gen Xers and Yers affected by,
       90–91
    in 1980s, 70
    statistics regarding, 82
Drucker, Peter, 18
Dublon, Dina, 149

early career, 182
elderly caregiving, 195, 250
employee(s)
    authenticity by, 184–186
    bottom-line impact of, 293–294
    "dual-focus," 264
    freedom of, 274
    global competition, 289
    meaning in the work performed
       by, 38–40, 273
    pride of, 274
    wellness promotion by, 271–272
    work-life balance by, 276
employee goodwill, 294
employment relationships, 15
enrichment effect, 34
entrepreneurs
    challenges for, 236–237
    intentional, 45
    latent, 45
    synergistic lifestyle, 207–208
    women as, 45–48, 236
    work schedule flexibility of, 236
executive development, 285
expertise building, 229–231

family
    importance to women, 59
    linear career effects on, 85

family business owners, 45
Family Medical Leave Act, 212–213
family track, 262
family-friendly firms
    advancement of women at,
       251–252
    in Canada, 259
    changes in, 244–245
    characteristics of, 244
    child care options at, 249–251
    flexible scheduling at, 247–249
    list of, 255, 263–264
    myths of, 246–256
    project-based work and salary
       systems at, 254
    rewards system at, 252–255, 258
    work-life programs, 245
family-friendly policies
    description of, 212–214, 244, 258
    in European countries, 259–260
    historical example of, 260–261
    social reprisal for using, 245,
       262–263
fatherhood, 213–214
Fels, Anna, 44
female-friendly programs, 287
feminism, 19
fight or flight response, 54
Fisher, Lucy, 48
Fletcher, Joyce, 55
flexible options, 312
flexible schedule
    benefits of, 247, 262
    employees who have, 248
    of entrepreneurs, 236
    examples of, 275–276
    failure to offer, 246
    importance of, 246, 257
    limitations of, 247
    prevalence of, 276–277
    technology influences on,
       248–249
France, 256, 260

franchisers, 45
free agents, 16–17
freelance work, 3
Friedman, Stewart, 213
Friedman, Thomas, 13, 288–289

Gallos, Joan, 52
Gen Xers and Yers
  adulthood delayed by, 224
  description of, 89–91, 152
  retention strategies for, 257–258
  success as defined by, 183
  work-family balance approach,
    212, 283
gender. *See also* men; women
  reasons for opting out of work-
    force based on, 310
  success definitions based on,
    182–183
gender discrimination
  costs of, 294
  description of, 40–44, 238, 252,
    286–287
gender roles, 11
George, Bill, 206–207
Germany, 260
Gilligan, Carol, 51–52, 78
glass ceiling, 40–42, 251
"golden middle age," 51
government policies, 283–284
Greenhaus, Jeffrey, 213

Hall, Tim, 10
Hamill, Madeline, 149
Hammel, Heidi, 233–235
Hammonds, Keith, 202
Hochschild, Arlie Russell, 28–29
Hollywood free agency model, 16–18
homemaker role, 49–50
household chores
  by men, 212
  by women, 28, 60
Hughes, Karen, 25

human resources
  evaluative questions for, 292–293
  Kaleidoscope Career practices,
    267–291
  outcomes measures for, 291–292
human resources accounting, 291

income, motherhood effects on, 27
influencing of others, 227–229
information economy
  global, 13
  intangible assets in, 14
  workplace changes created by, 13
intangible assets, 14
intentional entrepreneurs, 45
"interactive time," 281
intrapreneurial, 47
intrapreneurship, 289–290
Italy, 256

Jacobsen, Nina, 48
job outsourcing, 294
job security
  loss of, 9, 70, 108
  loyalty fostered by, 15
job sharing, 276
Johnson, Madolyn, 272

Kaleidoscope Career
  ABC model of, 113–121, 297
  Alpha pattern
    by men, 134–144, 147
    by women, 148–151
  authenticity. *See* authenticity
  balance. *See* balance
  benefits of, 296–298
  Beta pattern
    by men, 151–152
    by women, 130–134, 147
  case examples of, 121–130, 134–144
  challenge. *See* challenge(s)
  changes during lifetime, 119–121,
    131–132

Kaleidoscope Career, *cont'd*
  company examples of, 267–268
  corporations, 239–240
  definition of, 111
  description of, 193, 296
  drivers of, 154
  employers' understanding of,
    153
  human resource practices,
    267–291, 295
  implementation of, 266–267
  for men, 134–144
  opt-out revolution and, 154
  organizational support for,
    274–275
  parameters of, 113–114
  portfolio examples, 121–130
  principles of, 111–112
  shifts in, 232–233
  strategic thinking and, 265–267
  value of, 153
  for women, 121–134, 232–233
kaleidoscope thinking, 14, 265, 290
Kanter, Rosabeth Moss, 13–14, 265,
  290
Kaye, Beverly, 269
Kossek, Ellen Ernst, 276

"late-blooming careerist," 62–63
latent entrepreneurs, 45
leaders
  traits of, 184
  wellness promotion for, 272
leadership style
  command-and-control, 80
  by women, 55–56
Lee, Mary Dean, 276
Leinen, Jerri, 161–165
Lepore, Dawn, 149
leveling off, 85
Levinson, Daniel, 49–50, 81, 160–161
liberated-by-technology worker,
  91–95

life cycle
  authenticity throughout, 176–181
  career planning and development
    over, 280
  gender differences, 295
lifetime
  challenges during, 119–121
  Kaleidoscope Career changes
    during, 119–121, 131–132
  men's careers during, 119–121,
    136
  women's careers during, 119–121
Life-Track thinking, 262, 293, 298
linear career
  classic pattern of, 72–78
  death of, 8–10, 28
  example of, 4–6, 135–137
  family effects of, 85
  limiting nature of, 2
  for men, 72–78, 108–109, 114,
    134–137
  new career vs., 71
  shortcomings of, 135
  traditional, 68
  women in, 159
Lombardo, Michael, 221
long-term employment relationships,
  15
loyalty, 15

Maier, Mark, 78
Mainiero, Lisa, 57, 109
male straitjacket, 80–82, 114
manufacturing age economy, 16
market expanders, 45
masculinity
  corporate model of, 78–80
  in workplace, 81
Matalin, Mary, 25
material success, 182
McCall, Morgan, 221
McGraw, Phil, 166
meaning in your work, 38–40, 273

men. *See also* stay-at-home dads
ambition of, 44, 103
authenticity by, 178–179
baby boomer, 89–90, 211
balance as defined by, 144–147,
209–211
Beta Kaleidoscope Career by,
151–152
brain studies in, 53–54
career approach of, 110
career change reasons for, 85–86
career experiences of, 308
career patterns for, 100–104
child rearing by, 29
compartmentalization by, 112,
146
competition-based focus of, 78
development of, 52
developmental opportunities
from work for, 237–238
father role of, 213
female domesticity effects on, 29
gen Xers. *See* gen Xers and Yers
household chores by, 212
liberated-by-technology workers,
91–95
masculinity model for, 78–80
midlife crisis for, 81, 160
neuroscience studies in, 52–54
in 1950s, 67–68
paternity leave by, 212–213, 245,
263
self-identity through work, 79, 81,
109
self-reflection by, 176
sequential approach to career
used by, 112
stereotype of, 80–81
success as defined by, 182–183,
208
traditional model of, 67–69
unemployment effects on, 83–85
work identity for, 79, 109

work-family conflict as viewed
by, 77–78, 89, 108
workplace realities for, 18–19
worldview of, 53
men's careers
changes during lifetime, 119–121
characteristics of, 110
evolution of, 18
linear, 72–75, 114, 134–137
predictability of, 11
self-descriptions, 75–76
traditional model of, 48–49, 57,
67–68, 72–75
women's careers vs., 77, 107–109
mentoring, 287
midlife
authenticity at, 160–165
rebalancing in, 161
midlife crisis, 81, 160
"mommy tax," 27
"mommy track," 261
Moore, Dorothy, 45, 236
Morrison, Ann, 221
Motek, 241–243
motherhood
leaving workforce for, 39–40
satisfaction from, 39–40
women's income affected by, 27
work vs., 26–30
motivation
challenge as basis for, 219–220,
227, 285
at work, 240

National Association of Female
Executives, 251
Netherlands, 256
neuroscience, 52–54
new careers
adapting to, 86–89
linear career vs., 71
Newman, Gary, 276
Norway, 259–260

off-ramps, 280–282
Ohlott, Patricia, 165
older parents, 195, 250
on-ramps, 280–282
"opt-out prioritizer," 62
opt-out revolution
  description of, 25
  Kaleidoscope Career model as
    reason for, 154
  reasons for, 310
  relational model of, 64
  relationalism as cause of, 56–61
"opt-outs," 279–280
organization(s)
  balance supported by, 284–285
  challenges offered by, 227, 288,
    290–291
  downsizings in, 70
  family-friendly policies in,
    212–214
  with female-friendly programs,
    287
  "jungle gym" structure of, 268
  Kaleidoscope Career supported
    by, 274–275
  life perspective in, 264
  restructurings in, 70
  social responsibility by, 270–271
  structural changes in, 268–269
  wellness promotion by, 271–272
  work-family balance benefits for,
    206–207
  work-life programs at, 245
organizational authenticity, 184–185
outsourcing of jobs, 294
overworkers, 220

parental leave, 262–263
parenting needs, 285–286
part-time work, 3, 36–38
Pascal, Ann, 48
paternity leave, 212–213, 245, 263
pay-for-performance systems, 252

Pfeffer, Jeffery, 264
Pleck, Joseph, 81
positive spillover effect, 34
Powell, Gary N., 57, 109
Price, Ann, 241–243
pride, 274
priority setting, 178
protean career, 10
Pruett, Kyle, 99
purpose
  consciousness about, 167
  search for, 167–168

"quiet time," 281

rebalancing, 161
relationalism
  activation of, 60
  definition of, 52
  importance of, 64, 79
  opt-out phenomenon associated
    with, 56–61
  women's careers affected by, 149
  at work, 54–56
relationships, 50–52
remote technology, 94
research methods, 299–306
"resilient careerist," 101–102
retirement, 282–283
rewards systems
  in family-friendly firms, 252–255,
    258
  traditional, 254–255
"river of time" model, 57, 110–111
Rousseau, Denise, 9
Ruderman, Marian, 165

sabbaticals, 272–273, 279–280
Sartain, Libby, 274
Schappel, Elissa, 203–204
schedule flexibility. *See* flexible
  schedule
Schwartz, Felice, 261–262

self-employed women, 2
self-identity
  challenge used for building of,
    223–224
  of men, 79, 81, 109
  questions regarding, 311
  through work, 79, 81, 109
  of women, 109
self-reflection, 176, 186
sexism, 42
single individuals
  advancement opportunities for,
    196–197
  married couples vs., 190–191
  negative stereotypes of, 191
  work-family conflict for, 190–191,
    195–196
single women
  balance by, 190
  career changes by, 60
  prioritization by, 131
  working mothers vs., 60
  work-life conflict for, 150–151,
    190–191, 195–196
sleep deprivation, 95
Smith, Maureen, 22–25, 237, 277–278
social responsibility, 270–271
Society for Human Resource Management, 248
Spillman, Rob, 203–204
spiritual growth, authenticity as
  hunger for, 168–171
spirituality
  hunger for, 168–171
  moral compass use of, 170
  in workplace, 168–169
stay-at-home dads. *See also* men
  career path of, 103–104
  case example of, 95–100
  characteristics of, 103
  description of, 11
  increases in, 95
  statistics regarding, 99

stay-at-home moms
  full-time employment transition
    to, 35–36
  part-time employment transition
    to, 36–38
  working women vs., 29, 49–50
"stop-outs," 279–280
stretch assignments, 224, 226
study information, 299–306
success
  age-related differences in, 182
  career, 181–183
  career advancement and,
    208–209
  definition of
    by men, 182–183, 208
    variations in, 208
    by women, 183–184, 208–209
  in early career, 182
  gender influences on, 182–183
  material, 182
  measuring of, 181–182
Super, Donald, 69–70
supercommuters, 192
supermom
  description of, 61–62
  myth of, 28, 30–33
Sweden, 259

tech-flex dad, 101
technology
  expertise building affected by,
    231
  flexible schedule affected by,
    248–249
  new careers offered by, 91–95
  older worker's knowledge of, 231
  sleep deprivation and, 95
  workweek increased by, 191
time, 16
"traditionalist," 63
Tulgan, Bruce, 82
Tumolo, Marie, 263–264

unemployment, 83–84
United Kingdom, 260
United States
  labor force shortage in, 295, 298
  work attitudes in, 260
unrealized dream, 173–174

validation, from challenges, 220–224
values setting, 178
videoconferencing, 257

wage gap, 28, 30, 40, 253
Walden, Dana, 276
Warner, Judith, 232–233
Warren, Rick, 167
wellness promotion, 271–272
Williams, Joan, 29
Williamson, Marianne, 167
Winfrey, Oprah, 168, 271
women. *See also* gender; single
    women; stay-at-home moms;
    working mothers; working
    women
  ambition of, 44–45, 103
  authenticity by, 178–179
  authenticity for, 160
  biobehavioral stress response in, 54
  biological clock influences on,
    50–51
  brain studies in, 53–54
  career advancement for, 251–252,
    257
  career approach of, 110
  career change reasons for, 85–86
  career experiences of, 308
  career success as defined by,
    183–184
  "career-primary," 261
  caregiving by, 27–28, 195
  challenges for, 232–233, 239
  development of, 51–52, 287–288
  developmental opportunities
    from work for, 237–238

difficulties for, 21–22
domesticity of, 28
dropping out of workforce by,
  197–198
as entrepreneurs, 45–48, 236
executive development opportunities for, 285
family values by, 59
"golden middle age" for, 51
homemaker role for, 49–50
household chores performed by,
  28, 60
Kaleidoscope Careers for,
  121–134
leadership style of, 55–56
leaving corporate jobs, 2
in midlife, 160–161
neuroscience studies in, 53–54
participation rate of, 2
part-time work by, 3
prioritization by, 110, 116, 133
priority setting by, 178
relational practices used by, 55
relationalism by, 52–53, 149
relationships valued by, 50–52
retention strategies for, 257–258
self-employed, 2
self-identity of, 109
success as defined by, 183–184,
  208–209
surveys of, 12–13
unemployment effects on, 83–84
values setting by, 178
verbal skills in, 54
wage gap for, 253
work-family balance by, 120,
  133–134, 146–147
workplace realities for, 18–19
worldview of, 53
women-owned businesses
  growth rate for, 45
  statistics regarding, 45
  venture capital given to, 40

women's careers
balance in, 116–117
changes during lifetime, 119–121
characteristics of, 107–108, 110
concept of, 57–58
contextual influences on, 114
elements of, 110
factors that affect, 48
kaleidoscope metaphor applied
to, 114
late-blooming careerist, 62–63
men's careers vs., 77, 107
opt-out prioritizer, 62
patterns for, 61–64
prioritization of, 110
reassessment of, 133
relational nature of, 108, 112
relationships' influence on, 51–52
summary of, 64–65
supermom heroine pattern, 61–62
unpredictability of, 10–11
variations in, 49
work
American attitudes toward, 260
as fulfilling, 38
challenges at, 118–119
designing of, 281
dissatisfaction at, 39
European attitudes toward, 260
at home, 201–202
increases in, 27
meaning at, 38–40
men's views on, 84
motherhood vs., 26–30
motivating factors, 240
relationalism at, 54–56
self-identity obtained through,
79, 81, 109
time devoted to, 191–192
work schedule flexibility. *See* flexible
schedule
workaholics, 219–220
Workaholics Anonymous, 220

work-family balance
adjusting approach to, 193–197
alternating approach to, 202–204
benefits of, 190
business decisions affected by,
266
concurrent approach to, 199–202
consecutive approach to, 197–199
description of, 188
difficulty of, 199
in Europe, 256, 259
by Gen Xers and Yers, 212, 283
government policies that support,
283–284
media portrayals of, 211
by men, 209–211
organizations that promote
benefits, 206–207
description of, 265
in work culture, 277
synergistic pattern, 204–208
work-family conflict
effects of, 243
gender and, 59
importance of, 2, 10, 117
increases in, 193–194
men's view of, 77–78, 89, 108, 146
for single individuals, 190–191
single person's approach to,
150–151, 195–196
women's view of, 120, 133–134,
146–147
working mothers
balance by, 188–189
child care for, 250
media portrayal of, 211
single women vs., 60
typical day for, 189
working women
advancement of, 41
brain drain of, 33–34, 237
caregiving by, 193
case examples of, 22–25, 42–44

working women, *cont'd*
  difficulties for, 21–22
  in France, 256
  gender discrimination against,
    40–44, 238
  imbalance experienced by, 117
  needs of, 194
  in the Netherlands, 256
  non-family reasons for leaving
    work, 38–39
  opting out by, 34, 38
  part-time work by, 36–38
  statistics regarding, 33–34
  stay-at-home moms vs., 29, 49–50
  stress on, 28
  in Sweden, 259
  transition to stay-at-home mom,
    35–36
  wage gap for, 28, 30, 40
work-life programs
  challenging jobs and, 245
  commitment to, 245

workplace
  demands of, 34
  flexible options in, 312
  gender discrimination in, 40–44,
    238
  glass ceiling in, 40–42
  male stereotype in, 81
  masculinity in, 81
  non-family reasons for leaving,
    38–39
  parenting skills transferred to,
    286
  relationalism in, 56
  spirituality in, 168–169
workweek
  increases in, 27
  technology effects on, 191
worldviews, 53